Cuban Counterpoints

WESTERN HEMISPHERE STUDIES

Series Editor: Mauricio A. Font
The Graduate Center and Queens College
The City University of New York

This series represents a joint publication initiative of the Bildner Center for Western Hemisphere Studies at The City University of New York Graduate Center and Lexington Books. The books published in this series endeavor to support the Center's mission of generating greater comprehension of contemporary issues in the Americas, creating an international dialogue on policy issues, and producing research on a range of topics that are both country and theme specific.

EDITORIAL BOARD
E. Desmond Arias, John Jay College of Criminal Justice
Margaret E. Crahan, Hunter College and The Graduate Center
Cristina Equizábal, Ford Foundation
Ted Henken, Baruch College
Alfonso Quiroz, Baruch College and The Graduate Center
Mark Ungar, Brooklyn College

TITLES IN SERIES
Reforming Brazil, edited by Mauricio A. Font with the assistance of Anthony Peter Spanakos and Cristina Bordin

Cuban Counterpoints: The Legacy of Fernando Ortiz, edited by Mauricio A. Font and Alfonso Quiroz

Cuban Counterpoints

The Legacy of Fernando Ortiz

Edited by
Mauricio A. Font
and Alfonso W. Quiroz

LEXINGTON BOOKS
Lanham • Boulder • New York • Toronto • Oxford

LEXINGTON BOOKS

Published in the United States of America
by Lexington Books
An imprint of The Rowman & Littlefield Publishing Group, Inc.
4501 Forbes Boulevard, Suite 200, Lanham, Maryland 20706

PO Box 317
Oxford
OX2 9RU, UK

British Library Cataloguing in Publication Information Available

Library of Congress Cataloging-in-Publication Data

Cuban counterpoints : the legacy of Fernando Ortiz / edited by
  Mauricio A. Font and Alfonso W. Quiroz.
    p. cm. — (Western hemisphere studies)
  Includes bibliographical references and index.
  ISBN 0-7391-0917-0 (alk. paper) — ISBN 0-7391-0968-5 (pbk. : alk. paper)
  1. Ortiz, Fernando, 1881–1969—Congresses. 2. Social sciences—Cuba—
Congresses. 3. Music and literature—Congresses. 4. Hybridity (Social
sciences)—Cuba—Congresses. 5. Acculturation—Congresses. 6. Cuba—
Civilization—20th century—Congresses. 7. Latin America—Civilization—
20th century—Congresses. 8. Cuba—Historiography—Congresses. 9. Blacks—
Cultural assimilation—Cuba—Congresses. I. Font, Mauricio A. (Mauricio Augusto)
II. Quiroz, Alfonso W. III. Series.
F1787.O79C83 2004
972.9106'092—dc22   2004018662

Printed in the United States of America

♾™ The paper used in this publication meets the minimum requirements of
American National Standard for Information Sciences—Permanence of Paper
for Printed Library Materials, ANSI/NISO Z39.48-1992.

Contents

Acknowledgments

This volume is the result of a truly collective effort. The collaboration of Jane Gregory Rubin, María Fernanda Ortiz, Miguel Barnet, Margaret E. Crahan, Jerry Carlson, José Matos, and Octavio di Leo was crucial to the realization of the symposium on which it is based. Alfonso W. Quiroz was responsible for the volume's overall editing and organization. He selected texts for publication, revised and edited translations, and was a commentator and member of the organizing committee of the symposium. Pamela Smorkaloff collaborated in the organization of the symposium and contributed to this volume's introduction. Gary Aguayo coordinated the activities of the symposium and performed word processing and editorial tasks. Finally, Sandra Black and Scott Larson provided essential editorial assistance with much appreciated diligence and efficiency.

The March 2000 Ortiz symposium included a rich program of Cuban classical and popular music, an exhibition of paintings by Ramón Menocal on the subject of transculturation, a thematic selection of Cuban films and videos coordinated by Jerry Carlson, and an exhibit of rare Ortiz photographs and memorabilia thoughtfully provided by María Fernanda Ortiz. We thank María Fernanda Ortiz for her support of these endeavors and for sharing valuable personal insights on her father's work and life.

The Ortiz symposium, and this text, would not have been possible without the generous funding of the Ford Foundation and the thoughtful efforts of Cristina Eguizábal. The Graduate Center and Queens College of The City University of New York, the Christopher Reynolds Foundation, the Reed Foundation, InterAmericas, Fundación Fernando Ortiz, and the Instituto de Literatura y Lingüística-Sociedad Económica de Amigos del País supported the project in various ways. The Reed Foundation also provided a grant for the translation of chapters in this volume originally written in Spanish.

Introduction: The Intellectual Legacy of Fernando Ortiz

Mauricio A. Font, Alfonso W. Quiroz,
and Pamela Maria Smorkaloff

The vast and original body of work left by Cuban intellectual Fernando Ortiz (1881–1969) focuses on the sociocultural and historical manifestations of the island of Cuba. However, the theoretical implications of his work surpass national boundaries. In essence, Ortiz's conceptions delineate a program for interpreting daunting Latin American complexities marked by a freshness of intellect and enduring sophistication. Arguably, the intellectual legacy of Fernando Ortiz is a fundamental pillar for a comprehensive explanation of Latin American uniqueness and continuing evolution. This is one of the key insights stemming from the "Fernando Ortiz Symposium on Cuban Culture and History," organized by the Cuba Project/Bildner Center of The Graduate Center, The City University of New York, March 20–22, 2000. This symposium gathered more than thirty intellectuals, from Cuba and elsewhere, interested in the work and legacy of Fernando Ortiz. For three days, these intellectuals, coming from the most diverse academic disciplines and perspectives, participated in intense, open, and sincere exchange. This collection of essays is one result of that memorable symposium.

Together, these studies not only contribute to the study of Ortiz's life, work, and legacy, but also fulfill a glaring need for a general reinterpretation of a truly unique Latin American scholar. The volume is also an effort to offer fresh perspectives on Ortiz's contribution to interdisciplinary cultural, historical, artistic, and literary studies of Cuba, Latin America, and other complex societies with growing global interconnections.

Ortiz's work has been internationally recognized since the 1940s and 1950s. However, there is no single monographic interpretation of his life and legacy. Such a project is, admittedly, a challenging and overwhelming task. The scope and specialization of Ortiz's interests, and the complex historical context in which he developed his ideas, demand an interpretative study of epic proportions. Very few individual intellectuals could accomplish this task for several reasons, one of the most important being the current scarcity of analytic building blocks for such a synthesis. Since the publication of Ortiz's master work, *Contrapunteo cubano del tabaco y el azúcar* (1940), leading intellectuals in Latin America, the United States, and Europe have hailed the value of his contributions. Nevertheless, the study of his legacy was neglected in the 1970s and 1980s except for reeditions of his major works, and even then mainly in Cuba. Only recently have there been encouraging signals of a renewed international interest in Ortiz's work.

Beyond the prologues to certain editions of his works, there is no current work in English that collectively reassesses Ortiz's intellectual universe.[1] Three volumes of studies, by now dated, were published in Spanish in the 1950s, in addition to several short academic articles and studies published in Cuba between 1959 and 1990.[2] Only one previous international conference—mainly devoted to Ortiz's connections with Italy (Genoa, 1989)—has had its proceedings published in Italian and Spanish.[3] In the 1990s, however, there was increased international interest in Ortiz's work. In 1998, the InterAmericas Society of Arts and Letters of the Americas produced a modern Ortiz bibliography in English (with Spanish and French versions) that includes a unique catalog of manuscripts and a biographical chronology.[4] Likewise, María Fernanda Ortiz, Don Fernando's daughter, has contributed to the publication of her father's works in Madrid.[5] Recent important projects for the restoration, access, and diffusion of Ortiz's works, manuscripts, and papers housed at the library of the Sociedad Económica de Amigos del País, are under way, as are similar significant efforts led by Miguel Barnet and the Fundación Fernando Ortiz in Havana.

This collective volume is an effort to address the current limitations of the scholarship on Ortiz. It seeks to refocus and update the international legacy of Fernando Ortiz, whose concept of "transculturation" remains a fundamental pillar for the analysis of new, complex, and eclectic Latin American societies and cultures. This revision is done from different perspectives, with the aim of expanding an interdisciplinary field of study that promises great returns in the near future.

BIOGRAPHY AND WORKS

Fernando Ortiz lived during a crucial historical transition between two centuries. He was educated in both a Creole American and a European intellectual tradition, but his research led him to the study of African cultural roots in Cuba, a country which at the time was itself in transition from colonial rule to independent status. Ortiz's personal evolution reflected the intellectual and historical shifts he was exposed to: his initial enlightened positivist ideas evolved toward a multidisciplinary scientific perspective. From the study of law and criminal behavior he diversified to the study of anthropology, religion, and music. From his early political involvement, characteristic of many Latin American intellectuals, he opted for contributing to the development of Cuban associations and civil society. He was intellectually open-minded, a liberal-reformist, and a true polygraph. A nonsectarian thinker, he stood firmly against racism. Ortiz's work, as most of the participants in the symposium agreed, represents a serenely rational model for several generations of Cuban thinkers who have tried to grapple with the past and present tensions of Cuban reality.

There is an intimate connection between Ortiz's Cuban and international experiences and the evolution of his works. Born in Havana on July 16, 1881, he traveled with his mother in 1882 to Minorca, where he lived for several years. As a young boy in Minorca, he developed a special sense of identity with distant Cuba. He later studied at the University of Barcelona, where he received his bachelor's degree in 1895. That year he returned to Havana where he studied penal law at the University of Havana until 1898, a period that coincided with the violent struggle for Cuban independence from Spain. He returned to Barcelona in 1899, where he received his law degree in 1900. He then went to Madrid and obtained his doctorate in law in 1901 with a thesis on positivist inspiration under the guidance of Professor Manuel Sales y Ferré.

In 1902, he returned to Cuba and experienced the critical and confused early years of the fledgling Cuban republic. He soon left the island again to perform consular diplomatic duties in La Coruña, Marseilles, and Genoa between 1903 and 1906. In Genoa, he established close connections with the positivist criminologists Cesare Lombroso and Enrico Ferri. In 1906, Ortiz returned to Cuba and published several articles on criminology as well as his pathbreaking *Hampa afro-cubana: Los negros brujos*, his first attempt to understand Afro-Cuban marginal behavior and culture. In 1907, he became a member of the prestigious intellectual and institutional community of the Sociedad Económica de Amigos del País. In 1908, he married María Ester Cabrera, the daughter of Cuban reformist-liberal intellectual Raimundo Cabrera, and began to teach law at the University of Havana. From 1910 to 1959, Ortiz directed the publication of the influential *Revista Bimestre Cubana*, an organ of the Sociedad Económica. Preoccupied with the corrupt political culture in Cuba, he published, in 1913, *Entre cubanos . . . (Psicología tropical)*, a social critique that proposed the urgent transformation of Cuban institutions through reformist means and increased attention to cultural, institutional, and educational issues.

During the same period, he contributed to the publication and republication of classic Cuban historical and reformist works from the nineteenth century. In 1916, with the publication of *Hampa afro-cubana: Los negros esclavos*, Ortiz laid the foundations for a historical and eclectic methodology that eventually led to his concept of transculturation. At the time he was also active in politics and served in the Cuban Congress as a member of the Liberal Party. Disillusioned, he resigned his seat in 1926. In 1923, he also published a historical-linguistic compilation entitled *Un catauro de cubanismos.* Subsequently Ortiz founded the influential anthropological and cultural journals *Archivos del Folklore Cubano* (1924), *Surco* (1930), and *Cultura Contemporánea* (1930). His *Proyecto de código criminal cubano* (1926) helped lay the foundation for a progressive reform of criminal justice in Cuba, and was a major contribution to the country's legal and institutional framework. In 1926, he also established the Institución Hispano-Cubana de Cultura, a major cultural institution that developed important links between Cuba, Spain, and the rest of Latin America. Ortiz was actively opposed to the dictatorship of Gerardo Machado and, in 1931, went into self-imposed exile in Washington, D.C., and New York City. In the United States, he engaged in a propaganda campaign against Machado and existing U.S. policy toward Cuba. With the fall of Machado in 1933, Ortiz returned to Cuba and engaged in active cultural politics during a time of political and educational radicalization. In 1940, Ortiz published his magnum opus *Contrapunteo cubano.* In the 1930s and 1940s, he also developed his vintage antiracist and antifascist positions.

Having become a widower in 1942, Ortiz married María Herrera y González de Salcedo that same year. In 1945, his second daughter, María Fernanda, was born. In 1946, he published his antiracist manifesto *El engaño de las razas.* At this point in his life, he intensified his anthropological, linguistic, and ethnomusicological studies of Afro-Cuban culture with a series of successive monumental publications: *La africanía de la música folklórica de Cuba* (1950), *Los bailes y el teatro de los negros en el folklor de Cuba* (1951), five volumes of his *Los instrumentos de la música afrocubana* (1952–1955), and *Historia de una pelea cubana contra los demonios* (1959). In 1954, he was granted a doctorate Honoris Causa by Columbia University. Other international institutions also recognized his lifetime of monumental work, including the University of Cuzao and UNESCO. Fernando Ortiz died in Havana on April 10, 1969, at the age of eighty-seven.

THEORETICAL AND METHODOLOGICAL RELEVANCE

Attempts at general interpretations of Latin America's complex and evolving societies and cultures have faced formidable challenges. From the ambitious envisioning of a "cosmic race," to recent culturalist formulations and theories of modernization, dependency, and revolution, no single abstract interpretation has satisfactorily deciphered the Latin American puzzle. In his body of work, Ortiz brought together the cultural-symbolic and material aspects of social life in a dialectical fashion. Afro-Cuban religion, forms of consciousness, customs, music, language, and life received his sustained attention. This suggests that Ortiz tended to treat these factors as ontological essentials, realities in themselves, irreducible to either the material or even historical aspects of the social. His work implies that cultural fixations—traditions, legacies, beliefs, and practices—serve as the basis for stable group and national identities, and require in-depth study. This concept of transculturation pointed to a constant give-and-take across primary cultural traditions. Race and national identity were themselves socially constructed categories in cultural flux.

As a result, a key aspect of Ortiz's approach is its unwillingness to resolve such tension and dissolve cultural counterpoints. Indeterminacy is present in Ortiz's treatment of the relationship of the cultural with the economic and the historical. Thus, he left us with an image of social organization and culture as a perennial problematic. It is telling in this regard that in his waning years during the 1960s, he would see the revolutionary process of that decade as "a crisis of transculturation." Indeed, *Contrapunteo cubano* treats economic and technological determinism in the production of sugar and tobacco as equally inexorably shaping cultural and social phenomena: both staples affect national identity and culture in predictable ways. However, by merely bringing them together to point out their differences, Ortiz returns us to the world of tension, interactions, and perplexity. In the end, then, social organization and culture are seen as pregnant with the possibility for change, from both the evolution of these modalities of production and from the clash between them.

HISTORICAL AND INSTITUTIONAL CONTRIBUTIONS

Ortiz understood, through his view of *ajiaco* (a typical Cuban stew), that Cuban and Latin American realities were still evolving from seminal ethnocultural ingredients brought together in a unique pot of encounter, conflict, survival, and collaboration. History, that laboratory of the human sciences, needed to be included in the core of his anthropological analysis. The material manifestations of history—the economy and trade that sustained the evolving American population—had to be integrated in a comprehensive, ambitious, and erudite canvas. A sense of rediscovered identity emerges from such an effort at historical research. Thus, Ortiz does not limit his approach to rigid deterministic historical perspectives. Material and ideological elements combined and continue to be combined in a particularly Latin American blend. From Ortiz, historians can learn the use of an extensive net that meticulously catches essential kernels of historical understanding relevant to the present.

It is precisely this long-term historical perspective, this understanding of the unfinished Cuban and Latin American process of combination and recombination, that allowed Ortiz to act with a different perspective from that of the opportunistic intellectual or politician. In Cuba, Ortiz's reformist contributions to the building of cultural, educational, and civil institutions underscore the Latin American need for institutional evolution. Education, science, and patience would guide the way toward a veritable Latin American progress. A good cook knows how to moderate the fire under a pot so that the true flavors coalesce rather than be scorched by radical flames. Though deeply attached to Cuban ways and nationalistic hopes, Ortiz also recognized the benefit of foreign influences in the Latin American concoction, as long as these external factors did not choke originalities and identities that had taken centuries to evolve, due to impatient ambition or ignorant force. The particular history and institutions that embody these traditions are at the roots of the unfinished search for a stable and synergetic consensus, so painfully absent in the Latin American saga and its hemispheric, inter-American relations.

LITERARY AND AESTHETIC IMPACT

Recent dominant trends in contemporary Latin American and Caribbean literature—trends such as syncretism, the carnivalesque, *lo real maravilloso*, theories of identity and culture—may well be situated within the Ortizian notion of transculturation as process. As summarized by Malinowski in his introduction to *Contrapunteo cubano*, transculturation

> is a process in which something is always given in return for what one receives, a system of give and take . . . a term that does not contain the implication of one certain culture toward which the other must tend, but an exchange between two cultures, both of them active, both contributing their share, and both co-operating to bring about a new reality.[6]

One could say that the entire history of twentieth-century literary expression in Latin America and the Caribbean has been one of a growing recognition of the real terms of cultural exchange. This is especially true from mid–twentieth century to the present, when writers from the region began to assert, actively and without apology, that the literature of the old world had been shaped by that of the new, just as new world letters had received the influences of the old. That is at the core of the literary manifestos of Alejo Carpentier, Aimé Césaire, José María Arguedas, Gabriel García Márquez, Roberto Fernández Retamar, and many others.

Latin American literature in the twentieth century reflects the process of transculturation as defined by Ortiz, through a movement away from nineteenth-century *romanticismo*, toward *indigenismo* and *lo real maravilloso*, both of which readily cast off notions of "acculturation" in order to address and embrace the much more complex and conflictive process of "transculturation" at work in Latin American reality. The movement away from "discovery" toward self-discovery; the radical rethinking of the 1960s concept of what constituted the very bases for identity; and the critique of José Enrique Rodó's *Ariel* as an essential symbol, in favor of Calibán, the indigenous inhabitant who resists "the civilizing mission," all parallel the dialectic at work in Ortiz's rejection of the concept of acculturation and the creation of his own alternative, transculturation. In *Contrapunteo cubano,* Ortiz identifies tobacco and sugar as the major forces at work in shaping both culture and society. Thus:

> The one requires continual attention, the other involves seasonal work; intensive versus extensive cultivation; steady work on the part of a few, intermittent jobs for many; the immigration of whites on the one hand, the slave trade on the other; liberty and slavery; skilled and unskilled labor; hands versus arms; men versus machines; delicacy versus brute force.[7]

This is but one example of the bold new perspective Ortiz brought to bear on Cuban society, one that embraced simultaneity, conflict, inherent contradiction, and hybridity. Ortiz's later work may appear to belong to the field of literary theory, ethnology, or musicology, or, in interdisciplinary fashion, all three at once. It always was intent on gaining a more complete and inclusive understanding of Cuban culture.

By the 1930s, new generations began to look to the interdisciplinary work of the mature Ortiz as a guide for their work. Ortiz was a contemporary of groundbreaking, interdisciplinary thinkers such as the Peruvian José Carlos Mariátegui and the Argentinian Ezequiel Martínez Estrada, whose work in Latin American sociology and social history informed subsequent literary production. Alejo Carpentier admits to having "devoured Ortiz's books," which led him to new sources of inspiration: inspiration encapsulated in the cry "*¡Abajo la lira, viva el bongó!*" (Down with the lyre, long live the bongó!).[8]

Numerous literary theorists and critics have acknowledged their debt to the Ortizian notion of transculturation, most notably the Uruguayan Angel Rama, of whose 1982 work, *Transculturación narrativa en América Latina,* critic Jean Franco has said that "[h]e adopted Fernando Ortiz's term 'transculturation' in order to argue that what occurs in Latin America is not simply the substitution of one culture for another, but rather a liberating of energy and creativity, a transculturation that has saved and transformed culture, language and popular beliefs." Franco affirms that "transculturation (defined as a particular form of intertextuality in orally transmitted cultures) has given us the great novels of Guimarães Rosa, Juan Rulfo and José María Arguedas."[9]

THIS VOLUME

This volume seeks to highlight the contemporary relevance of Ortiz's intellectual legacy from different perspectives and voices. Consequently, it is organized in five parts in accord with major themes developed by the individual contributions. These five parts are subdivisions in disciplinary and interdisciplinary fields explored in Ortiz's body of work and methodological approaches. Each part begins with a short introduction that summarizes the major ideas and propositions of its individual chapters.

The first part, "Life and Education," gathers new biographical studies on Ortiz as well as fresh contributions toward piecing together his early intellectual evolution while he lived in Spain. The second part, "Interpreting Cuban History," includes fresh historical perspectives on Ortiz's approaches to history and the Cuban historical, intellectual, and political context in which he participated. The third, "Social Sciences and Law," centers on the original disciplinary contributions of Ortiz in the study of social realities with a special emphasis on the contemporary relevance of Ortizian formulations to Latin American studies. The fourth part, "Racial Diversity, Religion, and National Identity," addresses Ortiz's contributions to the study of racial issues, religious manifestations, and the formation of identities thereof. Finally, Part V, "Literature and Music," explores the influential interaction of Ortiz's work with literary and musical genres.

This volume's bibliography consists of a chronologically organized selection of Ortiz's works, most of them cited by the contributors in order to provide an overview of his main contributions to different fields of knowledge. A second section of general bibliography lists published secondary literature, manuscript, and audio and visual sources cited by the contributors to this volume. For a complete bibliography of Ortiz's works please refer to *Miscelanea II* (InterAmerica, 1998). The director of this project, Jane Gregory Rubin, envisioned the bibliography as a fundamental contribution to the conference that gave birth to this volume. A list of the contributors, with short biographical information on each of them, is available in the last pages of the volume.

NOTES

1. Apart from the classic introduction by Bronislaw Malinowski to the first English edition of Ortiz's *Cuban Counterpoint: Tobacco and Sugar,* trans. Harriet de Onís (New York: Knopf, 1947), see Julio Le Riverend, "Ortiz y sus contrapunteos," prologue to *Contrapunteo cubano del tabaco y el azúcar* (Caracas: Biblioteca Ayacucho, 1978) and *Contrapunteo cubano* (Havana: Editorial Ciencias Sociales, 1991), and Fernando Coronil's introduction to a recent English reedition of *Cuban Counterpoint* (Durham, N.C.: Duke University Press, 1995).

2. *Miscelánea de estudios dedicados a Fernando Ortiz* por sus discípulos, colegas y amigos con ocasión de cumplirse sesenta años de la publicación de su primer impreso en Menorca en 1895, vols. I–III (Havana: Sociedad Económica de Amigos del País, 1955–1957); Araceli García-Carranza, *Bio-bibliografía de Don Fernando Ortiz*

(Havana: Instituto del Libro, 1970); Diana Iznaga, *El estudio del arte negro en Fernando Ortiz* (Havana: Instituto de Literatura y Lingüística, 1982); *Transculturación en Fernando Ortiz* (Havana: Editorial Ciencias Sociales, 1989).

3. Enrico Basso and Giustina Olgiati, eds., *Fernando Ortiz. Atti del convegno* (Genova, May 11–12, 1988) (Genoa: Civico Istituto Colombiano, 1989).

4. *Miscelánea II of Studies dedicated to Fernando Ortiz (1881–1969)* (New York: InterAmericas, 1998).

5. Fernando Ortiz, *Contrapunteo cubano* introduction by María Fernanda Ortiz, with notes and critical edition by Enrico Mario Santí (Madrid: Música Mundana Maqueda, 1999; Madrid: Editorial Cátedra, forthcoming); *Los instrumentos de la música afrocubana* (Madrid: Música Mundana Maqueda, 1996); *La africanía del folklore cubano* (Madrid: Música Mundana Maqueda, 1998); and *Los bailes y el teatro de los negros* (Madrid: Música Mundana Maqueda, 1998).

6. Malinowski, "Introduction," in Ortiz, *Cuban Counterpoint* (1947), x–xi.

7. Ortiz, *Cuban Counterpoint* (1947), 6.

8. Alejo Carpentier, "El recuerdo de Amadeo Roldán" in *Ese músico que llevo dentro* (Havana: Letras Cubanas, 1980), cited in *La isla infinita de Fernando Ortiz*, ed. by Antonio Fernández Ferrer (Alicante: Instituto de Cultura Juan Gil-Albert, 1998), 15.

9. Jean Franco, "Angel Rama y la transculturación narrativa en América Latina," *Sin Nombre* vol. XIV, no. 3 (1984): 69, cited in Fernández Ferrer, ed. *La isla infinita*, 29–30.

I

LIFE AND EDUCATION

The heterodox style of Fernando Ortiz as a lawyer, anthropologist, and essayist grew out of a tradition of transatlantic migration and his own early childhood experience in Minorca. Ortiz's daughter, María Fernanda Ortiz, relates that even while in Minorca, he cultivated his passion for Cuba, and when he returned there in 1906 he realized that "like any other Cuban I was also confused." This realization led to his insatiable thirst for interdisciplinary studies. Miguel Angel Puig-Samper Malero and Consuelo Naranjo Orovio reconstruct Ortiz's intellectual formation in Spain, during the early years of the twentieth century, emphasizing the influence of the Spanish and Italian schools of criminology. Octavio di Leo proposes that Ortiz's intellectual interest on Afro-Cuban themes began during his initial legal studies in Madrid where he examined the reality of Spanish prisons and visited the Overseas Museum. María del Rosario Díaz asserts, based on manuscript sources in Havana, that Ortiz had begun to work on a study of the Chinese underworld in Cuba around 1902 at the same time he was starting to do research on Afro-Cuban criminal activities.

1

Fernando Ortiz, My Father

María Fernanda Ortiz Herrera

Fernando Ortiz was not only my father. He was also my friend, my confidant, and my tutor through "the school of life," as he used to say. Despite our age difference (I was born when he was sixty-four years old), I was very close to him and to my mother, María Herrera. We were a close, happy family. I never entered or left my house without looking for my father, whether he was alone or entertaining people, simply to kiss him and tell him what I was up to. He was always interested in my problems and gave me his attention. He always encouraged me to learn, study, and choose a degree, whichever interested me the most. When I chose molecular biology and genetics, he was thrilled. He would tell me, "Life, that is a real mystery." He would make sensible and demanding observations: "The approaching new world is about knowing, not having; one must study and be well prepared." However, when he saw me busy studying, he would say, with immense understanding, "It is incredible how much work students have to do these days." If he saw me stressed over my exams, he would attempt to calm me down: "Don't worry, go to bed, get some rest. Don't worry about being outstanding. I have seen many outstanding students being failures in life."

Above all, my father was a Cuban. He was born in Havana in 1881. At his birth my grandfather solemnly declared, "One more insurrectionist," but my grandmother had a premonition: "He will be plenipotentiary consul of a free Cuba." With time this was to be true (my father was the Cuban consul in La Coruña and then in Genoa), and if my grandfather's assertion never occurred it was only because my father was always opposed to violence and weapons. Even though he was never a revolutionary, he was an eternal "inconformist," as he would say; and a *bembón*, as Cubans generally say, because he would always say what he thought, since he believed that opposing views and being able to express them was necessary for a person's intellectual progress and for the general development of mankind.

At the age of fourteen months, my father went to live in Ciudadela, on the Spanish island of Minorca. There he spent his childhood and completed his primary and secondary education. His tutor was the great educator Juan Benejam, and he published his first text, *Principi y Prostes*, in Minorcan in 1895. That same year my father returned to Cuba, and began studying law at the University of Havana. Due to the grave problems in our country toward the end of the century, my grandfather decided to send him to Spain again, where he received his degree in law at the University of Barcelona. Later, in 1901, he obtained his Ph.D. in law from the University of Madrid. These initial years in my father's life, as is the case in anyone's, were to prove decisive in his education. Curiously, I believe that the great affection he held for Cuba began while he was in Minorca, thanks to his Cuban mother who so desired her son to represent a free Cuba. Following Cuban independence, when the time came to choose nationality, my father opted to be Cuban, but he remained fond of Spain and felt deeply for Spain's problems as well as Cuba's. As Gastón Baquero accurately stated in 1997 during the presentation of the new edition of *Los instrumentos de la música afrocubana* in Madrid, "One must not forget that Fernando Ortiz was 100 percent Cuban, but also 100 percent Spanish."

It was probably when my father returned to Cuba that he realized that while he was absent he had somewhat idealized Cuba. It was then that he found that there was a lot to be done. He was completely shaken by the configuration of the new Cuban nation and the reform of his Creole class. My father transmitted the love he felt toward Cuba to me when I was very young. I want to illustrate this with an example: My father was an adept painter (a hobby very few have known about). When I was around three years old, we would paint together while I sat on the arm of the couch in front of his desk. The first things he taught me to paint were the Cuban peasant's hut (*bohío*), the royal palm tree, and the Cuban flag with its solitary star. My father understood the notion of patriotism; he taught me its meaning and taught me to cherish it. He also encouraged me to identify key public figures in our history. His speech in the Sociedad Económica de Amigos del País, on January 9, 1914, illustrates the point:

> If you wish to recover the lost ideal you must turn to the memory of Saco, the father of our sociology; to Arango, the father of our economy; to Espada, the father of our charity; to Varela, the father of our philosophy; to Las Casas, the father of good government.[1]

My father's work, filled with research in the areas of anthropology, ethnography, sociology, economics, and law, was almost entirely dedicated to his country. He studied its aboriginal inhabitants, the African influence in our society, music, dance; he portrayed the country's economic problems, associated with the sugarcane and tobacco industries, in important and plea-surable texts such as *Contrapunteo cubano del tabaco y el azúcar*, repub-lished recently in Madrid by EditoCubaEspaña. However, he also left a legacy of projects, speeches, and books that are still relevant today, not only for Cuba but also for the world. I would like to mention his text *El engaño de las razas* (1946), in which he defends the protection of human rights, even before the signing of the Declaration of Human Rights in 1948. Through his beloved Sociedad Económica de Amigos del País, he defended the need to improve the education system in Cuba. He strove to promote cultural ex-change through the Institución Hispano-Cubana de Cultura, especially be-tween Cuba and Spain, and welcomed the valuable knowledge that any for-eign nation could provide. The Hispano-Cubana was a free institute, open to all ideologies. His objectives and ideals in life, which he tried to instill in me, were knowledge, culture and more culture, the expression of ideas, respect, tolerance, and furthering the knowledge of our country.

My father was a learned and cultured man, yet also modest despite his enormous level of culture. He was never afraid of admitting his ignorance regarding specific issues and would always encourage the person he was talking with to thoroughly research the matter under discussion. He would correct his analysis or hypothesis, always through genuine conviction or through finding new information after long hours of research, but never due to intellectual complacency. My father's honesty and modesty are reflected throughout his work. I was moved when Professor Castellanos of Miami agreed with this observation.

His inquiring spirit and zeal for research, which led him to search for answers to all kinds of social, political, or other quandaries, led him to find coherence in unusual and challenging topics. As he acknowledged, these were two qualities that always attracted him and were ubiquitous in his work. My inquisitive stage, the age of questions through which all children pass (often perturbing adults), was different for me in that my father always encouraged me to continue searching for answers. He was always willing to share his intellectual craving. He did so not only with distinguished intellectuals but also with me, my friends, and all those who approached him searching for answers and craving knowl-edge or seeking advice. Everyone was welcome regardless of gender, age, creed, or race (as he often stated in *Ultra,* the magazine published by the Insti-tución Hispano-Cubana de Cultura, a magazine that he founded and directed for many years). Despite his continuous exchange of opinions with many peo-ple in discussion groups during different stages of his life, he never indulged in teamwork, never intended to lead a school of thought, and he was certainly an unconditional follower of anyone or anything.

My father taught me, or at least attempted to teach me, to think. He believed that thought was every human being's right and obligation. According to him, thinking is one of the hardest things to do because we are all conditioned by our background, education, and increasingly by the media. "Thinking is suffering, it involves creating," he used to tell me. "Look, girl (*chica*), you listen to everyone's ideas, and then do your own cooking (*cocinadito*) and reach your own conclusions."

My father always opposed "sectarianism." He would insist that respect for others was essential for coexistence and progress. "Your rights," he would say to me, "end where other people's rights begin, and you must respect the views of others, even if you disagree with them." My father's respect for others was so large that he never told me what to do. When I sought his advice, he would express his own personal view and would inevitably add, "But you must decide, use your own judgment."

While still in good health, there was nothing that he enjoyed more than the company of a keen listener, to talk with absolute freedom about anything with anyone who showed interest in learning. In addition to teaching me to respect and tolerate the views of others, my father also taught me another of his principles: that I had to learn to defend my own position and convictions, and express them with educated manners and the firmness of being honest, especially to myself.

My father's views on defending one's convictions are clearly reflected in his texts on Afro-Cuban music, as a response to the view that the black drums "did not produce" music. My father contended that the drum did produce music. This was the inspiration behind *La africanía de la música folklórica de Cuba* and *Los bailes y el teatro de los negros en el folklore de Cuba*, which we have reedited with Editorial Música Mundana in Madrid, as well as the five volumes of *Los instrumentos de la música afrocubana*.

I want to clarify that my father studied our process of "transculturation"—a concept that he introduced for the first time in 1940[2]—and the African influence in Cuba with scientific method and great respect, but he was never involved in the everyday praxis of these matters, as some have tried to suggest.

Another prominent characteristic was his complete ideological independence, the importance of which he made me understand. In the 1920s, he was a representative of the Cuban Liberal Party. He told me that after a few years he abandoned it, disappointed to find that politics was full of corruption; he discovered that he would be unable to aid his young country if he was in politics, and after that he never participated in party politics. When I was young, hearing him speak about political parties, I remember asking him, "Dad, what are you?" and he replied, with his great sense of humor, "I'm a nonconformist," and "What party is that?" He laughed and said, "No, I don't belong to any political party." "And why?" This last question remained unanswered. I thought he had to belong to some party; as far as I was concerned, all "adults" could talk about politics, and everyone talked about parties. Some years later, when we discussed the issue again and when I was a better conversationalist, I asked him again, "Why do you not belong to any political party?" He said, "Because, *chica*, when you become part of a political party, you cease to be free, you are no longer able to say what you think, and you must follow the group's discipline." My father did not wish to compromise his beliefs. The fact that he abandoned party politics did not mean that he had lost his commitments. He was always committed: to Cuba, to himself, and, of course, to his family.

I do not know of any other magazine in any language that can be compared to *Ultra* as to useful information, interesting material, and universal cultural values for the general reader. There is nothing like it published in English. As he used to point out, he had been accused of almost everything. I believe that even today his views are misinterpreted. I believe that in order to understand my father's truly liberal spirit, references to his "Mensajes" in the journal *Ultra* are essential. I would ask all scholars who approach my father's work to study this magazine, not partially, but as a whole. In 1939, Stella Clemence, a writer and a book fan, director of the Harkness Collection and the Latin American section of the Library of Congress in Washington, D.C., referred to *Ultra* in the following terms: "I encourage you to read these messages by Fernando Ortiz and the content and diversity of the articles published in *Ultra*. I believe that the real value of Ortiz's scholarship lays there, reflected in his work and his teachings."

My father, as I have already stated, was an eternal "disagreer," and while he physically could, he fought for Cuba's moral, social, and racial integrity; he fought for our "*cubanidad*," as he used to say. He was a man who approached all problems, even his own and those of his family, with a wide perspective, with the attitude of a genuine daily thinker. He was a great Cuban, a great confidant, a great friend, and a great father.

I hope that Fernando Ortiz's work will be a reference for future generations in Cuba and that his ideals of a unique, united, free, culturally rich Cuba, where all trends of thought can flourish, may become a reality for this great nation we have before us. In closing, I would like to quote my father's words in the section "Afirmaciones de Cultura" of *Ultra* in 1936:

> Without mutual tolerance, which is the livening factor behind culture, science is reduced to chatter, religion to sterile 'fanaticism,' justice to oppressive despotism, and the power behind social rhythm turns into a suffocating, repelling beast.[3]

NOTES

1. Fernando Ortiz, *Seamos hoy como fueron ayer: Discurso pronunciado el 9 de enero de 1914 en la Sociedad Económica de Amigos del País* (Havana: La Universal, 1914).

2. Fernando Ortiz, *Contrapunteo cubano del tabaco y el azúcar* (Havana: José Montero, 1940).

3. "Afirmaciones de Cultura," *Ultra* 1, no. 1 (1936): 79–81.

2

Spanish Intellectuals and Fernando Ortiz (1900–1941)

Consuelo Naranjo Orovio and
Miguel Angel Puig-Samper Mulero

The influence of the Italian positivist scholars, particularly Cesare Lombroso and Enrico Ferri, has often been associated with Fernando Ortiz's anthropological work. This influence is clearly reflected in the prologue of Ortiz's *Hampa afro-cubana, Los negros brujos* (1906), and in his involvement in an Italian magazine directed by Lombroso.[1] However, there is less awareness of the influence the first Spanish criminologists and sociologists had on Ortiz's work and his education in the universities of Madrid and Barcelona. This chapter analyzes Ortiz's educational and intellectual experience in Spain, and the interactions between him and Spanish intellectuals during important stages of his early and mature career.

After his elementary and high school education in the Institute of Mahon, on the island of Minorca, Ortiz returned to Cuba for his college preparatory studies and first years of studies in law at the University of Havana, at the time of Cuba's war for independence in 1895–1898. He subsequently moved to Barcelona, where he finished his law degree in 1900, and then went on to Madrid for his Ph.D.[2] In Madrid, he came in contact with renowned Spanish positivists, many of them from the Instituto Libre de Enseñanza. These intellectuals had been developing Spanish Krausism—which was first introduced by Julián Sanz del Río and continued by Francisco Giner de los Ríos—into Krauspositivism. The latter ideology preserved certain notions of the primitive Krausism (such as the notion of organicity and evolution of society), as well as some of its ideals (such as the belief in social regeneration through education), while flirting with the theoretical views of the new positivism and Spencerian evolutionism.[3]

FERNANDO ORTIZ AND THE SPANISH "LOMBROSO"

Among Ortiz's professors in Madrid, it is important to mention the influence of Rafael Salillas. In 1900, Salillas became the director of the Criminology Laboratory of the School of Philosophy of Law in the Universidad Central de Madrid, then chaired by Francisco Giner de los Ríos. Giner himself had encouraged new approaches to criminalist anthropology within the Instituto Libre de Enseñanza. Its *Boletín* had published aspects of these new penal sciences in articles by Joaquín Sama, Pedro Dorado Montero, Alfredo Calderón, and Concepción Arenal. Their goal was to disseminate the ideas of the Lyon School led by Lacassagne, the Krauspositivists, the Italian positivists, and Correctionalism, the latter probably being the most influential among the Giner de los Ríos's group.

In 1886, after a period spent considering the reform of judicial institutions for the insane in collaboration with fellow positivist doctor Luis Simarro, Salillas began publishing a series of articles dealing with criminal life in Spain in *Revista General de Legislación y Jurisprudencia*. Salillas was also well known for his lectures on anthropology in criminal law at the Ateneo in Madrid, the sanctuary of local positivism. In 1896, he published *El delincuente español: el lenguaje (estudio filológico, psicológico y sociológico con dos vocabularios jergales)*; two years later he published the second part, *El delincuente español: hampa (Antropología picaresca)*; concluding his trilogy with *La teoría básica bio-sociológica* in 1901. All of these texts were clearly influenced by Lombrosian and Spencerian positivism, but with an emphasis on Spanish national peculiarities, something similar to what Fernando Ortiz would attempt eight years later in *Hampa afro-cubana* with regard to the roots of criminal behavior in Cuba. The seal of this Spanish Lombroso in Ortiz's work is evident, both in his positivist perspective and in the selection of themes for his earlier works. Even after Salillas's death, Ortiz was interested in Salillas's notes relating to an 1901 article published in the *Revista de Legislación y Jurisprudencia* on the *ñáñigos*, the black secret societies in Cuba, as evinced from a letter Ortiz wrote to José María Chacón in 1927.[4] Salillas had also discussed the theme in a lecture delivered at the Ateneo in Madrid a few years before.

Salillas's teaching career began in the Criminology Laboratory of the Giner de los Ríos program, at the same time Fernando Ortiz was studying philosophy of law in the University of Madrid. From information that Salillas himself published in the *Revista de Legislación y Jurisprudencia* between 1900 and 1902, as well as in the *Anales del Laboratorio de Criminología* (Madrid, 1899–1900), we know that the laboratory dealt with childhood crime and Lombroso's views on the origins of moral insanity and crime, the relationship between alcohol and moral insanity, and the notion of abnormality as described by Morel, Lombroso, Garófalo, Marro, Durkheim, and Ferri. Before founding the School of Criminology in 1903, Salillas collaborated with Giner himself, as well as Simarro and fellow professor Constancio Bernaldo de Quirós, a Spanish criminologist and sociologist who was one of Giner's youngest disciples and someone who also left an imprint on Ortiz's work.[5]

CRIMINOLOGY AND SOCIOLOGY: CONSTANCIO BERNALDO DE QUIRÓS

Young Bernaldo de Quirós was in charge of the foreign publications section in the *Revista General de Legislación y Jurisprudencia*, where he published the works of the Italian positivists (Lombroso, Ferri, Nicéforo, Manzini) between 1898 and 1901. Texts such as *Las nuevas teorías de la criminalidad* (1898) and *La mala vida en Madrid: Estudio psico-sociológico* (1901) were the result of Bernaldo de Quirós's work in the Salillas lab, which he pursued with the cooperation of J. M. Llanas. Llanas also followed the Salillas and the Nicéforo and Sigheli (*La mala vida en Roma*) schools of thought, which were based on the "fieldwork" of marginal groups, much in the same way as Ortiz would do later in the case of Havana.[6]

After Fernando Ortiz settled down in Cuba in 1902, he continued to correspond with Bernaldo de Quirós, a Spanish criminologist and sociologist who would soon redirect his research toward rural sociology, as a result of his work in the Social Reforms Institute. This new institution was led by Gumersindo de Azcárate, another pillar of Spanish Kraussism, who had lectured Ortiz on Comparative Legislation in Madrid and was one of the first theorists in the discipline.[7]

Ortiz sent his doctoral thesis to Bernaldo de Quirós on April 4, 1902. Later Ortiz also sent him the prospectus of *La Cultura Latina*, a magazine founded by Francisco Federico Falco, an Italian criminologist living in Cuba, which published contributions by Lombroso, Ferri, Tarde, and Dorado Montero.[8] Ortiz also communicated information regarding scientific activities on the island, which was of interest to Bernaldo de Quirós, as it was useful for the revision of his text *Nuevas teorías de la criminalidad*. In 1903, Ortiz publicized and reviewed an article by Bernaldo de Quirós on alcoholism in *Azul y Rojo*. In his review, Ortiz comments on the virtues of Bernaldo de Quirós article, the originality of his work, and his translations of Lombroso, Ferri, and Nicéforo. He places Bernaldo de Quirós among the most renowned criminologists, along with Dorado Montero and Salillas.[9]

Subsequent letters Ortiz wrote to Bernaldo de Quirós follow the Cuban intellectual's professional itinerary after he was appointed Consul in Coruña in 1903. From Coruña, Ortiz wrote to Bernaldo de Quirós to inform him of his arrival in Spain, which opened new opportunities for them to work together. In 1905, Ortiz returned to Cuba to continue his intellectual endeavors. In

1906, Ortiz sent Bernaldo de Quirós his article on "La mala vida cubana," which was undoubtedly influenced by Bernaldo de Quirós's "La mala vida en Madrid." That same year, Quirós published another article in *Derecho y Sociología,* by Ortiz's invitation. The Spanish criminalist returned the gesture by inviting Ortiz to publish his "Identificación criminológica" in the Criminal Sciences Library series. However, Ortiz's work was published in Havana in 1913 by the La Universal publishing house, under the title *La identificación dactiloscópica. Informe de policiología y de derecho público, seguido de las instrucciones técnicas para la práctica de la identificación y del decreto orgánico No. 1.173 de 1901,* and republished in Madrid in 1916 by Daniel Jorro, on Bernaldo de Quirós recommendation.

Furthermore, Bernaldo de Quirós wrote a review of *Los negros brujos* in *La Lectura* in 1906 and promised he would write another one for a German journal of criminal anthropology directed by Dr. Hellwig. From Havana in 1908, Ortiz sent Bernaldo de Quirós a copy of his recently published *Para la agonografía española: Estudio monográfico de las fiestas menorquinas.*[10]

ENCOUNTER WITH SPANISH PHYSICAL ANTHROPOLOGY

We also have evidence of Ortiz's relationship with physical anthropologist Federico Olóriz. Olóriz was renowned for founding an anthropological museum-laboratory attached to the Faculty of Medicine in Madrid and for his works on anatomy and anthropology, especially his *Manual de Técnica Anatómica* (1890), *Distribución geográfica del índice cefálico en España* (1894), and *La talla humana en España* (1896). As a result of these texts, he was considered to be one of the pioneers of the biogeographic perspective in Spanish anthropology. He was also the author of various texts dealing with issues that interested Ortiz during this early stage, including *Dactiloscopía* (1908) and *Manuel pour l'identification des délinquents de Madrid* (1911).[11] Ortiz shared with Olóriz his work on Afro-Cuban rebellions and Minorcan festivals.[12]

KRAUSPOSITIVISM AND CRIMINAL LAW:
PEDRO DORADO MONTERO

Apart from the group in Salillas's lab, to which Ortiz was linked through Giner and the Instituto Libre de Enseñanza, Ortiz was also directly influenced by the work of Dorado Montero, a professor at the University of Salamanca. Dorado had made himself known in Spain through his involvement in disseminating articles on Italian criminal positivism in magazines such as *Boletín de la Institución Libre de Enseñanza, Revista General de Legislación y Jurisprudencia, La España Moderna*, and *Nueva Ciencia Jurídica*, and above all for his book *La antropología criminal en Italia* (Madrid, 1889).[13] Despite his role in disseminating Italian positivism, Dorado maintained a critical positivist criticism of Lombroso's school and gradually narrowed his work toward a more eclectic view nearer to Krauspositivism.

Dorado was also influenced by British evolutionists—Darwin and Spencer—from whom he discovered the importance of the empirical method and the notion of society as an evolving organism. This background is evident in his sociological work, especially in *El derecho penal en Iberia* (Madrid, 1901). However, Dorado never forgot, and in fact he gradually incorporated the ideals of the Giner group. Following Krause and Röder, he considered punishment good and argued the importance of education in social transformation. Dorado thus agreed with the correctionalist views held by Giner and Arenal in his quest for reconciling the Krausist metaphysics of his teachers with the new criminal positivist views, something seemingly impossible.[14]

Letters preserved in the Biblioteca Nacional José Martí and in the archive of the University of Salamanca show that Ortiz and Dorado begun their correspondence in 1900. In 1900, Dorado answered Ortiz's queries on sources and bibliography for his work on the civil reparation of crime victims, which was the subject of his doctoral thesis. Dorado recommended that Ortiz should consult the records of international conferences on crime, the publications of the Société des Prisons de París, and the works of Demogue, Barrows, Tallaik, Leonardo Bertano, and the Scuola Positiva.[15] Reading Ortiz´s thesis, one can see that Dorado's recommendations were followed. Before traveling to Havana, Ortiz sent Dorado a copy.

Ortiz maintained contact with Dorado while working in the Cuban consulates in Coruña and Genoa. From Genoa, Ortiz notified him in 1904 that he would be publishing *La Cultura Latina*. Upon returning to Havana in 1906, Ortiz sent his *Hampa afro-cubana* to Dorado for his "authorized criticism" of what would be—according to Ortiz—a great work involving studies such as "Negros curros," "Los negros ñáñigos," "Los negros criminales," "La negra prostituta," and "La mala vida de los chinos en Cuba." Ortiz wanted to conduct a detailed study of crime in the island, "so rich in original observations." In August 1906, Dorado rushed to respond and congratulate Ortiz for the quality of his text and his dedication to research. He also inquired after the magazine *Derecho y Sociología*, in which Dorado had published the article "El derecho ¿es la fuerza?" that same year.

In October 1906, Dorado announced that he would be writing a review of Ortiz's book in *Revista de Legislación*. Dorado also expressed his solidarity regarding the United States' intervention in Cuba's fight for independence by stating, "I trust that you will emerge victorious from the test which, as a nation, you appear to be subjected to at present." In November 1906, Ortiz also received the text that Dorado had mentioned in previous letters, *De criminología y penología* (published in Madrid in 1906), which contained a number of articles, such as one dealing with the crime culture (*matonismo*) in Spain. Ortiz intended to use these works for writing *Los negros curros*, as he believed that these characters were nothing but the crystallization of Andalucian *matonismo* within the African and colonial context of Cuba. Ortiz thanked Dorado for including his works in a bibliography of *Revista de Legislación de Madrid* and told Dorado of his future involvement with Bernaldo de Quirós on a project for identifying criminals.[16] In 1908 Dorado confirmed that he had received Ortiz's text *Para la agonografía española* and asked him whether he had received, in turn, *El correcionalismo penal y sus bases doctrinales*. During the next year, Ortiz praised Dorado as a true master in a note, published in *Cuba y América*, in which he also referred to the state of criminal anthropological studies in Spain.[17]

The receipt of Ortiz's *La reconquista de América: Reflexiones sobre el panhispanismo* one year after its publication served as an opportunity for Dorado to reply on June 13, 1911 to Ortiz's stern stance against the revival of Spanish cultural imperialism. Although he understood the recent historical circumstances of the quarrel, Dorado noted that he thought Ortiz's words were too hostile, not only toward Spanish imperialists but also toward Spain. At the same time, he advised Ortiz not to take the "Oviedans" too seriously— a probable reference to Rafael Altamira and his group. Dorado considered that their entire campaign revolved around "games of artifice."

In his last letter from Salamanca on June 28, 1913, Dorado again congratulated Ortiz for his text *La identificación dactiloscópica*, which he considered to be the best project he had seen in the field, and also asked whether he had received his *Psicología criminal*, which Dorado had sent in 1912.[18]

THE SOCIOLOGY OF MANUEL SALES Y FERRÉ

Another Spanish intellectual whom Ortiz admired and studied under was Manuel Sales y Ferré, one of the most prominent representatives of Krauspositivism. Sales is considered to be the founder of sociology in Spain. He had a brilliant intellectual evolution ranging from pure Krausism to positivism, with a strong influence from Spencerian evolutionism. His views were reflected in several publications in the fields of anthropology and prehistoric studies, some of which were also published in the *Boletín de la Institución Libre de Enseñanza*. Sales had an intense academic life in Seville, where he founded the Ateneo and a technical-scientific library of Krausist inspiration. He moved to Madrid in 1889 to head the Sociology Department. The first few years in Madrid he published *Estudios de Sociología* (Madrid, 1889) and *Tratado de Sociología* (Sevilla, 1894–1897), books with a clear positivist perspective. In 1900, he was appointed vice secretary of the International Institute of Sociology in Paris.

Sales founded the Sociology Institute of Madrid in 1901, where Ortiz delivered lectures on November 27 and December 7, 1901. Ortiz later published them as part of his *Para la agonografía española* (1908), in which his sociological concerns become evident through his studies of popular festivals. Following the model of Tylor and Raúl de la Grasserie, Ortiz produced a detailed ethnographic study that tackled the survival of folkloric forms to envision extinct social relationships.

A letter written by Sales to Ortiz, dated Madrid, April 29, 1902, reads:

> I received your farewell letter, dated December 29, and then a second one, dated March 12, informing me of your arrival.
>
> We are grateful for the kind memories you hold for all of us, and correspond to them deeply regretting your absence. The Institute is running well, though financially less stable. I hope it will not delay in starting its publications; we will send you copies.
>
> Everyone remembers you and wishes your prosperity, especially your true friend. If your engagements enable you to work on Sociology, do not hesitate to send us a copy of your work.[19]

When Sales died, Ortiz wrote about him for the January 1911 issue of Havana's *El Fígaro*. Ortiz described himself as Sale's disciple and remembered his lectures and the Sunday group excursions led by Sales with admiration and pleasure. Thanks to the excursions of the Sociology Institute, Ortiz managed to fathom the great landmarks of Spanish history and acquire knowledge on modern criminal science from the "infected galleries of the correctional facility in Alcalá de Henares, where Don Manuel left me so that I could experience it for several days and study it closely."[20]

His relationship to Sales provided Ortiz knowledge of social life in all its expressions, "families in humble homes; poverty in hospitals and asylums; the army in barracks; criminals in jails and correction centers; the clergy in cathedrals and sacristies; arts in monuments and museums." From the purest of positivisms, Ortiz noted that his master taught him and his fellow students sociology as if it were the anatomy, physiology, and pathology of townships. With regard to Sale's political ideology, Ortiz mentioned his republicanism, skepticism, and Americanism, with the ever-present premise of the regeneration of Spain.[21]

FERNANDO ORTIZ'S DOCTORAL THESIS: THE ITALIAN POSITIVISTS

Apart from seeking advice from his Spanish professors for his doctoral thesis, Ortiz also contacted Enrico Ferri and Rafaele Garófalo requesting a bibliography on civil reparation for the victims of crime. Ferri answered in a letter from

Rome dated February 6, 1900, recommending his text *Sociologia criminale*, published in Torino; Garófalo advised him to consult his text *Nuovi studi sulla riparazione dovuta alle vittime del reato*, published by the Scuola Positiva in 1892. There Ortiz found other authors of interest, such as Melchiore Gioia and Herbert Spencer. Garófalo, then procurator general of Rome's court, recommended consulting the essays presented before the penitentiary conferences in Paris and Brussels.[22]

Ortiz submitted his doctoral thesis before the Faculty of Law of the Universidad Central in Madrid on December 13, 1901. The theme was "Olvido que se ha tenido de la víctima del delito" ("Neglect Suffered by the Victims of Crime"), which was later published in Madrid under the title *Base para un estudio sobre la llamada reparación civil: Concepto y división del daño personal del delito. Id. De su resarcimiento: Necesidad social de que éste sea efectivo* (1901) (Basis for the Study of So-called Civil Reparation). Although biographies of Ortiz suggest that he had some problems with the members of the panel that judged his thesis, the records indicate that he received outstanding marks. It is worth remembering that the panel's president, Vicente Santamaría de Paredes, belonged to the same ideological group as Ortiz's tutors in Spain; he was a shareholder in the Instituto Libre de Enseñanza, later a collaborator of the Social Reforms Institute, and a relevant member of the organicist and evolutionist theories in sociology. It is not difficult to understand Santamaría's affinity with Ortiz's positions in his doctoral thesis.[23]

As his Spanish and Italian tutors recommended, in his doctoral thesis Ortiz used the works of the main representatives of Italian positivism, Lombroso, Ferri, Garófalo, Rossi, Carrara;[24] French criminalists Lacretele, Tarde, Lanessan, Greau, Littre, Féré; English evolutionists Darwin, Spencer, and the anthropologist Lubbock; and Bernaldo de Quirós's *Las nuevas teorías de la criminalidad*.

The Italians' influence began to show in young Ortiz's first articles, published in Havana by the journals *Azul y Rojo*, *Cuba y América*, *Derecho y Sociología*, *El Mundo Ilustrado*, and *El Fígaro*. In these articles, Ortiz praised Lombroso and his scholarship, and he expressed his views on the presidium in Havana and other aspects of criminology and criminal anthropology, always from a positivist perspective.[25]

His first active work with Italian positivists began in 1905, with the piece "La criminalita dei negri in Cuba," in the *Archivio di Psichiatria, Medicina Legale ed Antropologia Criminale* (Torino), which was directed by Lombroso. Ortiz's article was followed by other articles, relating to suicide among blacks and criminal superstition in Cuba. That year he also published *Los negros brujos* in Havana, with a prologue that was published in the same journal in 1906 by Lombroso. In four letters, written in 1905 and 1906, Lombroso wrote to Ortiz to congratulate him on the publication of *Los negros brujos* and the journal *Derecho y Sociología*, as well as for applying the notion of atavism in black witchcraft. In one of the letters, Lombroso confirmed that he had received Ortiz's text on "El suicidio de los negros, la criminalidad y la violación," which he insisted should be submitted for publication in the *Archivio*. Lombroso also suggested that he should research craneal-fisiognomic and tactile anomalies among blacks, as well as hypnotic spiritual phenomena, witchcraft, and the use of certain food substances and fetishes that could affect the nervous system.

After sending *Los negros brujos* to Ferri, Mariani, Nicéforo, and Abele de Blasio, Ortiz received various letters in 1906 praising his contributions to psychology and anthropology. Nicéforo also commented that he had read the text with great pleasure, as well as Ortiz's article on Lombroso in the *Archivio,* which he had reviewed for the *Picolo de Trieste*. Nicéforo stated that he had witnessed the same phenomena in Europe that Ortiz had noted among blacks in Cuba when studying criminal life, local customs, and primitive forms of witchcraft. Acknowledgment of Ortiz's work reached such a high level that in 1906, Mariani, the editor of the *Archivio*, requested his signature for an Album of Honor to be presented to Lombroso. In another letter in 1906, Mariani helped Ortiz contact other renowned criminalists Guillermo Ferrero, Antonio Marro, Abele de Blasio, and Bruno Franchi. Between 1908 and 1910, Ortiz received letters from Mariani and Ferri Blasio, confirming that they received his publications and requesting that he send them physical anthropological objects from Cuba. Also, Mariani kept him informed on the organization of the Criminal Anthropology Congress, and Antonio Russo thanked him in 1910 for his potential contribution to *Il Progresso del Diritto Criminale* of Palermo, then under the direction of Emanuele Carnevale.

In 1913, Ortiz began corresponding with one of Lombroso's daughters, Gina Ferrero Lombroso. She confirmed the receipt of *Identificación dactiloscópica* and published one of its chapters in the *Archivio* in 1914 under the title "Le origini antiche della dactiloscopia."[26] A complete copy of *Identificación dactiloscópica* was translated into Italian and placed at the Criminal Anthropology Library. In another undated letter, Ferrero commented on the difficulty of finding an academic translator for Ortiz's book, which was why this text was never actually published in Italian.

Despite World War I, Ortiz continued to exchange his publications with Italian professors. In 1915, he received a letter from Marcelo Finzi, Ferrara's teacher, thanking him for sending *Identificación dactiloscópica*, which Finzi was considering using in one of his lectures at the Scientific Police and Criminal Studies Institute in the University of Bologna. During that same year, Mariani confirmed he had received *La filosofía penal de los espiritistas: Estudio de filosofía jurídica* (Havana, 1915), which was edited by Ortiz, and mentioned the book in the Cuban Collection, *La Habana antigua y moderna*.[27]

The letter that perhaps brought Ortiz the most satisfaction during this period was one from Ferri in 1926. According to Ortiz, Ferri praised *Proyecto
de código criminal cubano*, which was about the 1921 Italian Criminal Code.
Ferri confided to Ortiz that Cuba could be at the level of the most civilized
countries in regard to the reform of the criminal justice system, far ahead of
countries such as Germany, Switzerland, Poland, Peru, Argentina, and others
that had recently introduced new criminal codes.[28]

SPANISH REVIEWERS OF THE CRIMINAL CODE PROJECT

In the spring of 1926, Ortiz asked José María Chacón to help him contact the
director of the *Revista de Legislación y Jurisprudencia in Madrid*, to inquire
about the possibility of publishing the *Proyecto* with a prologue by one of the
two most prestigious Spanish criminalists: Quintiliano Saldaña or Luis
Jiménez de Asúa.[29] The former had been a professor of criminal anthropology
at the University of Madrid since 1911 and a former professor at the School of
Criminology founded by Salillas. Saldaña was renowned for developing a
criminal biotypology more advanced than that of the Italian scholars; as a
criminalist, he was responsible for the reform of the criminal code in Spain
and thus very interested in Ortiz's project, which he favorably quoted in *El
atentado social* and *Capacidad criminal de las personas sociales*. Despite the
failure of a Spanish publication of the *Proyecto*, Saldaña maintained a good
relationship with Ortiz, whom he met in Madrid in 1928, and sent him his *La
criminologie nouvelle* (Paris, 1929), a text used at the University of Paris.[30]

When Ortiz attempted to send Jiménez de Asúa his *Proyecto* however,
there were problems. Jiménez de Asúa, a professor of criminal law in the
University of Madrid, had recently traveled to Cuba, and upon his return to
Spain he was deported to the Chafarinas Islands. In a letter dated May 18,
1926, Ortiz confided:

> I had written a letter with a copy of my project on the Criminal Code, but on the
> very same day in which I intended to send it we learned of your deportation,
> and therefore abstained from sending it, as it was unlikely to reach you easily,
> due to censorship and other security measures which are usually applied to no-
> toriously dangerous individuals. According to your government you fall in this
> category. Cubans and Spanish alike regretted the news here as I doubt there is
> any Spaniard visiting Havana after independence who has won more sympathy
> for your nation than you have, without the recourse to racial, religious or lan-
> guage ties, but simply through the showing of self worth and the community of
> ideas with the young American spirits.

Aside from thanking him for his support, which would continue over the
years, Jiménez de Asúa sent Ortiz a copy of an article which he had pub-

lished in *La Libertad* in Madrid, on "La reforma penal en Cuba" ("The Penal Reform in Cuba"), in which he praised Cuban criminalists, including Ortiz, and favorably critiqued the project for the new Cuban criminal code.[31]

ORTIZ AND SPANISH REGENERATIONISM: MIGUEL DE UNAMUNO

Miguel de Unamuno was another influence on Ortiz, despite their somewhat ambiguous relationship, especially in regard to the quest for American *regeneracionismo*.[32] In response to Ortiz's letter dated May 7, 1906, in which Ortiz praised Unamuno for his article "The Burial of Don Quijote," Unamuno sent Ortiz the following letter, dated June 1, 1906:

> My dear friend:
> Trusting that you had not yet read it, yesterday I sent you a copy of my Vida de D. Quijote y Sancho, a text in which I have discussed many of the views you approach in your article "La vida de las ideas" in El Mundo.
> Through this article I have been able to witness the horrible damage which this culture of *choteo* [teasing] creates, becoming, as you put it, *la desgracia criolla* [the Creole disgrace], and the terrible custom of qualifying anything which rises above the vulgar ideals of routine life as a *bobería* [silliness]. Argentineans use the term *macanas*, which means the same as *boberías*.
> It is a very peculiar thing that we Spaniards and Hispanic-Cubans spend our entire time contemplating the so called practical sense of other cultures which make progress and grow, and have not actually realized that this is due to their idealist spirit; it is due to their poetry that they progress. To us, poetry is merely a punch line—usually not poetic at all—and we do not conceive it as part of ordinary life. . . .
> The first thing one must teach people here is to have faith and confidence in themselves. This faith alone can defeat ridicule and sabotage. Courage to face all the saboteurs who conform to their routine is the greatest value of all. This is why I enjoy your comment on the bobos. When their saboteurs are silenced, they will receive the blessing of others.
> You must continue to fight against that brutal sense of false pragmatism, against the spirit of Sansón Carrasco, who is destroying the Spanish speaking world. Once we lose the flower of poetry we drown among one dead leaf after another.[33]

Following Ortiz's reply on July 16, 1906, in which he mentions posting a copy of *Hampa afro-cubana* and requests a portrait, on August 3 Unamuno replied:

> My dear friend:
> I am sure that your *Hampa afro-cubana*, which I hope will arrive soon, will interest me, as I have heard about it and it strikes me as very curious. I will let you know my views on it, and indeed hope to make them public.

I am glad that you enjoyed my text on D. Quijote and Sancho's Life.

I followed your suggestion and wrote yesterday to D. Severino Sollow from the Wilson Library, sending him copies of my two texts, so that he may sell them for a commission. I will continue to do the same with anything I produce from now on. I am sending you a photograph of myself, as you requested, and would appreciate it if you would tell me what you wish to do with it.

Bobadilla (Fray Candil) was here about one month ago, and he assured me that Havana was now the cultural revelation of Spanish speaking America. And if this fact is not so well known, it is only due to the fact that Cubans tend to be more reserved and less exhibitionist.

This must be so, as I receive almost twice as much material from Cuba than from Argentina and Chile or from anywhere else in America, and have heard of Cuban writers that I barely know. This effort to remain reserved is not a good thing. . . . Time is essential, and the only way of getting the better of it is by making yourself known as soon as you can.[34]

Ortiz's reply was published in *El Fígaro* next to a fragment of Unamuno's letter and his photograph on September 23, 1906. Ortiz disagreed with Unamuno's opinion, based on the information supplied by Bobadilla, regarding the supposed shyness of Cuban intellectuals, pointing out that these intellectuals' real fault was that they tried to stand out much too quickly, due to a kind of infantile vanity, self-indulgence, and lack of intellectual ideals. Ortiz went so far as to state:

The questions that concern scientists and governments in Europe and North America are ignored by the masses and our clay idols here. The political parties that we have to bear do not actually have substantially different views or programs, and all of us, whether Guelph or Ghibelline, are dragged along by this or that planet, rotating in more or less concentrical orbits around budgets, fearful that a crossing comet may shed light on the poverty of our solar system. We classify these people as abstainers, and treat them as traitors because they disturb the slumber of our digestion or they channel the impulses of our hunger.[35]

Ortiz also regretted the fact that the general public despised the *boberías* of intellectuals as well as their foreign appeal, as summed up by the colloquial expression "the country does not need the sympathy of foreigners." Such regrets were similar to those expressed by Unamuno in *Vida de D. Quijote y Sancho*.

Four years later, Ortiz contacted Unamuno to request a prologue for his *Entre cubanos* in which he intended to compile a series of regenerationist articles expressing "rage and desperation at the invincible sleepiness which overcomes us and prevents us from indulging in cultural life." Ortiz also sent Unamuno a series of articles published in *El Tiempo* so that he could see the true "Americanizing" and "de-Hispanizing" work of certain Cuban intellectuals, themselves determined to achieve regeneration in Cuba from an Americanist position, and contrary to the Hispanizing views Rafael Altamira had tried to propagate in his voyage to Cuba. Ortiz confirmed the arrival of Unamuno´s prologue in July 1911. In the end, however, the prologue could not be included in the edition of *Entre cubanos*, because in it Unamuno made reference to all the articles which Ortiz had sent him, including those already published in *La Reconquista de América*. Ortiz requested another prologue that Unamuno was not able to deliver.[36]

Although it was not published except as part of Unamuno's complete works, his prologue is interesting to the extent that it attempts to show certain key differences between the regenerationist notions on the two sides of the Atlantic, in this case between the notions of Ortiz and those of Unamuno. While Unamuno defends a concept of culture capable of defeating "race," in the same way as Ortiz does, he appears more reluctant to accept the de-Hispanizing political program Ortiz was developing at the time, which was bent on some form of "Saxonization" of the Cuban society parallel to the "Europeanization" of Spain. Unamuno favored modernization, as long as Hispanic cultural roots were preserved, primarily through a common language. That was something Ortiz did not agree with at the time. Unamuno stated that:

> I am convinced that language is the blood of the spirit, that thoughts are words, that each language carries, condensed through the pressure of centuries, a conception of life and the universe itself, and that he who talks in Spanish internally, thinks in Spanish, believe it or not, desire it or not.[37]

Wary of Ortiz's criticisms of intrusions by some Hispanizing intellectuals regarding the situation in Cuba and its possible solutions, Unamuno clearly maintained that Cuban regeneration should rest in the hands of Cubans. He wrote to Ortiz:

> Hyperbole, *choteo*, eroticism, mundane vanity—these are all symptoms of the same illness, that sleepiness or laziness, which may in itself be yet another symptom. Of what, I wonder? I must leave this question unanswered. It is not my duty, but the duty of the children of that country, to seek the answer to this question. This is a challenge, which Fernando Ortiz, among others, must undertake. His patriotism will undoubtedly guide him in the right direction. Or so I trust.

Just as Dorado had done, Ortiz began to distance himself from Italian positivism and its theories of biological determinism. The views of Giner de los Ríos were essential in the evolution of these two intellectuals: While Dorado explored the correctionalist theories upheld by Giner and Arenal within criminal law, Ortiz insisted on including social issues along with anthropological aspects of the "bad life" as determinants in the cultural and ethnical evolution of Cubans, something his Spanish mentors were already exploring in Spain.[38] Ortiz believed that analysis of social phenomena was essential for understanding history. It is also worth noting that Ortiz never directed his research toward morphology and craneometry, which clearly differentiated him from the Italian criminalists.

The progress of Ortiz's theoretical perspectives resulted in a radical modification of his convictions, methodology, and topics. As such, positivism gradually gave way to a more balanced scientific approach to society and individuals. By 1920, Ortiz can be viewed as a fully formed intellectual who expressed a Cuban national sentiment based on the study of psychological and social factors.[39] His criticism of the study of society based on race and not culture occurred simultaneously with his attacks against racial categories, which he deemed artificial and conventional and which he considered a category of culture.[40] It was precisely the study of cultures and not races that led Ortiz to define Cubanity as a category of culture, a culture in which the fusion of all ethnic contributions would lead to the integration of all social forces which were a part of this island and its nationality.

POLEMICS AND COLLABORATION
WITH SPANISH INTELLECTUALS

Ortiz's interaction with Spanish intellectuals of the "regeneration" group also featured important polemics. One of the best known is the one he carried on with University of Oviedo historian Rafael Altamira. Altamira visited Cuba in 1910 where he engaged in a rhetoric that, in the opinion of many Cubans struggling to consolidate Cuban nationality and sovereignty, was too charged with Spanish bias (*españolismo*).[41] He advocated a "common Hispanic homeland" based on the common spirit of both peoples and a common language, which should encourage unity and not separation.[42] Altamira also encouraged the forgetting of "dark" events in the history of Spain in America and alerted his peers to the dangers of North American expansion and its attacks on the interests of Hispanic Americans and Spaniards, as well as what he called "our racial heritage."[43] In Ortiz's mind, Altamira's words regarding race—the "moral unity of race," "Spanish roots," and the "mission of Spain"—echoed the voices of traditional and regressive Spain, a continuous allusion to a common homeland, that for the Cuban anthropologist had long ago ceased to exist. For Ortiz, these words lacked intellectual content but were pregnant with political significance. To him they were the expressions of the new Spanish expansionism, of the so-called Pan-Hispanism and they collided head-on with his integratory and nationalist ideals. He condemned the attitude of certain Spanish intellectuals who, taking advantage of Altamira´s presence in Cuba, tried to revive the ghosts of the past by remembering heroic deeds and ignoring the country's problems.[44] In *Reconquista de América (The Reconquest of Spain)*, a collection of articles regarding his differences with Altamira, Ortiz defended arguments against the term *race* and in favor of culture and science. These arguments would later grow more consistent. Ortiz's criticism centers on the notion of "historical community" employed by Pan-Hispanists, as well as the views of a number of Spanish intellectuals who continued to exalt Spanish heroic deeds (*gestas*) without considering Cuban sensibilities. Ortiz proposed a rapprochement between Spain and Cuba on the bases of culture and civilization: "deprived of an intense and dominant civilization, race is an armor with no warrior inside; language, a mouth with no tongue; religion, a bell with no toll."[45]

In his criticism of Pan-Hispanism as an expansionist ideology, Ortiz brandishes his dynamic conceptions of culture and vindicates the original American and Cuban cultures. Based on these assessments, leaving aside paternalism and ghosts from the past, Ortiz proposed a model for building relations between countries. Finally, Ortiz wondered with skepticisms if there was any such thing as a Spanish race.

Despite these disputes, Ortiz maintained a close connection with Spain through the intellectuals who abandoned chauvinistic and racial rhetoric, and who worked in favor of science and culture. Proof of these contacts is the continuous correspondence between Ortiz and different Spanish authors, criminologists, criminal lawyers, historians, anthropologists, and sociologists. In response to Ortiz's interest, expressed through José M. Chacón, Emilio Cotarelo, who in 1925 was the secretary of the Real Academia de la Lengua Española, proposed the organization of an Academia in Cuba. It would be similar to the one in Spain, where sixteen people would work alongside Ortiz and Dr. Pichardo. Ortiz welcomed this suggestion as a "very positive benefit for Hispanic culture and the protection of the language." In July of that same year, Fernando Ortiz was appointed an honorary member of the Academia de Jurisprudencia y Legislación Española.[46]

His close connection to Spain was evident on several other occasions. One of them was the visit of Adolfo Bonilla San Martín to the Academia de la Historia de Cuba in 1925. Ortiz intended to establish an open dialogue beyond that of race, a prominent subject among intellectuals and politicians in Spain. He suggested the study of a common history as a means of approaching the traditions of Spain and thereby understanding those of Cuba, but without resorting to the argument of other intellectuals who stated that race was the common element among Hispanic countries. He wanted to establish cultural and scientific relationships based on equality, not on subordination, and on mutual knowledge—not only knowledge of Spain, but on respect of each other's history and the singularity of Cuban history.

In 1928, on the occasion of his visit to Spain, Ortiz again criticized the manner in which the Spanish government tried to approach Spanish America by invoking religion and race. Still, he believed that an alliance with Spain was a historical imperative. Searching the common past for the possible causes of the current state of relations between the two nations, Ortiz's thinking grew closer to that of some Spanish intellectuals. He recognized the vices and qualities of the Cuban people in Spanish history and advocated the strengthening of a Latin culture with its own voice. Thus, he commented, "Cuba, in not few respects, is more Spanish than Spain itself."[47] Despite this, he refused to accept the propaganda that certain politicians and intellectuals created around religion, language, and race. He retorted that despite inquisitorial and racist fanatics, there was neither a Spanish religion nor a Spanish race. Likewise, in a short interview after his trip to Spain that year, Ortiz opposed Americanism and classic Hispanic-Americanism.[48]

In 1929, Benjamín Jarnés commented on Ortiz's trip in *Revista América*, stressing Ortiz's words in favor of culture and not race, "purgatives, not balsams. Open air, not chains. Vitality, not stagnation." Continuing this thought, Jarnés argued that the term race was mostly formed by negative historical elements and not by living substance. Remembering Ortiz's observation "culture can attract, race can't," he argued the shortcomings of considering race as the common link between countries.[49]

THE INSTITUCIÓN HISPANO-CUBANA DE CULTURA

Ortiz was pivotal in the initiative to establish Spanish-Cuban relations at the intellectual level, from the early twentieth century until the arrival of Spanish exiles in Cuba as a result of the Spanish Civil War (1936–1939). With regard to his connection to the Spanish cultural world and his correspondence with Unamuno and Dorado, among others, one must differentiate between two distinct stages. In the first stage, up to the 1920s, Ortiz adopted a very critical position toward Spanish culture, favoring Americanization over Hispanization. On the one hand, Ortiz admired Altamira for his efforts at modernizing Spain through Europeanization and scientific renovation. On the other hand, at the time of Altamira's trip to Cuba in 1910, Ortiz criticized his effort to persuade Spanish American countries to re-Hispanize themselves in order to counteract the aggressive penetration of Anglo-Saxon culture. Ortiz countered that if Spain needed to Europeanize, then Cuba and other Spanish American countries would be required to Americanize so as to achieve modernity.[50]

Gradually Ortiz moderated his early radical views and became disillusioned with the idea that all modernity would come from the North. The example in other Latin American countries, such as Argentina, Uruguay or Mexico, where exchange institutes with Spain had been established, led Ortiz to an important decision. On November 12, 1926, he proposed the creation of the Institución Hispano-Cubana de Cultura (IHCC) in Havana during a lecture at the Sociedad Económica de Amigos del País, an institution he then presided over and considered the "Cuban daughter of the Enlightenment." The official establishment of the IHCC was approved ten days after with the main objective of

> endeavoring to increase the intellectual relations between Spain and Cuba through the exchange between scientists, artists, and students, the founding of professorships, and publicizing activities geared toward the intensification and diffusion of our own culture.[51]

The IHCC, which Ortiz founded in Havana on November 22, 1926, emerged in the midst of the Sociedad Económica as a result of Ortiz's intellectual commitment to other Spanish-speaking nations and specifically Spain. It was an independent association, free of political allegiances, that attracted prestigious Spanish intellectuals who came to Cuba as fellows and professors. In 1928, the institution launched its own journal, *Mensajes de la Institución Hispanocubana de Cultura*, and in 1930 it sponsored another publication, the monthly *Surco*. Among the first Cuban members of the IHCC, apart from its founder, were Ramiro Guerra, Jorge Mañach, Juan Marinello, Carlos Loveira, Herminio Portell Vilá, Israel Castellanos, Ramón Grau San Martín, and José C. Millás. Among the Spanish members residing in the island were Bernardo Solís, M. Solís Mendieta, and Aquilino Entrialgo, the owners of the well-known store El Encanto; José Solís, the deputy director of the *Diario de la Marina*; Pedro Sanjuán, the founder of Havana's Symphonic Orchestra; Alfredo Blanco, of the Galician Center; and Joaquín Sisto and Ceferino Morán, the owners of the store Fin de Siglo.[52]

Female membership at the IHCC was initially small but would later be important. Anthropologist Lydia Cabrera was among the important female scholars to join. Cabrera was a member of the IHCC's Feminine Advisory Committee, which had eleven members, among them Hortensia Lamar, René Méndez Capote, Lily Hidalgo de Conill, and Pilar Morlón.

Concerning economic support, the IHCC received numerous financial contributions from private donors, such as the publishing house Cultural S.A., Casino Español, Centro Asturiano, Centro Gallego, and Centro Andaluz. Also, the steamship company Compañía Transatlántica Española granted transportation fares with a 40 percent discount for invited professors traveling to Havana.[53] Avelino Gutiérrez of the Institución Cultural Española in Buenos Aires provided an additional donation.[54] A tacit agreement was also established between Ortiz and Manuel Aznar to announce the activities of the IHCC in the *Diario de la Marina* of Havana.

Institutional support included local agreements with the University of Havana and with the Junta para la Ampliación de Estudios e Investigaciones Científicas (JAE) in Madrid to represent the IHCC in Spain and cooperate in the organization of courses. Other institutions, such as the Spanish Cultural Institute (Institución Cultural Española) in New York and the Hispanic-Mexican University Exchange Institution (Instituto Hispano-Mexicano de Intercambio Universitario), also expressed willingness to link activities.[55]

In an interview in the *Diario de la Marina* on the occasion of the IHCC's inauguration, Ortiz declared the objectives of the new institution to be free of political bias, sectarianism, unilateral schools, and propaganda and to be strictly at the service of art and science. The institution would not spend time or resources in "songs to race, language, history, or the empire of Cervantes"; it would encourage intellectual work and study. Ortiz also announced that he had already invited Spanish professors Blas Cabrera and Fernando de los Ríos, at the time in Mexico, to participate in the inauguration of the IHCC. Ortiz also expressed the desire to collaborate with José Ortega y Gasset, Navarro Tomás, Gregorio Marañón, Américo Castro, Gustavo Pittaluga, Federico de Onís, and Menéndez Pidal on conferences and courses in Havana and to sponsor Cuban scholars sent to Spain to enhance their studies.

The dictatorship of Gerardo Machado (1925–1933) forced Ortiz to leave Cuba and reside in New York and Washington, D.C. (1931–1933). From abroad, he unsuccessfully attempted to continue publishing *Surco*. Upon his return to Cuba, he reorganized the IHCC, which started operating once again in 1936. During this second stage, the institution counted among its members several women who had been very active at the Lyceum, a prominent gathering place for Cuba's leading female intellectuals. Elena Mederos de González even became vice president of the IHCC. The new objectives of the institution were published in *Ultra* (Havana, 1936–1947). This journal became the institution's organ and published the proceedings of its conferences, publicized its activities, and diffused knowledge and current scientific advances. On November 1, 1939, "Hora Ultra" aired on the radio as a cultural program in which Cuban and foreign intellectuals participated, including Spanish professors residing in Cuba. In 1926, Chacón was nominated delegate and correspondent of the IHCC in Madrid with the objective of strengthening relations with Spain.[56] Ortiz asked Chacón to contact Menéndez Pidal and Ortega to inform them that his objective was to establish a Hispanic American exchange circuit: Montevideo, Buenos Aires, Santiago, Lima, Mexico, and Havana, for which he required the JAE's assistance.

Committed to his tasks from the very beginning, Chacón constantly informed Ortiz on the negotiations and internal dynamic of the JAE, its problems and conservative detractors, as well as on the decisions adopted in Spain with regard to America.[57] One such decision was the creation of the Cultural Relations Board (Junta de Relaciones Culturales) in 1926, within the Spanish Ministry of State, independent from the JAE and designed to diffuse and extend Spanish culture.[58] The debate that the creation of this new board produced led Chacón to recommend to Ortiz that he tactfully keep the institutes in touch. Ortiz replied that he would only maintain contact and exchanges with the JAE.[59]

To get the project moving, Ortiz contacted Santiago Ramón y Cajal, the president of the JAE in March 1927, informing him that he wanted the JAE to represent the IHCC in Spain, and pointing out that his decision had been based on the scientific prestige of the JAE.[60] Ortiz also informed Ramón e Cajal about the IHCC's scientific program, which would feature the participation of renowned Spanish scientists and intellectuals. Professors were requested to give ten lectures on cultural and scientific issues for associates of the IHCC, and an additional five or six lectures at the University of Havana. In exchange, they would receive two thousand pesos and steamship fare.

To establish networks and connections and to ensure flexible and economic trips for the Spanish professors, Ortiz was constantly in contact with the Cultural Institute in Mexico, the University of Puerto Rico, and the Instituto de las Españas, later renamed the Hispanic Institute (Instituto Hispánico), directed by Federico de Onís at Columbia University in New York. In 1927, Ramón y Cajal wrote to Ortiz, congratulating him on the creation of the IHCC and thanking him for honoring the JAE with the mission of representing it in Spain. Ramón y Cajal also wired Ortiz a message of "total agreement with the orientations and ideals you propose," adding that the JAE shared the same principles: scientific work with independence from politics, religion, and nationality.[61]

Personal relations and interaction between Ortiz and the JAE's José Castillejo also grew strong with time. In his letters, Ortiz addressed Castillejo as his "ideal friend," and they wrote to each other several times per month. Some of these letters show the routine workings and problems facing the IHCC and the JAE. In reference to the IHCC's efforts to increase its membership and obtain funds to purchase its own building, Ortiz asked Castillejo to send Spanish artistic and educational films for bimonthly showings.[62] In another letter, Ortiz informed Castillejo about the achievements of Spanish scholars such as Professor Luis de Zulueta, who established IHCC branches in Santiago, Matanzas, Sagua, and Manzanillo and encouraged the creation of those in Camagüey and Santa Clara. He also informed Castillejo that the Spanish ambassador had notified him that the Spanish minister of state had granted three free tickets per year for Spanish professors to travel and work with the IHCC; the IHCC was required to send proposals for each individual guest to the Spanish minister of public education.[63] This offer of free tickets did not materialize, and the IHCC's financial limitations forced Ortiz to request aid for tickets from the Spanish embassy in Havana.

Within the JAE, critics targeted Ortiz's position that the IHCC alone should select the exchange scholars. Chacón immediately communicated this to Ortiz, who wrote to Castillejo to clarify the objectives of the IHCC. Ortiz also commented that, contrary to other cultural institutions, the IHCC was not composed exclusively of Spanish individuals whose only objective was to show the American youth the positive values of contemporary Spanish mentality. Ortiz understood the hostility that the IHCC could trigger in Spain, as its objective was "culture and the spiritual improvement of my country." He reminded Castillejo that the IHCC counted on Cubans and some Spaniards who "back us, and have as their primary objective the spiritual advance of Cuba and for which we want to open up sources of culture from all horizons." This, he argued, was one of the reasons why the leadership of the IHCC should control the decisions regarding the selection of speakers. Additionally, the IHCC acted not only as an agency for the extension of studies but also as a lecture society, and therefore it had to offer its associates lectures that met their interest. The IHCC commitment was not only with Spain, although Spain had certain preference, but also with the rest of Latin America. Lastly the IHCC financed two annual scholarships in Spain, some of which were brokered by the JAE in Madrid.

The exchange program began in January 1927 with lectures by Fernando de los Ríos and Blas Cabrera. Cabrera spoke on "The Evolution of Stars," and de los Ríos spoke on the "Intellectual Renaissance of Spain." Cabrera gave two further lectures in the Aula Magna of the University of Havana: "Organization of the Atom and the Periodical Classification" and "Magnetic Properties and Atomic Structure of the Elements." Ríos proceeded with his other lectures at the university, the Spanish Casino, and the National Theater of Havana, and then moved on to the IHCC branches of Cienfuegos and Sagua la Grande. Over time, the program grew to include many prominent intellectuals.

On scientific topics, apart from the participation of Cabrera, the IHCC also invited a Catalan expert on tuberculosis, Luis Sayé, who gave a lecture in June at the Teatro Principal de la Comedia on "New Social Aspects of the Struggle against Tuberculosis." The impact of Sayé's participation in Havana resulted in the selection of Rita Shelton, the first Cuban scholar to study in Madrid; she then decided to work with Sayé in Barcelona as a member of one of the most important medical circles at the time.[64] Another Cuban scholar, Arsenio Roa, went to the Universidad Central in Madrid to work with the economist Flores de Lemus. Toward the end of the year, the IHCC achieved one of its main goals: the appearance of Gregorio Marañón in Havana. Marañón gave a successful cycle of lectures in the Teatro Payret on issues relating to sexuality. The lectures gathered over three thousand people, according to Madrid's *El Sol.*[65]

In 1928, a number of Spanish scientists and intellectuals continued arriving in Havana, some of them traveling from Mexico, where a close link with Spain had been established. For example, the chemist José Casares Gil, a founder of the Spanish Society of Physics and Chemistry, arrived from Mexico in April to give three lectures in Havana on the theoretical principles of chemistry, the study of the constitution of matter, and the use of chemistry in war.[66] Other speakers included Francisco Bernis, a professor of political economy and secretary of the General Council of Banking in Spain, and Antonio Fabra Rivas, a member of the International Labor Office of the League of Nations.[67] Scientists included Roberto Novoa Santos, a professor of general pathology at the Universidad de Santiago de Compostela, who arrived in Cuba as a JAE fellow thanks to the initiative of Castillejo.[68] Novoa's lectures also took place at the IHCC branches of Santiago and Manzanillo. These lectures were apparently the most controversial, as he not only dealt with issues of pathology, but also discussed "The biological Status of Women." He became the subject of the protests of a number of Cuban feminists, including pediatrician Hortensia Lamar who claimed that Novoa should be refuted in a counterlecture.[69]

Another lecture that received much attention was that of Américo Castro, who gave a long series of lectures on Spanish literary history. His work was widely discussed by the local press as being valuable for Cuban university students.[70]

The following year María de Maeztu, director of the Residencia de Señoritas, visited Havana. Sponsored by the JAE, she primarily visited teaching centers in Cuba and gave a series of lectures for the IHCC.[71] Other participants included musician Joaquín Turina;[72] the art specialist José Pijoán, a disciple of Giner and organizer of the Institut d'Estudis Catalans;[73] and Camilo Barcia Trelles, a former JAE fellow in international law, founder of the Asociación Francisco de Vitoria, and professor at the International Law Academy in The Hague.[74] Among the scientists, visitors included Francisco Durán Reynals, a disciple of Ramón Turró who had been a JAE fellow at the Pasteur Institute in Paris and the Rockefeller Institute in New York, where he conducted important research on immunity, bacteria, and cancer.[75]

In March 1930, Federico García Lorca visited Havana at Ortiz's personal invitation. García Lorca gave two lectures on Góngora at the Teatro Principal de la Comedia, one on the mechanics of poetry, another on Spanish lullabies, and a third on the *cante jondo*, sometimes playing the piano during his lectures.[76]

In December 1930, Ortiz was forced into exile, and during his absence, the activities and membership of the IHCC decreased substantially. Several visits by Spanish scholars were canceled, but other lecture series were held, including that of Salvador de Madariaga in May 1931. Additional one-time lectures by Cuban intellectuals took place, including one by Rita Shelton, who spoke on the problems of eugenics. Ortiz returned the following year, but his efforts to reactivate the IHCC did not bear fruit until 1936. That year Ortiz founded a new journal, *Ultra*, which became a channel of expression for his intellectual interests as well as for the IHCC.

The inaugural act of the IHCC's new phase took place on May 24, 1936, with a lecture on "The Significance of the Spanish Revolution" by Spanish ambassador Félix Gordón Ordás.

At the outbreak of the Spanish Civil War, the IHCC continued its cultural tasks but combined them with providing assistance to Spanish exiles arriving in Cuba. One of the first to arrive on the island was the poet Juan Ramón Jiménez, alongside his wife, Zenobia Camprubí. He arrived in November 1936 from Puerto Rico as a personal guest of Ortiz. Jiménez gave three lectures for the IHCC on "The Pleasurable Work (or Political Poetry)," "The Spirit of Contemporary Spanish Poetry," and "Evoking Valle Inclán." Finally, Jiménez organized a Cuban poetry festival in 1937 that resulted in the publication of *La poesía cubana en 1936*.[77]

During the initial stages of the war in Spain, the IHCC also studied the possibility of inviting Ortega y Gasset and Marañón to Cuba, but without success. One invitation that did materialize was that to Ramón Menéndez Pidal in January 1937. Over the next months Menéndez Pidal gave a series of lectures on the history of Spanish literature. These lectures were much praised by José M. Chacón in the journal *Lyceum*.[78] This publication also published the first articles by Luis Amado Blanco following his exile on the island.[79] The IHCC also welcomed musicologist Regino Sainz de la Maza and Adolfo Salazar, who had already cooperated with the IHCC in 1930.[80] Attempts were made to bring the poet Pedro Salinas to Cuba from the United States, where he had lived in exile since 1936, lecturing at Wellesley College.[81]

During this period, the institution used its contacts to attempt to help Spanish academics as much as it could. In April, Ortiz contacted "The Society for the Protection of Science and Learning" in England to secure lectures for refugee Spanish professors. Soon afterward he contacted Federico de Onís making a similar request and asking for help from the United States.[82]

In May 1937, Gustavo Pittaluga, living at the time in Geneva, was invited by the IHCC to give lectures in Cuba.[83] As on other occasions, the IHCC acted as host and intermediary between the Spanish scholar and Cuban academic institutions where he also held conferences. In Havana, Pittaluga gave a series of lectures in locales leased by the IHCC, such as the Teatro Campoamor. His lectures were published in *Lyceum* and *Ultra*.[84] He designed a series of courses and seminars in clinical hematology, and lectured at the Faculty of Medicine at the University of Havana and in the Finlay Institute. In the Faculty of Medicine, he gave lectures and taught one practical course for students in their final year. Pittaluga's notes were published under the title *Conferencias de hematología: recopiladas por el Dr. Víctor Santamaría* (Havana, 1938) with a preface by Pedro Domingo and an introduction by Santamaría.

Among the intellectuals visiting Havana in 1938, Claudio Sánchez Albornoz delivered a series of six lectures for the IHCC between March and April under the general title "From Medieval Spain to Contemporary Spain." Summaries of his lectures were published in *Ultra* despite the author's irritation at not being able to proofread the texts before their publication.[85]

Américo Castro collaborated again with the IHCC in 1938. Castro's second visit had been inexplicably postponed, leading him to believe that there were pressure groups in Cuba opposed to his "ideology."[86] Toward the end of that year, Luis Recasens Siches, a professor of law, lectured on "Society and Law in Human Life,"[87] and José M. Ots Capdequí lectured on "Legal and Economic Bases in the Social Organization of the Indies." The latter had maintained contact with Ortiz since 1929, while cultivating an active exchange in the *Revista Bimestre Cubana* for publications from the Hispanic-Cuban Institute of American History in Seville (Rafael González Abreu Foundation).[88]

At the beginning of 1939, Luis de Zulueta returned to Cuba from exile in Colombia to deliver a series of lectures which were soon published in *Ultra*.[89] Also published were lectures by playwright Alejandro Casona and a tribute to poets García Lorca and Antonio Machado, held at the Teatro Encanto and performed by Ortiz and Spanish poets Manuel Altolaguirre and Luis Amado Blanco.[90] During that same year Álvaro de Albornoz, a former Spanish minister of development and justice, presented a course on political doctrines.[91] Ortiz continued to correspond with other exiles, among them his friend José Pijoán, who informed him of various matters from New York and promised to travel to Havana as soon as possible.[92] At the end of the Spanish Civil War in 1940, Ortiz promoted the creation of the "Cuban Alliance for a Free World" within the IHCC as a mechanism for "defending the ideals of freedom, democracy, and social justice as fundamental for civilized and peaceful life among people."

Ortiz's intellectual background, based on the most progressive Spanish traditions, and his efforts to continue sincere intellectual exchanges with Spanish scholars were fundamental for the fruitful continuation of modern Hispanic-Cuban intellectual ties during his lifetime.

NOTES

This work is part of the Proyectos de Investigación BHA2000-1334 (MCyT) and 06/0091/2000 (CAM). It is part of a forthcoming book on the cultural and scientific relations between Spain, Cuba, and Puerto Rico, 1920–1945. In Havana, assistance provided at the Sociedad Económica/Instituto de Literatura y Lingüística and the Biblioteca Nacional José Martí (Sala Cubana) was essential. We would like to express our thanks to the directors and library staff of both institutions, and to the researchers who helped in the transcription of documents: Leida Fernández, Yolanda Díaz, Enrique López, María Antonia Marqués, and Zoila Lapique. We would also like to thank Herminia Reinat, the director of the Sala Zenobia y Juan Ramón Jiménez, Biblioteca de la Universidad de Puerto Rico, Río Piedras; and Carmen H. Pinzón Moreno, the heir of Juan Ramón Jiménez, for allowing use of the Juan Ramón Jiménez's papers in Puerto Rico.

1. Fernando Ortiz, *Hampa afro-cubana: Los negros brujos. (Apuntes para un estudio de etnología criminal)*, 2d ed. (Madrid: Editorial-América, 1917). The first edition of this book in 1906 began the Hampa Afro-Cubana series, which included *Los negros esclavos, Los negros horros, Los negros curros, Los negros brujos*, and *Los negros ñáñigos*. On the intellectual influences on Ortiz's work and his own conceptions, see Consuelo Naranjo and Miguel Angel Puig-Samper, "Delincuencia y racismo en Cuba: Israel Castellanos *versus* Fernando Ortiz" in *Ciencia y fascismo* ed. Carmen Ortiz and Rafael Huertas (Aranjuez: Ediciones Doce Calles, 1998), 11–21; Aline Helg, "Fernando Ortiz ou la pseudo-science contre la sorcellerie africaine á Cuba" in *Cahiers de l'Institut Universitaire l'Etudes du Développement* (Paris: Presses Universitaires de France, 1990), 241–49; Jorge Ibarra, "La herencia científica de Fernando Ortiz," *Revista Iberoamericana*, nos. 152–153 (1990), 1339–51; García-Carranza, *Biobibliografía*, references his work.

2. The file on Ortiz's *Licenciatura* degree in law, by the Universidad Literaria de Barcelona, exists in the Archivo General de la Administración, Alcalá de Henares, Sección de Educación, AGA 16.374, exp. 67. The accreditation papers of Ortiz's Ph.D. in law, by the Universidad Central de Madrid, in Archivo de la Universidad Complutense de Madrid, was made available to us by its chief archivist, Mr. Olivares.

3. See Juan López-Morillas, *El krausismo español: Perfil de una aventura intelectual*, 2d rev. ed. (Madrid: FCE, 1980). On the *Institución Libre de Enseñanza*, there are numerous studies; see the essential works by Vicente Cacho Viu, *La Institución Libre de Enseñanza* (Madrid: Rialp, 1969) and Antonio Jiménez-Landi, *La Institución Libre de Enseñanza y su ambiente: Los orígenes* (Madrid: Taurus, 1973). For studies on the Spanish criminal anthropology, see Miguel Ángel Puig-Samper and Andrés Galera, *La antropología española en el siglo XIX* (Madrid: CSIC, 1983), and Andrés Galera, *Ciencia y delincuencia* (Sevilla: CSIC, 1991). On the introduction of Lombroso's ideas in Spain, Luis Maristany, *El gabinete del doctor Lombroso (Delincuencia y fin de siglo en España)* (Barcelona: Editorial Anagrama, 1973). On Krauspositivism, Diego Núñez Ruiz, *La mentalidad positiva en España: desarrollo y crisis* (Madrid: Túcar Ediciones, 1975).

4. "Otro asunto, Rafael Salillas, el eminente antropólogo y criminalista español, publicó hará unos 30 años en una revista española un artículo acerca de los ñáñigos. Por carta me dijo que sólo era ese trabajo una parte de un estudio ya listo e inédito, que iba a publicar. No lo hizo. Y ese estudio quedó inédito. Yo voy a trabajar este año en ultimar un muy extenso libro *Los ñáñigos*, y se me ocurre que Ud., tan afortunado rebuscador de papeles viejos, podría dar, entre los que dejó al morir aquel sabio, con las cuartillas inéditas, dibujos, etc. ¿Tendríamos esa suerte? Si logra averiguar el paradero de sus familiares, acaso sea fácil, podrán informarle quizás los viejos funcionarios de prisiones, o sus editores (V. Suárez entre otros). Me interesa dominar este asunto para poder agotar en lo posible el tema del ñañiguismo. Es una cosa realmente original, que ha de intrigar a los antropólogos y sociólogos." See Zenaida Gutiérrez-Vega, *Fernando Ortiz en sus cartas a José M. Chacón* (Madrid: Fundación Universitaria Española, 1982), 68.

5. Manuel Antón, "Don Rafael Salillas: Nota necrológica" in *Actas y Memorias de la Sociedad Española de Antropología, Etnografía y Prehistoria*, vol. II (1923), 89–93; Pedro Dorado Montero, "Sobre el último libro de Salillas y la teoría criminológica de este autor" *Revista General de Legislación y Jurisprudencia* XCIII (1898): 483–99, and XCIV (1899): 46–78; M.D. Fernández Rodríguez, *El pensamiento penitenciario y criminológico de Rafael Salillas* (Santiago de Compostela: Universidad de Santiago de Compostela, 1976); Andrés Galera Gómez, "Rafael Salillas: medio siglo de antropología criminal española," *Llull* IX (1986): 81–104.

6. J. L. García Delgado, "Estudio preliminar" in Constancio Bernaldo de Quirós, ed., *El espartaquismo agrario y otros ensayos sobre la estructura económica y social de Andalucía* (Madrid: Ed. de la Revista de Trabajo, 1973), 10–51; Fermín del Pino Díaz, "Antropólogos en el exilio" in J. L. Abellán, ed., *El exilio español de 1939* (Madrid: Taurus, 1978), vol. VI: 13–155.

7. Azcárate was the author of *Concepto de la Sociología* (1891) and "Plan de la Sociología" (1899), which shared Giner's orthodox approach in *La persona social: Estudios y fragmentos* (1899). Among the works of Bernaldo de Quirós, see *La picota* (Madrid: Suárez, 1907), where he quotes Fernando Ortiz, his *Bandolerismo y delincuencia subversiva en la Baja Andalucía*, published in *Anales* by the JAE in 1913, and especially *El espartaquismo agrario andaluz* (Madrid: Reus, 1919). Also Gumersindo de Azcárate: *Concepto de Sociología* (Madrid: Fortanet, 1891), and "Plan de la Sociología," *Boletín de la Institución Libre de Enseñanza* XXIII (1899). See Patricio de Azcárate, *Gumersindo de Azcárate: Estudio biográfico documental* (Madrid: Tecnos, 1968); Francisco Giner de los Ríos, *La persona social: Estudios y fragmentos* (Madrid: Suárez, 1899).

8. Fernando Ortiz, "Los modernos criminólogos Americanos," *Cuba y América* (Havana) 14, no. 6 (February 7, 1904): 154–56; no. 11 (March 13, 1904): 277–80; no. 12 (March 20, 1904): 322–24.

9. Fernando Ortiz, "El alcoholismo," *Azul y Rojo: Revista Ilustrada* (Havana) 2, no. 8 (February 22, 1903): 8.

10. Biblioteca Nacional José Martí, Havana (hereafter BNJM), C. M. Ortiz, no. 348; various correspondence.

11. On Olóriz, see Elvira Arquiola, "Anatomía y antropología en la obra de Olóriz," *Dynamis* I (1981): 165–77.

12. Letter from Federico Olóriz to Fernando Ortiz from Miraflores, Madrid, July 21, 1910, BNJM, C. M. Ortiz, no. 348.

13. Andrés Galera Gómez, "Dorado Montero, Pedro" in Carmen Ortiz García and Luis Ángel Sánchez Gómez, *Diccionario histórico de la antropología española* (Madrid: CSIC, 1994), 264–66.

14. Although now old and difficult to find, it is useful to consult the excellent text written by Mariano and José Luis Peset Reig, "Positivismo y ciencia positiva en médicos y juristas españoles del siglo XIX. Pedro Dorado Montero," *Almena* (1963): 65–123. An interesting monography appears in Juan Andrés Blanco Rodríguez, *El pensamiento sociopolítico de Dorado Montero* (Salamanca: Centro de Estudios Salmantinos–CSIC, 1982).

15. BNJM, C. M. Ortiz, no. 348.

16. Archives of the Universidad de Salamanca, "Cartas de Fernando Ortiz con Pedro Dorado Montero," Caja VI, 5–9. We are grateful to Severiano Hernández for his cooperation in finding these documents.

17. Ortiz, "Desde Salamanca," *Cuba y América* 25, no. 21 (February 12, 1908): 3.

18. BNJM, C. M. Ortiz no. 348.

19. BNJM, C. M. Ortiz no. 348.

20. In the records, there is a letter written by the director of the correctional facility in Alcalá de Henares, Pedro Bruyé, to Fernando Ortiz, dated January 21, 1902, in which he thanks Ortiz for sending a copy of his doctoral thesis and congratulates him on obtaining his doctorate.

21. Ortiz commented, "Como casi todos los maestros de la actual juventud española, que es esperanza de España, fue hijo del Krausismo, de aquella filosofía alemana que Sanz del Río llevó a su patria, aprendida en universidades germanas, y que tanta influencia ejerció en la juventud de los días revolucionarios de septiembre. Sobre su base profundamente filosófica, Sales y Ferré, impulsado por su propia vocación y por su cátedra de historia universal en la universidad de Sevilla, consagróse a los estudios históricos; y de esa cópula de investigaciones de filosofía y de historia, resultó en su temple positivista, la fe en la sociología. Su tratado de sociología, aparecido después de una porción de trabajos de índole histórica, fue la fusión de sus conocimientos en un solo crisol. Spencer, Bachofen, McLenan, y especialmente el norteamericano Morgan, le marcaron los nuevos horizontes y a ellos se lanzó con audacia y fruto." Fernando Ortiz, "Sales y Ferré," *El Fígaro* XXVII, no. 4 (January 22, 1911): 47. See also Manuel Núñez Encabo, *Manuel Sales y Ferré: Los orígenes de la Sociología en España* (Madrid: Edicusa, 1976); Rafael Jerez Mir, *La introducción de la sociología en España: Manuel Sales y Ferré, una experiencia frustrada* (Madrid: Ayuso, 1980).

22. BNJM, C. M. Ortiz, no. 348.

23. Vicente Santamaría de Paredes, *El concepto de organismo social* (Madrid: Real Academia de Ciencias Morales y Políticas, 1896).

24. José Luis Peset y Mariano Peset, *Lombroso y la escuela positivista italiana* (Madrid: CSIC, 1975).

25. InterAmericas, *Miscelánea II*; García Carranza, *Bio-bibliografía*.

26. Fernando Ortiz, "Le origini antiche della dactiloscopia," *Archivio* 35 (1914).

27. BNJM, C. M. Ortiz, no. 348. Correspondence between Ortiz and the Italian scholars exists for the period 1905–1917, in Italian.

28. Fernando Ortiz, "El proyecto de código criminal cubano," *Revista Bimestre Cubana* XXI, no. 5 (September–October 1926): 681–705.

29. Gutiérrez-Vega, *Cartas a Chacón*, 55–57.

30. BNJM, C. M. Ortiz, no. 403–4.

31. BNJM, C. M. Ortiz, no. 181.

32. Carlos Serrano, "Miguel de Unamuno y Fernando Ortiz. Un caso de regeneracionismo transatlántico," *Nueva Revista de Filología Hispánica* XXXV, no. 1 (1987): 299–310.

33. BNJM, C. M. Ortiz, no. 333.

34. BNJM, C. M. Ortiz, no. 333.

35. Fernando Ortiz, "A Unamuno," *El Fígaro*, no. 38 (September 23, 1906): 481.

36. "Cartas de Fernando Ortiz con Miguel de Unamuno," Casa Museo Unamuno, Archivo, Salamanca, Sign. 02/29.

37. Miguel de Unamuno, *Obras completas* (Madrid, 1966), vol. 3: 982–86.

38. Manuel Tuñón de Lara, *Medio siglo de cultura española (1885–1936)* (Madrid: Tecnos, 1977); Javier Varela, *La novela de España: Los intelectuales y el problema español* (Madrid: Taurus, 1999).

39. Ibarra, "Herencia científica"; Helg, "Pseudo-science."

40. Fernando Ortiz, "Los factores humanos de la cubanidad," *Revista Bimestre Cubana* XIV, no. 2 (1940): 161–86; and Fernando Ortiz, *Estudios etnosociológicos* (Havana: Editorial de Ciencias Sociales, 1991).

41. Altamira said this book was the "Libro rojo de la labor americanista," a task compared to a diplomatic mission. Chapter 7 deals with his visit to Cuba, where he gave many lectures in different institutions: Rafael Altamira y Crevea, *Mi viaje a América* (Madrid: Librería General de Victoriano Suárez, 1911).

42. Altamira, *Mi viaje*, 433.

43. Rafael Altamira y Crevea, *La huella de España en América* (Madrid: Editorial Reus, 1924). This book is a compilation of Altamira's articles and lectures produced during his visit to the Universidad de la Plata, Argentina.

44. Fernando Ortiz, *La reconquista de América: Reflexiones sobre el panhispanismo* (París: Librería P. Ollendorff, 1910); Ortiz, "Panhispanismo," *Revista Bimestre Cubana* 70 (1955): 55–59.

45. Fernando Ortiz, *Entre Cubanos: Psicología tropical* (Havana: Editorial Ciencias Sociales, 1986): 107 (1st ed., 1913).

46. Fernando Ortiz was a member of various academies. He was president of the Academia de Historia de Cuba, created in 1910, from which he resigned in 1929. He was also a member of various Spanish academies: the Real Academia de la Lengua, Ciencias Morales y Políticas, Historia, and Jurisprudencia y Legislación. While Ortiz was the president of the Academia de Historia de Cuba (1925–1929), a committee was established to seek information on the history of Cuba in Spanish archives. The task was directed by José María Chacón y Calvo, the secretary of the Cuban embassy in Madrid, where he lived from 1918 to 1936. The Academia de la Historia de Cuba made an inventory based on the monthly lists of documents provided by Chacón: BNJM, C. M. Ortiz, no. 403.

47. BNJM, C. M. Ortiz, no. 403: 13.

48. "I believe it is too simple to talk to the descendants of the Indians of race to impose on them Spanish culture. It is not a question of ignoring a precedent, false in the majority of cases; let us try to gain them through the truth, and the only truth is that they imbibe science and knowledge through Hispanic culture"; see "Cultura, cultura y cultura, en lugar de raza, religión e idioma," *El Mundo* (December 12, 1928): 1 and 23.

49. "Raza, grilletes," *Revista América* 37 (1929): 196–97.

50. Ortiz, *Reconquista*. See M. A. Puig-Samper and C. Naranjo, "Fernando Ortiz: herencias culturales y forja de la nacionalidad" in *Imágenes e imaginarios españoles en el Ultramar español*, ed. Consuelo Naranjo Orovio and Carlos Serrano (Madrid: CSIC-Casa de Velázquez, 1999), 192–221.

51. "La Institución Hispano Cubana de Cultura," *Revista Bimestre Cubana* 21, no. 6 (1926): 896–913.

52. BNJM, C. M. Ortiz, no. 246: Hispano Cubana de Cultura, Juntas-Actas-Permisos-Citaciones, IX.

53. "Memoria, 1926–1927," *Mensajes de la Institución Hispano Cubana de Cultura* 1, no. 1 (1927): 41–45.

54. BNJM, C. M. Ortiz, no. 203: Hispano Cubana de Cultura II, Actas.

55. "Memoria, 1926-1927," *Mensajes de la Institución Hispano Cubana de Cultura* 1, no. 1 (1927): 63–65.

56. BNJM, C. M. Ortiz, no. 407: Correspondencia Variada.

57. The letters Chacón y Calvo wrote to Ortiz, and some copies of those written by Ortiz to Chacón, can be read at the BNJM. The vast majority of the letters sent from Havana to Chacón have been edited by Zenaida Gutiérrez-Vega, who in 1964 consulted Chacón's archives in the flat in which he once lived in Madrid. See *Fernando Ortiz en sus cartas a José M. Chacón (1914–1936, 1956)* (Madrid: Fundación Universitaria Española, 1982).

58. Debate over the role of JAE in: "La Junta para la Ampliación de Estudios," *Diario de la Marina* 95 (January 15, 1927), and in "Creación del patronato," *La Voz* (December 28, 1926); see also *La Voz* (March 2, 1927).

59. BNJM, C. M. Ortiz, no. 407: Correspondencia Variada.

60. BNJM, C. M. Ortiz, no. 261.

61. BNJM, C. M. Ortiz, no. 261.

62. BNJM, C. M. Ortiz, no. 261.

63. BNJM, C. M. Ortiz, no. 261.

64. José Cornudella, "Obra científica y sanitaria del académico honorario prof. Luis Sayé," *Anales de Medicina y Cirugía* 53, no. 233 (1973): 247–53; José Oriol Anguera, "Obra científica y sanitaria del académico honorario prof. Luis Sayé Sempere," *Anales de Medicina y Cirugía* 53, no. 233 (1973): 253–59; G. Manresa Formosa, "Obra científica y sanitaria del académico honorario prof. Luis Sayé Sempere en Hispanoamérica," *Anales de Medicina y Cirugía* 53 (1973): 260–65; Pedro Domingo Sanjuán, "En recuerdo de Luis Sayé Sempere," *Anales de Medicina y Cirugía* 56, no. 243 (1976): 19–28; José Cornudella, "Lluis Sayé i Sempere," *Anales de Medicina y Cirugía* 56, no. 243 (1976): 46–50.

65. *El Sol* (22 Dec. 1927); BNJM, C. M. Ortiz, no. 294.

66. BNJM, C. M. Ortiz, no. 294 and 297. The program developed by Casares Gil in the Instituto Hispano Mexicano de Intercambio Universitario is registered in the JAE file in the Residencia de Estudiantes (RE), Madrid, Archivo de la Secretaría de la Junta para la Ampliación de Estudios e Investigaciones Científicas (ASJAE), 32-332.

67. RE-ASJAE, 50-2.

68. BNJM, C. M. Ortiz, no. 261 and no. 407.

69. BNJM, C. M. Ortiz, no. 183 and 320; RE-ASJAE, 106-29; and Junta para Ampliación de Estudios e Investigaciones Científicas, *Memoria correspondiente a los cursos 1926–7 y 1927–8* (Madrid: JAE, 1929), 135–37.

70. BNJM, C. M. Ortiz, no. 294 and 297; RE-ASJAE, 34-428.

71. RE-ASJAE, 90-39.

72. RE-ASJAE, 144-211.

73. RE-ASJAE, 115-419.

74. RE-ASJAE, 15-90; BNJM, C. M. Ortiz, nos. 177 and 241.

75. RE-ASJAE, 45-219.

76. BNJM, C. M. Ortiz, no. 309.

77. Documents on Juan Ramón Jiménez's stay in Cuba in the Sala Zenobia and Juan Ramón Jiménez, Biblioteca de la Universidad de Puerto Rico; see also Cintio Vitier, *Juan Ramón Jiménez en Cuba* (Havana: Ed. Arte y Literatura, 1981), and Zenobia Camprubí, *Diario. 1: Cuba (1937–1939)* (Madrid: Alianza Tres-EDUPR, 1991).

78. José M. Chacón y Calvo, "Los días Cubanos de Menéndez Pidal," *Lyceum* 5–6 (1937): 5–8.

79. Luis Amado Blanco, "Biología de la moda," *Lyceum* 8 (1937): 28–45.

80. BNJM, C. M. Ortiz, no. 330.

81. BNJM, C. M. Ortiz, no. 330.

82. BNJM, C. M. Ortiz, nos. 246, 289, and 360.

83. Manuel Tuñón de Lara, *Medio siglo de cultura española (1885–1936)*, 3d ed. (Madrid: Editorial Tecnos, 1977), 152–53, 28; BNJM, C. M. Ortiz, no. 325.

84. Gustavo Pittaluga, "El libro y la cultura," *Lyceum* 2, no. 8 (December 1937): 9–17; "El mito de la sangre" (lecture of December 2, 1937, in Teatro Campoamor) in *Ultra* 4, no. 20 (February 1938): 179–80.

85. Correspondence with Sánchez Albornoz in BNJM, C. M. Ortiz, no. 330.

86. BNJM, C. M. Ortiz, no. 294.

87. BNJM, C. M. Ortiz, no. 327.

88. An account of the creation of the Instituto Hispano-Cubano de Sevilla can be found in *Archipiélago* (November 30, 1928): 120. In March 1939, Ots Capdequí wrote to Ortiz from Paris to inform him that he was moving to Colombia with his entire family. The relationship between the two continued while Ots remained in exile in Bogota. They wrote to each other frequently in 1945; Ortiz helped Ots obtain a temporary visa in Cuba en route to Puerto Rico, where Ots had been appointed visiting professor: BNJM, C. M. Ortiz, nos. 186, 322, 323, 346, and 404.

89. The lectures were published in *Ultra* 6, no. 33 (March 1939): 268–79. The letter in which Ortiz announces his arrival in Cuba: BNJM, C. M. Ortiz, no. 336. For a condensed biography, A. Jiménez-Landi, "Luis de Zulueta y Escolano," in *Cartas, 1903–1933* by Miguel de Unamuno-Luis de Zulueta, ed. Carmen de Zulueta, 343–73 (Madrid: Aguilar, 1972).

90. *Ultra* 7, no. 37 (July 1939): 83–88.

91. *Ultra* 7, no. 38 (August 1939): 177–80.

92. BNJM, C. M. Ortiz, no. 346.

3

It All Started in Madrid

Octavio di Leo

Fernando Ortiz owes much to Cuban literature. But, as with most obvious things, this debt has been little studied and remains unspoken. For such a prolific writer, with such a wide spectrum of interests developed over a lifetime, Ortiz made his own method of literature.[1] I therefore begin with the first name cited in his first book, *Hampa afro-cubana: Los negros brujos* (1906). This text was the first part of a "Black Trilogy," which remained unfinished at his death in 1969. It began with a prologue, written by the Italian criminologist Cesare Lombroso, and the first name Ortiz quoted was the Spanish writer Rafael Salillas (1855–1923).

What do we know about Salillas? In the 1880s, Salillas was appointed inspector of the penitentiaries of the Crown and reviewed, among other prisons, Ceuta, in northern Africa. As a result of his travels, he published *La vida penal en España* in 1888, a book that gave him a reputation as a criminal anthropologist. The prison of Ceuta became the model for his ideas for penitentiary reform in Spain: "The prison of Ceuta," he says, "is the mother of all prisons."[2] Due to the history of constant harassment, the prison was contained within the walls of the barracks, which conferred on Ceuta the status of a "penitentiary city." This made the integration of the prisoners into the social network of the city easier, which was ultimately Salillas's idea for a reform.

In the same book, he describes the opposite of the Ceuta model, the prison of Alcalá de Henares, which was built behind the university and next to the women's reformatory, or *casa galera*. Between the *casa galera* and the prison there happened to be a small garden that became a meeting point for amorous prisoners from both sides of the garden. Here the lovers intercepted letters from, waited for, or betrayed each other. At times it was an

Eden, at times an *hortus conclusus*. A subtle line in the book gives us an idea of its style: "female prisoners wash the clothes of their convict neighbors, and each bundle (*hato*) becomes a problem (*lío*)."[3] The correspondence Salillas collected in *La vida penal* went beyond the limits of a prison report and exceeded the purposes of the anthropology of his time.

The gaze of a voyeur who finds pleasure in letters is one of the oldest topics of literature. In fact, while describing the characters he found in the correspondence from Alcalá, Salillas related them to those the *pícaro* Guzmán de Alfarache found in the Naples prison in the sixteenth century. And it is to the "good memory of Mateo Alemán," a master of Spanish picaresque, that Salillas dedicates his *Hampa: Antropología picaresca* (1898). Salillas also analyzed the picaresque psychology of the gypsies, "princes of our ingenuities," and put together two lineages that would pass from 1898 Spain to independent Cuba in the writings of Fernando Ortiz: the picaresque novel and social evolutionism.

Ortiz visited the prison of Alcalá de Henares in 1900 while studying law in Madrid. Like any law student in Madrid in those days, the name *Ceuta* must have sounded familiar to him. The stories Ortiz (over)heard about the prison in Ceuta could hardly be quoted, but oral historiography, as proved by Jan Vansina in Central Africa, can also be told on another scale: the beginning and end of life, within the limits of kinship. Noam Chomsky said once in an interview that kinship systems are the mathematics of the illiterate.

During his last trip to Ceuta[4] in October 1889, Salillas interviewed several Cuban prisoners who belonged to an all-male secret society that originated among the people of the coast of Calabar, in equatorial West Africa. In Cuba, these men were known as *ñáñigos*, but their African name was *Abakuá*. In the works of Ortiz and later on in those of Lydia Cabrera, the name of Salillas is often associated with the study of those secret societies. Salillas started publishing the results of his research on Ceuta in 1901.[5] According to García Carranza, Ortiz wrote over one thousand pages on the *ñáñigos* that remain unpublished.[6] That text could give a clue to the whereabouts of those interviews by Salillas, which became the original myth of Afro-Romance anthropology.

The first documents about the establishment of an Abakuá society in Cuba go back to 1835 and to the Havana district of Regla. When Ortiz wrote about the Cuban *hampa* or underworld, the *ñáñigos* were the talk of the town. With the migration of the former slaves from the interior to the cities or, to put it in Alejo Carpentier's words, from the "diabetic giant" to the capital, something unexpected happened on the island. Secret societies, devoid of their religious links and freed from forced labor in the sugar plantations, were seen as having criminal associations on the new urban horizon.

According to the golden rule of these societies, if one of its member or *ecobios* happened to be attacked by another faction of the Abakuás, the brothers under oath should come to his defense. That explains why several men belonging to one or the other faction of the *ñáñigos* were killed in Havana. Texts that followed that of Ortiz were more vehement in their condemnation of the crimes, such as a treatise by the police inspector Rafael Roche, who in 1908 decided that the Abakuás were the bête noire of post-slavery Cuba.[7] With an arsenal of photographs and coarse vocabulary, Roche proposed a method for recognizing the *ñáñigos* by their tattoos and their slang—in other words, by the marks of body and language. Ironically enough, it wasn't until the arrival of Lydia Cabrera, who as a woman was banned from the secret rites, that the real stories told by and of those Cuban Abakuás became public in 1970.[8] Some of her informants attributed the wave of *ñáñigo* terror after the abolition of slavery to the entry of white members into the societies, the first of which was the legendary Andrés Petit, in 1875.

Until 1880, every year on the Epiphany, or *Día de Reyes*, African descendants were allowed to parade to the Palacio de Gobierno. For the occasion, they danced, sang, and dressed in costume.[9] The rest of the population was used to the spine-chilling masks of the Abakuá ritual, the so-called *íremes* or *ñañas*, from which the pejorative *ñáñigo* is derived. Stories about these *íremes* and about the murder of the "*niña* Zoila" were manipulated to scare an entire generation of Cuban children.

In 1904, when Ortiz was living in Europe and writing in the *Archivi di Psichiatria*, edited by Lombroso, a white girl named Zoila was killed on a sugar plantation by a Congo (not an Abakuá) sorcerer (*brujo*) by the name of Bocú. The story of this murder is a constant reference in Ortiz's *Hampa afro-cubana,* and is used to justify a regional branch of the criminal anthropology invented by Lombroso, which Ortiz was eager to call "tropical criminology." Soon afterward, upon his return to Cuba, he would change his mind. In 1902, as an example of how the *Zeitgeist* had already taken a different course, one of the anarchists in Joseph Conrad's *The Secret Agent* says:

> Lombroso is an ass [. . .]. Did you ever see such an idiot? For him the criminal is the prisoner. Simple, is it not? What about those who shut him up there forced him in there? Exactly. Forced him in there. And what is crime? Does he know that, this imbecile who has made his way in this world of gorged fools by looking at the ears and teeth of a lot of poor, luckless devils? Teeth and ears mark the criminal? Do they? And what about the law that marks him still better the pretty branding instrument invented by the overfed to protect themselves against the hungry? Red-hot applications of their vile skins-hey? Can't you smell and hear from here the thick hide of the people burn and sizzle? That's how criminals are made for your Lombrosos to write their silly stuff about.

Lombroso, in fact, had coined the term *polizia scientifica*, an euphemism for his criminal anthropology, and one of its main goals was the abolition of secret societies.[10] Seen in retrospect, it prefigured the Italian fascism of the 1920s. But Ortiz's own developments, in language and context, were already closer to those of Salillas, for whom slang was the most revealing feature of the *hampa*. Talking of the *hampa* in Spain, Ortiz described its slang, the *germanía*, as "*un reino dentro de otro reino*,"[11] which in turn related the Abakuá societies to Freemasonry and the Mafia. He soon realized, however, that any positivistic study of criminal slang would leave aside a whole field of secret spells and incantatory formulas which every sacred language consists of, and he proposed a theory of linguistic change that included the ritual function of language, thus going far beyond his purposes as a criminologist:

> The principles that gave birth to the sacred slangs, of which that of the *brujos* is an illustration, deny the possibility of their frequent variation. The god is unable to understand a series of articulated sounds with a key it does not know; neither can priests among themselves, or the faithful while hunting or fishing, use those improper sounds; neither would the praising periphrasis make sense, nor would prayer (*oración*) have the virtue of obliging the gods. . . . The survival of ancient languages and words in these tongues also demonstrates without dispute their general stability. Thus, the greater the degree of cohesion among the priests and the faithful, the greater the stability of the slang. This occurs with criminal slangs: the most lasting are those used by criminal associations; compare in Spain the use of the ancient *germanía* with the scarce and more variable speeches of Spanish criminals today, whose associations are disappearing.[12]

From this rich passage, I would like to expand on the concept of *oración*, because in the original Spanish it has a double connotation: that of the prayer to invoke the divine and also the minimum unit of syntax. These two meanings will be particularly useful in the 1920s, when both poets and anthropologists would try to incorporate the different African languages used in the liturgies across the island into a new way of writing. In other words, it will be a bridge between the oral and the written traditions of Cuba.

By the time Ortiz had published *Hampa afro-cubana* in Madrid and returned to Cuba, he had spent three-quarters of his life in Europe: first in Minorca, where he was taken at the age of one by his mother and where he wrote compositions at school in the dialect of the island, and later in Barcelona, Madrid, Coruña, Marseilles, and Genova. As the first oral historian of Cuba, he had no other choice than to invent his precursors: "I started doing research," he says, "but soon I realized that, like all Cubans, I was confused."[13] Nothing suited him better in this task than revisiting the island after a long stay abroad. It gave him a panoramic view and the opportunity to redefine the map of Africa from the perspective of Cuba. That view took shape in Spain in Madrid, in Alcalá de Henares, and in the mythic Ceuta of Salillas. It was his idea of a "penitentiary city" that we find again in *Hampa afrocubana*: "if there were a true criminal colony in Cuba, the problem [of the isolation of the *brujo*] would almost be solved, as *brujos* could take up special tasks, isolated from the other categories of criminals."[14]

After his formative years in criminology, Ortiz realized that in order to write a social history of Cuba, he had to interview the *"negros de nación,"* understand the ritual use of their musical instruments, study their languages, and describe the structure of their secret societies. The nineteenth-century abolitionist prose, ranging from the literary circle of Domingo del Monte in the 1830s to Cirilo Villaverde's *Cecilia Valdés* (1882), certainly knew the mysteries of black Cuba. But the descriptions came from the educated sons of the masters, and, with the exception of the autobiography by an ex-slave (Manzano, 1839), they were written in the third person. Among Ortiz's achievements was the realization that in order to eventually rescue the first person in Afro-Cuban storytelling, he had to make use of interviews. This was something he had learned from Salillas's adventures in Ceuta and from Raymundo Nina Rodrigues's excursions to the *terreiros,* or temples, of Bahia in Brazil.

Nina Rodrigues had written a milestone article in 1897, about and during the millenarian protests in Canudos, Bahia, in which self-proclaimed prophet Antonio Conselheiro posed the first test for the young republic after the abolition of slavery, by keeping the national army on guard. Euclides da Cunha's notes as a war correspondent in Canudos would eventually turn into the canonical *Os sertões* (1902), describing the circumstances in the life of Antonio Conselheiro as an "agent of history." Likewise Nina Rodrigues, trained as a forensic doctor, felt the causes of the revolt were in Conselheiro's mind. In his article "A loucura epidêmica de Canudos," he characterized the disease of the millenarist Messiah as endemic and hereditary. Nina Rodrigues became a criminologist par excellence in Brazil and started publishing scientific papers in Europe. He died during a visit to Paris, in 1906, at the age of forty-four. He was on a mission to buy new technology for the morgue of the Medicine School in Bahia, and it was the first time he had left the country. His career had begun to take off while he was engaged in fieldwork on the *terreiros* of Salvador. We know, for instance, that his favorite informant was Martiniano Eliseu do Bonfim, an old Yoruba who after being freed returned to Lagos, spent several years learning the customs, and came back to Salvador. He eventually became a *babalaô* or priest surrounded by the prestige that his trip across the Atlantic and the knowledge of an African language had given him.[15]

Fernando Ortiz knew the work of Nina Rodrigues and quoted it several times in important passages of his own writings. The Brazilian, from the standpoint of legal medicine, and Ortiz, from that of criminal law, aimed in the same direction: the inclusion of the black people into the legal system following the end of slavery. And both, at the beginning of their careers, were convinced of the need to fulfill the plan of European anthropology by dividing the *oikoumenes* into ethnographic provinces. The discovery of the Africans in Ibero-America made the integration of the young republics of Brazil and Cuba into the ethnographic literature at the turn of the century possible. Epistemological validation, however, came together with political recognition: in the positivistic universe, the authority of the scientific community meant as well a place in the concert of nations.

Yet Afro-Romance anthropology, as much as Malinowski's ethnography in the western Pacific, was born *in extremis*, when the object of the study was about to disappear. Nina Rodrigues and Ortiz were aware of the fact that no one before them had accepted the challenge of systemizing the geoethnical origin of the Africans in Brazil or Cuba. Even before Malinowski's elegy to the Argonauts of the South Seas, they both wrote a swan song for the people who were about to vanish from the map of the world: the last Africans in Brazil and the last Africans in Cuba. Once they disappeared, poets and storytellers would have only one choice: writing by heart. And for them this posed one of the most intricate dilemmas of literature: not only to write as the last Africans spoke, but to do it when they spoke no more.[16] In *Los negros esclavos* (1916), the second part of his *Hampa afro-cubana*, Ortiz gives his own version of Afro-Cuban historiography:

> I have been unable to obtain a full report regarding the diverse origins of the cargoes of ebony. . . . I will merely provide an indication of the names of the African regions which I have seen quoted in the work of Cuban authors and ancient documents which I have consulted, with certain clarifications and observations regarding their location in Africa, largely unknown given that no one before me has delved into this theme publicly, and I consider it to be essential for Cuban anthropology.[17]

This set the pace of a toponymical adventure in Africa. Beyond the organization of the material into long catalogs and in alphabetical order, Ortiz seems to imply that the only sources for this imaginary *atlas africanus* were the written ones, both domestic and foreign.[18] Among the vernacular sources of *Los negros esclavos*, there was a map of Africa designed by Esteban Pichardo, a Dominican polymath, in 1866. We learn about this unseen map, however, only through a footnote in Ortiz, which gives the scientific source a literary character, as an apocryphal quotation.[19] Pichardo's map divided the western coast of Africa into the five "nations" of Mandinga, Gangá, Lucumí, Carabalí, and Congo. With its obvious limitations, it counts as the first map in the toponymical chain. The French doctor Henri Dumont was another precursor from the nineteenth century in systematizing the geographic origin of the Africans in Cuba. Simultaneously with *Los negros esclavos*, Ortiz started publishing Dumont's 1866 report (same year as Pichardo's map) in the *Revista Bimestre Cubana*.[20] Dumont visited hospitals and sickbays at different sugar plantations where he examined and photographed slaves following Pichardo's classification of nations. He then arrived at the statistic conclusion that slaves, more than freed laborers and certainly more than white people, could live more than one hundred years. Dumont's figures authorized and spread the myth of longevity in nineteenth-century Cuba. In ethnography, longevity plays a key role because it narrows down the infinite versions and diversions of oral history to the limits of individual biography. It is nonetheless true that the interviewer must face other obstacles, such as translation and self-censorship. But by resorting to a witness, he reduces the margin of error every transmission entails. The more we move away from that "*tiempo-España*," as colonial times were called in Cuba, the more crucial the longevity of the informants becomes. And it was longevity that built a bridge between the nineteenth and the twentieth centuries, between the colony and the republic.

A connection also existed between the clinical case studies by the pathologist Dumont, the type described in the first writings of Ortiz, and the stylized (*Auto*)*Biography of a Runaway Slave* (1966) by Miguel Barnet. Barnet tells readers of his *Biography* that he has omitted the repetitions in the account of the maroon, "but what if repetition is an essential part of Montejo's rhetoric, a mnemonic device, a formula like those present in oral literature, particularly in epic poems?"[21] Unlike Lydia Cabrera, however, for whom the juxtaposed voices of her informants kept their oral tone because they had been transcribed from interviews, the first-person account of the ex-slave Esteban Montejo is indistinguishable from Barnet's *ego scriptor*. This new assimilation of anthropology and literature, which contributed to the widening circle of readers of ethnography, also offered Barnet the possibility to position himself as the last link in the series that, after the medical attempts of the nineteenth century, was initiated by Fernando Ortiz in 1906. Soon the oral map of Africa wouldn't be drawn from written sources alone but also from stories told by Africans themselves.

After discovering their interlocutors, anthropologists felt the need to fill the linguistic gap between themselves and their informants with the writing of dictionaries. In the history of Cuban dictionaries, Pichardo's *Diccionario provincial casi-razonado de vozes cubanas* (1836) starts with the series of Africanisms incorporated into the national language. It gathers many indigenous words, although the native speakers were long extinct in Cuba, but mixes up the words of African origin, whose speakers were well alive.

In nineteenth-century Cuba, there was a linguistic continuum that ranged from peninsular Castilian or Creole, on one end, to a multiplicity of African languages, on the other, with *bozal* or pidgin in between. This *bozal* became increasingly similar to standard Spanish, and eventually only managed to survive in those places where the black population remained more or less stable, such as certain areas in Matanzas.[22]

The dictionary by Pichardo begins with an autobiographical prologue, in which he describes his journey through the Caribbean: "Born at the heart of the island of Santo Domingo, emigrating with my family as a child to the interior of Cuba, I spent my first years in the populous and very Créole city of

Port-au-Prince; I have traveled across the Island [Cuba] by land and sea, as well as in Puerto Rico."[23] The fact that he had been to the three Spanish-speaking islands confers Pichardo with the authority to compare and later write down the words he hears in his dictionary.

Fernando Ortiz wrote his own dictionary in 1923, which he called *Catauro de cubanismos*. The term *catauro* refers to a kind of backpack made of the bark of the *palma real* tree, which is of the utmost importance in Afro-Cuban mythology. The *guajiro* or peasant puts his belongings for his journeys through the island in the *Catauro*. Thus, the *Catauro* was meant to be a pocket dictionary of Cuban idioms. Ortiz's definitions remind us of the thesaurus by Covarrubias, a key paradigm for Spanish since the early seventeenth century, where philological erudition goes together with explanation by hearsay. As a result, he incorporates the pidgin into the Cuban Spanish. In this sense, the *Catauro de cubanismos* is the first Afro-Cuban dictionary.

The lexicographical notes of the *Catauro*, which Ortiz calls "cubicherías," would reappear in his second dictionary, the *Glosario de afronegrismos* (1924), which contains only African words imported to Cuba during four centuries of slave trade. As is his want, every time he explores a new field, Ortiz warns readers of his *Glosario* that nobody before him had examined the linguistic influence of Africa in Spanish America. But at the same time, aware of the fact that he is not a linguist, he applies the information he collected on the geographic origin for *Los negros esclavos* to formulate an Afro-Cuban protolinguistics:

> We do not consider that the African linguistic nomenclature has been sufficiently established in all cases, nor can we assure that the entries in this glossary are the definitive for the etymology of African words. We are unable to afford the luxury of dealing with, for example, words derived from the Bantu, Olofo, Yoruba, and other; and even less so, on the basis of the common expressions of place or origin which we conserve here, when talking of the derivations from the Congo, Mandingo, Calabar, or Lucumí.[24]

Of the many terms Ortiz recovers from oblivion, I explore one that was particularly meaningful to him, *cocorícamo*, which from republican Cuba goes back to the Spanish Golden Age.[25] In 1929, Ortiz published an extensive note about the history of this African word in the Spanish language. By giving a brief synthesis of the African diaspora, he showed a thorough knowledge not only of the written sources but also of the oral ones.

Unless otherwise proven, the term *coco* traveled to Spain from Africa and the West Indies, through the Bantu blacks, known as Congolese and Angolas, who influenced the Spanish language. These influences came from those continents to Spain, during the fifteenth, sixteenth, and seventeenth centuries, via the impact on the language of white children, who the blacks bred in America, and that of adults, with whom they mingled in dance and love. At their return to their original places in Spain, these white Spaniards in turn transmitted their infantile or vulgar terms to their fellow countrymen, following their long stay in the coastlands of the New World. Now they were *indianos* and blackened in their language due to the dense African slave population, which inhabited the coastal areas where the Indians once lived.[26]

Coco is a term that travels from Bantu languages, which covers the fearsome, from the fierce beasts, the flying birds, the extraordinary and powerful insects, the clinging arm, and the strong claw, to the ghost which imagination creates. Fear of the *coco* is fear of all that is "supernatural," a sacred fear. I must end my evaluation by situating this term, which we have discovered in multiple similar terms in Cuba, within contemporary anthropology. The *cocorícamo* is nothing more than what ethnographers today refer to as *mana*.[27] In this way, philology offers Ortiz the opportunity of remaking the journey of the Africans to Spain, be it from Africa or from Spanish America. He felt entitled to defy both the *Diccionario de la Real Academia* and the first chronicler of Indies, Fernández de Oviedo. The former had given the word *coco* an Aimara origin, and the latter, in his *Historia general y natural de las Indias,* had compared the coconut to the monkey, from which the term *macaco* derives.

If, in twentieth-century anthropological jargon, "the Cuban *cocorícamo* is the *mana* of the Melanesians," we should keep in mind that the word *coco,* whatever its route to Spain might have been, carried by a Bantu language, is already found in the anonymous Lazarillo de Tormes, as early as 1554. When Lázaro, quintessence of the Spanish *pícaro,* talks about his stepbrother's fear of the black father, he described the following scene:

> I remember that when my black stepfather was working, as the child saw that my mother and myself were white, and not his father, he ran fearfully towards my mother and said, "Mother, *coco!*" He replied, laughing, "Son of a bitch!" Although young, I realized what my brother had said, and told myself, "How many in the world run from others because they do not see themselves!"

There is a further entry for *cocorícamo* proposed by Lydia Cabrera in her *Cuentos negros de Cuba,* whose animal fables could easily be related to the medieval Spanish tradition, as to the collection of stories by the German ethnologist Leo Frobenius in his *Black Decameron* (1910). The main character in the story told by Cabrera is a tortoise, Jicotea, who makes a musical instrument to attract the other animals of the forest in order to eat them. This popular trickster of the Yoruba tradition explains what his instrument is made of: "I call it '*cocorícamo.*' I've made it so to speak with my good and evil heart."[28] We can conclude that, underlying the findings of anthropologists, there was a tradition that came to Cuba from Spain—the picaresque, one of the richest in this language, and that gave them a frame for understanding the ambiguities of the African trickster. Ortiz's thesis is that the *pícaro* is the vehicle of pidgin.

In the first issue of *Estudios Afrocubanos*, a magazine published in Havana
in 1937, Ortiz explains the choice of the symbol for the publication. It was a
Greek urn with a double profile, a black woman on one side and a white
woman on the other, "reproducing the historic Janus-like urn from the sixth
century B.C., by the potter Charinus, because it is the most ancient object in
which the two great races of the Afro-Cuban lineage are equal for the human
satisfaction." The two faces of Janus, the Latin god that keeps watch of the
doors, became from then on the feature Ortiz looked for in the African
iconography in order to prove the syncretism in Cuba.

Among the Janus-type representations of the African black, those of a religious character in the regions near Nigeria and Calabar are of particular interest. In these regions, and within their secret societies, some of which still
remain in Cuba, there are very typical masks with two faces. Those sacred
masks of Calabar have not reached Cuba, as far as we know. But we do have
some pictures of the sacred Yoruba imagery that have Janus-like motifs.[29]

But to choose a pre-Christian symbol to represent the Afro-Cuban repeats
an operation dear to Frobenius, who in 1911 had identified the history of the
black continent with the Platonic fable of the Atlantis. During the nineteenth
century and the beginning of the twentieth, in Cuba and the other Spanish
colonies, the wind blew from the classics. That neoclassical period could be
called "Janus in Cuba."

Soon it was the turn of the avant-garde in Europe who, exhausted from
looking back, decided to head to more exotic lands and discovered African art.
Ironically enough, that fashion also arrived in Cuba, where the cities of Havana
and Santiago had been worshipping the syncretic Madonnas of Regla and Caridad del Cobre. Therefore, the revival of Janus was not enough to represent the
crossbreeding in Cuba and was replaced by an African god. This way the trickster of the Yoruba pantheon, the ambivalent Elegbá, took over from the two
faces of Ortiz's urn. This period of the discoveries of the African without the
mediation of a Mediterranean mystique could be called "Elegbá in Cuba."

Janus and Elegbá share the role of guardians. To the Latin god, a by-
cephalic one, a temple is dedicated in Rome. The *orishá* Elegbá keeps watch
over the doors and rules the gossiping; he is consulted on when to act and
how; and every *oración* in the Afro-Cuban liturgy begins and ends with him.
Both deities arrived in Cuba by sea: Janus, in the books from Europe, Elegbá,
in the stories and songs from Africa.

If Afro-Cuban studies were born with Fernando Ortiz, it is also true that
thanks to the generation that followed, Afro-Romance anthropology became
Afro-Cuban literature as well. The most notorious of his followers are Lydia
Cabrera (1900–1988) and Rómulo Lachatañeré (1909–1952). The biographical map of both writers coincides in a date, 1939, when Cabrera returned to
Cuba after a long stay in France, where she published her first book, *Contes
négres de Cuba* (1936). It was also in 1939, as a result of his forced exile, that

Lachatañeré arrived in New York. In terms of their texts, Ortiz wrote the prologues for both of their *opera prima*. By sponsoring the entry of Lachatañeré and Cabrera into the scientific-poetic community of Afro-Cuban studies, like Malinowski with his African disciples in England, Ortiz extended his sphere of influence. His two prologues (to *¡Oh, mío Yemayá! Cuentos y cantos negros* [1938], by Lachatañeré, and to the Spanish version of Cabrera's book, *Cuentos negros de Cuba* [1940]) should be read in tandem. They are a symptom of Ortiz's own developments, from the criminological view of Cuba in distant 1906 to the apology of the counterpoint in the late 1930s. By reading the two prologues, we see how he collects the fruits of his pioneering work in the upcoming generation and also how Cabrera and Lachatañeré show in their stories the literary sources of their mentor's anthropology.

As a volunteer for the Allies during World War II, Lachatañeré went to Africa to evacuate fallen soldiers. At the end of the war, anthropologists such as Boas, Herskovits, Benedict, and Bascom, all at Columbia University, encouraged him to continue his work. It was in New York that he cherished the project of expanding his field of study to the rest of the Caribbean as an ethnographic photographer. In 1952, however, on his way back from a research trip in Puerto Rico, his plane crashed into the sea, cutting short his promising career. Ortiz insisted on spelling his family name in the French fashion (Lachatagnarais), as a statement of the unity of the Caribbean world. He recognized Haiti's influence on Cuba since at least the revolution of 1794. One of the descendants of those Haitians from Oriente was Rómulo Lachatagnarais. Today perhaps he would have enjoyed the glory of a pioneering documentary maker, like Jean Rouch in the French Sudan or Pierre Verger, who after starting as a photographer for the Musée de l'Homme in Paris became the indispensable historian of the Middle Passage between Bahia and the gulf of Benin.

Lachatañeré's first book, *¡Oh, mío Yemayá!*, tells the saga of the Yoruba deities as known in the Cuban oral tradition. Unlike Cabrera, who until her death declared having never learned an African language, during his years in America, Lachatañeré studied Yoruba history and language. And because of his familiarity with the English rather than with the French, he read the *History of the Yorubas* by the ex-slave Samuel Johnson, who had become an Anglican reverend in Nigeria. It is in his prologue to Lachatañeré's first book that Ortiz plays with the classical idea of fable—a story with a moral. Oral fables, he says, lack the exegesis that follows a holy book. Tradition has it that the paradigm of ancient fable writers began with a mulatto slave from the sixth century B.C., whose name was Aesop. Ortiz makes Lachatañeré the mulatto fable writer of modern Cuba. In the same prologue, he writes:

> This book [*¡Oh, mío Yemayá!*] would be highly unintelligible and little appreciated, even for literary pleasure, if the reader did not have some prior and even remote knowledge regarding its origin, themes, genre, or intentions. As the

Egyptian *Book of the Dead*, or the adventures of the Greco-Roman Gods, or certain Hebrew texts in the Old Testament, can not be read without bordering tediousness and a sense of banality, unless the mind is prepared to approach a literary text with a religious meaning.[30]

Afro-Cuban fables, after all, also require a religious approach. Here Ortiz shows that he became especially interested during that period in the religious systems of the island. At the same time, something had preoccupied him since the writing of his first dictionary: the translation of "some languages remote in space and time, agglutinative, overflowed by metaphors and very musical" to the language of Cuba. In this sense, his 1938 prologue for Lachatañeré already contains the prologue he would write two years later for Lydia Cabrera. Ortiz confesses in his prologue to ¡*Oh, mío Yemayá*! that he already knew the French version of *Cuentos negros de Cuba*. The history behind Cabrera's text shows itself best in Ortiz's preoccupations with translating, since her stories describe a singular sequence that moves "from the African languages in Guinea, predominantly Yoruba and Ewe, to the Afro-Cuban dialect of Spanish, from this to standard Spanish, and finally to French."[31] In short, telling a story in Cuba supposed the translation of a translation, as if the versions and diversions inherent to oral transmission would never cease to occur, not even on the written page.

At the time of his death, Ortiz was working on the third part of his Black Trilogy, *Los negros curros*, published posthumously in Havana in 1986 on the basis of articles with the same title published in *Archivos del Folklore Cubano* (1926–1928). As a work of literary archaeology, it represents his greatest effort in tracing the lost tongue of the *curros*, a type of Havana braggart from Seville that disappeared at the end of the nineteenth century. In order to reconstruct their background on both sides of the Atlantic, Ortiz reviews the Africanisms in the Spanish dances and plays from the sixteenth and seventeenth centuries. And with his usual sharpness, he associates the Spanish Golden Age with twentieth-century Cuba. The connector, as one would expect, was African music.

Within the verses of those songs, the most characteristic tunes can be distinguished. Centuries later, in the twentieth century, these tunes would have to be resurrected by Afro-Cuban poetry, at a time when black poets and musicians had managed to create a favorable atmosphere, socially similar to that of the Spanish age: verse structure, percussion refrains sometimes onomatopoeic in sound, acute rhymes, and, in general, predominant musicality integrated with literary expressions.[32]

But as Carpentier comments, to say "African music is like saying 'medieval knights'"[33] implies something, but it doesn't explain much. Carpentier, a musicologist himself, had started his career as a writer by collecting data on Abakuá initiation rights in the outskirts of Havana, which later inspired his first librettos for the stage. Where Ortiz best develops his idea of "*consustan-*

ciación," or integration of music and literature, is in his *La africanía de la música folklórica en Cuba* (1950), which complements and gives breadth to Carpentier's history of Cuban music. This text immediately became a reference book on Afro-Cuban ethnomusicology. It was by means of the music that the poetic movement of the 1920s and 1930s came to conquer an audience. If we think of Nicolás Guillén's 1934 poem "Sensemayá" with the subtitle "Canto para matar una culebra," or "Song for killing a snake," we learn from Ortiz that it actually belonged to a popular genre in colonial Cuba. On *Día de Reyes*, the *comparsa* or traveling ballet used to choose a subject, the most common of which was either the snake or the scorpion, and an expert dancer would carry a huge figure representing the dangerous beast along the procession. The songs that accompanied that dance were to encourage the killing of the beast, and so the expressions "*matar el alacrán*" or "*matar la culebra*" passed to Afro-Cuban poetry. In 1937, Ortiz explains the connections (the counterpoint) of the same ritual on both sides of the Atlantic.

In Cuba, there are no serpents, vipers, or other harmful ophidian to kill. The scarce *majás*, *jubos*, and little snakes that inhabit these Greater Antilles are harmless; they even visit the bedclothes of the peasant hut and never disturb the dwellers. It is in Africa that these animals cause fears and provoke people to brew potions. "Killing the snake" has been the theme of a dance and a song that was very popular in festivities of Havana's blacks in the last century, in their famous celebration of *Dia de Reyes*, and in their carnivalesque entertainments.[34]

In that very tradition of performing a ritual, during those years of Afro-Cuban euphoria, there had been attempts at performative poetry in Havana. The undisputed muse of Afro-Cuban poets was Eusebia Cosme. In 1936, after attending one of her performances, the journalist Rafael Marquina called her "a black priestess of a white Eucharist . . . when Eusebia Cosme recites she is in a 'state of grace.' And everything in her is pure and almost religious. Hearing her it seems we are witnessing in mesmerizement a quintessential liturgy of recreation."[35] Ortiz, however, warns us from the exaltation of such a poetic act outside of its religious context.

But in the new poetics, we insist, there is no longer the emotional splendor and aesthetic of the collective liturgical act, as for example, a solemn *Tantum ergo of a Corpus Christi* in a medieval church, or the processions worshipping Cybele in Tartesios, expressing a maximum euphoric and communal exaltation of life. . . . Black gods would not understand a white language. Neither does Afro-Cuban lyric have a female poet, and one can not expect that when it does, the sacred inspiration would turn into Elegua love verses. The same culture that will enable black poetry to germinate will be far from similar to the emotions contained in African pieces. Due to this, Afro-Cuban lyrics do not have poetic dialogues with the all-powerful beings of the superhuman mystery. These mulatto poets "do not summon the saint."[36]

The dilemma of putting a religious experience into words, which had been the main question for the mystical poetry in sixteenth-century Spain, reappears in twentieth-century Cuba. And while retelling the main act of Eusebia Cosme's performance, her interpretation of the poem "Sensemayá," Ortiz condenses in five words the new version of Cuban poetry: "language, melody, rhythm, pantomime, and drama."

Finally, it was the same kind of expressive complex that the main interpreter of Ortiz's discoveries, Lydia Cabrera, describes in her groundbreaking book, *El monte* (1954), while recalling the visit of Federico García Lorca to Cuba in 1930. The Spanish poet remained speechless (and later on quite lyrical) after seeing the *íremes* and witnessing an initiation rite of an Abakuá society.

> I do not forget the fear that the *íremes*, with their white cyclopean eyes, produced in Federico García Lorca, nor the delirious poetic description of poetry that he gave me after witnessing a *plante*. If a Diaghilev had been born on this island, he surely would have made this *ñañigo* devil dance in the stages of Europe.[37]

And it was, in fact, on the European stages that the cycle of discoveries of the Africans in Cuba was symbolically completed. For Lorca, whose point of view did not significantly differ from the Cuban poet Emilio Ballagas, a procession in Havana had the charm of the exotic. It was the face of Africa that he could not find in Andalusia. For Carpentier, whose first writings were the result of his experience of the religious ceremonies of the Abakuá, Diaghilev was the choreographic point of reference for the Parisian avant-garde and the ideal reader of his librettos. And for Ortiz as much as for Cabrera, the *oración* as liturgy and literature gave them the chance to penetrate the Abakuá enigma.

It is a paradox that African Cuba was first discovered in Europe. Around 1900, while Fernando Ortiz was studying law in Madrid, excited by the wonders of criminology and the underworld of the Spanish prisons, he saw the *íremes* for the first time in his life.[38] He was immediately asked by his Spanish friends and colleagues to tell them the story behind those masks. But he could say very little about a ritual and people he did not know. So the polymath set to work, and the literary method of Ortiz became a virtual anthropology. It was virtual because he drew a map of Africa without having ever been to Africa and because his approach to things Cuban took shape elsewhere. At the Museo de Ultramar, he started looking with new eyes at his island, which was no longer his mother's paradise lost but the island of the *íremes*. And it all started in Madrid.

NOTES

1. Roberto González Echevarría (oral intervention at the Ortiz Symposium, New York, March 22, 2000).

2. Rafael Salillas, *La vida penal en España* (Madrid: 1888), 244.

3. Salillas, *La vida penal*, 275.

4. The other usual destination for Cubans deported to Africa until 1898 was the island of Fernando Póo—renamed Bioko in 1973.

5. Rafael Salillas, "Los ñañigos en Ceuta," *Revista General de Legislación y Jurisprudencia* 98 (1901): 337–60. See Antonio Fernández Ferrer, *La isla infinita de Fernando Ortiz* (Alicante: Instituto de Cultura Juan Gil-Albert, 1998), 20.

6. Araceli García Carranza, Norma Suárez Suárez, and Alberto Quesada Morales, *Cronología Fernando Ortiz* (Havana: Fundación Fernando Ortiz, 1996), 18.

7. Rafael Roche Monteagudo, *La policía y sus misterios en Cuba* (Havana: 1908).

8. Lydia Cabrera, *La sociedad secreta abakuá narrada por viejos adeptos* (Miami: Colección del Chicherekú, 1970).

9. Fernando Ortiz, "La fiesta afro-cubana del 'Día de Reyes,'" *Revista Bimestre Cubana* XV (1920): 5–26.

10. Cesare Lombroso, *L'uomo delinquente* (Torino: Bocca, 1876): 288.

11. Fernando Ortiz, *Los negros curros*, ed. Diana Iznaga (Havana: Editorial de Ciencias Sociales, 1986 [1926–1928]), 115.

12. Fernando Ortiz, *Hampa afro-cubana: Los negros brujos (apuntes para un estudio de etnología criminal), con una carta prólogo del Dr. C. Lombroso* (Madrid: Librería de Fernando Fe, 1906), 139.

13. Fernando Ortiz, "Por la integración cubana de blancos y negros," lecture at the Club Atenas in Havana, December 12, 1942, in *Ultra* 13 (1943): 69–76.

14. Fernando Ortiz, *Orbita de Fernando Ortiz*, ed. Julio Le Riverend (Havana: UNEAC, 1973), 244.

15. A proper revision of Nina's work, however, came out only in 1999, from the Brazilian historian of anthropology Mariza Corrêa, *As ilusões da liberdade: A escola Nina Rodrigues e a antropologia no Brasil* (Bragança Paulista: Instituto Franciscano de Antropologia, 1999).

16. "Assim, o conhecimento etnográfico dos africanos vindos escravos para o Brasil, o qual não me consta tenha sido tentado antes de meus estudos, projeta larga e intensa luz sobre todos estes fatos, conferindo a cada qual uma fisionomia histórica justa e racional"; Raymundo Nina Rodrigues, *Os africanos no Brasil* (São Paulo: 1933), 70.

17. Fernando Ortiz, *Hampa afrocubana: Los negros esclavos (Estudio sociológico y de derecho público)* (Havana: Revista Bimestre Cubana, 1916), 40.

18. Rafael Rojas mentioned the scrupulous taxonomies of Ortiz regarding the European immigration to Cuba, which apply also for the African slave trade (Ortiz Symposium, March 20, 2000).

19. Ortiz, *Hampa afrocubana*, 62.

20. Henri Dumont. "Antropología y patología comparada de los negros esclavos" (memoria inédita referente a Cuba, 1866), *Revista Bimestre Cubana* 10, no. 3 (1915); 11, no. 2 (1916).

21. Roberto Gonzalez Echevarria, *Myth and Archive: A Theory of Latin American Narrative* (New York: Cambridge University Press, 1990), 167.

22. Isabel Castellanos, "Abre kutu wiri ndinga: Lydia Cabrera y las lenguas afrocubanas," in *En torno a Lydia Cabrera* (Miami: Ediciones Universal, 1987), 214.

23. Esteban Pichardo, *Diccionario provincial casi-razonado de vozes cubanas* (1836), xii.

24. Fernando Ortiz, *Glosario de afronegrismos* (Havana: Imprenta El Siglo XX, 1924), xiv.

25. Fernando Ortiz, *Nuevo catauro de cubanismos*, ed. Angel Lluis Fernández Guerra and Gladys Alonso, posthumous ed. (Havana: Editorial de Ciencias Sociales, 1974), 148.

26. Fernando Ortiz, "El cocorícamo y otros conceptos teoplásmicos del folklore afrocubano," *Archivos del Folklore Cubano* 4, no. 4 (1929): 298.

27. Ortiz, "El cocorícamo," 308–9.

28. Lydia Cabrera, *Cuentos negros de Cuba* (Havana: 1940), 81.

29. Fernando Ortiz, "El emblema de la Sociedad de Estudios Afrocubanos," *Estudios Afrocubanos* 1, no. 1 (1937): 11.

30. Fernando Ortiz, "Prólogo," in *¡Oh, mío Yemayá! Cuentos y cantos negros* by Rómulo Lachatañeré (Manzanillo, Cuba: Editorial El Arte, 1938), xxvii.

31. Ortiz, "Prólogo," xxvii.

32. Ortiz, *Los negros curros,* 176.

33. Alejo Carpentier, *La música en Cuba* (Havana: Letras Cubanas, 1988): 268.

34. Fernando Ortiz, "La religión en la poesía mulata," *Estudios Afrocubanos* 1, no. 1 (1937): 41.

35. Ortiz, "La religión en la poesía mulata," 60.

36. Ortiz, "La religión en la poesía mulata," 53.

37. Lydia Cabrera, *El monte* (Havana: 1954), 211.

38. Fernández Ferrer identifies the masks and dresses for the Abakuá ceremony at the Museo de Ultramar (then at the Parque del Retiro in Madrid) as belonging to the Trujillo and Monagas collection. For some, according to María Fernanda Ortiz (Ortiz Symposium, March 22, 2000), those *íremes* were copies of the original masks brought from Havana by one of the last captain generals.

Many foreign students sought recommendations from professors close to Ortiz, so as to be taught by him personally. For example, Manuel Pedro González wrote to Ortiz, from the University of California, on June 21, 1947:

The essential objective of this letter is to introduce you to its bearer, Mr. Edward D. Yeatman, a graduate of our university who is currently preparing for his Ph.D. Mr. Yeatman is an intelligent and dedicated student who wishes to write his thesis on Afro-Cuban poetry. This is why he will be traveling to Havana to attend various courses in your Summer School program, especially the one which you are offering and the one offered by Medardo Vitier on nineteenth-century Cuban literature. He is also keen to collect as much information for his thesis as possible. He already knows who you are and what you represent for Cuban culture, particularly for Afro-Cuban culture. Only you, with your wisdom and advice, are able to guide him towards the correct information and sources. I would be grateful for any cooperation you may provide on this matter.

Apart from regular lectures, the Summer School provided opportunities for visiting places of interest, taking field trips, and attending complementary lectures on different topics, essay and film sessions, Cuban art exhibitions, theater productions, and so on. The organizers carefully designed each extracurricular activity so that it would complement lectures in fields such as Cuban history, geography, economics, and other matters. Ortiz's involvement in these ventures is illustrated by the following announcement:

Students are encouraged to take up the invitation of the Fine Arts Circle and visit the Cuban Painting and Sculpture exhibition, especially organized by the Summer School. The exhibition will close Thursday, August 14. Students are expected to attend the inauguration of the Cuban Modern Art exhibition at the Lyceum, Tuesday 12 at 6 p.m., as well as all the events following it, as specified in the program. On Wednesday 13, at 9 p.m. Dr. Fernando Ortiz will give a lecture in the Medicine Amphitheater, in the "Angel Arturo Aballí" building . . . on illustrations of drum music and ritual Afro-Cuban dancing. All those who wish to attend are welcome.

PROGRAM STRUCTURE

As previously mentioned, Ortiz capitalized on the opportunity that his courses provided for disseminating basic concepts about Cuba, its history, culture, population, and other topics he researched throughout his life. Ortiz was also able to convey to his students the direct findings behind his research, sometimes even before he published them.

He compiled an incredible amount of information for over half a century, meticulously organizing it in hundreds of files that are now part of his personal archives. The archive contains all kinds of valuable data, as well as original drafts of unfinished parts of unpublished texts. It contains his famous bibliographic cards, or *"papeletas,"* as he used to call them in the fashion of Ramón Menéndez Pidal's methodology; cuttings, address books, letters, photographs, paintings, prints, engravings, official documents, musical pieces, galley proofs, manuscripts of other authors—in short, anything that could shed light on a specific topic.

The information stored in the files on "Antilles," "Indians," "Blacks," and "ethnography courses," which never became books as such, were valuable sources that enabled Ortiz to design his courses. In my view, these courses included all those contributions to science and culture, which he had worked on during his inquisitive stages. The data and information in them ranged from the beginning of the century, when Ortiz was concerned with black Cubans and their incorporation in the *"mala vida,"* to the seeds of what became his theory of transculturation, his most important contribution to science. When viewing the themes and bibliography for the course, "Ethnographic Factors in Cuba" (see below), one can see the presence of texts for key topics, with the added bonus that Ortiz had been involved with other authors, whether in the writing process, by writing prologues, or in some other fundamental way.

Ethnographic Factors in Cuba[3]

- Cuban ethnography—general introduction: Races. Ethnic groups. Cultures. Transculturation.
- The Antilles. Ethnic mosaic. Geography. Races. History. Cultures. Languages. Religions. Policies.
- Cuba. Its ethnical factors.
- Cuba. The Indians. Various Indian immigrations. Their various cultures. Latest discoveries and theories.
- Cuba. The Indians. Social survival. Economic survival. Extractive economics. Agrarian. Culinary survival.
- Cuba. The Indians. Industrial survival. Crafts. Weaving. Textiles. Utensils.
- Cuba. The Indians. Religious survival. Tobacco. Its Indo-Cuban significance and transculturation of blacks and whites.
- Cuba. The Indians. Field Trip to the Anthropology Museum.
- Cuba. White ethnic components. Cultures. Social impact on the Indians. Destruction of the Indians. Hispanic domination. Other white ethnical components.
- Cuba. Blacks. Language survival. Vocabulary. Grammar. Writing. Literary survival. Folklore. Poetry.
- Cuba. Blacks. Artistic survival. Music. Instruments.
- Cuba. Blacks. Artistic survival. Song and dance.
- Cuba. Blacks. Artistic survival. Arts. Games.

- Cuba. Blacks. Social survival. Family. The carabelas and cúmbilas. The comadrajos. The curros.
- Cuba. Black townships. El Día de Reyes. The comparsas.
- Cuba. Blacks. Religious survival. Cults. Saints. "Sincretismo." Ñañiguismo.
- Cuba. Blacks. Field trips to museums.

Course Bibliography

Fernando Ortiz. *Los factores humanos de la Cubanidad.* 1940.
Fernando Ortiz. *Las Antillas: Tratado de geografía física y humana de las Antillas.* Volume XVI of the *Geografía Universal* directed by Vidal de la Blanche. 1933.

Indians
J. A. Cosculluela. *Cuatro años en la Ciénaga de Zapata.* 1916.
M. R. Harrington. *Cuba antes de Colón.* Spanish trans. 2 vols. Habana, 1936.
R. Herrera Fritot. *Culturas aborígenes de las Antillas.* Habana. 1936.
Fernando Ortiz. *Historia de la arqueología indocubana.* Habana. 1936.
Roberto Agramonte. "Los indios de Cuba. Aspecto sociológico." In *Curso de introducción a la historia de Cuba.* Habana. 1937.
Cornelius Osgood. *The Siboney Culture in Cayo Redondo.* Cuba. 1942.
Irving Rouse. *Archeology of the Maniabon Hills, Cuba.* New Haven. 1942.
Fernando Ortiz. *Contrapunteo cubano del tabaco y el azúcar.* Habana. 1941.
Fernando Ortiz. *Las cuatro culturas indias de Cuba.* Habana. 1943.

Blacks
Fernando Ortiz. *Los negros esclavos.* Habana. 1906 [sic].
Fernando Ortiz. *Los negros brujos.* Madrid. 1906.
Fernando Ortiz. *Glosario de afronegrismos.* Habana. 1916.
Fernando Ortiz. "El cocorícamo." Conferencia.
Fernando Ortiz. "La música sagrada de los negros Yoruba en Cuba." Conferencia.
Fernando Ortiz. "Los cabildos afrocubanos." 1926.
Fernando Ortiz. "Las comparsas." 1938.
Fernando Ortiz. "Martí y las razas." Conferencia. Habana. 1940.
Fernando Ortiz. "Por la integración cubana de blancos y negros." Conferencia.

Articles [Journals] and Statistics
Population censuses (especially census of 1917).
Archivos del Folklore Cubano. 5 vols.
Estudios Afro-Cubanos. 4 vols.
Revista Bimestre Cubana. 51 vols.

NOTES

1. Printed summary of the course in carpeta no. 133, Cursos de etnografía, Archivo Fernando Ortiz, Sociedad Económica de Amigos del País-Instituto de Literatura y Lingüística José A. Portuondo Valdor, Havana (SEAP-ILL).

2. Ellen Irene Diggs, "Fernando Ortiz: La vida y la obra," M.A. thesis, Facultad de Filosofía y Letras, Universidad de La Habana, 1944; Sala de Etnología, BNJM.

3. Carpeta no. 133, Cursos de etnografía, Archivo Fernando Ortiz, SEAP-ILL.

II

INTERPRETING CUBAN HISTORY

A historical perspective is central to Ortiz's most important works and public actions. His pivotal concepts for studying Cuban social reality are suffused with historical content. In this section, Rafael Rojas argues that Ortiz was inspired by a transcultural and historically based nationalism, different from more rigid forms of Cuban nationalism and José Martí's racial perspectives. Marifeli Pérez-Stable analyzes the historical relevance of Ortiz's political career during the early Cuban republic, his intellectual leadership in civic movements, and his ultimate disillusion with Cuban politics. Carmen Almodóvar underscores that Ortiz's preferred method in dealing with Cuban social and political problems was the promotion of pedagogy and education rather than internal war. José Matos Arévalos uncovers a rare and unpublished project by Ortiz on the realm of economic history, and he traces Ortiz's historiographical roots among Cuban liberal-reformist historians of the nineteenth century. Finally, Jean Stubbs reclaims the importance of tobacco history, in contrast to the dominant history of sugar, through the analysis of postcripts to the classic Ortizian counterpoint.

5

Transculturation and Nationalism

Rafael Rojas

A first reaction when considering Ortiz's work is to stand in awe at its immense diversity. Ortiz alone represents the incarnation, in the Cuban culture's narrative tradition, of the textual metamorphosis described by Michel Foucault in which a document turns into a monument.[1] Law and criminology, ethnology and sociology, languages and archeology, literature and politics, and anthropology and history create a rare multiplicity of forms of knowledge from where that Cuban tradition stems.[2] María Zambrano uses the metaphor of a tree to illustrate the wholeness of José Lezama Lima's work. Likewise, Manuel Ulacia refers to the nature of Octavio Paz's poetry, in his ability to traverse different areas of history and culture. But in both cases the symbolic axis of the author-as-tree metaphor resides in the tree's trunk. In Ortiz, however, the interpretative value lies in the branches or, more precisely, in the roots themselves.

Let us imagine for a moment what Cuba's intellectual history would be without Enrique José Varona and Jorge Mañach, without Elías Entralgo and Roberto Agramonte, without Alejo Carpentier and José Lezama Lima, without Lydia Cabrera and Manuel Moreno Fraginals. Even in that desert, Ortiz's work alone would be sufficient to link Cuban culture to modernity. Ortiz's legacy envelops the mystery of a fully modern intellectual adventure in the Caribbean and even in Spanish America. This notion of modernity is put to the test in what Habermas would call the dialectics between the self-assurance of having a place in the world and the ability to move to other epistemological latitudes.[3] Ortiz's nomadism is reflected in his cultural anthropology texts relating to Cuban folklore, in works such as *La africanía de la música folklórica de Cuba*, or *Los bailes y el teatro de los negros en el folklore de Cuba*; in a unique book dealing with the history of mentalities, his

Historia de una pelea cubana contra los demonios, which preceded for a full decade the historiographic path opened by Jacques Le Goff and Georges Duby, Carlo Ginzburg and Robert Darnton; in essays such as *La crisis política cubana: Sus causas y remedios*, or *En la tribuna: Discursos cubanos*; and in mixed texts, halfway between anthropology, history, and economics, such as his renowned *Contrapunteo cubano del tabaco y el azúcar* and *El huracán, su mitología y sus símbolos*.[4]

However, Ortiz's modernity lies not so much in the expansive nature of his texts, but more in the shadows he projects, in the trail of readings he leaves behind or in that vast expanse of interpretations that open up around him: an unusual example, in Cuban culture, of the mixture of two ample records—what is read and what is written.[5] Let us consider, for example, the case of *Contrapunteo cubano del tabaco y el azúcar*. In its first edition, (Jesús Montero, 1940), Ortiz's text was preceded by a prologue written by Cuban historian Herminio Portell Vilá and an introduction by the British-Polish anthropologist Bronislaw Malinowski, who was, until his death in 1942, a professor at Yale University. Both considerations of the same text emerged from different reference points and were directed at a different public, without provoking any tension.

Portell Vilá attempted to comment on the nationalist implications of the *Contrapunteo*, within the context of an important restructuring in tariff and trade in Cuban sugar exports to the United States. Malinowski commented on the theoretical contribution of the term *transculturation* to Western anthropology and Ortiz's affinity with functionalist scholars and the functionalist methodology, which Malinowski and Alfred Reginald Radcliffe-Brown had founded in England, and which was adopted by sociologists Robert Merton and Talcott Parsons in the United States.[6]

Portell Vilá perceived in *Contrapunteo* an

> authentic doctrine, undoubtedly true, in the fact that sugarcane, its industrial process, and the system that is organized around it, form an external issue in Cuba, something alien to the country, and which serves foreign interests before national interest and entails human exploitation, undue privilege, and protectionism.[7]

This nationalistic perception was partly triggered by the text's binary nature, and also by the Cuban economic reality, then affected by the revolutionary process of the 1930s, Franklin Delano Roosevelt's New Deal, and the outbreak of World War II. The suspension of the sugar quota system, decreed by the Costigan-Jones Act of 1934, and the increase in the U.S. sugar tariff, triggered a reduction of income, unemployment, a fall in salaries, and an increase in prices in Cuba. All this caused an interesting division between the elite political classes who believed that "without sugar there was no country," and the elite intellectual classes who, since the mid-1920s, demanded the abolition of the *latifundio* and a redefinition of the notion of economic sovereignty with regard to the United States.[8] Other republican scholars, such as Ramiro Guerra, Emeterio Santovenia, Francisco Ichaso, and even Emilio Roig de Leuchsenring, would have agreed with Portell Vilá's criticism of the "synonymity between sugar and nation," leading to "the identity between national interests and the sugar industry's interest."[9] In this circle of liberal republican intellectuals, Ortiz's *Contrapunteo* was perceived as an argument against agricultural monoproduction and in favor of agricultural diversification and industrialization.

Malinowski's views were not addressed to the public in Cuba, but rather to the Anglo-American academic sphere and, to a lesser extent, to a reduced portion of the political classes in the United States linked to foreign affairs. First, Malinowski, who was invited to Cuba by Ortiz, acknowledged that the notion of transculturation was invented by Ortiz and that it made more sense than other terms, such as "cultural change," "acculturation," "diffusion," and "migration or osmosis of cultures," given its detachment from European ethnocentrism.[10]

In sections of *Contrapunteo*, Ortiz could not conceal his pride at the fact that the term he invented was being disseminated throughout Western anthropological academic centers. "The proposed neologism transculturation, wrote Ortiz, "was presented before the undeniable authority of Bronislaw Malinowski, the great contemporary master of ethnography and sociology, and he approved of it. With such a sponsor, we will not hesitate in adopting the mentioned neologism."[11] Ortiz felt that Malinowski had authorized him, and Malinowski highly valued this authorization because it incorporated Ortiz in the canon of the functionalist methodology. This is why the Yale professor overemphasized that Ortiz was "a true functionalist, aware of the fact that the aesthetics and psychology of the sensorial impressions must be taken into account alongside habitat and technology," or that he was "a good functionalist because he refers to history when it is essential."[12]

However, there is a crossroad where the nationalist ideological perception adopted by Portell Vilá, and the epistemological functionalist perspective adopted by Malinowski, so far running in parallel, subtly clash. Portell Vilá understood that his criticism regarding sugar, as a factor of domination and alienation, entailed actions toward economic independence from the United States and the extirpation of a "parasite which extracts the vital juices from the nation," as he would put it in prose.[13] Malinowski, on the other hand, assumed that the term *transculturation*, in establishing a two-directional dialogue between two or more cultures, entails not independence but interdependence with regard to the United States.[14] The author of *Magic, Science, and Religion*, familiar with the changes of Roosevelt's diplomatic policy toward Latin America during his years at Yale, used his introduction to the

Contrapunteo to engage transculturation in foreign policy and to suggest that interdependence between bordering nations should develop new symbolic openings. "Cuba, alongside Mexico," concluded Malinowski, "is the nearest of Latin American neighbors where the 'good neighbor policy' should be implemented in the intelligent, cautious, and generous manner that U.S. statesmen and even magnates are occasionally capable of."[15]

A radical political interpretation of both perspectives could show that, while Portell Vilá maintained a nationalist, pro-independence view, Malinowski, inclined to stand by British anthropological notions, had a more imperialistic view. However, in the two reeditions of *Contrapunteo*, corrected and lengthened by Ortiz himself and printed in Cuba after Fidel Castro's nationalist revolution—one by the Universidad Central de Las Villas (1963) and another one by the Consejo Nacional de Cultura (1963)—Portell Vila's prologue was removed, while Malinowski's introduction remained.[16] The answer to this apparent conundrum is simple: The nationalist historian Portell Vilá had emigrated to the United States, rejecting Marxism-Leninism as the official ideology of the state. Ten years after those reeditions, historian Julio Le Riverend adopted many views of Portell Vila's nationalist perspective, without quoting him, naturally, but inscribing them within a Marxist-Leninist interpretation of Ortiz's anti-imperialism, in his prologue to Ortiz's collection of essays entitled *Órbita de Fernando Ortiz*, published by the official authors and writers' union, UNEAC.[17]

However, this incidental paradox obliges one to reconsider Ortiz's notion of nationalism and, in general, all nationalisms in Cuban culture. By this I mean an interpretative modification, as Montserrat Guibernau recommends, from the singular to the plural, from that abusive topic "Cuban nationalism" to a typology of nationalisms in Cuba.[18] To say that Fernando Ortiz was a nationalistic intellectual is to state the obvious: The real challenge in a sophisticated analysis is to attempt to illustrate what kind of nationalism he defended.

Without even meaning to, Malinowski pointed out that if the *Contrapunteo* was not read "transculturally," a discourse antinomy could result between the nationalistic narration and the transcultural one. Effectively, the excessively binary rhetoric Ortiz adopted to narrate the secular struggle between "Don Tabaco" and "Doña Azúcar" appears to, at certain stages, suggest—as it did to Portell Vilá—that tobacco was a metaphor for nationalism, and sugar was an allegory for the antinational. In one of the most difficult sections of the book directly related to this dilemma one can read, "in trade: for our tobacco, the whole world is a market, yet our sugar has only one market. Centripetal and centrifugal. Cubanity and foreignness. Sovereignty and colonialism. High crown and humble sack."[19] However, in other sections of the text, including the title, Ortiz maintains that Cubanity is not in one or other archetype, in one or other allegory, but in the collision, in their rubbing against each other—basically, in the transculturation of sugar and tobacco. This is why, for example, he mentions that sugar and its derivatives produce a "miscegenation of flavors," that "sugar was mulatto since its origin, because in its production the energies of white men and black men blended" and that "the black man's arm and sugarcane are two binomials in the same economic equation of our country."[20] Fernando Ortiz, a dialogic thinker, was reluctant to accept manicheisms and stereotypes. In the construction of Cuban national identity he never excluded—together with Manuel Moreno Fraginals—the economic, political, and social processes in sugar production, despite its infernal discourse of "manicheism, land ownership, colonialism, labor trafficking, super capitalism, absentism, foreigness, corporativism, and imperialism."[21] This is why he ended his essay predicting the marriage between Don Tabaco y Doña Azúcar and its trinitarian offspring: rum.[22]

An adequate solution to the tension between nationalism and transculturation would be a dialectic of transcultural nationalism. It is clear that when Ortiz writes that memorable phrase, "the true history of Cuba is the history of its intricate transculturations," he reveals a porous, tempered, and permeable narrative of national identity in the island.[23] A cautious reader will observe that when he uses the plural *transculturations*, Ortiz is alluding to, first, a mutation within a sedentary population, produced between the Ciboney Paleolithic and the Taino Neolithic, and, then, an infinite cycle of immigrations that begins with the arrival of the first Spaniards and Africans in the sixteenth, seventeenth, and eighteenth centuries and continues with the incorporation of the French, British, German, Italian, Chinese, Jewish, Polish, North American, Russian, and other immigrant populations in Cuba during the last two centuries.[24]

This idea is better explained in his lecture *Los factores humanos de la cubanidad* where Ortiz uses the metaphor of the *ajiaco* to illustrate that endless process of blending and filtration of different cultures within one single nation. One must again insist, given the erroneous interpretations that this text has had, that Ortiz does not find the base of Cubanity in the broth, but in its cooking, not in "the sauce of the new and synthetic succulence formed by the fusion of human lineages," but rather in the "very complex process of its formation, both integrative and disintegrative."[25]

This notion of a permanent cultural construction, in which the clash and hybridization between agents never dissolves fragmentary identities into a homogenous whole, is the epistemological bridge between Fernando Ortiz and the postmodern anthropology of Clifford Geertz, James Clifford, and Dennis Tedlock.[26] The first postmodern interpretations of the *Contrapunteo*, as is well known, have been by Antonio Benítez Rojo, who above all emphasizes the element of fiction in the text. More recently, the postmodern approaches of George Yúdice, Román de la Campa, Fernando Coronil, and Peter Burke, who, more inclined toward postfunctionalist anthropology, have retooled the notion of multiculturalism in the United States through Ortiz's transcultural nationalism.[27]

The rejection of the process of synthesis, as a discursive fiction that turns national identity into a teleological narrative, is so evident in Ortiz that it is impossible to find in his essays a recycling of the myth of the "fundamental mulatto character of the Cuban." [28] *Ajiaco* underlines the blending of cultures ("blending of cookery, blending of races, blending of cultures"), but it is not a synonym of being or becoming mulatto (*mulatez*).[29] Interpreting *mulatez* as an allegory of nationality is equivalent to destroying a complete and diffuse whole, because, as Ortiz points out, the nation "is never made" and its mass is never "integrated." Thus, his lucid conclusion, which has so often been misread: The infinite migratory tissue of Cuban society always "differs," and will always differ, "from the consolidation of a definitive and basic national homogeneity."[30] Therefore, this transcultural nationalism is different from an ethnic nationalism, as is projected in *La raza cósmica* by the Mexican José Vasconcelos, whose argument, according to Ortiz, was "pure paradox." [31]

NOTES

1. Michel Foucault, *La arqueología del saber* (Mexico City: Siglo XXI), 51–64.

2. Gilles Deleuze and Félix Guattari, *Mil mesetas: Capitalismo y esquizofrenia* (Valencia: Pretextos, 1997), 9–29.

3. Jürgen Habermas, *El discurso filosófico de la modernidad* (Madrid: Taurus, 1989), 11–35. Also consult Arendt's text on Walter Benjamin in Hannah Arendt, *Hombres en tiempos de oscuridad* (Barcelona: Gedisa, 1990), 158–78.

4. Julio Le Riverend, "Fernando Ortiz y su obra cubana," prologue to Fernando Ortiz, *Orbita de Fernando Ortiz* (Havana: UNEAC, 1973), 49–51; Isaac Barreal, "Prólogo," in Fernando Ortiz, *Etnía y sociedad* (Havana: Editorial Ciencias Sociales, 1993), vii–viii.

5. Following Bloom, it could be stated that through his reading, Ortiz becomes a canonical author: Harold Bloom, *El canon occidental: La escuela y los libros de todas las épocas* (Barcelona: Anagrama, 1995), 11–22. See also Jacques Derrida, *La diseminación* (Madrid: Editorial Fundamentos, 1975), 41; and Giuglielmo Cavallo and Roger Chartier, *Historia de la lectura en el mundo occidental* (Madrid: Taurus, 1998), 534–49.

6. Fernando Ortiz, *Contrapunteo cubano del tabaco y el azúcar: Advertencia de sus contrastes agrarios, económicos, históricos y sociales, su etnografía y su transculturación*, prologue by Herminio Portell Vilá, introduction by Bronislaw Malinowski (Havana: Jesús Montero, 1940), ix–xxiii.

7. Ortiz, *Contrapunteo*, x.

8. Ortiz, *Contrapunteo*, xi.

9. Ortiz, *Contrapunteo*, x.

10. Ortiz, *Contrapunteo*, xv.

11. Ortiz, *Contrapunteo*, 142.

12. Ortiz, *Contrapunteo*, xxi.

13. Ortiz, *Contrapunteo*, x–xi.

14. Ortiz, *Contrapunteo*, xii.

15. Ortiz, *Contrapunteo*, xii.

16. Regarding the editions of *Contrapunteo*, see "Prólogo" by María Fernanda Ortiz Herrera, daughter of the author, in a beautiful reedition under her care: Fernando Ortiz, *Contrapunteo Cubano del tabaco y el azúcar* (Madrid: Música Mundana Maqueda, 1999), i–ix. See also Fernando Ortiz, *Contrapunteo cubano del tabaco y el azúcar* (Santa Clara: Universidad Central de las Villas-Dirección de Publicaciones, 1963), ix.

17. Ortiz, *Orbita*, 39.

18. Montserrat Guibernau, *Los nacionalismos* (Barcelona. Editorial Ariel, 1996), 9–14.

19. Ortiz, *Contrapunteo*, 7.

20. Ortiz, *Contrapunteo*, 31, 80, 81.

21. Ortiz, *Contrapunteo*, 71.

22. Ortiz, *Contrapunteo*, 131.

23. Ortiz, *Contrapunteo*, 137.

24. Ortiz, *Contrapunteo*, 137–42.

25. Ortiz, *Etnía y sociedad*, 6.

26. Clifford Geertz, James Clifford, et al., *El surgimiento de la antropología posmoderna* (Barcelona: Gedisa, 1992), 63–77, 141–70, and 275–88.

27. Antonio Benítez Rojo, *La isla que se repite* (Barcelona: Editorial Casiopea, 1998), 183–90; Román de la Campa, *Latin Americanism* (Minneapolis: University of Minnesota Press, 1999), 64–96; Fernando Coronil, "Introduction" to Ortiz, *Cuban Counterpoint* (1995), ix–lvi; Peter Burke, *Formas de historia cultural* (Madrid: Alianza Editorial, 2000), 202–3.

28. Rafael Rojas, *Isla sin fin: Contribución a la crítica del nacionalismo cubano* (Miami: Ediciones Universal, 1998), 105–22.

29. Ortiz, *Etnía y sociedad*, 6.

30. Ortiz, *Etnía y sociedad*, 20.

31. Ortiz, *Etnía y sociedad*, 7.

6

The Early Republic

Politics, Civic Culture, and Sovereignty

Marifeli Pérez-Stable

Fernando Ortiz's work is indispensable for understanding Cuban culture. My concerns, however, lie elsewhere, though culture also enters the profile I raise in this essay. I am concerned with politics as Ortiz was early in his career. He was a member of the Liberal Party in the Cuban House of Representatives between 1916 and 1923. He participated in various reformist movements during the 1920s, and finally departed politics—and Cuba temporarily—in 1930, repulsed by the *cooperativismo* of 1928, Machado's personality cult, and the regime's heightened repression. In 1916, he entered the political fray with hope but without blinders. Writing around 1910, Ortiz noted: "Incoherence and disintegration in the ruling classes, ignorance among the ruled: this is our stigma."[1] He well understood—how could he not as the early republic unfolded—the terrible toll *caudillismo* took on Cuba's political society and defended as salutary the formation of multiple, idea-based parties. Ortiz simply wrote:

> We should get used to measure the merit and force of parties, not based on the men that integrate them but on the ideas that motivate them and the creeds they disseminate. A handful of altruist believers is worth more than a legion of skeptics who are only moved by expectations of bounty. We would not be scared if in Cuba the different parties, socialist, clerical, Semitic, military, federalist, labor, even racist and monarchical parties, even parties intending to resurrect Spanish loyalism and the incorporation to Spain, as long as these were based on ideals. The real danger does not lie in multiple parties who aspire for the truth, nor in those who even err; it lies in political personalism, which we inherited from Spain, because personalism in politics almost always leads to deceit.[2]

Ortiz also had a keen awareness—again, how could he not, given the circumstances of the republic's foundations—of the peculiar ascendancy the

United States had over Cuba. Writing about the U.S. intervention in Nicaragua in 1911, Don Fernando noted:

> The anemic creatures of a dying imperialism, we have remained stultified in a tropical lethargy, and will wake up from it maybe too late when a second imperialism absorbs us into its twister. Cuba and Nicaragua, victims of the same ailment, will steadily bleed. Only an intense and well-diffused civilization could rescue us: being cultured we would be strong. Let us be so.[3]

Open-eyed, Ortiz still believed political action by men like him could mitigate the ills gnawing at the republican entrails. He was elected to the House of Representatives in 1916, the year Alfredo Zayas should have become the duly elected president of Cuba. The Liberal Party won the November tally, but the Conservatives refused to turn over the executive's reins as Mario García Menocal declared himself the winner a month after ballots were cast. Liberals, however, gained entrance to Congress and the provincial and municipal governments. The election, in fact, had been fairly honest; fraud marred the presidential assumption of office. Unsurprisingly, the stolen election touched off a political crisis reminiscent of 1905–1906 when Tomás Estrada Palma's Moderates had prevented Liberal José Miguel Gómez from entering the Presidential Palace, preferring instead to turn Cuba over to the United States. The year 1917—the first of Don Fernando's political career—marked a critical turning point in the political development of the young republic. As argued later in this chapter, the winds of renovation that would sweep Cuban society in the 1920s were first felt as Menocal illicitly remained in command with the blessing of the Woodrow Wilson administration. Honest Liberals and Conservatives cringed at Menocal's brazenness and the recurrent Liberal knack to resort to armed insurrection. A bipartisan group of renowned personalities—Manuel Sanguily, Manuel Márquez Sterling, Enrique José Varona, Carlos Manuel de la Cruz, Cosme de la Torriente, Juan José de la Maza y Artola, Enrique Loynaz del Castillo—tried unsuccessfully to found a new political party. Though I have not found Ortiz's name associated with this effort, I am certain he was, or would have been, a part of the nascent movement for renewal.[4]

One of the consequences of the reelection crisis was the arrival in Havana of General Enoch Crowder in 1919; the general remained until 1922 and supervised the most flagrant U.S. intromission in Cuba's domestic affairs. Don Fernando's unflinching nationalism did not prevent him from working with Crowder on a new electoral code, the principal thrust of which was the reorganization of political parties to weaken the *caudillos'* stranglehold. While still a representative, Ortiz prescribed a list of political reforms to strengthen Cuba's institutional lattice; the Crowder electoral code built upon these prescriptions.[5] Don Fernando never considered the imperious side of U.S. diplomacy as the only face of the United States. He recommended:

Strengthening the national sentiment, without saintly quixotic illusions or anachronistic xenophobia. The best guarantee for Cuban independence is a cultured, just and honest government, based on popular aspirations and acting in cordial reciprocity with the United States.[6]

Ortiz did not run for reelection in 1922 and thus left the House of Representatives. He did not give up the hustings, though. In 1923, the Junta Cubana de Renovación Nacional issued a manifesto for Cubans ("Manifiesto a los cubanos"), the first of a salvo of protests that civil society launched against the political system during the first half of the decade. Don Fernando was the Junta's president and the author of the searing document. Interestingly, the manifesto reflected on the state of the nation from within: the nationalism it clamored was what civic conscience Cubans—as citizens and as leaders—should bring to the public arena for the greater good of *la patria*. The Junta unequivocally affirmed that national renovation began at home.

We Cubans want a republican life, new public ideas, new governmental practices, new legislative directions, new schools, new wealth, new codes, all in all a new civic spirit to revive, as a purifying fire, the energies of the Cuban people; to consolidate the republic and finish the task of the liberating revolution, providing Cuba with a truly free and democratic government, defended by a vigorous national civilization and a resilient political probity.[7]

Government and opposition left indelible marks on the 1920s. Social and political movements of various stripes raised the banner of reform and eventually the cry of revolution. The catalyst for what would become the revolution of 1933 was Gerardo Machado's effort to retain power against the constitution's grain and public opinion. *Caudillismo* reached new heights around Machado's persona as he was lavished with honors unrelated to his merits and disconnected from the brewing opposition—Doctor Honoris Causa, Egregio (Egregious), Salvador de la Patria (Savior of the Motherland), Hombre Cumbre (Pinnacle Man), Primer Obrero de Cuba (First Worker of Cuba).[8] By 1928, the two-party system imploded as Liberals and Conservatives joined hands in *cooperativismo* to support the president's bogus reelection; the pact split the parties and paved the way for the emergence of a new political class in the 1930s. By 1930, Ortiz was exasperated and left Cuba altogether. His parting essay clamored for Machado and Congress to resign, the establishment of a provisional government, and a truly Cuban solution to the national crisis. The latter was a reference to the *cooperativistas'* claim to their agreement as a Cuban solution (*solución cubana*). Ortiz retorted that a real solution could not be another situation of Cuban dubiousness (*cubaneo*).[9] Don Fernando, of course, remained a public intellectual of exceptional stature until his death and did not eschew political matters; he would, however, never again directly partake in the political arena.

In 1923, Ortiz addressed a prestigious gathering at the Academia de Historia and urged his audience to look beyond politics in the study of Cuban
history; said Don Fernando: "To reconstruct the history of Cuba based on the
precise knowledge of its ethnic, demographic, and cultural foundations, beyond its squalid political structure." Cuban culture, he argued, had been analyzed "under the light of the age-old bonfire" of the struggles that gave
Cuba its freedom. Other lights needed to be brought upon the past to fully
and justly encompass it.[10] He was probably right—at least for then. But,
presently, I am going to do precisely what Ortiz decried in 1923—will put
Don Fernando's political career in the context of republican politics between
1902 and 1928. Cuban historiography has been too centered on the economy, on social movements, and on the weight of the United States. We need
a political understanding of the island's past for the simple reason that it is
through political action that people make and remake their own history.

This study consists of three sections. The first outlines the contours of
what I am calling the civic movement of the early republic nurtured by two
strands of nineteenth-century *cubanidad*, the ideal of a civil republic that inspired important sectors of the separatist movement, and the preeminence of
a civic culture that the frustrated *autonomistas* promoted. The second dwells
on three critical moments in the so-called first republic, the 1905–1906 crisis
provoked by the fraudulent Estrada Palma reelection, the 1917 crisis around
Menocal's usurpation, and Machado's aborted *cooperativismo*. The third section concludes by raising issues, themes, and comparative perspectives on
Cuban politics in the early decades after independence.

A CIVIC MOVEMENT FOR A CIVILIAN REPUBLIC

Historians have rightfully underscored how Cuba's less than full independence in 1902 disappointed nineteenth-century separatist ideals. The Platt
Amendment unambiguously conditioned the island's sovereignty. Yet, the
republic of *caudillos* that vitiated the civil and civic aspirations of important
sectors of the separatist community was just as contravening of Cuba Libre.
If the Platt Amendment mediated national sovereignty, the post-1902 political class clearly transgressed the republican ambitions of *independentismo*.
Rescuing this civic tradition, which encompasses the persistent and ad-
mirable labor of the *autonomistas*, is essential for understanding the trajectory of the early republic.

On May 20, 1902, the Cuban republic was born under a constitution that
contained the singular amendment whereby the United States retained the
right of intervention. It was not self-evident exactly how that right would be
applied and under what conditions. Good government, many honorable
Cubans considered, would render the odious amendment moot and perhaps

lead to its repeal. Good government, moreover, was intrinsic to Cuba's anti-colonial struggles. In late April and early May 1902, as Estrada Palma trekked through Cuba in an exceptional caravan of popular rejoice, the Platt Amendment took second place to the extraordinary event that was about to happen: the inauguration of the republic on May 20. As he went from Oriente to Havana, the first president harped on the themes of "union and harmony" to safeguard national sovereignty and preempt the *caudillismo* rampant in Latin America; Cuba's would be a *república civilista*.[11] The early republic's civic movement—and Fernando Ortiz heartily partook in it—upheld good government as the best crucible for progress and the most effective antidote against U.S. intervention. Central to this movement was the proposition that relations with the United States could be constructed; Cubans could temper the always-difficult interactions between a great power and a small nation by dutiful self-government. Manuel Márquez Sterling put it pithily: "The civic spirit is, after all, the ultimate expression of a consolidated independence."[12] His 1917 article, "Against Foreign Interference, Domestic Virtue" ("A la ingerencia extraña, la virtud doméstica") encapsulated the movement's spirit.[13]

Good government, thus, was as valid a litmus test for the successful passage from colony to republic as full national sovereignty. Self-government would perforce depart from the standards established by the captain generals—despotic, personalist, arbitrary, corrupt, exclusionary, and repressive—if it were to fulfill the promise of Cuba Libre. Part and parcel of colonialism has always been the denigration of the capacities of the colonized for self-rule. Spain demeaned the Cuban racial *ajiacos* an insurmountable obstacle for civilization, and not a few *independentistas* shared these doubts. The calls to abolish slavery and extend full citizenship, indeed, put a brake on *independentismo* through the better part of the nineteenth century. One of the stellar achievements of the post-1878 anticolonial movement was precisely the forging of an inclusive and self-confident *cubanidad*, which identified racism with colonial backwardness.[14] That which was crafted among tobacco workers, the intelligentsia, the petty bourgeoisie, and some wealthy *criollos* on the island and in the diaspora in the 1880s and early 1890s, and, after 1895, on the battlefields was a sense that Cubans could, indeed, do it. The political success of the Partido Revolucionario Cubano (PRC, Cuban Revolutionary Party) and the military feats of the Ejército Libertador gave substance to Cuba Libre. The battle, however, was also about ideas and self-image.

There is no more exemplary text in that respect than *Cuba y sus jueces* by Raimundo Cabrera. First published in 1888 in response to an anti-Cuban tract written by the Spaniard Francisco Moreno, *Cuba y su gente*, Cabrera's book became the first Cuban best-seller, quickly going through seven editions. *Cuba y sus jueces* is a blow-by-blow account of Cuban achievements against the tide of Spanish backwardness and conveys an unflinching faith in the bounties a free Cuba would enjoy. Said Cabrera: "All that is bad in this much-slandered Cuban society is what it retains as a Spanish colony, and the little good that it has sprouts spontaneously from its American environment."[15] Many *mambises* carried *Cuba y sus jueces* in their saddlebags.

The Platt Amendment aside, the novice republic started out reasonably well. Estrada Palma ruled during generally auspicious times: Economic reconstruction proceeded apace; the national treasury soon registered a surplus; the first Cuban administration built upon—and even surpassed—the record of John Brooke and Leonard Wood, the two U.S. governors of Cuba between 1898 and 1902; about a quarter of the state budget was spent on public education; the health profile of Cubans continued to improve; and Don Tomás's road construction program tripled the kilometers paved during the U.S. occupation.[16] U.S. intromission in Cuban affairs was modest; Cuba, in fact, maneuvered the possibility of a trade agreement with Great Britain to obtain the reciprocity treaty with the United States that beet producers were opposing. In brief, Estrada Palma ruled the new republic acceptably for three years. In the fourth year, a storm gathered: the president's closest associates schemed, connived, and strong-armed Don Tomás's reelection. The crisis, which I discuss in the next section, overshadowed the administration's accomplishments, and together with subsequent U.S. intervention, did more harm to Cuba's fledgling sense of nationhood than the Platt Amendment. Cuban annexationists and resident Spaniards deemed the occupation irrefutable proof that Cubans were incapable of self-government. U.S. and world opinion confirmed preconceived notions of Cubans as ill-behaved children, but most importantly, the 1905–1906 crisis and the 1906–1909 occupation reinforced a colonial mentality in many Cubans. The foundation that Don Tomás laid in the first three years of his administration fissured when he refused to compromise with the Liberals. A terrible casualty was the nascent sense of pride and confidence in Cuba Libre, and a cloud of pessimism befell the republic.

The civic movement was elitist. Many of its advocates decried universal suffrage just as firmly as they or their precursors had denounced slavery as "two mistaken and completely opposed institutions."[17] Populism—part and parcel of universal suffrage—was inimical to good government: demagoguery was the *políticos'* easiest currency. Grandstanding supplanted leadership. Politicians proved themselves highly incompetent "for the patriotic objectives of the country's consolidation, but highly able to take advantage of the simplicity of their less educated countrymen."[18] Culture, education, and a consciousness-raising crusade were imperative to raise the quality of citizenship. So was white immigration—the civic movement fully partook of the racist assumptions commonplace in the early twentieth century. A public, secular education was the medium to forge the new citizen that Cuba Libre needed. *Cuba Contemporánea, Revista Bimestre*, and other publications deplored the neglect education had suffered after the Estrada Palma administration. Trelles, in fact, identified the republic's retrogression first and foremost in educational terms: between 1903 and 1922, the number of teachers increased from 3,500 to 6,000, while the number of soldiers from 3,000 to 13,000; budget expenditures on education declined from 25 percent to 15 percent; those on the military increased from 10 percent to 24 percent.[19] The problem was leadership, a political class that would replicate in the republic the task so ably undertaken by the separatist and *autonomista* elders in the nineteenth century.[20] A civic vanguard would lead a neophyte citizenry to exercise their rights prudently, encouraging the "singular abilities of our people towards the organized exercise of their rights and freedoms."[21] Carlos de Velasco noted: "How many things would be done better than they are done now if the people understood well their concerns and gave each man what he deserved!"[22] The *civilistas* argued that an honest enough political class ("somewhat more prudence in the handling of the national treasury") would make a difference in U.S.–Cuba relations and in ordinary Cubans' faith in the republic.[23]

In 1892, article 4 of the Cuban Revolutionary Party's program affirmed:

> The Partido Revolucionario Cubano does not intend to perpetuate, with new forms or alterations more apparent than essential, the authoritarian spirit and the bureaucratic composition of the colony. It rather seeks to establish on the basis of the frank and cordial exercise of man's legitimate capacities, a new country of genuine democracy, capable of conquering, through the order of real work and a balance of the social forces, the dangers of sudden freedom in a society originated from slavery.[24]

The civic movement fully embraced the PRC's modern, civilian élan. But the *civilistas* harked further back to the Camagüeyan leader Ignacio Agramonte's opposition to military supremacy during the Ten Years' War (1868–1878):

> The doctrine of the Camagüeyans, dangerous and harmful as it may have later been, even supposing that it had caused the failure of the Revolution of 1868, was the right one, as it taught Cubans to feel a holy terror for everything that resembled tyranny, despotism, and a true military dictatorship.[25]

Republican failings, then, harked of the colony, and the times called for strengthening the new habits to extirpate the old ones acquired over centuries when all Cubans were slaves. In spite of these failings, Cuba was patently better off *libre* than under Spain. Culture and education in a civic republic would allow growing numbers of Cubans to feel "independence as an inviolable faculty of the spirit."[26] For the *civilistas*, the crisis of 1905–1906 was excruciating: Estrada Palma had been a good president, but his intransigence and then his willingness to surrender the republic were unacceptable. Still, Don Tomás remained a guiding light of sorts, a mark that *cubanos libres* could, indeed, as Cabrera had so impassionedly argued in his best-seller, do it.

CRITICAL MOMENTS:
THE FIRST REPUBLIC'S ABORTED PACTS

The early republic never quite established an institutional and ideological common ground to center the political system. Elite conflicts were marred by the opposition's "fears of exclusion" and the government's "temptation to hegemony"; mechanisms of consensus were weak or short-lived.[27] A lack of trust within the elites was not unusual in Latin America in moments of transition or expansion of political participation. What is distinctive about Cuba is the inability of the political system to gain a foothold along a stable institutional path à la Mexico, Costa Rica, or Venezuela, or to consolidate a military core of either the "Sultanistic" variety, akin to Nicaragua and the Dominican Republic, or of the populist bent of Brazil and Argentina. Cuba's "contradictory developmental path" took other turns, and we need to fully grasp their political character.[28]

In this study, I mention three moments of potential elite pacts (an essential component of political stability) that failed to deliver. The "might have beens" of history are always enticing, but we cannot overextend their powers. Nonetheless, these three moments shed light onto Cuba's political dais from the ground up, rather than by appealing to the deus ex machina of U.S. imperialism or the determinism of sugar monoculture.

These three moments were Estrada Palma's reelection in 1905, the Liberal revolt in 1906, and the second U.S. occupation (1906–1909). Estrada Palma's aversion to *caudillismo* rendered tense executive-legislative relations during his administration. Veterans controlled the House of Representatives, and most were Liberals. Although nonpartisan, the president held the Liberals in low esteem. In the eyes of Don Tomás and his conservative allies, liberal demagoguery and universal male suffrage threatened the governability of the republic and pointed Cuba down the same road as the doomed Latin American republics. His supporters' ambitions and his own fears of the unruly mob (*la turba multa*) led Estrada Palma to condone all-out purges of Liberals from municipal governments and to mount the grossly fraudulent elections of 1905. Like the first in 1901, Cuba's second presidential contest was uncompetitive. When confronted with the fait accompli of an electoral sham, the Liberals withdrew and eventually took up arms against the government. In 1906, Estrada Palma preferred a U.S. intervention to a compromise that would have inevitably favored the Liberal cause.

A civilian republic was at the core of Martí's program for Cuba *Libre*. However, sovereignty and governability were often at odds. In 1902, the civic march exemplified *civismo* as the best platform to defend national sovereignty. At the same time, the liberators occupied a special place in Cuba Libre; their expectations and grievances steered important aspects of early republican politics. Yet, the liberators embodied *caudillismo* and militarism, reminiscent of the Latin American syndrome and, more important,[14] the immediate past of Spanish colonialism. When the War of 1895 ended, Cuba Libre civilians did not command the same respect as the *mambises*, and *civilismo* stood on shakier ground than caudillismo. Good government proved to be an elusive circle. Under the Platt Amendment, the temptation to resort to the United States as mediator of elite conflicts undermined sovereignty and diminished the incentives for elites to find a compromise among themselves. In turn, U.S. intervention diminished Cubans' sense of efficacy as a nation and as citizens.

Disbanded though it was, the Ejército Libertador retained considerable mobilizational capabilities. During the civic march, these were put in evidence as officers and soldiers greeted Estrada Palma, displaying armaments supposedly turned over to the U.S. Army when $3 million were disbursed for that purpose. In a matter of weeks in 1906, the Liberals gathered thousands of armed men against the Estrada Palma administration and threatened a takeover of Havana. The government's initial hesitation to use force undoubtedly facilitated the opposition's mobilization. Yet, once Estrada Palma drafted a militia force, many soldiers quickly abandoned its ranks and joined the rebels. The Liberals represented *independentismo* and commanded widespread popular support, thanks to their war record and as the victims in the recent electoral hoodwink. Public opinion was decidedly Liberal in the early republic. The rapid military mobilization reflected as well the character of the War of Independence, where some thirty-four thousand soldiers (a majority nonwhite) conducted a guerrilla war, which gathered sufficient support among rural Cubans for Spain to dislocate tens of thousands in the ferocious *reconcentración* (forced transfer of rural populations to urban settings) as a way of severing the *mambises'* lifeline. War had been a politically inclusionary and mobilizational experience amid a society that had undergone considerable socioeconomic transformation after 1878. Moreover, many ordinary Cubans were available for a call to arms; in a society lacking pervasive traditional ties and marked by the recent experience of guerrilla war, armed struggle constituted a reasonable strategy for political opponents to gain control of the national government. State coffers, after all, not only provided an exclusively Cuban source of capital accumulation but also, and more importantly, the only means for distributing favors and building the foundation of a political class. The absence of traditional social ties significantly marked the character of early republican politics.

When the Liberals rebelled in 1906, both sides expected the *guerrita* to be over soon via U.S. intervention. All were surprised at the reluctant imperialism of Teddy Roosevelt, about which the historical record is unequivocally clear: The United States did not want to intervene and in fact supported a compromise among Cubans. How could the intervention have been averted? During his term, Estrada Palma could have been an able politician, using state resources to consolidate the political class and the republic, but the "antipolitics" sentiments that would mount in Cuban society in the decades leading to 1959 had an early manifestation in Don Tomás. His fiscal conservatism and civilian sensibilities kept him from building up the army, so he was ill prepared to put down the rebellion. When he did not use full force to put down the Liberals, the revolt spread. Estrada Palma could have compromised with the Liberals. A compromise had, in fact, been negotiated between Menocal and Zayas whereby all officials elected in 1905 except for the president and vice president would resign, new elections would be scheduled, and the Liberals would lay down their arms. This is the most crucial moment in Cuba's early political development. Such a compromise would have been a pact between Cuban elites and set a precedent for turning over the government to the opposition, two essential ingredients of political stability and eventual democracy.

On both sides of the conflict, voices were heard regarding the importance of settling the conflict to avoid U.S. intervention. Initially willing to settle, Estrada Palma quickly and intransigently retracted. Roosevelt emissaries William H. Taft and Robert Bacon shared the conservatives' misgivings about the Liberals but were appalled by the incumbent's flagrant fraud. When Taft and Bacon recommended a compromise on the terms worked out by Menocal and Zayas, Estrada Palma resigned and left the United States no choice but to intervene. Perhaps Don Tomás considered that a second intervention would finally secure annexation and, subsequently, good government. Even under the Platt Amendment, though, successful negotiations among Cubans in 1906 might well have tracked the republic along a different path of political development. Don Tomás used to bemoan the fact that Cuba was a republic without citizens. Calixto Masó, a distinguished Cuban historian, turned Estrada Palma's woes upside down: What Cuba lacked in 1905–1906 was leadership.[29]

In contrast to the first, the second U.S. occupation was a civilian affair. Charles Magoon, much maligned by Cuban historiography, carried out a politically sensible program: Expanding state rolls to accommodate the Liberals was imperative if the United States was ever to leave Cuba. He certainly did not teach Cubans how to be corrupt, there was plenty of schooling in this regard in the colony during the first few years of independence in spite of Estrada Palma's austerity. Moreover, corruption was part and parcel of turn-of-the-century politics everywhere. The second occupation revived annexationism in certain quarters, including the Spanish community (*colonia española*), but the United States left in 1909 with a clear antiannexation message. From thence forward, the political paradigm would be the republic, perhaps the only salutary outcome of the definitely avoidable occupation of 1906–1909.[30]

The second moment was Menocal's counterfeit reelection in 1917. In 1913, the Conservative administration had been met with great expectations; the

Liberals' four years in power had lent credence to Conservative fears. José Miguel Gómez widely extended the maze of arrangements whereby incumbents did well for themselves. The Liberals unabashedly, if erratically and self-servingly, intoned a populist, nationalist rhetoric that did little to advance the cause of ordinary Cubans or of the nation. The ongoing feud between Gómez and Zayas—not a platform of principles—was the central mark of the Liberal Party. The Conservative Menocal was, in fact, elected because of this feud. Gómez mobilized the army in favor of Menocal on election day, preferring his fellow *mambí* veteran in the presidency over his Liberal nemesis who lacked military credentials. Menocal, however, did not live up to expectations: though initially curbing corruption, his administration continued the governance pattern established by the Liberals. By most accounts, *políticos* multiplied their schemes and deals; state budgets ballooned without commensurate public benefits.[31] Elections were scheduled for 1916, and the perennial issue of reelection reared into public debate in 1915. After some apparent hesitation, Menocal decided to seek a second term, and the stage was set for a repeat of 1905–1906. As in 1912, the Liberal candidate was Zayas.

If in 1905–1906 Conservatives under the aegis of Estrada Palma could adduce with some credibility that their continuation in office was the only guarantee of good government, a similar rationale had little basis in 1916 except that the Cornell-educated Menocal inspired confidence in Washington and in most quarters of Cuba's active classes (*clases vivas*). The reelection maneuver starkly underscored the salient weaknesses of Cuban politics: The political class had no internal arrangement for the alternation of power. State control not only provided the means for personal enrichment but also the sinecures to consolidate the political machinery. A combination of fraud and repression resulted in Menocal's reelection. The Liberals immediately appealed the outcome to the Central Electoral Board, which evaluated the evidence and ruled mostly in favor of the challengers. Conservatives appealed to the Supreme Court, which again dictated that the Liberals had made a strong case and called for new elections in Las Villas and Oriente. Free and fair contests would almost certainly have tilted the presidential outcome in favor of Zayas, and the Conservatives well understood their disadvantage. Imaginary electors (*electores imaginarios*) were a routine remedy to make up for the gap in popular support. In 1919, when electoral rolls were revised, the following were among the names appearing on rosters: Cristóbal Colón, Arsenio Martínez Campos, Antonio Cánovas del Castillo, Emilio Castelar, Valeriano Weyler, and Simón Bolívar.[32] Honest Conservatives like Enrique José Varona and Cosme de la Torriente raised stinging criticisms of Menocal's brazenness, previewing the fury of honest Liberals in 1928 who broke with Machado over *cooperativismo*. The 1916 electoral affront, in fact, fleetingly anticipated a reverse *cooperativismo*: a group of honest *políticos* from both parties announced their intention to create a new party committed to the "cleaning up of politics." The effort came to naught.[33]

Between November and February, there were various attempts to settle the conflict. Recalcitrant, Menocal implied nonetheless he might yield if the Liberals had someone other than Zayas to assume the presidency. Zayas, of course, had received the citizenry's sanction at the polls in November 1916. In the end, the United States supported Menocal, but Washington was much more evenhanded until February than is usually portrayed. What made the Wilson administration support Menocal was the February insurrection. Then the talk became one of defending "constitutional government" against violent rebels and protecting U.S. property. A contingent of five hundred marines landed in Oriente near U.S.-owned sugar mills and, in passing, helped disarm some Liberal rebels. Whatever the merits of opposing armed rebellion, the fact is Washington supported a Cuban administration that had transgressed electoral procedures. U.S. support of Menocal also undermined the verdict handed down by Cuban institutions to settle the conflict in the Liberals' favor.

The year 1917 did not become 1906 for several reasons. Menocal stated clearly that he would not tolerate an insurrection and then delivered. In 1917, Cuba had a president who did not hesitate to exercise the powers of his office. The army proved to be loyal to the Conservative administration, even though most officers and soldiers were probably Liberals. Moreover, Menocal succeeded in recruiting more soldiers and mobilizing a citizen militia. Though public opinion leaned toward the Liberals, ordinary Cubans basically sat out the conflict in the relative comfort of economic prosperity. Miguelista (pro–José Miguel Gómez) Liberals precipitated the revolt instead of allowing the new elections to take place as planned, in part because Gómez thought that the rebels would quickly succeed and his hand would then be strengthened in relation to Zayas. Gómez counted on the desertion of the army, the quick spread of the insurrection, and a U.S. intervention, which would ultimately favor the Liberals as had happened in 1906–1909. But the army did not desert Menocal, and the rebels established themselves in Camagüey and Oriente but only modestly elsewhere. As the government restrained the rebellion, the urgency of a U.S. intervention eased.

What followed the 1917 crisis was the most flagrant period of U.S. intervention in Cuban affairs. In Márquez Sterling's cutting phrases a "plural regime" resulted from "the usurper oligarchy,"[34] Martínez Ortiz noted the following regarding Cuba's relations with the United States:

> The only danger for Cuba is its proximity to a great power without counterweight in the continent; fortunately, however, its interests are not antagonistic but rather complementary to those of Cuba and, additionally, its model of government is trustworthy. Cuba's personality will never succumb to violence. This great power's own interests lead it towards peace in the island and never to use Cuba as a pretext for creating a colonial state. Only a chronic state of non-government, a period of social disintegration, could determine an indefinite direct action.[35]

Leading lights of the civic movement, like Márquez Sterling and Fernando Ortiz, came to the rescue of the *patria* during the Zayas–Crowder administration. The first, deploring the Crowder mission and Zayas's corruption, nonetheless, cooperated with Zayas in the administration's efforts to extricate Cuba from the Crowder grip. The second, deploring Zayas and deeming the "moralization" program proposed by Crowder laudable, collaborated with the U.S. emissary. What Crowder set out to do, after all, was nothing new to the civic movement: his program had been advocated by Cubans in its entirety well before the U.S.S. *Minnesota* entered Havana harbor. Reform from above, however, was short-lived.

By the time Gerardo Machado was elected in 1924, Washington was moving away from the "big stick" and "dollar diplomacy." Though not yet ready to enunciate a Good Neighbor Policy, Republican administrations during the 1920s increasingly grasped the diminishing returns of constant interventions. Machado's election was well received in Washington, among Cuba's *clases vivas*, and in public opinion. Conservative loser, Menocal, congratulated Machado after the election—a first in the republic. Initially, Machado awakened new hopes, though social movements of various sorts had already despaired of reforming the republic within the established bounds. Whether or not Machado had two faces—a good one the first few years, and a dictatorial one after 1928—the fact that *cooperativismo* remained in office at the expense of partisan loyalties and popular support fatally wounded the political class. *Cooperativismo*, nonetheless, could have been a consensus solution, a viable pact. In Mexico, the revolutionaries were just beginning to lay the foundation of the PRI (Institutional Revolutionary Party), which turned out to be a spectacular political success. This third critical moment in the republic demands reinterpretation in view of early republican politics and comparative perspectives. The would-be PRI mobilized society, *cooperativismo*, entailed a countermobilization of citizens and elites.

ISSUES, THEMES, AND COMPARATIVE PERSPECTIVES

Being part of a larger work-in-progress, this chapter does not have a conclusion. It is a small piece of a larger puzzle that does not yet have a clear profile. It is easier to start with what I do not want to do, which I hope is implicit in these pages. A unifying framework around U.S. domination, sugar monoculture, and national sovereignty has largely constricted Cuban historiography. I do not seek an alternate unifying logic to Cuba's contradictory developmental path, and I believe politics provides an open-ended, contingency-sensitive reading. A politics-centered analysis is crucial in order to give internal factors their rightful place.

Cuba's longer colonial term under Spain and subsequent peculiar relationship with the United States have favored the analytical preeminence of external factors. Status issues—sovereignty, autonomy, and annexation—dominate much of the historiography on the nineteenth century. Historians of the republic up to 1959, writing before or after the revolution, accord with an overarching centrality to the degrees of sovereignty Cuba experienced. The presence of the United States via military occupation, civil interventions, or capital investments, has commanded the able attention of historians and social scientists.

Cuba's socioeconomic profile has similarly been accurately drawn, even if conclusions about the character of the island's developmental path and the origins of the revolution vary widely. Emphasizing U.S. preponderance and/or socioeconomic factors has usually meant that the role of Cubans themselves in shaping their own history has not been sufficiently considered. I am by no means suggesting that politics alone suffices. Without it or without giving it due attention, however, we may well have a grand view of the forest, without any inkling of the ways and moments the various trees came together. Politics—pace Don Fernando's entreaty in 1923—may well offer a much-needed corrective in the field of Cuban history.

Regarding early republican politics, I offer the following observations, which I hope to ultimately weave into an interpretive framework. Nineteenth-century status issues—independence, autonomism, annexation—marked the character and culture of Cuban politics and set the context for republican politics. Cuba developed "modern politics" under colonialism: nascent political parties, civilian-military conflicts, reform versus armed rebellion, and extension of citizenship rights. From the outset, Cubans quickly learned that domestic purposes required international actions: They lobbied in Madrid (for autonomy) and in Washington and New York (for annexation and independence).

Cuba's independence struggles were, in essence, a precursor of twentieth-century national liberation movements. The War of 1895 especially mobilized a cross-class, multiracial, island/diaspora coalition, which raised an army thirty-four thousand strong and conducted an extraordinary public relations campaign in the United States and elsewhere. The war was an inclusionary, participatory experience that set similar expectations for the republic. Wars, however, are devastating: more than thirty thousand Cubans died in the Ten Years' War, and some three hundred thousand people fell victims of battle, disease, and dislocation in the War of 1895. In proportion to population, the latter figure was higher than U.S. losses during the Civil War.

Modern politics, modern warfare, a slave-based capitalist transformation, an international moment of rapid trade and investment expansion, and the U.S. coming of imperial age all combined to set a context for the founding of the republic markedly different from those established in the rest of Latin America seventy-five years earlier. Latin American nineteenth-century conservatives in Cuba have no real counterpart. The island had no oligarchy to speak of, no sedentary peasantry, and cities—not only Havana and not only in Cuba—played too central a part in national formation. Cuban liberals, at the same time, were not exactly like their Latin American correlates, as continental liberalism did not start out from a platform of universal male suffrage. The pivotal threads were the formation/transformation/breakdown of Cuba's political class; the institutional and cultural character of political society; and patterns of inclusion, a populist, patrimonial political system amid a highly mobilized society.

Pre- and post-1959 historiographies have more in common than meets the eye: Teleology weighs both down. Before 1959, historians formed what I am calling a "waiting for the nation" school, a Caribbean version of a Jeffersonian economy, civic democracy, and populist political culture. After 1959, the continuities between nineteenth-century struggles for independence and social justice and the revolution of 1959 are tightly drawn. Teleologies are fantasies. No society bears a hidden destiny of any kind; teleologies, moreover, explain nothing. Cuban historiography is trapped in a spider web. Two possible ways out are empirical research and alternative paradigms, the latter intended, not to generate a new teleology, but to allow an open-ended, contingency-sensitive look at the pieces. Understanding Cuba in bits and pieces (*en y a pedazos*) is a much more stimulating intellectual challenge than the Cuba on history's tracks that has received so much attention.

NOTES

1. Fernando Ortiz, "La irresponsabilidad del pueblo cubano," in *Entre cubanos: Psicología tropical* (Havana: Editorial de Ciencias Sociales, 1987), 28.

2. Fernando Ortiz, "Más partidos políticos," in Ortiz, *Entre cubanos*, 100–1.

3. Fernando Ortiz, "Nicaragua intervenida," in Ortiz, *Entre cubanos*, 77–78.

4. Calixto C. Masó, *Historia de Cuba* (Miami: Ediciones Universal, 1998), 500.

5. Fernando Ortiz, "La crisis política cubana sus causas y sus remedios," in Julio Le Riverend, ed., *Orbita de Fernando Ortiz* (Havana: UNEAC, 1973), 99–119.

6. Ortiz, *Orbita*, 112.

7. "Manifiesto a los cubanos," in Hortensia Pichardo, ed., *Documentos para la historia de Cuba* (Havana: Editorial de Ciencias Sociales, 1973), vol. 3: 149.

8. Masó, *Historia de Cuba*, 520.

9. Fernando Ortiz, "Bases para una efectiva solución cubana," in Ortiz, *Orbita*, 135–42.

10. Fernando Ortiz, "Las nuevas orientaciones históricas e inmigratorias de Cuba," in Rubén Martínez Villena, ed., *En la tribuna (discursos cubanos)* (Havana: Imprenta El Siglo XX, 1923), 208, 212.

11. Marifeli Pérez-Stable, "Estrada Palma's Civic March: From Oriente to Havana, April 20–May 11, 1902," *Cuban Studies/Estudios Cubanos*, vol. 29.

12. Manuel Márquez Sterling, *Doctrina de la República* (Havana: Secretaría de Educación, 1937), 27.

13. Carlos Márquez Sterling, *A la ingerencia extraña, la virtud doméstica: Biografía de Manuel Márquez Sterling* (Miami: Ediciones Universal, 1986), 204–6.

14. Ada Ferrer, *Insurgent Cuba: Race, Nation, and Revolution, 1868–1898* (Chapel Hill: University of North Carolina Press, 1999).

15. Raimundo Cabrera, *Cuba y sus juices: Rectificaciones necesarias* (Havana: Librería Cervantes, 1922), 22.

16. Carlos M. Trelles, *El Progreso (1902 a 1905) y el Retroceso (1906–1922) de la República de Cuba* (Matanzas: Imprenta de Tomás González, 1923), 6.

17. José Sixto Solá, "El pesimismo cubano," *Cuba Contemporánea*, December 1913: 281.

18. Carlos de Velasco, "El problema negro," *Cuba Contemporánea*, February 1913: 77.

19. Trelles, *Progreso*, 12.

20. Fernando Ortiz, "Seamos hoy como fueron ayer," in Rubén Martínez Villena, ed., *En la tribuna: Discursos cubanos* (Havana: Imprenta El Siglo XX, 1923 [1914]), 37–56.

21. Mario Guiral Moreno, "El saneamiento de las costumbtres públicas y la educación cívica del pueblo," *Cuba Contemporánea*, February 1917: 109.

22. Carlos de Velasco, "La obra de la revolución cubana," *Cuba Contemporánea*, July 1914: 281.

23. Miguel de Carrión, "El desenvolvimiento social de Cuba en los últimos veinte años," *Cuba Contemporánea*, September 1921: 25.

24. Pichardo, ed., *Documentos*, vol. 1: 481.

25. Julio Villoldo, "La República civil," *Cuba Contemporánea*, March 1918: 193.

26. Márquez Sterling, *Doctrina de la República*, 93.

27. Alexander W. Wilde, "Conversations among Gentlemen: Oligarchical Democracy in Colombia," in Juan J. Linz and Alfred Stepan, eds., *The Breakdown of Democratic Regimes: Latin America* (Baltimore: Johns Hopkins University Press, 1978), 46.

28. Tim McDaniel, "Response to Goodwin," *Theory and Society* 23 (1994): 791.

29. Masó, *Historia de Cuba*, 470.

30. For an excellent history of the early republic, see Rafael Martínez Ortiz, *Cuba: Los primeros años de independencia*, 2 vols. (Paris: Editorial Le Livre Libre, 1929); for the Taft–Bacon report on their mission, see William H. Taft, *Cuban Pacification. Report of William H. Taft, Secretary of War, and Robert Bacon, Assistant Secretary of State, of What Was Done under the Instructions of the President in Restoring Peace to Cuba* (Washington, D.C., December 11, 1906); for the early republic, see also Charles A. Chapman, *A History of the Cuban Republic* (New York: Octagon Books, 1969), and José M. Hernández, *Cuba and the United States: Intervention and Militarism, 1868–1933* (Austin: University of Texas Press, 1933).

31. Trelles, *Progreso*, 18, cites Menocal's budget expenditures over eight years as 600 million pesos; Gómez spent 140 million pesos over four.

32. Manuel Márquez Sterling, *Las conferencias del Shoreham* (Mexico: Ediciones Botas, 1933), 30–31.

33. Masó, *Historia*, 500.

34. Márquez Sterling, *Conferencias*, 38–48.

35. Martínez Ortiz, *Cuba*, vol. 1: 342–43.

7

The Political Ideas of Fernando Ortiz (1906–1933)

Carmen Almodóvar

Fernando Ortiz belonged to the generation born between 1880 and 1895, the so-called first republican generation. This generation represented the new revolutionary conscience. Although Ortiz, who had been called the "third discoverer of Cuba," did not get involved in the "necessary war," he did identify with José Martí's ideals and patriotism. A man of Ortiz's intellectual stature could not be unconcerned with his surroundings, and he did not ignore the social and economic crises that affected his country, or its internal political fluctuations, or the links that tied the republic to the will of Washington.

Ortiz was part of the sizable group of renowned Cuban intellectuals of his generation who were influenced by positivist notions at the dawn of the twentieth century, and who earnestly believed that it was possible to eliminate the vices and evils inherited from colonialism through liberal reformism. They also felt capable of tackling the problems arising from the creation of the republic.

In this brief synthesis, I do not intend to review the entirety of Ortiz's work through the period 1906–1933 to trace the footsteps of his political ideals. I will only refer to the titles that concretely underline his views on this topic. In this sense, *Entre cubanos: Psicología tropical* (1913) is a mandatory text for analysis. This is one of the first and most consulted of his works. Although irrelevant from a social-scientific perspective, given the context in which it was written, I believe that it is a good starting point for understanding the political ideals of the learned Ortiz. This text was published in 1913, the same year the essay *Contra el yankee*, written by Julio César Granadilla, appeared in the island's bookshops. This latter work made an isolated claim for the economic independence of the country as an essential measure for overcoming the deterioration of the emerging republic.

The essays compiled in *Entre cubanos* were written mainly between 1906 and 1908 and previously published in newspapers and magazines of the time. This text provided readers with a description of the nature, personality, and attitude of those born on the island. Cubans were witnessing their history as it unrolled in those critical years of republican trial and error. Within the pages of this text on the "tropical psychology" of Cubans, Ortiz emphasized the need for education and culture as essential weapons in Cuba's evolution. He called for solidarity, criticizing the media for being immersed in "personal selfishness," and exhorting Cubans to continue "being themselves" in the process of renewing themselves. He decisively criticized Cuban jesting or *choteo*, classifying it as the "great Creole tragedy" and a double-sided weapon. He called for Cubans to wake up, work, and abandon the apathy he believed affected the citizenship.

Ortiz's criticism in *Entre cubanos* was wholly constructive; his objectives were not in any way related to historian Francisco Figuera's "dissection" of the Cuban personality in his polemical book *Cuba y su evolución colonial*. Ortiz did not ignore the historical past, or consideration of the future possibilities, following the U.S. intervention in Cuba. In *Entre cubanos* he dealt with these issues. This text may be considered to be Ortiz's plunge into the political scene at the time when he also acknowledged that social mobility was subjected to "unavoidable and inevitable historical laws."

In 1914, during the 121st anniversary of the Sociedad Económica de Amigos del País, Ortiz looked back to the golden age of that institution. Taking it as an example of cultural performance, he claimed that "the work of a dedicated, well-meaning group of men can turn an exhausted factory into a country and a nationality." Ortiz wanted to encourage his contemporaries to renew the achievements of the past and to convince them to strive for the same. Among other issues, he emphasized that faith in culture had weakened, that there was a lack of a robust social brain, and that the Cuban political parties lacked intellectual creativity in their programs. Ortiz stated that faith alone did not suffice if the country were to be saved but that passionate work and dedication were required, as Cuba's salvation depended on Cubans themselves.

In 1915, Ortiz began to actively participate in politics. Two years later, he was elected to the House of Representatives. The author of *Los factores humanos de la cubanidad* (1940) had a long way to go to link what he had written before 1917 with his publications in *Heraldo de Cuba* in 1919 and his national reform program, *La crisis política cubana, sus causas y remedios* (1919). This road involved Cuba's role in World War I, among other issues. Ortiz delivered a speech on the subject in the House of Representatives on April 17, 1917, and another one on obligatory military service on June 18, 1918. The second of these speeches emphasized the urgent need to consolidate independence in the country, as Cuba was small and young. Time after time he criticized Cuban diplomacy and protested against the statements made by Albert Bushmell Hart, a professor of international law at Harvard University. Hart had stated that the United States had rights over the island, as it was within the borders of its "empire." Ortiz later looked back to those days of "counterpoints" in the Cuban Congress to confirm that the U.S. government and U.S. public opinion did not share the "Prussian" views of the Harvard professor.

In *La crisis política cubana*, Ortiz initially analyzed the causes that had led the country to the critical stage in which it found itself. He classified these causes according to their origin: political, historical, and sociological. He then suggested possible cures for overcoming those vices affecting political life in the republic. The usurpation of the presidency by Mario García Menocal and his successful fight against the 1917 liberal insurrection, thanks to U.S. support, were issues that Ortiz believed could not be ignored when evaluating the causes of the political downfall of Cuba in the late 1920s.

As far as international causes were concerned, he did not ignore the continual U.S. intervention in Cuban internal administrative issues through its so called "notes," with the blatant intention of controlling Cuban national wealth. Ortiz criticized "secret" diplomacy, U.S. hegemony, and the political chaos, arguing that the Cuban republic had practically fallen in the hands of a U.S. "proconsul." Ortiz suggested, as an international cure, that a relationship of mutual respect should be established between the governments of Cuba and the United States. He noted that the attitude displayed by Washington, in relation to the liberal uprising and the outbreak of civil war in February 1917, had left its mark.

La crisis política cubana also reveals the author's great concerns over labor legislation operating on the island at the time. Ortiz pronounced himself in favor of the eight-hour work day and the improvement of women's working conditions and pregnancy protection. Some of these views, published in *Heraldo de Cuba*, had been published previously in the pamphlet *Las actuales responsabilidades políticas y la nota americana* (1918). In this short text, he considered Menocal's statements on electoral guarantees, approved by the U.S. minister in Cuba, "dangerous for Cuba's future."

At the end of World War I, Ortiz delivered an unforgettable speech in the House of Representatives: *Cuba en la Paz de Versalles* (1920). His eloquent words revealed an acute Creole wit. Certain paragraphs contained severe criticisms of Cuban representation at the Versalles conferences: "Cuba was never heard because it never spoke, it obtained nothing because it asked for nothing, and it did not triumph because there was nothing to defeat." He criticized the Versalles Treaty because the "equality of nations" had been violated, different categories were established among nations, and those that were excommunicated were not admitted to the League of Nations. He cited clear examples: Russia, Mexico, and Santo Domingo. He referred to article

10 of the League of Nations' constitution, the backbone of this international organization, which stated "all states are obliged to guarantee territorial and political independence against foreign aggression." He then warned the members of Cuba's Congress that this article would only "have the value which the United States can bestow to it."

He also commented on the regimen of labor, the last topic discussed in Paris. He mentioned Cuba's backwardness regarding labor legislation, in which "the laborer continues to be merchandise, even if the treaty proclaims that he can no longer be treated as such." Finally, Ortiz encouraged Cubans to forget past hatreds and senseless ambitions in order to gain respect for their national sovereignty.

Ortiz did not ignore national, global, and regional changes, specifically in the postwar period, the United States' intervention in the Caribbean, the Russian Revolution, the emergence of the first trade unions, and the Cuban economic crisis. In this decisive stage, Ortiz developed more profound critiques, integrating the liberal "left" component of his party with the determination to implement his ideas on "national renovation."

A number of his prominent speeches and lectures between 1912 and 1923 were compiled in two volumes, published in 1923 under the title *En la tribuna: discursos cubanos*. The prologue of this compilation was written by the poet Rubén Martínez Villena, who had led the "Protest of 13" ("protesta de los 13") at the Cuban Science Academy in 1923. The young revolutionary clearly summarized Ortiz's role in the times of crisis and renovation Cuba was undergoing. Martínez Villena emphasized that Ortiz had worked for his *patria* in times of peace; he was an example of culture and honesty to youth willing to save their motherland. Ortiz proceeded to head the civil association *Junta de Renovación Cívica* in 1923. In general, its manifesto denounced the corruption that existed in all levels of the republican government.

In 1923, the relentless Ortiz became president of the Sociedad Económica de Amigos del País, a post he retained until 1932. It was there that he organized a program of lectures with the intention of opening an academic debate on the polemical topic of Cuban decadence. His book on Cuban decadence, *La decadencia cubana* (1924), was based on an unforgettable lecture he had given on the subject. Ortiz warned the audience that he had radicalized his views. He had dug into the factors that had contributed to the weakening and "evident intellectual, moral, and economic decadence of Cuban society." He did not limit himself to touching just the surface; Ortiz searched for the roots of the difficulties faced by the nation. He noted that 53 percent of Cubans were illiterate; 68 percent of children did not go to school; there was not a single rural school in Cuba, an agricultural nation; over 20 percent of the candidates running for political parties in the previous elections had criminal records; and "according to public judicial sentences the police corps were full of criminals." He thus concluded, "Cuba is falling into the abyss of barbarity."

When discussing economic problems, Ortiz emphasized the influence of foreign investment in the island, pointing out that two thirds of the sugar industry was in U.S. hands. Sugar lands "were not to be burnt down by their owners, as in the Ten Years' War, because active capital in Cuba was not a social force integrally connected to others." He continued, "almost 17 percent of the national territory belonged to North Americans. . . . The mines, railways, telephones, and especially banks are all foreign."

The battle Ortiz fought to stop Cuba from drowning in a deep "decadence" was not one that he waged alone. The Minorist group, and especially the *Revista de Avance*, were also struggling against this decadence. The Minorists denounced false values, called for the total renovation of the arts at all levels, spoke out about political problems, and made their gatherings, or *tertulias,* the ideal scenarios for debating political and cultural issues. During this period Ortiz worked with left-wing scholars, and, as did other cultural figures in Cuba, he adopted "more defined" views of the future, as historian Julio Le Riverend notes in the prologue to the 1978 edition of *Contrapunteo cubano.*

Starting in 1925, the nation faced a turbulent decade. Gerardo Machado became the president of the republic in May 1925 and immediately forgot about the reform program he had promised the nation. The "regenaration" program became an open attack on all those who failed to obey the ruler's wishes and decisions. The opposition reacted immediately. From the beginning of 1926, the spokesmen for the Machado regime maneuvered politics to ensure that Machado stayed in power. Machado himself insisted time and time again that he had no intention of running for reelection; yet he astutely cleared a path to staying in power, arguing that he "would only remain in power if the people wanted him to do so." Amid this atmosphere of political tension Ortiz traveled to Washington, D.C., to attend the Third Pan American Conference. Toward the end of 1926, Ortiz promoted the foundation of the Institución Hispano-Cubana de Cultura, which became an important part of Cuban cultural life. Even when concentrating on the struggle against racism and xenophobia, Ortiz did not forget Machado's abuses. Condemned to an "imposed" regime, Ortiz resorted to a self-imposed exile in 1930.

He made an anthological speech in the Town Hall of New York on November 8, 1931: published under the titles *American Responsabilities for Cuba's Troubles* (1931) and *Las responsabilidades de los Estados Unidos en los males de Cuba* (1932). Here Ortiz stated that all public liberties in Cuba had been suppressed and, except for a small group of people, Cubans were crying out, "Down with Machado!" The key part of his speech, however, was his denouncing of the U.S. government as responsible for the island's problems: "There is no excuse for this because it can be confirmed not only by facts but also by the very text of a public law governing Cuba and its links to the United

States, by a treaty." He continued by noting, "The Platt Amendment has since 1917 ensured that successive usurping governments stay in power against the public will of Cubans." The radical nature of his arguments was evident both in terms of internal matters and the country's foreign policy. Perhaps his political activities, developed mainly while he was a theorist among the left wing of the party denominated "the old shoe" (*la chancleta*), had influenced his intellectual views. While in the United States, he wrote several articles describing the grave situation in Cuba. His speech in Washington on December 10, 1932, *Lo que Cuba desea de los Estados Unidos* (1932) (What Cuba Wants from the United States) deserves special attention. In this speech, he delved into the roots of the Cuban problem, starting with the political and economic dependence of the is-land on the United States. He denied that Cubans wanted a proconsular or military intervention; he advocated for the elimination of U.S. influence in Cuba, stating that it was harmful because Cuba "is definitely being influenced by the controlling mechanisms of the enormous political and economic forces of the North American people, directly or through diplomacy." He then summarized his position by saying that the Platt Amendment should be abrogated immediately. In issues relating to the economy, Ortiz requested that the reciprocity treaty should be revised, to establish a truly reciprocal tariff policy.

In 1933, at the end of the Machado dictatorship, Ortiz returned to Cuba to resume his unfinished work. At the First National History Congress, he was acclaimed for "his valuable historical works and his moral and civic nature; one should add, also for his faultless humanism." During World War II and until his death in 1969, Ortiz proved that Rubén Martínez Villena was not mistaken when he wrote:

> Tomorrow, when the good conquer
> ("the good always win in the end");
> when the misty horizon clears
> and the dust of false idols disappears,
> when men using intellectual or
> patriotic masks, who are nothing but
> iodine and sawdust, are forgotten,
> the memory of Fernando Ortiz will remain,
> bearing his talent and commitment.
> And his image will remain standing among the rubble,
> and will be selected by the young as one of the
> pillars on which the New Republic will stand.

8

Economic Historian and Editor of Cuban Classics

José Matos Arévalos

In the Cuban intellectual tradition, history has been the object of important research and appraisal. The works of José Martín Félix de Arrate, Antonio José Valdés, and Ignacio Urrutia are well known; they have been dubbed the "three first historians of Cuba." Other examples are the monumental *Historia de la esclavitud* by José Antonio Saco, *Apuntes para la historia de las letras* by Antonio Bachiller y Morales, and the invaluable *Historia de la isla de Cuba* by Pedro José Guiteras. These historians, in their effort to establish the origins and development of the Cuban nation, were influenced by the ideals and methods of their respective times.

With the emergence of the Cuban republic, scholars reflected on the social events that molded the country during the nineteenth century, including historical monographs on the war of independence or the history of the provinces and townships, and biographical essays on the great Cuban leaders and thinkers. Even though the diversity of historical topics was considerable, the traditional, descriptive historical perspective always reigned. There was an exaltation of individual heroism without the intention of establishing the logic of historical events.

In the 1920s, however, the study of Cuban history underwent a renovative process that began with the works of Emilio Roig de Leuchsenring, Ramiro Guerra, and Fernando Ortiz. Roig, from an anti-imperialist perspective, studied the relationship between Cuba and the United States. Guerra, in his famous manual *Historia de Cuba* (1921) and in his essay *Azúcar y población en las Antillas*, approached national history—until then thought of as a series of facts in chronological order—from the basis of political and economic analysis. Finally Ortiz, critical of the notions of traditional history and an advocate of new methodological perspectives, evaluated and interrelated economic and political phenomena.

This level of self-consciousness among Cuban scholars coincided with a similar transformation of historical studies under way in Europe. In Cuba, this new way of thinking about history was characterized by an interest in historical reference, the reconstruction of national history, and the exaltation of the values of the country's revolutionary and nationalist tradition.

AN UNPUBLISHED PROJECT
OF CUBAN ECONOMIC HISTORY

It is within this context that Fernando Ortiz initiated the writing of an interesting and revealing project on Cuba's economic history. The unpublished manuscript exists today in the archives of the library of the Sociedad Económica and Instituto de Literatura y Lingüística in Havana. It constitutes proof of the evolution in Ortiz's thinking toward a conception of history that overcame the limitations posed by his earlier positivist perspective.

Ortiz titled the project "The First Historical Revolution in Cuba (Introduction to Cuban economic Development)" ("La primera revolución histórica de Cuba [Introducción a un estudio de la evolución económica de Cuba])." In its unfinished condition, it offers insight into Ortiz's approach to organizing his material. He would first classify the quotations, economic data, newspaper cuttings, photographs, and other research notes. Only later did he begin drafting preliminary ideas, and afterward he would add new information and make new considerations. This is how Ortiz carried out his book-writing career in this period, working on two or more books at a time.

Ortiz's unfinished manuscript does not form a volume. It consists of mainly notes, which show a logical plan for a text on Cuba's economic development. Despite this, it contains opinions that show the prevalence of new historical conceptions. The title itself introduces a perspective that deviates from traditional Cuban studies. Also, among the papers that form this unpublished project are a number of notes taken from Karl Kautsky's *Los fundamentos del cristianismo* (New York, 1925), confirming Ortiz's theoretical inclination toward Marxist philosophy to explain the role of economic production, public property, and the social classes of the slave system in Roman society during the empire.

Ortiz understood the need to evaluate the social and economic phenomena, without neglecting the subjective dimension of historical processes or the internal nature of social contradictions. Based on this new perspective, and aiming to understand the conformation of Cuban culture, Ortiz abandoned traditional historical conceptions and criticized the existing historiography in these terms:

The history of Cuba, like that of many other countries, has also been thought as being forged through the centuries by its main characters, and supernatural mystery as in biblical stories, the work of heroes as in chivalric literature, or personal sacrifices as in romantic and sentimental novels.[1]

In addition:

The history of Cuba has been reduced to that of its political domination, to its superior structure: this would be equivalent to reducing the geography of Cuba to its valleys and mountains. Today the historiographical science places deeper and more positive demands; it requires the consideration of the true or decisive causes in historical phenomena and the links between them. It therefore demands a detailed analysis of the economic bases of Cuban society in order to explain its civil formation.[2]

In reference to external phenomena in relation to internal contradictions in Cuban society, Ortiz later wrote:

It is preferable to examine the foreign contradictions of the Spanish rule in Cuba not through the simple chain of external events, but from the inside, from Cuba's entrails, and look outwards, in the same way as a person looks out from a ship to study the course of its voyage: the sudden changes in direction, the maneuvers of its crew, the landmarks it passes, the speed of the current under it, the winds that push it along, the shallows that threaten it, and the anchorages that offer fair weather and human comfort.[3]

The reconstruction of national history, based on economic and social assumptions, was a methodological necessity for understanding the role of economic structures of different cultures in the formation process of the Creole economy during the initial years of Spanish colonization. To gain this knowledge, Ortiz studied the economy of the "Indian society": family, agriculture, transport, historical level of culture, the use of metals, domestic animals, housing, trade, labor, and social classes. In the same way, he studied "Castillan society" in order to establish the origins of the formation and development of the capitalist economy in Cuba. The different models of society that he depicted demonstrated the contradictory origins of this mixed economy, "as it was not possible to reproduce Castillan society neither was national or municipal mercantilism possible . . . nor was feudalism possible."[4] The formation of the economy in the island was rife with numerous cultural and economic conflicts, and capitalism arose from the violent clash of civilizations. Ortiz called this process Cuba's first historical revolution:

In the Hispano-Cuban clash of the sixteenth century, economic progress from the Taino-Siboney economy to the Castillan economy was so sudden, and the adaptation process so hastened, that it was only possible through great conflicts; the mass being subjugated was not able to adapt and perished.[5]

This idea, on which Ortiz comments but does not elaborate, is dealt with in "Presentación y glosa de Fray Bartolomé," a prologue to the book *Bartolomé de las Casas: pensador político, historiador, antropólogo* by Lewis Hanke (Havana, 1949). Ortiz's introduction shows both a historical value and the continuity of his thoughts on this matter:

> The distance between the two horizons was enormous, in the magnitude of millenniums, in the evolution of culture. The clash was unbearable for the Americans. It was not only due to the strife of wooden weapons against iron arms, arrows against guns, indigenous hoes [coa] against iron tools, and canoes against caravels, nor due to the overpowering wheel, sails, and horses and other Old World beasts of burden; nor was it due to the crossing of infectious diseases reciprocally ignored and causing great mortality among both contending groups. The overwhelming and decisive factor was the impossibility of urgently adapting the simple social and economic order of the Indians, deprived of greed, coins, capital, and salaries, to that of the Europeans moved by the eagerness of the already triumphant mercantile capitalism. In that sudden contact of conflicting cultures, both conquerors and conquered failed, unable to combine their social mechanisms, and the awesome 'destruction of the Indies' occurred.[6]

Returning to Ortiz's unpublished manuscripts, one can see that he was laying the general guidelines for understanding the first historical revolution in Cuba. He accomplished this by examining the process of appropriation and division of the land, a problem Ortiz tracked from the conquest up to the second decade of the twentieth century. Ortiz developed these ideas at the time of Machado's government; through them he revealed the political and economic context underlying his work. In using his historical knowledge as a political tool, he stated:

> In the current system of salary workers, a capitalist minority dominates the proletariat through the appropriation of lands. In the initial regime of the conquest the conquerors established their domination by becoming capitalists through the forced possession of the only workers in the island, the Indians. Nowadays land is taken and laborers are said to be legally free; yesterday, the Indians were owned and the land remained legally free. Social repercussion was rooted in the privileged ownership of the instruments of production and, therefore, of wealth.[7]

Ortiz touched other issues in this project, including the economic and political role of the first towns (*villas*) established in Cuba, the social and economic importance of the administration of the properties of the deceased (*bienes de difuntos*) in the Indies, and the economic significance of contraband in Cuba's history. One section, titled "The First Historical Revolution in Cuba," illustrates the depth with which Ortiz studied Cuban historical themes as the basis for his famous *Cuban Counterpoint* and other texts in which his conception of history is predominant. The history of Cuba, he asserts, is a process where ethnic groups, classes, economies, ideas, religions, and superstitions are articulated, and the Cuban identity emerges as a new qualitative factor.

THE CUBAN BOOKS SERIES

A study of the Cuban Books Series (Colección de Libros Cubanos), which was created and directed by Ortiz, enables us to take another look at his interest in reconstructing and maintaining the history and cultural traditions of Cuban people. Analysis of its various publications permits a new assessment of its significance. The general bibliography elaborated by the Biblioteca Nacional José Martí for the period between 1917 and 1936—the so-called empty years[8]—provides the context for Cuban Books Series. During that time numerous texts on Jose Martí appeared, works on the experiences of the War for Independence circulated, and a revaluation of Cuban historical studies occurred (after its initial stages in the 1920s, this latter tendency achieved maturity after 1930). Likewise, works on education and pedagogy proliferated, as well as works highlighting the most relevant Cuban intellectuals and independence leaders.

At the time, José Martí was Cuba's most studied intellectual figure, but a bibliography on Martí mainly demonstrates biographical data and specific analysis of his work. Priority was given to his poetry, aesthetics, literary values, teaching ideas, and eloquence. As Julio Antonio Mella noted, there was a clear absence of studies dealing with the truly revolutionary essence of Martí's thought. Scholars such as Antonio Saco, Carlos Manuel de Céspedes, Domingo del Monte, Antonio Maceo, and Félix Varela and others led the interest in Martí. Most of these were historical and biographical accounts.

Efforts at recovering essential Cuban thought were isolated and mainly descriptive, although one must acknowledge the rigor of Carlos Trelles's *Biblioteca histórica de autores cubanos* and the well-informed works of Domingo Figarola Caneda and José Fernández de Castro. Before the publication of the Cuban Books Series, the only project that contemplated the recovery of Cuba's historical memory was Ortiz's own 1913 project, the Cuban Books and Unpublished or Rare Documents Series (Colección Cubana de Libros y Documentos Inéditos o Raros). In this project Ortiz addressed the need to republish out-of-print Cuban texts, such as *Lo que fuimos o lo que somos* by José María de La Torre. This series was also designed to encourage the publication of manuscript works, which according to Ortiz were being "forgotten or devoured by moths." This is how José María Callejas's unpublished *Historia de Santiago de Cuba* was rescued from oblivion. The same happened to the interesting book of testimonies by Lola María Ximeno. Finally,

Ortiz sought to publish books on Cuba written by foreigners and which rarely reached the island, such as *Historia de la esclavitud en Cuba* by Hubert S. Aimes. The 1913 series remained active until the 1930s. However, for unknown reasons, very few volumes were actually published.

In 1927, Ortiz launched the Cuban Books Series in collaboration with renowned bibliographers,[9] and the works published partly coincided in subject matter with the previous Colección Cubana de Libros y Documentos Inéditos o Raros. However, in the new series, only important Cuban texts such as *La historia de Cuba* by Pedro J. Guiteras are included, not unpublished manuscripts. The new series is similar to the previous one because it also published works on Cuba written by foreigners, such as Samuel Hazard's *Cuba a pluma y a lápiz* (*Cuba with Pen and Pencil*, 1871), and Alexander von Humboldt's *Ensayo político de la Isla de Cuba* (*Political Essay on the Island of Cuba*, Spanish edition, 1827, French and English editions, 1826).

Ortiz contributed to the publication of more than forty-two volumes in the Cuban Book Series, among them *José Martí: Poesías*, with a biography and introduction by Juan Marinello; *José Martí: Ideario*; *José Martí: Epistolario*; *Iniciadores y primeros mártires de la revolución Cubana* by Vidal Morales; the works of José de la Luz y Caballero; poetic works of José María Heredia, Plácido, and Julián del Casal; and José Antonio Saco's *Contra la anexión*, and *Historia de la esclavitud*. The publication of these texts alone illustrates the close links Ortiz was seeking to establish between the twentieth century and past traditions of Cuban scholarship as a means for giving ideological continuity to revolutionary and progressive thought. This is why he began the Cuban Books Series with the reedition of *La historia de Cuba* by Guiteras, a deeply patriotic and nationalistic historian.

Ortiz introduced new methodological issues in the different prologues he wrote to the series' publications. He first proposes to establish a method for evaluating historical sources, a critical analysis of the documents, in reference to the chronicles of conquerors and Cuban voyagers. He took the role of an active historian, not only in the reedition of the historical texts but also in questioning them as documents and seeing them as resulting from circumstantial and human contradictions.

In 1927, Ortiz wrote, "Particularly the pre-history of Cuba and its pre-Columbian civilizations require a remodeling because the chronicles of the conquest and its almost medieval visions are still being accepted in their literal sense."[10] He pointed out that:

> Cuban economic life until Charles III and its restructuring, almost entirely extralegal in terms of widespread contraband, is open to the analysis of its significance; the convulsions of the island's nationalism, since their birth with the Economic Societies [Sociedades Económicas de Amigos del País] until the bloody convulsions of Guiteras's time, must soon be enlightened, linking them further to the modern patterns of human thought and the accidents of the world's economy.[11]

This proposal in the introduction to Guitera's *Historia de Cuba*, the first volume in the Cuban Books Series, was based on a social and economic perspective of Cuban history. Ortiz argued that the colonial economy could only be understood by considering society's internal dynamics, and by observing the links between the universal and particular factors, and between the economy and the world's current economic ideas.

Another aspect of Ortiz's historiographical perspective appeared in his prologue to Saco's *Contra la anexión*. He proposed to analyze the works of Cuban intellectuals as expressions of their responses to the ideological challenges of their times; analysis, he suggested, should not obscure these intellectuals' ideas or request something from them that their historical backgrounds did not provide for. Following this methodology, Ortiz updated the debate over nineteenth-century reformist ideology and highlighted the national values of anti-Annexationism. At the same time Ortiz considered different factors that influenced the formation and development of Saco's political personality. He argued that a well-argued and detailed study should show the importance of understanding the individual in his historical rhythm. Detaching a writer's texts from the context in which they were produced would often render them confusing, disjointed, or disoriented. If we frame them within the historical conditions that inspired them, however, we begin to understand Saco's ideas. Yet, comprehending all the tones and clarity of Saco's views still requires some sense of the burning intimacy that filled his letters.[12]

Ortiz cautiously studied many of Saco's views regarding Cuban independence, the abolition of slavery, and the debated issue of his "racism." Ortiz showed the contradictory views present in Saco's work and Ortiz was able to differentiate between what was circumstantial and what was permanent in Saco's political thought. Ortiz highlighted his liberal ideals and his attachment to political "possibilism" in an unprecedented way, as well as his clear definition of Cuban nationality. According to this definition, Cuban nationality is not limited to a segment of white colonial society; instead it has historical sense and transcends due to its universality. According to Saco, "The notion of immortality is sublime, it prolongs the existence of individuals beyond burial, and nationality is the immortality of a people and the purest origin of patriotism."[13]

Ortiz focuses on the central aspects of Saco's thought, and on the concept of nationality—not limiting it to its ethnic aspect but understanding it in its axiological, ethical, and cultural dimensions. One can affirm that Ortiz's historical conceptions are based on Saco, who was an advocate of Cuban reformism, and developed his historical ideas in texts such as *Colección de papeles científicos o históricos, políticos y de otras ramas sobre la isla de Cuba* (some of which went unpublished), and his monumental *Historia de la esclavitud* (*History of Slavery*). In these works Saco centers his ideas around the issue of slavery, which was so closely linked to the reality of nineteenth-century Cuba.

In *Historia de la esclavitud*, Saco universalized Cuban issues, culture, and history, thus constructing a history of slavery in other places that was deeply critical of the Spanish colonial system. In his historical studies Saco developed the idea, cherished by Ortiz, that facts acquire true value when studied in relation to general issues. This idea enabled Saco to analyze the events of Cuban national history with a greater level of objectivity. Thus, in developing an argument for the abolition of slavery, Saco inserts the Cuban experience into his historical analysis of slavery in Asia and Europe: that is why the analysis of free work and its advantages were central to his notions. He needed to establish the historical value of salaried work for social transformation.

Saco, and later Ortiz, conceived of history as a political resort, as an ideological weapon that guided being Cuban. For them history was not only scientific knowledge, or the memory of the Cuban people, but also a mechanism with a "social purpose" for the transformation of Cuban society. Saco's example provided an important background for Ortiz's historical studies, especially his encyclopedic spirit and his ability to integrate various historical studies into a focused object of research. Saco's work on slavery and its history confirmed Ortiz's ideas regarding Indian labor in the New World, and Saco's insights into vagrancy in Cuba and his ethnographic articles were quoted by Ortiz to correct the historical errors of foreign authors who wrote about Cuba.

Both authors understood and studied the works of Fray Bartolomé de las Casas. Saco wrote an article in Madrid entitled "La Historia de las Indias por Fray Bartolomé de las Casas y la Real Academia de la Historia de Madrid" (1865), long before this unpublished work of Las Casas was published in 1875. In his *Historia de la esclavitud,* Saco included many quotes and references from manuscripts by Las Casas to reclaim the humanism of this defender of Indians in America, and to refute the Black Legend that had misused his work. Ortiz followed Saco's footsteps from a new theoretical perspective.

Ortiz believed that Saco's political work during the nineteenth century complemented the revolutionary works of Martí. Both Saco and Martí remained at the center of his reflections on Cuba's political issues. In 1929, during Machado's dictatorship, Ortiz wrote:

> Saco and Martí, these are the fathers of Cuban freedom, always perceptive and aware of, never fooled by, their predictions. The ideology of Cuban civic spirit was constructed, from the time of dark slave factories to the dawn of an independent nation, first around Saco and afterwards around Martí.[14]

Saco and Ortiz did not express their essential views in a specific doctrine; they emanated rather from their scientific and political activity. This is why we are unable to find a theory of history in Ortiz without first approaching the problems that occupied his attention. Each of Ortiz's concepts offered a plethora of references to the history of Cuban thought and the social, cultural, and practical activities of Cuban society.

NOTES

1. Fernando Ortiz, "La primera revolución histórica de Cuba (Introducción a un estudio de la evolución económica cubana)," unpublished manuscript, Archivo Fernando Ortiz, SEAP-ILL, Havana.

2. Ortiz, "Primera revolución histórica," Archivo Fernando Ortiz, SEAP-ILL.

3. Ortiz, "Primera revolución histórica," Archivo Fernando Ortiz, SEAP-ILL.

4. Ortiz, "Primera revolución histórica," Archivo Fernando Ortiz, SEAP-ILL.

5. Ortiz, "Primera revolución histórica," Archivo Fernando Ortiz, SEAP-ILL.

6. Fernando Ortiz, "Presentación y glosa de Fray Bartolomé," *Revista Bimestre Cubana* 70 (1955): 203.

7. Ortiz, "Primera revolución histórica," Archivo Fernando Ortiz, SEAP-ILL.

8. The years between the bibliographic annuals of Carlos Trelles, which include Cuban books up to 1916, and those of Fermín Peraza, which begin only in 1937 (1917–1936) are the so-called empty years.

9. José María Chacón y Calvo, Juan M. Dihigo, A. M. Eligio de la Puente, José A. Fernández de Castro, Francisco González del Valle, Max Henriquez Ureña, Félix Lizaso, Juan Marinello, M. Isidro Méndez, Juan Pérez Abreu, Emeterio S. Santovenia, Adrián del Valle, and Enrique José Varona.

10. Fernando Ortiz, "Prólogo," in *Historia de la isla de Cuba* by Pedro José Guiteras (Havana: Cultural, 1927), vol. 1: vi.

11. Ortiz, "Introducción bibliográfica."

12. Fernando Ortiz, "Prólogo," in *Contra la anexión* by José Antonio Saco (Havana: Cultural S.A., 1928), vol. 1: ix.

13. José Antonio Saco, *Contra la anexión* (Havana: Cultural S.A., 1928), vol. 2: 12.

14. Fernando Ortiz, *José Antonio Saco y sus ideas cubanas* (Habana: El Universo S.A., 1929): 207.

9

Tobacco in the *Contrapunteo*

Ortiz and the Havana Cigar

Jean Stubbs

The last decade of the twentieth century was one in which the island of Cuba was catapulted once more onto the international cultural arena. In the late 1990s, the *son* stole back the show from *salsa* through the octogenarian Buena Vista Social Club.[1] The revival of the *son* was predated by other Cuban revivals, two of which are of concern here: Fernando Ortiz and the Havana cigar. The Ortiz revival, and its contrapuntal critique of postcoloniality, modernity, and postmodernity, was largely literary and anthropological. Tobacco, like sugar, was relegated to a secondary plane. Yet Ortiz, in developing the *Contrapunteo*,[2] dwelt on tobacco, even more than sugar, and especially on the cigar, to construct his counterpoint and concept of transculturation, which have been at the heart of the Ortiz revival.

I look first at the Ortiz revival and the *Contrapunteo*. I then chart the history behind the Havana cigar revival, recentering Cuba's tobacco product par excellence in the *Contrapunteo*. My story is of a new Cuban counterpoint, within tobacco itself—more precisely, between what I have come to call the "offshore" and the island Havana cigar, involving island and émigré Cubans, for non-U.S. and U.S. markets. It is contrapuntal with the work of Ortiz and my own earlier work.[3] In centrifugal fashion, there is the main story and two complementary essays. The first spans a century (1895–1995) of Florida *Habano* history and is framed by two tobacco embargoes. The second functions as a representational play, which raises key questions for our understanding of Cuba's "national" history. I conclude by posing a hypothetical question: What would Ortiz, in true contrapuntal fashion, have made of these latter-day developments?

ORTIZ AND THE *CONTRAPUNTEO*

The Ortiz revival began among the Cuban-American academic community in the United States with the work of Gustavo Pérez-Firmat and Antonio Benítez-Rojo.[4] Both drew on postmodernism, and, while in historical and anthropological context, their analyses were linguistic and literary.

Pérez-Firmat argued that Cuban national identity is translational not foundational, highlighting how the Ortiz metaphor of the *ajiaco*, a stew of Amerindian origin, the culinary emblem of Cuba, was not so much *fusión* (a melting pot fusion) but *cocción* (an incessant simmering concoction). It is not difficult to see how powerful a current of thinking this might be for Cuban emigrés, like Pérez-Firmat. It legitimized their *cubanía*, in the Ortiz sense of the term (the spiritual or desired condition, the "conscious, ethical identification" with what is Cuban), as opposed to their *cubanidad* (the civil status, or "generic condition," of being Cuban).

Benítez-Rojo interpreted transculturation through chaos theory, whereby in nature order and disorder are not the antithesis of each other but rather mutually generative phenomena to argue that, within the sociocultural fluidity and the apparent disorder of the Caribbean, seen largely through the prism of Cuba, there emerges an "island" of order. This repeats itself, in the paradoxical sense it appears in the discourse of chaos, whereby every repetition entails the unpredictable flux of transformative change, transition, and return. He characterized the Caribbean above all as a region of performance, whose coherence is that of *mestizaje*, understood as both cultural and racial mixing, not as a synthesis but as a "concentration of differences," "generalized promiscuity," and the "impossibility of a stable identity."

In his preface to the new English-language edition of *Counterpoint*,[5] Fernando Coronil heralded Ortiz as a thinker ahead of his times; in tune with the fluidity of the contemporary world, fashioning binary opposites as metaphors, or tropes, for events, ideas, and interpretations that were in constant flux. Coronil applied the postmodernist maxim that each reading of the book opens up a different book. Ortiz, he argued, would have welcomed a perspective that "recognizes its provisionality and inconclusiveness, the contrapuntal play of text against text and of reader against author."[6] He paid tribute to Ortiz "by engaging in this transcultural exchange, as Ortiz's book does, in counterpoint with the historical conditions of its own making."[7] For him, *Contrapunteo* was written in times of international and domestic upheaval, which frame its concerns and help explain its allegorical character. Yet, *Counterpoint* "proposed neither unambiguous solutions nor a blueprint for the future."[8] This was precisely its attraction over half a century later, in a much-changed world "in which globalizing forms of capital accumulation and communication are met both with transnationalizing and reconfigured nationalist responses, have unsettled certainties associated with the belief in modernity."[9]

One interesting dimension of the revival has been the extent to which Ortiz is interpreted as giving primacy to harmony over conflict, especially that of the races, a highly charged notion in Cuba's crisis 1990s, as discussed in Pérez Sarduy and Stubbs.[10] As we enter the new millennium, this message is a sobering one, wherein what emerges uppermost is a less harmonious and more conflictual and contended terrain of racial paradigms facing Cuba (and the world). Nonetheless, while interpretations of Ortiz's work vary widely, on and off the island, his utopian vision remains a beacon to many, as does his notion of the *Contrapunteo.*

Pérez-Firmat values *Contrapunteo* for its conceptual, "textual" counterpoint. Ortiz, he declares, was not a good "scientist," in that many of his conclusions were based on incomplete data or erroneous assumptions. In the impact of tobacco and sugar on the history of Cuba:

> Ortiz found a subject on which he could exercise his relational talent to best advantage. The contrasts between tobacco and sugar are both determining and representative. They are determining inasmuch as the peculiarities of the two industries have done much to shape the course of Cuban history; and they are representative because the counterpoint of the two products symbolizes many of the defining features of the Cuban character.[11]

The literary precedent, the dispute between Carnival and Lent, sets up an allegorical drama in which *Don Tabaco* and *Doña Azucar* enact a long sequence of literal and figurative contrasts. Not least among them is sugar as a centripetal, centralizing force reproducing the relationship between the exploitative metropolis and the exploited colonies, and tobacco as a centrifugal, decentralizing force signifying autonomy, freedom, and independence. Tobacco is quality and distinctiveness, "the best," as opposed to "the most" for sugar.

Benítez-Rojo begins his discussion of Ortiz and the *Contrapunteo* with a latter-day quote from French historian Fernand Braudel: "Interdisciplinarity is the legal marriage of two neighboring sciences. But as for me, I am for generalized promiscuity."[12] Benítez-Rojo sees this in tune with the new history and multidisciplinary pluralism of today. His preferred reading of *Contrapunteo* is "not only as a socio-economic study of tobacco and sugar, but rather as a text that tries to speak to us about Cuban, and by extension Caribbean, experience."[13] In drawing attention to the structure of *Contrapunteo,* he signals its two parts. The first sets up the binary opposition; the second treats it as a discursive strategy, since tobacco and sugar do not in fact inhabit such extremes. *Contrapunteo* evades the canon of "for or against," "true or false" that characterize the analytical models modernity uses most: "When Ortiz says that 'to study Cuban history is fundamentally to study the history of sugar and tobacco as the visceral systems of its economy,'[14] he is suggesting to us 'another' mode of investigation whose prototype would be that of the *Contrapunteo.*"[15]

Tobacco, Coronil reiterates, functions as the counterpoint to the socio-economic power of the sugar mill accumulated under capitalist production. When Ortiz speaks of tobacco, he discards all allusions to capitalist power and evokes an indigenous, primitive mode of production that has mystery and rite of passage, religion and magic, harmony and sacred dance: "The proud cigar band as against the lowly sack."[16] The countercontrast to capital's growing domination of Cuban society is a utopian solution to the fairy tale, because "there never was any enmity between sugar and tobacco," a fruitful marriage, compromise and fusion, rather than conflict or transformation, "the intermeshed transmigrations of people":

> The more Ortiz tells about tobacco and sugar, the more the reader learns about Cubans, their culture, musicality, humor, uprootedness, baroque manner of re-fashioning their identities by integrating the fractured meanings of multiple cultures. The two commodities become highly complex metaphorical constructs that represent at once material things and human actors, or, Ortiz "uses the fetish power of commodities as a poetic means to understand the society that produces them" presenting "a counterfetishistic interpretation that challenges essentialist understandings of Cuban history."[17]

A NEW CIGAR COUNTERPOINT

It has been over thirty years since I embarked on the research for my own tobacco monograph. As a British historian, I was influenced by the British Marxist school of history and by empiricism—the need for empirical evidence. My London-based reading of the English-language *Cuban Counterpoint* was for background documentation. As my research progressed, the text, wonderful though it is, jarred with what I was discovering. Primarily concerned with twentieth-century tobacco history, I began to delve into the nineteenth century in an attempt to understand phenomena that presented themselves as significantly other than the "accepted truths." Only now, as I return to Ortiz, having espoused a more relativist, dare I say almost post-modern, approach to Caribbean and Cuban history, do I realize the extent to which those "truths" derived from Ortiz, when Ortiz himself never posited them as such. When I wrote the book, it seemed fitting to take my opening quote from Ortiz: [18]

> Out of the agricultural and industrial development of these amazing plants were to come those economic interests that foreign traders would twist and weave for centuries to form the web of our country's history, the motives of its leaders, and, at one and the same time, the shackles and the support of its people. Tobacco and sugar are the two most important figures in the history of Cuba.[19]

I titled chapter one "Don Tabaco: 1817–88," as it covered the period on which the classic Ortiz counterpoint most held sway. In reflection, the rest of the book was structured in such a way as to challenge the Ortiz position, though overtly only once, in chapter 6, "The Peripheral Mode of Production." The target of my attack was Ortiz's insistence on the delicate process of tobacco agriculture and industry, which made it less lucrative to foreign capital and therefore more Cuban: tobacco signified freedom and national sovereignty in opposition to the slavery and colonizing influence of sugar.

At the time of writing my book, dependency theory had given way to core/periphery thinking, and *Tobacco on the Periphery* seemed an obvious title for what I was observing.[20] I charted what now appears to me an almost linear approach of the inevitability of foreign domination over an industry in decline. That line was broken with the 1959 revolution, but it has also been fragmented, both before and since, in multiple directions, perhaps none so dramatic as in the 1990s.

When the book manuscript was read for publication, I was struck by one reader's comment: that what we needed was the full story of the "Havana Cigar Universe." The reader was Cuba's historian Louis Pérez, and his comment was grounded on the Havana cigar history of Key West and Tampa. Haunted by his comment, I embarked on a larger on- and off-island cigar history, which became compelling with the 1990s cigar revival: behind the 1990s cigar cool lay a swashbuckling, godfather-type history of fires, hurricanes, and revolutions, but also a subtext of a more harmonious kind. This led me to rethink received wisdom on Cuba's "national" history, as well as my own earlier work and that of Ortiz.

If we take the classic Ortiz counterpoint of tobacco symbolizing all that sugar was not in particular nationalism, freedom, and independence the picture I paint is somewhat different. It is one in which the Havana cigar has long been at the heart of political and economic rivalries, linked with foreign and local capital and labor, and with out-migration at key turning points in Cuban history. The synopsis of my story runs as follows. Late nineteenth-century independence and the 1959 revolution created Cuban communities and economies abroad, centered around products like tobacco. These in turn came to constitute serious competition for, while also being interlocked with, island production. Today, as in the past, parallel production and marketing systems of identical or similar brands, and the cultural and labor practices associated with them, raise issues of identity and reconciliation in the context of both political nationalism and economic pragmatism.

Cuban tobacco was developed with Spanish, German, British, and French capital, for European, North American, and world markets. It formed part of a nineteenth-century world cigar tobacco economy whose tobacco blends were produced as far afield as Cameroon, Turkey, Java, and Sumatra and whose key retail outlets were London, Amsterdam, Bremen, and New York.

The backdrop to Cuba's First and Second Wars of Independence from Spain (1868–1878 and 1895–1898) was an out-migration to the United States, the Caribbean, and Central America. Cuban tobacco interests came together in the settler countries, providing a familiar means of livelihood for the displaced migrant community and an economic and political mainstay for the independence struggle at home. Over time, rival economic and political interests built up, with trading and other advantages over a home country in turmoil. U.S. capital investment came fast in Cuban tobacco, swallowing up tracts of Cuban tobacco land and major manufacturing companies. There were "independents" who held out, but the industry as a whole never regained its former glory. Thirty years later, the 1930s depression and labor unrest culminated a process whereby U.S.-owned manufacturing withdrew from Cuba to the United States.

The mass migratory phenomenon reemerged with the 1959 revolution. Newer Cuban tobacco "host communities" grew up in the Dominican Republic, Nicaragua, Honduras, Costa Rica, and Ecuador, joining older established ones in Jamaica, Mexico, and the United States—Florida, New Jersey, and Connecticut.[21] Smaller manufacturers, dealers, growers and workers proved to be as astute as larger monopoly capital in finding fertile ground for overseas business. They profited from the post-1959 internal economic upheaval in Cuba that was the product of insurrection, agrarian reform, and nationalization, plus the tight trade embargo that was the political response of the United States (and for a while the whole area) to the Cuban revolution. Western European markets became a battleground for disputed Havana cigar brands. At the same time, the Eastern European bloc and key Third World countries emerged as Havana cigar partners.

Thirty years on, a new chapter opened when the demise of the Eastern European socialist bloc in 1989 signaled the end of Cuba's special trade and aid. At the same time, the United States took steps to tighten and extraterritorialize the embargo in the form of the 1991 Torricelli and 1996 Helms-Burton Acts. As external geopolitical realities compounded internal weaknesses, the Cuban revolutionary government devised a structural adjustment strategy, courting non-U.S. trade and investment. The Havana cigar became a key player in the Cuban strategy for the 1990s, as Cuban production plummeted, and battles fought in international courts over market brand names were but the more visible tip of a cigar war. A U.S. cigar revival was gaining momentum, involving the two U.S. cigar giants—Connecticut-based General Cigar and Fort Lauderdale-based Consolidated Cigar—along with émigré Cuban tobacco interests, in the Dominican Republic, followed by Honduras, Nicaragua, Mexico, and Connecticut, in all-out competition with Cuba.

As of the late 1980s, the state-owned Cuban tobacco sector blazed the internal adjustment trail with the disaggregation of tobacco land from cooperatives back into private smallholdings. In 1994, part-dollar payments were introduced as an incentives package for the tobacco sector, and a new holding company, Habanos S.A., was set up to handle overseas marketing ventures. Both measures followed fast in the wake of two landmark "credit for tobacco swap" deals struck between the Cuban state tobacco enterprise, Cubatabaco, and its French and Spanish parastatal tobacco counterparts, Societé Nationale des Tabacs (SEITA) and Tabacalera Española, S.A. A European cigar marketing deal was struck in Britain with Hunters & Frankau. By 1997, Cuba was investing heavily in tobacco to help meet a world market demand in excess of supply. Heightened U.S.–Europe rivalry in the contemporary world of American cigar politics was mirrored by that within the Havana cigar universe, though with global capital mergers, national policies notwithstanding. A new twist came in 1999 when Tabacalera Española and Seita formed Altadis (Alianza de Tabacos y Distribución), which bought 50 percent of shares in Habanos S.A. Tabacalera Española had earlier that year bought Consolidated Cigar Co. and was thereby heavily involved in both the Havana and clone Havana cigar business.

A TALE OF TWO EMBARGOES (1895–1995)

The Havana cigar counterpoint of island and offshore production is graphically illustrated by Florida cigar history, framed by two U.S. embargoes on Cuban tobacco imports: the lesser-known embargo of the early 1890s and the current forty-year embargo dating back to the early 1960s. The first helped establish Florida as a major Havana cigar tobacco-growing, manufacturing, and retail state. The second culminated in Florida's deagriculturalization and deindustrialization in the cigar sector. The century as a whole, from the 1890s to the 1990s, was one of successive boom–bust processes. These were initially in Florida itself, in Gadsden County (1890s–1970s), the Tampa Bay area (1890s–1990s), and Miami (1960s–1990s). Then, as growing and manufacturing that had come from Cuba once again moved offshore, they were transplanted to the Caribbean and Central America (Nicaragua, Honduras, Mexico, Dominican Republic, Jamaica, Costa Rica, and Ecuador) as part of wider processes of regionalization and globalization, controlled mainly from the United States and for the lucrative U.S. market.[22]

If cigar tobacco growing was short-lived around the Tampa area, it was to remain in northern Florida up until the 1970s. Cuban tobacco was first introduced there in 1828, but it was later in the nineteenth century that a hybrid Havana-Sumatra seed, shade-grown, Georgia–Florida wrapper was developed, paving the way for 1880s–1890s expansion. Alongside the better-known manufacturing histories of Key West, Tampa, and Martí City, today Ocala,[23] is the untold growing history of Gadsden County, with its tobacco towns of Havana, Sumatra, Amsterdam, and Quincy, linked to machine manufacturing in Jacksonville and Tampa,[24] the latter becoming the 1950s cigar smoke capital of the world.[25] The corollary to this agricultural development was a state infrastructure of tobacco agricultural research and extension.[26]

In 1960, the United States broke diplomatic ties with Cuba and, in 1962, declared an embargo on tobacco imports from the island. Before then, steps were being taken to prepare for such a contingency. In January 1961, the United States Department of Agriculture's Tobacco Research and Marketing Advisory Committee recommended that a study be conducted to determine the effect on the cigar industry and tobacco farmers if supplies of Cuban tobacco were no longer available and also the effect of a change in duty rates. High priority was given to the project, and a study group sought the views of growers, manufacturers and dealers in compiling a seventy-one-page *Special Study on Cigar Tobacco* in November of that year.

According to the report, all except about 0.5 percent of cigars sold in the United States were produced in factories in the United States and Puerto Rico. Cuba was the source of nearly one-fourth of cigar tobacco (31 million pounds out of a total of 135 million pounds). Of the 7 billion cigars sold in a typical recent year, 4.7 billion—some two-thirds—contained Cuban tobacco. Around 670 million were made entirely of Cuban or predominantly Cuban tobacco: the "clear Havanas" (100 percent) and the "Havana filler" cigars (100 or near 100 percent Cuban filler but not the binder and wrapper). These predominantly "Cuban tobacco cigars" used about 45 percent of all Cuban imported tobacco. The other 55 percent was used in "blended filler" cigars in varying proportions, which varied from 20 to 50 percent Cuban tobacco. If imports were to cease, "clear Havana" manufacturers saw their problems as "extremely difficult and probably insurmountable."[27]

A February 1962 University of Florida Circular from Cooperative Extension Work in Agriculture and Home Economics to All County Agents and Assistants (February 9, 1962) referred to the fact that "Small scale tests have been made in the Quincy area to produce a wrapper similar to that produced in Cuba, through modification of curing techniques." This was also reflected in a May 1962 article in the *Tampa Tribune* titled "Specialists Eye Growing Cuban Tobacco in Florida." It reported that Florida agricultural experiment stations at Quincy and Gainesville were experimenting with Cuban seed that had been obtained.[28]

In the 1950s, Tampa was again a source of overseas support for Cuban revolutionary organizations (the 26th of July movement was a case in point), and the Havana cigar industry was still the largest single employer in the city, with thousands working in cigar manufacturing and related fields (box making, label printing, etc.). This changed dramatically as the industry relocated. In May 1962, the *Tampa Tribune* ran articles titled "Cigar Firms Hope for Survival, but Workers Despair—Manufacturers Feel They Have Chance to Hold onto Market; Employees See No Place to Turn" and "Future Bleak for Jobless

Unwanted Ex–Cigar Workers."[29] More than six thousand cigar makers lost their jobs, and, by 1971, the cigar industry was disappearing as a factor in the economic life of Tampa Bay. A few small *chinchales* had opened in the intervening years, but most of these were for the tourists and not considered an integral part of the industry. Villazón was more typical, having opened two factories in Honduras for the manufacture of handmade Havanas: Hoyo de Monte Rey and Punch. The Armenia Avenue factory stayed in West Tampa, but to produce only machine-made cigars. By the 1980s, it was increasingly the newly developed homogenized leaf that was being used, driving yet another nail in the coffin of the quality handmade cigar and craft cigar maker.[30]

The outcome was that, as recorded in the 1992 U.S. census, there were only 27 U.S. cigar companies, making primarily machine-made cigars with a total employment of 2,600. By the late 1990s, companies fell into two broad categories. The first comprised the two major U.S. players. One was Consolidated Cigar, which in the 1970s acquired rights to the Cuban brands Montecristo and H. Upmann. The other was General Cigar, which purchased Villazón in 1996, and in 1998 was with Cubatabaco in the courtroom over Cohíba cigars and in precedent-setting talks in Mexico City. The second category comprised smaller Tampa- and Miami-based Cuban American and American companies, such as the Fuente-Oliva-Newman consortium in Tampa and Padrón in Miami.[31] All were interlocked with production in the Dominican Republic, Honduras, Nicaragua, Jamaica, Mexico, Ecuador, and Costa Rica.

Unsurprisingly, the more recent company is easier to piece together than labor history. There is no wealth of labor studies available for the earlier period.[32] Only now is a Cuban American labor history emerging for the post-1959 period,[33] and thus far it does include tobacco. Yet, consider the following from the May 1, 1977 *Miami Herald*:

> Experienced "tabaqueros" roll lots of cigars daily for small shops. . . . Long Hours and Small Pay: Tobacco Business Keeps Rolling—Teodoro Santana learned as boy of 15 in Jovellanos, then Havana, and for the past seven years at Padrón, West Flagler. . . . Most of the tabaqueros working in dozens of small cigar shops sprinkled throughout Little Havana, and in four or five shops that produce several million cigars a year, like Santana, are products of a time and place foreign to younger Cubans with American ideas of pay and work conditions. "It's slave-like work, and the young people don't want to do it," semi-retired Santana said. "Just as the rollers are of an era past, so are their employers, many of whom began amassing their knowledge by following their fathers through the fields in Cuba. . . . The rollers are all dying off," said Pérez-Carillo Sr. Many companies, he said, "already import many of the cigars they sell from Latin American countries, where poor people are still willing to labor all day long for a pittance."

Florida's minimum wage policy was often invoked by companies to explain why they "had" to go offshore. But this was lucrative business, transformed through technology, experimentation, litigation, and labor practices, to the extent that much of today's cigar rolling bears little resemblance to that of a century ago.

What is striking about the offshore cigar sector is a pragmatism as regards the end of the embargo. The 1990s cigar hype was such that neither island nor offshore production could meet demand, though demand peaked in the late 1990s, and the bubble may soon burst. In the event of any normalization of U.S.–Cuba relations, the Florida–Havana cigar best-case scenario is to be able to import the island's leaf while limiting the import of island-manufactured cigars, but in all probability this would be resisted by Cuba and non-U.S. Havana cigar importers, especially those in Europe. Arguably, some U.S./ non-U.S. importers are now so interlocked that they are already able to sidestep the embargo.

¿HABANO O NO?

The cigar advertisements featured in the 1992-founded New York glossy *Cigar Aficionado* were key to the 1990s U.S. cigar boom. They ranged from a suggestive Carmen rolling cigars on her thighs to "Agnes, have you seen my Don Diegos? A word of warning, don't let your Don Diegos out of your sight," with Agnes in pre-Lewinsky-type image.[34] Don Diegos, handmade in the Dominican Republic for Consolidated Cigar, were now owned by Tabacalera Española. Some were more explicit: "The only thing sexier than sex is a cigar. . . . On one end, the fire. On the other, a Lady. In between, the ultimate pleasure. Let your senses take over, enjoy La Diva Cigars." La Diva was being made in the Dominican Republic with a Connecticut wrapper. Or, "You never forget the first time," accompanied Don Sixto cigars, made in the Cuban tradition of generations of the Plascencia family.[35]

In the late 1990s, Tabacalera de García, a subsidiary of the Fort Lauderdale Consolidated Cigar, ran a two-page ad for Montecristo La Corona: "Born in Cuba. Perfected in the Dominican Republic."[36] Theirs was but one in an aggressive marketing campaign meant to bolster the real quality *Habanos* as those made outside Cuba. By the 1990s, counterfeit cigars had become big business, as brand battles in trade disputes centered around the leaf and the Havana seed that has been taken, licitly and illicitly, for growing trials.[37] There were also two epicenters of Havana seed leaf production: the Partido/Vuelta Abajo region of western Pinar del Río and the central Vuelta Arriba in Cuba, and the central Cibao in the Dominican Republic. There were also growing areas in Mexico, Nicaragua, Honduras, Ecuador, and Brazil, replacing the earlier Florida–Georgia area in the United States, though Connecticut remained.

The Dominican Republic was not historically considered a producer of quality cigar leaf. In 1962, however, an émigré Cuban tobacco agronomist, Napoleón Padilla, who was part of the Washington reconstruction plan after the fall of Trujillo, helped found the Instituto del Tabaco in Santiago de los Caballeros in the Cibao.[38] Thirty years later, when Cuba was facing the depths of its post-1989 crisis and dislocation, Cuban American family businesses such as the Fuentes saw long years of hard investment and effort in the Cibao bear quality Havana seed leaf and cigars, and that is what their advertising drew on: "Chateau de la Fuente: Birthplace of a Dream"; "Never Before Was There Such a Cigar . . . The Most Sought After Cigar on Earth" (October 1999). With close ties to Tampa (Newman) and Ecuador (Oliva),[39] their family business was producing cigars in the early 1990s that arguably surpassed the quality of many from Havana, and it continues to come close to this day.

Cigar advertising and cigar labels constitute a telling iconography.[40] The 1990s U.S. cigar imagery was a far cry from that of the nineteenth century. One only has to see the finely embossed romantic imagery of labels of old: Royal Palm–lined plantations where the leaf was grown and, for the London market, the House of Lords or Buckingham Palace, equaled almost by the size and elegance of palatial buildings in Havana, such as that of Aldama, where the cigars were made. There was classical romance, as in *Romeo y Julieta*, and humor as in Punch, who was surrounded by depictions of white, male cigar workers, all rather dapper young Hispanics, at a time when the workforce included children, convicts, soldiers, enslaved Africans, and indentured Chinese immigrants. More politically, in 1897, a year before the end of Cuba's Second War of Independence, one label celebrated three of Cuba's great generals in the war: Calixto García, Máximo Gómez, and Antonio Maceo. Idyllic images were painted of Cuba's relationship with the neighboring United States, far removed from the reality of today, a century later, after forty years of hostilities, broken diplomatic relations, and embargo. Perhaps more in tune with history, an omen of what was to come, the American eagle could also be seen 'embracing' the Cuban flag.

Key West, the southernmost of the Florida Keys, located only ninety miles from Cuba, was the first port of call for émigré manufacturers and workers to develop a Cuban cigar industry, and was also home to Cuban émigré nationalist and labor unrest.[41] In the 1890s, Spanish manufacturers undercut national and class strife by moving to Tampa, whose town patricians were working aggressively to attract the industry. West Tampa and Ybor City became resplendent,[42] as symbolized by Ybor City's Cuban Club from its early twentieth-century heyday.[43] Cuban traditions continued, such as that of the reader in the factories, paid by the workers to read to them while they labored; news in the morning, novels in the afternoon.[44] By 1930, however, the industry was headed for decline due to the Depression, mechanization, and relocation. The advent of the cigar machine cemented a process of feminization and deskilling of mechanized cigar rolling, which had started with the introduc-tion of the *bonches*, or bunching molds, in hand rolling.[45] The big losers in the Tampa story were the Afro-Cubans, who gradually fell foul of U.S. South-style segregation, driving a wedge into the community that had fought together on a nationalist and worker ticket.[46] In the 1960s, local historians rescued Ybor City from developers and opened a museum, complete with cigar makers' cottages, but the commercialized attraction was almost entirely Hispanic in its re-creation of the past.[47] Only a lowly building on the outskirts of the reno-vated center boasted a plaque to the Marti-Maceo Society, founded in 1904 by Afro-Cubans holding on to the dream of a united Cuba.[48]

José Martí visited the Ybor factory in 1892 to fund-raise for his newly cre-ated Cuban Revolutionary Party.[49] Descendants of Cubans proudly recall how their worker forebears donated their day's wages to the cause for inde-pendence. Martí also went to Jamaica to raise support among the Cuban émi-gré community of tobacco manufacturers, workers, and growers, visiting the Temple Hall Cuban tobacco-growing colony not far from Kingston, the cap-ital.[50] Jamaica was the refuge for a number of Cuba's more famous indepen-dence leaders, including Maceo.

The 1990s cigar revival included the brand Temple Hall Estates, whose la-bel bears the founding date of 1876, during Cuba's first War of Indepen-dence, from 1868 to 1878, when the first Cubans founded the Jamaican cigar economy. There was also Macanudo, among the best Jamaican cigars, made under the supervision of Benjamín Menéndez,[51] a master cigar maker who also once made Partagás. In the late nineteenth century, there was Partagás in Havana and Partagás in Key West. In Havana at the time of the revolution, Partagás was made by Cifuentes, who then left Cuba in 1960. A photo of Ci-fuentes Jr., much used in 1990s ads, claimed "Fidel Castro thought I had left with only the shirt on his back. But my secrets were locked in my heart." Ci-fuentes took his tobacco knowledge to the General Cigar Company in Ja-maica and the Dominican Republic, along with some clever marketing of Partagás, "the cigar that knew Cuba when: Made in the Dominican Republic under the supervision of Ramon Cifuentes, the same master cigar-maker who made those legendary cigars over 30 years ago in Cuba" (Summer 1994). Be-hind Macanudo and Partagás was Ed Cullman and his Cullbro Tobacco,[52] the parent company of General Cigar and a leading producer of the Connecticut wrapper. Cifuentes and Menéndez joined the company in the early 1960s, and in the 1970s, the company launched Partagás, claiming the brand name was theirs.

Fidel Castro gave up smoking in the early 1980s, in a drive to encourage the smoking Cuban population to smoke less on health grounds, but in the early days of the revolution he could always be seen smoking a cigar. So could Che Guevara who, while Argentine, developed a taste for Cuban ci-gars. Castro was the target of several CIA assassination attempts, one of which was to have him smoke an exploding cigar, and another to make him look foolish by injecting substances into the cigar that would cause his beard to fall out, or LSD, which would make him speak gibberish. So serious were these attempts that an elegant Miramar mansion became a top-security cigar factory, whose workforce was composed of the women of his male security guards. That was the origin of the now famous Cohíba cigar, later marketed commercially, a story much retold in the cigar press. The present manager of the Cohíba factory, Emilia Tamayo, is one of four women cigar factory managers today. Cohíba is now big outside Cuba, too: made in the Dominican Republic and marketed in the United States by Cullbro, who registered Cohíba in the United States before the Cubans had gone commercial with the brand.

No post-1959 émigré Cuban story would be complete without Miami. However, Miami was not a major cigar player. Initially, small concerns catered to little more than the local Cuban émigré community. One exception was Padrón, who, out of his small Miami business, went on to grow tobacco in Nicaragua. The Nicaraguan economy is a post-1963 phenomenon, thanks to a generous offer made to émigré Cubans by Anastasio Somoza on land around northern Estelí. After the 1979 Sandinista revolution, the area became a battlefield for the contras, and much of the tobacco moved north, to southern Honduras, around Danlí. Padrón and son, however, are among the few still there. A recent ad campaign of theirs ran, "Seeds of Survival. Despite wars in Nicaragua and bombings in Miami."[53] Padrón took a beating for going public against the embargo and for normalization of U.S.–Cuba relations.

The more the cigar revival gained in momentum, and the more island Cuba featured in this, the more the old-time Miami Cuban American Lobby was prone to become incensed with *Cigar Aficionado*. The issue carrying editor Marvin Shanken's cover feature interview with "el jefe" Fidel Castro[54]—an issue that also covered counterfeit cigars—so enraged parts of the Cuban community that it was de facto barred from sale in Miami. Five years later, an issue was given over largely to Cuba, including interviews with key Cuban figures and a feature on Cuba's cigar summit, as well as general reportage. Its cover highlighted precisely what the lobby did not want: an end to the embargo and the opening up of travel to Cuba.[55] To this, the response of the Miami-based Cuban American National Foundation came in the form of a page ad reading, "Lift the smoke screen, not the embargo."[56] It came in an issue that also carried a debate about Cuba generated around the time of John F. Kennedy's presidency.

By the late 1990s, *Cigar Aficionado* circulation had risen to half a million, with sell-out issues whose glossy covers and inside pages featured cigar-smoking stars (Arnold Schwarzenegger, Tom Selleck, Alfred Hitchcock, Groucho Marx, Charlie Chaplin, Jack Nicholson, Bill Cosby, Whoopie Goldberg,

Demi Moore, Madonna, Janet Jones, Susan Lucci, to name but a few); sports-men, including a very elegantly attired El Duque, one of Cuba's leading base-ball players who had recently crossed over to the United States[57]; and politi-cians such as Britain's Winston Churchill, who has *Habanos* named after him.[58] The theme of cigar-smoking famous people had, of course, been clev-erly taken up earlier by the London-based Cuban writer Guillermo Cabrera Infante[59] and in other works: one amusing caption ran, "The psychoanalyst Jacques Lacan, famous for the meanderings of his thought, smoked only twisted cigars of the *culebras* type."[60]

Cigar World is London's less big-time glossy answer to *Cigar Aficionado*, and it is edited by London-based Hunter and Frankau's Simon Chase. The caption to a photo of Chase at the Avelina plantation in Cuba ran as follows: "Any resemblance between this photo and pictures of the Fuente family in their plantations is entirely intentional."[61] The U.S. market is for the Fuentes' H. Upmann, with some clever advertising: "When a cigar can make you for-get about Havana . . . that's One-Upmannship"[62]; and "Ever wonder what those cigar makers did after leaving Cuba? One upmannship?"[63] Hunters & Frankau, who once owned H. Upmann in Havana, and in 1994 celebrated with the Cubans its 150th anniversary,[64] continued to handle its London market. Chase is Britain's man in Havana and has been one of the master-minds behind the now yearly *Habano* Festival, which in 1999 raised $750,000 in a cigar auction for the Cuban health system. One of the items auctioned was a Vegas Robaina humidor. Alejandro Robaina is one of the Pinar del Río smallholders to have benefited from the 1990s tobacco recu-peration program, with an incentive package including part-dollar pay-ments. In 1999, he was declared *Habano* man of the year for the quality of his leaf, which included the successful new strain Habana 2000,[65] and Vegas Robaina was a new brand of *Habanos* named after the tobacco from his family farm.[66]

A NEW COUNTERPOINT?

What would Don Fernando have made of all this? The reader will by now have recognized how the new Cuban counterpoint within my on- and off-island cigar story resonates with Ortiz revisited, whether Pérez-Firmat's translational incessant *cocción*, Benítez-Rojo's transformative chaos and rep-resentational promiscuity, Coronil's provisionality and counterfetishism of text, or Martínez Furé's imaginary dialogue with Don Fernando himself. And so I set myself up as Doña Juana in counterpoint with Don Fernando. I haven't gone into the business, I don't smoke, but my thirty-year addiction to researching Havana cigar history and the 1990s Havana cigar revival put me on the fashion catwalk, and state of the art technology enabled me to create my own virtual cigar world with a cigar band in my very own image. In my story, there are no metanarratives, no cut-and-dried extremes, no unambiguous solutions or blueprints for the future; rather, within globalizing capital, there is a transnationalizing and reconfigured response of the "proud cigar band," a fluidity, a provisionality, an inconclusive *cubanía* that carries within it the possibility of a certain harmony rising against injustice. Robaina travels the world with his tobacco, just as Buena Vista's Compay Segundo, an inveterate smoker of *Habanos*, plays London, New York, and Havana's *Habano* Festival 2000 Gala Dinner. The economics of transnational mergers and the slick advertising images, plus the culture associated with enjoying cigars (as with music, dance, and sport), might just harmonize erstwhile hostile politics. I take pleasure in thinking Don Fernando would have been drawn to such a latter-day allegory of that Cuban commodity par excellence, the Havana cigar.

NOTES

This essay forms part of wider research for a monograph on the island and offshore Havana cigar, 1868–1998. I am grateful for support and financial assistance from my own University of North London and from a British Academy small research grant in summer 1997, and for being awarded two Rockefeller Scholarships, one at the Caribbean 2000 program at the University of Puerto Rico and one at the Cuban Research Institute, Florida International University, in the spring and summer of 1998, as well as a Visiting Fellowship at the Caribbean Center, Royal Institute of Linguistics and Anthropology, Leiden, in autumn 1998. My thanks go to many colleagues for their support and encouragement and for generously contributing to my work in so many ways.

1. A companion article linking offshore developments with the 1990s tobacco reforms can be found in Jean Stubbs, "Turning over a New Leaf? The Havana Cigar Revisited," *New West Indian Guide* 74, no. 3 (2000): 4.

2. Fernando Ortiz, *Cuban Counterpoint: Tobacco and Sugar* (Durham, N.C.: Duke University Press, 1995).

3. Jean Stubbs, *Tobacco on the Periphery: A Case Study in Cuban Labour History, 1860–1958* (London: Cambridge University Press, 1985).

4. Gustavo Pérez-Firmat, *The Cuban Condition: Translation and Identity in Cuban Literature* (Cambridge: Cambridge University Press, 1989); Antonio Benítez-Rojo, *The Repeating Island: The Caribbean and the Postmodern Perspective* (Durham, N.C.: Duke University Press, 1992) (1st ed. 1990).

5. Fernando Ortiz, *Cuban Counterpoint*.

6. Ortiz, *Cuban Counterpoint*, xi.

7. Ortiz, *Cuban Counterpoint*, xi.

8. Coronil in Ortiz, *Cuban Counterpoint*, xi–xii.

9. Coronil in Ortiz, *Cuban Counterpoint*, xii.

10. Pedro Pérez Sarduy and Jean Stubbs, eds., *Afro-Cuban Voices: On Race and Identity in Contemporary Cuba* (Gainesville: University Press of Florida, 2000). See also Pedro Pérez Sarduy and Jean Stubbs, *AFROCUBA: An Anthology of Cuban Writing on Race, Politics and Culture* (Melbourne: Ocean Press/Latin America Bureau/Center for Cuban Studies, 1993).

11. Pérez-Firmat, *The Cuban Condition*: 47.

12. The quote is taken from Francis Ewald and Jean-Jacques Brochier "Una vie pour l'histoire," *Magazine Littéraire* 212 (1984): 22.

13. Benítez-Rojo, *The Repeating Island*, 152.

14. Ortiz, *Cuban Counterpoints*, 13. Benítez-Rojo takes this and subsequent quotes from the Caracas edition: Ortiz, *Contrapunteo cubano del tabado e el azúcar* (Caracas: Biblioteca Ayacucho, 1978).

15. Benítez-Rojo, *The Repeating Island*, 158.

16. Coronil in Ortiz, *Cuban Counterpoint*, xxi; Ortiz, *Cuban Counterpoint*, 7. Espino Marrero, *Cuban Cigar Tobacco: Why Cuban Cigars Are the World's Best* (Neptune City, N.J.: T.F.H. Publications, 1996).

17. Coronil in Ortiz, *Cuban Counterpoint*, xxvii.

18. Stubbs, "Turning over a New Leaf?" v.

19. Ortiz, *Cuban Counterpoint*, 4.

20. Interestingly, a later general text on tobacco in history took as its subtitle "The Cultures of Dependence." Jordan Goodman, *Tobacco in History: The Cultures of Dependence* (London: Routledge, 1993). For tobacco history, see also V. G. Kiernan, *Tobacco: A History* (London: Hutchinson Radius, 1991).

21. We know relatively little about these histories. For Jamaica, see Jean Stubbs, "Political Idealism and Commodity Production: Cuban Tobacco in Jamaica, 1870–1930," *Cuban Studies* 25 (1995). For Mexico, see José González Sierra, *Monopolio del humano: elementos de la historia del tabado en México y algunos conflictos de tabaqueros veracruzanos: 1915–1930* (Xalapa, Mexico: Veracruz University, 1987). The United States will be discussed later.

22. *The Tobacco Leaf* (August 4,1897); press cuttings taken from the Tony Pizzo Collection, University of South Florida, Tampa; *The Tobacco Leaf* (May 18, 1898); M. F. Hetherington, *History of Polk County, Florida* (Chulmota, Fla.: Mickler House Publishers, 1971), 79.

23. Michael Bure and Mary Ellen Moore, *Tampa: Yesterday & Tomorrow* (Tampa: Mishler King, 1981); A. Stuart Campbell, *The Cigar Industry of Tampa, Florida* (Tampa: University of Tampa, 1939); Karl H. Grismer *Tampa: A History of the City of Tampa and the Tampa Bay Region of Florida* (St. Petersburg: St. Petersburg Printing, 1950); Charles F. Harner, *A Pictorial History of Ybor City* (Tampa, Fla.: Trend Publications, 1975); L. Glenn Westfall, *Don Vicente Martínez Ybor, The Man and His Empire: Development of the Clear Havana Industry in Cuba and Florida in the Nineteenth Century* (New York: Garland, 1987); L. Glenn Westfall, *Key West: Cigar City U.S.A.* (Key West: Historic Key West Preservation Board, 1984).

24. Swisher and Havanatampa.

25. Hampton Dunn, *Yesterday's Tallahassee* (Miami: EA Seeman, 1974). Armando Mendez, *Ciudad de Cigars: West Tampa* (Tampa: Florida Historical Society, 1994).

26. The University of Florida, Gainesville, became the state agricultural flagship college. Florida Agricultural Experiment Station booklets held at University of Florida range from 1892 to 1972 and covered tobacco culture, strains, and disease.

27. United States Department of Agriculture, *1961 Special Study on Cigar Tobacco*, 2. I am indebted to colleagues at the University of Florida for facilitating access to departmental agricultural holdings that contain a copy of the report.

28. *Tampa Tribune*, May 27, 1962.

29. *Tampa Tribune*, May 27, 1962.

30. *Tampa Tribune-Times*, April 4, 1982.

31. The broader émigré cigar success story is reflected in James S. Olson and Judith E. Olson, *Cuban Americans: From Trauma to Triumph* (New York: Twane; London: Prentice Hall International, 1995). It is, however, a story yet to be pieced together in its entirety. I was surprised to find scant reference to cigar or tobacco in the University of Miami Special Cuba Collection on the post-1959 period. The collection is, however, a unique and invaluable source of press clippings and ephemera for the period as a whole.

32. Nancy A. Hewitt, "Varieties of Voluntarism: Class, Ethnicity, and Women's Activism in Tampa," in Louise Tilly and Patricia Gurin, eds., *Women, Politics, and Change* (New York: Russell Sage Foundation, 1990); Nancy A. Hewitt, "'The Voice of Virile Labor': Labor Militancy, Community Solidarity, and Gender Identity among Tampa's Latin Workers, 1880–1921," in Ava Baron, ed., *Work Engendered: Toward a New History of American Labor* (Ithaca, N.Y.: Cornell University Press, 1991); Durward Long, "La Resistencia: Tampa's Immigrant Labor Union," *Labor History* 6, no. 3 (Fall 1965); Durward Long, "The Historical Beginnings of Ybor City and Modern Tampa," *Florida Historical Quarterly* 45, no. 1 (July 1966); Durward Long, "The Open-Closed Shop Battle in Tampa's Cigar Industry, 1919–21," *Florida Historical Quarterly* 47, no. 3 (October 1968); Durward Long, "Labor Relations in the Tampa Cigar Industry, 1885–1911," *Labor History* 12, no. 4 (1971); Durward Long, "The Making of Modern Tampa: A City of the New South," *Florida Historical Quarterly* 49, no. 4 (April 1971); Robert Ingalls, *Urban Vigilantes in the New South: Tampa, 1882–1936* (Knoxville: University of Tennessee Press, 1988); Gary Mormino and George E. Pozetta, "'The Reader Lights the Candle': Cuban and Florida Cigar Workers' Oral Tradition," *Labor's Heritage* (Spring 1993); Louis Pérez, "Reminiscences of a Lector: Cuban Cigar Makers in Tampa," *Florida Historical Quarterly* 53, no. 4 (April 1975); Louis Pérez, Jr., "Cubans in Tampa: From Exiles to Immigrants, 1892–1901," *Florida Historical Quarterly* 47, no. 2 (October 1978); Gerald E. Poyo, "Key West and the Cuban Ten Year's War," *Florida Historical Quarterly* 57, no. 3 (January 1979); Gerald E. Poyo, "The Anarchist Challenge to the Cuban Independence Movement, 1895–1890," *Cuban Studies/Estudios Cubanos* 15, no. 1 (Winter 1986); Gerald E. Poyo, "Evolution of Cuban Separatist Thought in the Emigré Communities of the United States, 1848–1895," *Hispanic American Historical Review* 66, no. 3 (1986); Gerald E. Poyo, *With All and for the Good of All* (Durham, N.C.: Duke University Press, 1989).

33. Louise Lamphere, Alex Stepick, and Guillermo Grenier, *Newcomers in the Workplace: Immigrants and the Restructuring of the U.S. Economy* (Philadelphia: Temple University Press, 1994).

34. *Cigar Aficionado*, Autumn 1993.

35. *Cigar Aficionado*, August 1997.

36. *Cigar Aficionado*, October 1999.

37. The brand battle was mirrored by the even more aggressive marketing of Bacardi against the island's Havana Club rum, winning in U.S. courts the right to sell their own identically named Havana Club brand. Significantly, Bacardi ads pandered to a lifestyle that went hand in hand with the new trendy cigars.

38. Napoleón S. Padilla, *Memorias de un cubano sin importancia* (Hialeah, Fla.: A.C. Graphics, 1988); Napoleón S. Padilla, *Cultivo del tabaco negro: sol y tapado* (Santo Domingo, Dominican Republic: Instituto del Tabaco de la Republica Dominicana, 1982).

39. The Newmans had long ago bought the Cuban cigar Cuesta Rey. A lengthy interview with Stanley Newman can be found in *Cigar Aficionado*, August 1997. Oliva was featured in *Cigar Aficionado*, Spring 1993.

40. For an earlier treatise on cigar iconography, especially with reference to film, see Guillermo Cabrera Infante, *Holy Smoke* (London: Faber & Faber, 1985). In the 1990s, a spate of coffee table and museum-piece books were brought out on the Havana cigar: Eric Deschodt and Philippe Morane, *The Cigar* (Cologne: Könemann Verlagsgesellschaft, 1998 [1996]); Eumelio Espino Marrero, *Cuban Cigar Tobacco: Why Cuban Cigars Are the World's Best* (Neptune City, N.J.: T.F.H. Publications, 1996); Enzo A. Infante Urivazo, *Havana Cigars 1817–1960* (Neptune City, N.J.: T.F.H. Publications, 1997); Narciso Menocal, *The Tobacco Industry in Cuba and Florida: Its Golden Age in Lithography and Architecture* (Coral Gables, Fla.: Cuban National Heritage, 1995); Antonio Nuñez Jiménez, *The Journey of the Havana Cigar* (Neptune City, N.J.: T.F.H. Publications 1998); Iain Scarlet, *A Puff of Smoke* (London: Robert Lewis, n.d.). For the history of Florida cigar lithography, see Narciso Menocal, *The Tobacco Industry in Cuba and Florida: Its Golden Age in Lithography and Architecture* (Coral Gables, Fla.: Cuban National Heritage, 1995).

41. Gerald E. Poyo, "Key West and the Cuban Ten Year's War." *Florida Historical Quarterly* 57, no. 3 (January 1979); L. Glenn Westfall, *Key West: Cigar City U.S.A.* (Key West, Fla.: Historic Key West Preservation Board, 1984).

42. Bure and Moore, *Tampa;* Campbell, *The Cigar Industry;* Grismer, *Tampa: A History of the City of Tampa;* Harner, *A Pictorial History;* Westfall, *Don Vicente Martínez Ybor.*

43. This was reflected in Tampa publications: *Tampa, Florida's Greatest City; Tampa's Hillsborough County, 1918–19.*

44. Mormino and Pozetta "'The Reader Lights the Candle'"; Pérez, "Reminiscences of a Lector" *Florida Historical Quarterly* 53, no. 4. The reader was found internationally among cigar workers. For Puerto Rico, see Angel Quintero Rivera, "Socialist and Cigarmaker: Artisan's Proletarianzation in the Making of the Puerto Rican Working Class," *Latin American Perspectives* 10, no. 2 (1983): 3. The fortunes of the Puerto Rican cigar industry were almost inverse to those of Cuba in timing, and generated their own struggles. See Juan José Baldrich, *Los que sembraron la no-siembra* (San Juan, Puerto Rico: Ediciones Huracán, 1988).

45. Hewitt, "The Voice of Virile Labor"; Hewitt, "Varieties of Voluntarism."

46. Susan Greenbaum, "Afro-Cubans in Exile: Tampa, Florida, 1886–1984," *Cuban Studies/Estudios Cubanos* 15, no. 1 (Winter 1985); Winston James, *Holding Aloft the*

Banner of Ethiopia: Caribbean Radicalism in Early Twentieth-Century America (London: Verso, 1998); Nancy Raquel Mirabal, "Telling Silences and Making Community: Afro-Cubans in Ybor City and Tampa, 1899–1915" in Lisa Brock and Digna Castañeda Fuertes, eds., *Between Race and Empire: Afro-Americans and Cubans before the Cuban Revolution* (Philadelphia: Temple University Press, 1998).

47. This is reflected in *Florida's Cuban Heritage Trail/Herencia cubana en la Florida* (Tallahassee: Florida Department of State, n.d.).

48. We have little reference to Afro-Cubans in the earlier Key West period. It is interesting to note, however, that Mario Sanchez' paintings *The Reader and the Cigar Makers* and *Manungo's Diablito Dancers* depict Afro-Cubans. See Kathryn Hall Proby, *Mario Sanchez: Painter of Key West Memories* (Key West, Fla.: Southernmost Press, 1981).

49. Poyo, *With All and for the Good of All*; Poyo, "Evolution of Cuban Separatist Thought;" Poyo, "The Anarchist Challenge;" Glenn L. Westfall, *Don Vicente Martínez Ybor: The Man and His Empire: Development of the Clear Havana Industry in Cuba and Florida in the Nineteenth Century* (New York: Garland, 1987).

50. Stubbs, "Political Idealism."

51. Behind Menéndez was an earlier history of Canary Islander migration into tobacco in Cuba.

52. Cullman and Cullbro were featured in *Cigar Aficionado*, Spring 1993 and Autumn 1994.

53. *Cigar Aficionado*, August 1997, 124–37.

54. *Cigar Aficionado*, Summer 1994.

55. *Cigar Aficionado*, June 1999.

56. *Cigar Aficionado*, October 1999, 216.

57. *Cigar Aficionado*, April 1999.

58. *Cigar Aficionado*, Autumn 1993.

59. Guillermo Cabrera Infante took up this theme in 1985.

60. Deschodt and Morane, *The Cigar*, 161.

61. *Cigar World*, Winter 1998/1999: 7.

62. *Cigar Aficionado*, Spring 1993.

63. *Cigar Aficionado*, Summer 1994.

64. *Cigar World*, Winter 1994/1995.

65. Habana 2000, along with its earlier strain Habana '92, were both featured in Espino Marrero, *Cuban Cigar Tobacco*. An earlier work on tobacco agronomy is Eumelio Espino Marrero and Torrecilla Guerra, *El tabaco cubano: recursos fito-genéticos* (Madrid: Instituto Cubano del Libro Editorial Científico-Técnica, 1999).

66. *Cigar World 2000*, Winter 1999/2000.

III

SOCIAL SCIENCES AND LAW

The three essays in this section probe Ortiz's conceptualization of the process of transculturation, as well as his interdisciplinary approach to informing it. Enrique S. Pumar focuses on Ortiz's legacy to the social sciences. To Pumar, the underlying structure of *Cuban Counterpoint* anticipates "many of the conclusions and research programs" of contemporary economic sociology and the sociology of development, and hence needs to be acclaimed as a masterpiece in economic sociology. Pumar finds that Ortiz's analysis has policy implications for liberal measures to promote independent agriculture, which, though rooted in the realities of the 1930s, still resonate today.

Fernando Coronil's essay concentrates on *Cuban Counterpoint* and the concept of transculturation. He examines Malinowski's treatment of Ortiz's concepts to probe anthropological theory itself as a transcultural phenomenon, molded by domination and power relations. Coronil highlights Ortiz's originality as a Latin American thinker who managed to present a positive view of the region from within. His theory represents a critical and even tense dialogue with metropolitan or European/Western anthropology.

The methodology of law was another important pillar of Ortiz's intellectual approach. As asserted by Alejandra Bronfman, Ortiz's earlier studies of law were methodically reformist. Although initially inspired by positivism, Ortiz's legal thought was also infused by his interest in the practices of Afro-Cubans and the origins and etiology of crime.

10

Economic Sociology and Ortiz's *Counterpoint*

Enrique S. Pumar

> Sugar is common, unpretentious, undifferentiated. . . . Tobacco may be
> good or bad, but it always strives for individuality.
>
> —Fernando Ortiz[1]

Fernando Ortiz is generally considered one of the most eclectic social scientists in Cuba's history. His notion of transculturation revolutionized the fields of cultural identity and ethnic relations. With regard to race, Ortiz was one of the first sociologists to illustrate how cultural formation combined with social capital to heighten the chances for cultural subsistence among the Afro-Cuban diaspora. In addition, eminent scholars such as Malinowski, Rama, and Portell Vilá, to name a few, have praised his scholarship. More recently, the work of Ortiz is attracting a well-deserved renaissance among ethnographers across academic disciplines, dedicated to the study of identity and nationhood. In Havana, the Fernando Ortiz Foundation houses a group of scholars dedicated to preserving and promoting his legacy and many intellectual contributions.[2]

To be sure, despite the solid reputation of his work among academic elite circles dedicated to the study of culture, it is fair to assert that Ortiz has not received the attention he deserves in other fields. For instance, among contemporary economic sociologists there are rarely any references to his work. Several factors account for this omission. For most of his life, Ortiz resided in Cuba and often found an intellectual outlet in Spain, which means that his work was not diffused as widely in other parts of Europe and North America as it was throughout the Iberian peninsula and Latin America. Most of his intellectual contacts who facilitated the promotion of his work were based in the Hispanic world where he is widely renowned.[3] Ortiz also remained in his native island until the end of his life in 1969. The first decade of the revolution was one of international isolation, marginalization, and segregation for many Cuban intellectuals, whose academic work was brushed aside by the primacy of ongoing political and ideological controversies between Cuba and its neighbors.

Perhaps the most important factor for his unplumbed popularity among some sociologists is that social scientists find it very hard to categorize his work into any single traditional academic discipline. Many still wonder if he should be regarded as an anthropologist or a sociologist, historian or ethnographer, or if he should be even categorized as a social scientist. His appreciation for interdependent academic traditions led him to adopt a multidisciplinary methodology and to investigate diverse issue areas. His work combines historical research and ethnography, with an interpretation of intersubjective meanings rarely displayed by any of his contemporaries. Let's not forget, finally, that the bulk of his scholarship was published at a time when academic disciplines were more entrenched than they are today. The social sciences were dominated by structural-functionalism, and proponents of this position were not very receptive to other nonconforming academic perspectives.[4] His lucid epistemology and the versatility of his formulations are comparable to many classic sociologists or, more recently, with Albert O. Hirschman and Joseph A. Schumpeter.

In this chapter, I call attention to the dimensions of economic sociology in Ortiz scholarship. This is one of the aspects most neglected by students of Ortiz. In particular, I focus my attention on his contribution to the notion of embeddedness. Thanks to the seminal works of Mark Granovetter, and more recently Alejandro Portes, the notion of embeddedness has regained currency in economic sociology today.[5] Through embeddedness, scholars understand that economic behavior and arrangements cannot be separated from the effects of social relations.[6]

My goals in this essay are twofold. First, I will show that Fernando Ortiz anticipated many of the arguments associated with contemporary developments within the literature on economic sociology. His pioneering contribution to embedded social action deserves much closer attention than it has received in sociology thus far. Second, I intend to demonstrate that, contrary to that of contemporary sociologists, his notion of the economics of social relations surpasses the middle-range scope of many recent approaches, and provides valuable insight into the eternal question of levels of development among nations.

I propose to fulfill these tasks by organizing my argument along the following lines. First, as an introductory background, I briefly review the current state of economic sociology to identify its major themes. Second, I measure the merits of Ortiz's scholarship, as illustrated by his masterpiece *Contrapunteo Cubano* (which I call *Counterpoint* hereafter), against the context of the major themes in economic sociology.[7] Third, I examine Ortiz's insights into the problem of national development. The chapter concludes with a recap of the relevance and weight of Ortiz's *Counterpoint* among the social sciences in Cuba and abroad.

ECONOMIC SOCIOLOGY: A REVIEW

The economics of social relations remains a topic of interest among sociologists. Both Marx and Weber made significant contributions to this brand of sociology. Since at least the nineteenth century, every key figure in the discipline of sociology has written at one point or another from an economic sociology perspective.[8] This statement also holds ground in the case of Durkheim's analysis of social integration and anomie. When sociologists wanted to react against the resurgence of neoclassical economics in the 1970s and 1980s, they revisited the work of Karl Polanyi, the Hungarian social scientist who established the substantivist school of economic anthropology.[9] The appeal of Polanyi's approach for contemporary economic sociologists lies in his conception of the self-regulating market as a social construction, meshed in social relations.[10] His critique of neoclassical economic arguments came in very handy to sociologists disgusted with the undersocialized conception of action promoted by microeconomics. In addition, Polanyi's institutional process operates at the same level of analysis as that of the interactionist focus on some neoclassical positions, such as public goods and game theory.[11] This means that Polanyi's critique carries more weight since it was conceived from a parallel analytical scope.

Polanyi conceives the market as an instituted social process embedded and enmeshed in economic and noneconomic institutions.[12] Every market, in his view, consists of reciprocal social relations, political redistribution, and price mechanisms dictated by social forces. Therefore, he viewed an atomistic conception of the self-regulating market, where choices are derived from material calculation and interests, as fallacious. Like Ortiz a few years before him, he analyzes nonindustrial markets from a historical perspective.

However, the similarities between the two scholars cease at this point. Polanyi conceives the development of markets in two well-defined stages. In traditional economies, the effects of market failures were social, since economic forces did not institutionalize market transactions; noneconomic structures predominated in the functioning of markets. On the other hand, more contemporary market arrangements are organized on economic principles. Here, Polanyi distinguishes between nineteenth-century classical liberalism and what he refers to as postwar embedded liberalism.[13] In the latter, the market was permitted to run its course, but the state became the rescuer of last resort to assure the political regime's own survival.

While Polanyi centers his analysis on the question of trade and money exchanges,[14] Ortiz directs his emphasis squarely on the social relations of production. This emphasis provides him several advantages, among them the ability to explore the root causes of inequality without indulging in human subjectivity. His comparative study of crop production makes his brand of sociology more relevant today, given the macro scope of more recent economic sociological theories. In addition, as I will elaborate later on, Ortiz's allegorical comparison of tobacco and sugar production sketches a theory of development and underdevelopment in need of further testing today. To be sure, one of Ortiz's major assertions is to investigate the social effects of production without indulging in vulgar determinism. He often inverts the relation between structure and superstructure and gives scientific prominence to the articulation of knowledge. As Ortiz asserts at one point in the book, "sugar came through the application of scientific alchemy; tobacco's origins are to be found in folklore."[15]

Ortiz disagrees with Polanyi on at least two other conceptual premises. At times, Polanyi gives the impression that exchange is a method of social integration and depicts the notion of reciprocal interests in the market as a self-regulating arrangement.[16] Ortiz, on the other hand, conceives markets as segmented and unequal. Markets are a function of production forces. In developing societies, it is often the case that multiple market arrangements are simultaneously coexisting within one territory. Given the transnational trading regimes usually associated with conditions of underdevelopment, developing markets are more hierarchically organized than what Polanyi conceived. Ortiz summarizes the juxtaposition of market arrangements as follows: "the production of sugar was always a capitalistic venture because of its great territorial and industrial scope. . . . Tobacco, child of the savage Indian and the virgin earth, is a free being."[17] In short, one of the reasons for the need to explore the work of Ortiz more thoroughly today is that he offers a richer historical alternative to the present ethnocentrism in contemporary economic sociology. He offers us the possibility of extending the economic sociological perspective to interpret issues associated with developing societies.

Besides being intimately related with the work of Polanyi, the field of economic sociology today revolves around three major research projects. While it is commonly acknowledged that Harrison White was responsible for reviving a general interest in the sociology of markets, Granovetter defined the basic premise of the contemporary economic sociology paradigm as "the problem of embeddedness" in his trend-setting 1985 article.[18] The article proposes a sophisticated explanation of how social networks penetrate economic transactions, in addition to proposing an elegant critique of the new institutional economics and prisoner dilemma modeling. Granovetter argues that social embeddedness is the process whereby social relations constrain economic action and institutions.[19] In short, the embeddedness view contradicts atomistic arguments of economic preferences and interests. One of the most penetrating insights Granovetter proposes in this article is his divergence with Polanyi's claim that embeddedness is lower in contemporary market societies.[20]

Richard Swedberg identifies two additional intellectual innovations that preoccupy economic sociologists today. These are (1) the structure of different economic organizations and (2) the role of culture in economic life.[21] After reviewing the state of organization literature, Nitin Nohria and Ranjay Gulati conclude, "a central element underlying much of institutional theory is the notion that organizations typically adopt institutionalized practices within their appropriate environment."[22] With regard to culture, Paul DiMaggio concludes in his assessment of the field that "culture plays many roles in economic life: constituting actors and economic institutions, defining the ends and means of action, and regulating the relationship between means and ends."[23]

The purpose of briefly reviewing contemporary economic sociology, and of identifying its major trends, is to set the stage for an interpretation of *Counterpoint* according to the three major themes present in the literature today. Not only did Ortiz discuss these three issues at length sixty-plus years ago, his remarks continue to reveal discerning conclusions about the impact of markets and productions on the course of socioeconomic development.

ECONOMIC SOCIOLOGY AND *COUNTERPOINT*: EMBEDDEDNESS, CULTURE, AND ORGANIZATIONS

According to David Frisby, to understand different traditions in sociology one needs to situate the formulation of ideas within the practical context of their emergence.[24] In the case of *Counterpoint*, its publications coincided with one of the most turbulent and ideologically fragmented periods in the history of Cuba. Ortiz experienced firsthand the effects of political sectarism when his formula for a government of national reconciliation under Grau failed to gain enough elite support by October 1933, mostly because of the mutual suspicion and legacy of resentments among political factions.[25] The medley of political disorder, philosophical rift, and the economic deprivation that dominated the postdepression years on the island, provided the historical background that gave way to the argument in *Counterpoint*. Ortiz was one of several scholars who turned to Cuban history to search for an answer to the despair they witnessed during the interwar years. In the first pages of the book, Ortiz reveals his intention to understand the peculiar historical trajectory of the island nation through the development of crop production. He does not hesitate to assert the centrality of tobacco and sugar in Cuban society. As he states, "the posing and examination of this deep-seated contrast which exists between sugar and tobacco, from their very nature to their social derivations, may throw some new light upon the study of Cuban economy and its historical peculiarities."[26] The transcendence of the truncated 1933 uprising also fosters in Ortiz, as in many of his contemporaries, a disdain for the foreign presence on the island. The uneasy coexistence between contradictory sugar and tobacco productions illustrates the struggle between the foreign and the native in Cuban society. In many respects, it is fair to conclude that the central theme in *Counterpoint* is the tension derived from embedded social relations in sugar and tobacco.

From the outset of *Counterpoint*, Ortiz forewarns the reader about the fact that these two crops do not stand alone throughout the history of Cuba. Their production is embedded in social relations. As he states:

> In the economy of Cuba there are also striking contrasts in the cultivation, the processing, and the human connotations of the two products. Tobacco requires delicate care, sugar can look after itself; the one requires continual attention, the other involves seasonal work; intensive versus extensive cultivation; steady work on the part of a few, intermittent jobs for many; the immigration of whites on the one hand, the slave trade on the other; liberty and slavery; skilled and unskilled labor; hands versus arms; men versus machines; delicacy versus brute force. The cultivation of tobacco gave rise to the smallholdings; that of sugar brought about the great land grants. In their industrial aspects tobacco belongs to the city, sugar to the country. Commercially the whole world is the market for our tobacco, while our sugar has only a single market. . . . The native versus the foreigner. National sovereignty as against colonial status.[27]

The market for sugar cannot be studied without investigating the profound social issues associated with the cultivation of this crop. Sugar production embodies mechanization, mass production, and the legacy of a plantation economy. The hierarchical organization of production in the *central* often translated into a command economic outlook and an undemocratic political culture. The constant demand for cheap labor brought slavery, migration, and multiculturalism to the island. More important, sugar symbolizes a way of life. As Ortiz asserts, sugar represents a larger interest with closed commercial ties to the United States than the primary market for Cuban sugar. Employment for sugar cutters is seasonal, pays little, and requires physical stamina but no formal education. Thus, sugar is a symbol of underdevelopment.

Tobacco, on the other hand, connotes expertise and skillfulness among small or individual growers. The long-standing Cuban tradition of reading to those employed in manufacturing tobacco empowered workers with a long tradition of revolutionary activism. One after another, independence movements recruited tobacco workers to fill their ranks. In addition, the cultivation of this crop requires a yearlong cycle of steady employment. In Cuba, this crop was not produced in large plantations as in Virginia. This means that growers were more in control of their own production cycle, and the industry was subjected to little, if any, foreign control. Many of the growers were also relatively more affluent and self-sufficient than the average sugar worker.

In addition to Ortiz's thinking about the centrality of production in social development, the continuous appeal of this book resides in his innovative discussion of cultural development and organizational isomorphism. The first of these topics is one of the most popular legacies of Ortiz's work. For him, cultural formation results from *transculturation*, a term he introduces in *Counterpoint* to depict the complicated process of transmission and diffusion of culture by different social groups coming to the new world.[28] To this day, *transculturation* captures the process of resettling in a new society more accurately than other terms in the spectrum of immigration discourse. It depicts how social values are the conglomerations of various cultural traditions coming together under one territorial space. In addition, this notion recognizes the transnational nature of population movements, a factor only recently considered in harness by sociologists.[29]

Transculturation is the force behind Cubans' unique national identity. However, it is important to bear in mind that in *Counterpoint*, Ortiz emphasizes another aspect of this process as well. Transnational population movements bring with them new modes of production that alter the social complexity of the host country. In other words, social embeddedness of production is one of the features that most resonates in the process of transculturation. Once again, we witness how Ortiz accentuates the question of enmeshed economic and social relations and the centrality of production in the social character of nations. For instance, with regard to the transculturation of tobacco, he has this to say:

> The history of tobacco affords an example of the most extraordinary processes of transculturation, by reason of the rapidity and extent to which the use of this plant spread . . . and the very profound change operated in its social significance as it passed from the cultures of the New World to the Old.[30]

If there is one factor where Ortiz could be condemned with regard to the transculturation, it is that he did not sufficiently problematize this notion in *Counterpoint*. While Ortiz speaks very clearly of the economic impact of the central characters in the history of Cuba, he neglects to examine the limitations of transculturation as a socializing process. Can we assume that transculturation diminishes or exacerbates social tensions in Cuba? If this process is ongoing, can one account for its variation, or is it a constant? Scholars need to address these and other similar questions for this concept to more profoundly resonate in social science discourse.

With respect to organizations, Ortiz is less forthcoming in *Counterpoint*. He treats the notion of isomorphism as a by-product of the reproduction of relations of production. Throughout his exhaustive contrast between tobacco and sugar, he assumes that different social actors engaged in production behave alike, pending their position in the hierarchical production chain associated with each crop. There is no careful differentiation of the characters among *vegueros* or *hacendados*. While this level of generality may hold at a macro level, beyond the surface, there are marked differences among actors even if they are engaged in the same branch of production. Other authors described different mechanisms of cultivation and labor arrangements throughout the evolution of the sugar industry.[31] One of the most measurable intellectual legacies of Ortiz's *Counterpoint* is the assertion of the primacy of the market in the organization of production without indulging in political rhetoric. This is one of the few classic social science texts in Cuba where the topic of politics occupied a secondary role. After *Counterpoint*, the market became a topic of persistent analysis in many of the classic social science texts published in Cuba.

Meanwhile, the study of tobacco and sugar opens several other lines of research for those scholars interested in organizational analysis. I'll mention two to illustrate this point. One possible research course is the relation between transculturation and organizational development. The reader of *Counterpoint* will be curious about the relationship between transculturation and the promotion of entrepreneurship. Here Ortiz offers an alternative to Schumpeter's view. Rather than emphasizing the functions of individual entrepreneurs in society, as Schumpeter does, Ortiz sees the process of transculturation as one of the engines behind the diffusion of social initiatives and innovations. This insight has been corroborated by the recent findings in the literature on enclave economies, which illustrates that the social capital that immigrants bring along often translates into economic resources and opportunities.

Ortiz further suggests another line of organizational research. Contrary to the findings of Osterman[32] and Doeringer and Piore,[33] Ortiz demonstrates that the primary reason for labor segmentation among developing societies is not necessarily the peculiarities of the labor market, but rather the social organization of production. Sugar requires a very different labor market than the specialized and more skill-intensive conditions of tobacco. As he asserts on page 65 of *Counterpoint*:

> Sugar was an anonymous industry, the mass labor of slaves or gangs of hired workmen, under the supervision of capital's overseers. Tobacco has created a middle class, a free bourgeoisie; sugar has created two extremes, slaves and masters, the proletarian and the rich.[34]

The analysis of Ortiz's discussion on embeddedness, cultural organization, and organizational developments demonstrates the enduring relevance of *Counterpoint* for contemporary economic sociology. Not only did Ortiz foresee many of the recent lines of research in the field, but some of his ideas could develop new research programs as well. Although I will not address the innovative application of the historical comparative method in Ortiz's work, it is worth mentioning that another of his assertions in *Counterpoint* marks one of the first instances in which the comparative methodology is systematically utilized throughout the social sciences in Cuba. In addition, judging from some of the economic sociology works published in recent years, the comparative analysis could still be considered a methodological novelty.

Having established the relevance of Ortiz's thinking for sociologists today, I would like to turn to a more interpretative posture to analyze how Ortiz frames the discussion of development and underdevelopment, and what possible solutions can be derived from his work.

TOBACCO (DEVELOPMENT)
AND SUGAR (UNDERDEVELOPMENT)

As I alluded to earlier, Ortiz depicts the contradictory social embeddedness of tobacco and sugar as the proper avenue from which to explain the despair of developing societies such as Cuba. These two crops connote two distinct modes of production and concomitant social relations. They also symbolize the struggle between the forces of progress and the legacy of tradition. It is clear that for Ortiz, some of the attributes characterized by his depiction of tobacco, in particular the native, skilled, and laborious relations of production, are a remedy for underdevelopment; whereas sugar, the traditional creature, correlates with the unfortunate reality among developing nations struggling to outweigh the effects of foreign interest, dependency, unskilled labor-intensive markets, and capital domination. Ortiz underlines the distinction between these two alternative paths of development when he states:

> In the production of tobacco intelligence is the prime factor; we have already observed that tobacco is liberal, not to say revolutionary. In the production of sugar it is a question of power; sugar is conservative, if not reactionary.[35]

Another aspect of the formula recommended by Ortiz for embarking on a sustained course of development consists of gearing state policies to support native technologies requiring specialized labor rich in human capital, as is the case with tobacco production. In addition, a dedicated cadre of producers who enjoy a certain degree of freedom to innovate must be adjoined to this equation. Rather than focusing on bilateral trading relations, Ortiz also favors diversified trading partners to override the disproportionate influences from one of the trading counterparts. Finally, Ortiz calls for an economy dominated by multiple small and medium-size holdings of roughly similar proportion.

Throughout the argument in *Counterpoint*, Ortiz emphasizes two related features, which underwrite the predominance of sugar despite its adverse effects on national economies. The first of these features is the imposition of sugar production by foreign interests.[36] Sugar, as Ortiz emphasizes time and time again, denotes foreign origin, character, and economy. The introduction of the sugar crop was promoted by the colonial administration and was later sustained by a close network of transnational interests among foreign financiers, underwriters, and absentee landlords vertically entangled with the local nobility. In the words of Ortiz, "the foreign control of the central is not only external but internal as well. To use the language in vogue today, it has a vertical structure."[37] Once again, this statement outlines the intricate relation between social forces and the configuration of production. One cannot distill market structures without accounting for the social interests that sustain them. The transnational aspects of Ortiz's embeddedness argument foresaw some tenets of the dependency paradigm by twenty plus years.

The other element of foreignness beneath the imposition of dependency controls is the adverse side effects associated with the status of being an offshore producer in the world economy. Ortiz makes the interesting observation that, as the sugar industry grew in magnitude in response to international demands, foreign entanglement became more solidified. In many respects, this assertion is reminiscent of one of the basic premises of dependent development; that is, relative prosperity does not translate in economic sovereignty. As Ortiz describes it, one of the effects of the great depression was to replace mercantilism with "supercapitalism." [38]

Accordingly, foreign controls exercised over the Cuban economy became more closely knotted with financial capital. Once again, Ortiz does not refrain his analysis to the economic aspects of this question alone. Rather, he goes on to describe the effects of this shift on the social composition of sugar producers. In his view, the insertion of financial capital into the (sugar) economy resulted in the gradual disappearance of tenant farmers, and the eventual proletarianization of the sugar worker.

In sum, Ortiz's notion of embeddedness surpasses the predominant middle-range scope of some of the current advocates of this term in contemporary sociology. The range of this economic sociology is transnational. His goal is to be able to provide a heuristic interpretation of the causes of underdevelopment among nations. In doing so, he again anticipates many of the arguments proposed much later by economic sociologists. His notion of how transnational networks between foreign and domestic interests function precedes many of the arguments of the dependency movement of the 1960s.

The economic sociology exposition in *Counterpoint* leaves the reader with a fatalistic conclusion about the prospects for development in Cuba and other neighboring societies. Ortiz provides us with a reasonable explanation for the fate of developing nations. Market structures initially inserted by colonial administrations, and later sustained by domestic and international interlocks, outweighed infant industries. The implication of this argument is that developing nations must provide support for middle-class local producers with progressive orientation. The overwhelming foreign presence throughout Latin America during the 1930s cultivated a sense of nationalism in Ortiz, which led to his critical reexamination of the configuration of production structures. His inference, like many other arguments in *Counterpoint,* still shapes subsequent generations of Cuban intellectuals.

CONCLUSION

This chapter departs from the assumption that Don Fernando Ortiz's writings have been tragically overlooked by many contemporary sociologists. This is particularly the case in economic sociology. This basic premise motivated me to demonstrate two points. First, Ortiz anticipated many of the conclusions and research programs in contemporary economic sociology. I demonstrated this postulate by identifying three major themes in current literature and then discussing Ortiz's contributions to each. Through my discussion of his depiction of the notion of embeddedness, I have made references to how Ortiz proposed similar lines of research than more contemporary proponents of the sociology of development.

Second, I set out to demonstrate that Ortiz's social structural position continues to be useful among scholars. This is the case for two reasons. From the start, Ortiz develops a perspective that is more macro in character than the interactionist scope of many economic sociologists today. Ortiz also offers an alternative point of departure to analyze social relations. Rather than focusing on exchange like Polanyi, he underlines the importance of relations of production without vulgar conjectures.

NOTES

1. Fernando Ortiz, *Cuban Counterpoint: Tobacco and Sugar* (Durham, N.C.: Duke University Press, 1995), 24.

2. Another indication of the renewed interest in Ortiz's work is the recent republication of *Cuban Counterpoint* by Duke University Press.

3. In 1911, Ortiz joined the American Sociological Society. His next, and last, academic trip outside the Hispanic world was in 1953 when he attended two international academic congresses, one in Oxford and the other in Vienna. See Araceli Garcia Carranza, Norma Suarez Suarez, and Alberto Quesada, *Cronologia Fernando Ortiz* (Havana: Fundación Fernando Ortiz, 1996).

4. Said, Edward W. 1993. *Culture and Imperialism.* New York: Alfred A. Knopf.

5. Mignolo, Walter D. 1993. "Colonial and Postcolonial Discourses: Cultural Critique or Academic Colonialism?" *Latin American Research Review* 28 (3): 120–31.

6. Granovetter, "Economic Action," 481–82.

7. Malinowsli, Bonislaw. 1943. "The Pan-African Problem of Culture Contact." *American Journal of Sociology* 48 (6): 649–65.

8. For an informative overview of the different traditions in economic sociology and their intellectual history, see Richard Swedberg, "Major Traditions of Economic Sociology," *Annual Review of Sociology* 17 (1991): 251–76.

9. Mark Granovetter, "The Nature of Economic Relationships," in Richard Swedberg, ed., *Explorations in Economic Sociology* (New York: Russell Sage Foundation, 1993), 4–5.

10. Alberto Martinelli, "The Economy as an Institutional Process," *Telos* 73 (1987): 131–46.

11. For an accessible review of this literature, see Avinash Dixit and Barry Nelabuff, *Thinking Strategically* (New York: Norton, 1991).

12. See Karl Polanyi, Conrad Arensberg, and Harry Pearson, eds., *Trade and Markets in the Early Empires* (New York: Free Press, 1957).

13. Karl Polanyi, *The Great Transformation* (Boston: Beacon, 1944).

14. Karl Polanyi, "The Economy as Instituted Process," in Karl Polanyi et al., eds., *Trade Market in the Early Empires* (New York: Free Press, 1957).

15. "Global Contagion." 1999. *The New York Times*, February 15, 1999.

16. Ramo, Joshua Cooper. 1998. "The Big Bank Theory and What It Says About the Future of Money." *Time*, Apr. 27.

17. Ortiz, *Cuban Counterpoint*, 56.

18. See note 1.

19. Granovetter, "Economic Action," 481–82.

20. Granovetter, "Economic Action," 482–83.

21. Swedberg, "Major Traditions," 269.

22. Nitin Nohria and Ranjay Gulati, "Firms and Their Environments" in Neil Smelser and Richard Swedberg, eds., *The Handbook of Economic Sociology* (Princeton, N.J.: Princeton University Press, 1994), 540.

23. Paul DiMaggio, "Culture and Economy," 19, 47.

24. David Frisby, *The Alienated Mind* (New York: Routledge, 1992), 1–25.

25. Luis E. Aguilar, *Cuba 1933* (New York: Norton, 1974), 189.

26. Ortiz, *Cuban Counterpoint*, 5.

27. Ortiz, *Cuban Counterpoint*, 6–7.

28. Ortiz, *Cuban Counterpoint*, particularly 97–103.

29. Alejandro Portes, "The Hidden Abode: Sociology as Analysis of the Unexpected," *American Sociological Review* 65 (February 2000): 1–18.

30. Ortiz, *Cuban Counterpoint*, 183.

31. One of the classic works on this aspect of the sugar industry is Manuel Moreno Fraginals, *El Ingenio* (Havana: Editorial de Ciencias Sociales, 1978).

32. Paul Osterman, *Employment Futures: Reorganization, Dislocation, and Public Policy* (New York: Oxford University Press, 1988).

33. Peter Doeringer and Michael Piore, *Internal Labor Markets and Manpower Analysis* (Lexington, Mass.: Heath, 1971).

34. Ortiz, *Cuban Counterpoint*, 65.

35. Ortiz, *Cuban Counterpoint*, 56.

36. Ortiz, *Cuban Counterpoint*, 70.

37. Ortiz, *Cuban Counterpoint*, 63.

38. Ortiz, *Cuban Counterpoint*, 63.

Fernando Ortiz and his parents, Rosendo Ortiz and Josefa Fernández. Havana, 1895.
© María Fernanda Ortiz Herrera.

Ortiz, Ph.D. in Law, University of Madrid, 1901. © María Fernanda Ortiz Herrera.

D. Juan Benejam, Fernando Ortiz's professor in Menorca. © María Fernanda Ortiz Herrera.

Photograph of Miguel de Unamuno dedicated to Ortiz, 1906. © María Fernanda Ortiz Herrera.

Fernando Ortiz with José María Chacón y Calvo, 1925. © María Fernanda Ortiz Herrera.

Fernando Ortiz and members of Okilapkua group at a lecture in the Campoamor Theater. Havana, May 30, 1937. This was the first time that Batá drums were played before a nonreligious public. © María Fernanda Ortiz Herrera.

Fernando Ortiz at the Sociedad Económica de Amigos del País de la Habana in an awards ceremony for students on January 9, 1949. © María Fernanda Ortiz Herrera.

Fernando Ortiz conference on Afrocuban music and dances, celebrated in the Aula Magna at the Universidad de la Habana in 1955. Ortiz with his daughter María Fernanda; Alicia Alonso; Dr. Clemente Inclán, President of Universidad de la Habana; Wilfredo Lam; Félix Dánger, his secretary for several years; Raúl Díaz, Batá drummer; and Mercedita Valdés, among others. © María Fernanda Ortiz Herrera.

Ortiz at his desk, in the library of his house at L and 27 in el Vedado, Havana. © María Fernanda Ortiz Herrera.

Fernando Ortiz at the Institución Hispano-Cubana de Cultura, with professors Charles C. Thompson (Washington), C.L. Haring (Harvard University), Concha Romero James (Unión Panamericana), J. Boch Gimpera (Barcelona), J. Berrien (Rio de Janeiro), G. Arciniegas (Bogotá), and secretary Conchita Fernández standing. Havana, 1941. © María Fernanda Ortiz Herrera.

Inauguration of President Rómulo Gallegos of Venezuela. From left to right: Jorge Mañach, Raúl Roa García, Rómulo Gallegos, Juan Marinello, Fernando Ortiz, and Rómulo Betancourt seated. Caracas, 1948. © María Fernanda Ortiz Herrera.

Fernando Ortiz with his wife María Herrera and his daughter María Fernanda. Christmas, 1945. © María Fernanda Ortiz Herrera.

Ortiz and his wife, María Herrera, with Lydia Cabrera and María Teresa Rojas. Vienna, 1952. © María Fernanda Ortiz Herrera.

Fernando Ortiz with Luis Muñoz Marín, governor of the Estado Libre Asociado de Puerto Rico, 1954. © María Fernanda Ortiz Herrera.

Ortiz with his wife, María Herrera; Alejandro Lipschutz and wife; Julio Le Riverend and wife; Juan Marinello and wife; José Antonio Portuondo and wife; Mariano Rodríguez Solveira; and María Fernanda Ortiz. Havana, 1962. © María Fernanda Ortiz Herrera.

Fernando Ortiz, as always, immersed in books, papers, and manuscripts. © María Fernanda Ortiz Herrera.

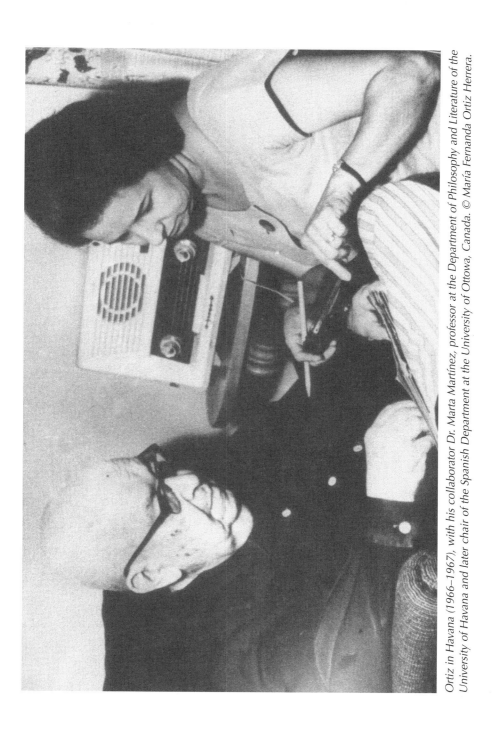

Ortiz in Havana (1966–1967), with his collaborator Dr. Marta Martínez, professor at the Department of Philosophy and Literature of the University of Havana and later chair of the Spanish Department at the University of Ottowa, Canada. © María Fernanda Ortiz Herrera.

Fernando Ortiz with his daughter María Fernanda, during the last years of his life. ©
María Fernanda Ortiz Herrera.

11

Transcultural Anthropology in the Américas (with an Accent)

The Uses of Fernando Ortiz

Fernando Coronil

In *Contrapunteo Cubano*, Ortiz examined Cuban history and culture through a playful counterpoint between tobacco and sugar, the two most important agricultural products in Cuban history since the Spanish conquest. In critical dialogue with metropolitan anthropology, he coined the term *transculturation* in order to examine the dynamics of colonial and neocolonial encounters, and to describe their destructive and creative role in the formation of Cuban culture. This essay is an effort to use *Cuban Counterpoint* to think about the present. I will focus on the concept of transculturation, how it was coined by Ortiz, how it traveled, particularly how it was received by Malinowski, and why I hope to return to Cuba again.

I have begun to develop a project on Cuba, tentatively entitled "Nation and Imagination: Images of Revolution and History," which concerns the politics of visual semantics, or the role that visual images have played in the definition and representation of personal and collective identities, in relation to the Cuban revolution static images. I have collected images such as photos, paintings, bills, stamps, posters, cartoons, and so on. I am particularly interested in the tension between official images of Cuban history and identity, produced for the state, and images produced by individual artists for the public—particularly during this transitional period, when there is an increasing commodification of art, as well as growing contestation concerning the meaning of the "revolution." Through this project, just as through my continuing work on Venezuela, I seek to examine transformations of national and collective identifications in an increasingly globalized context. In this essay, I explore aspects of this *globalizing* world, in part because the study of the images themselves is still nascent, but mostly because I feel that understanding globality is essential for understanding current national and collective imaginings.

This will take me away from the evocative images themselves, as I have begun to delve into the opaque world of derivatives.

In effect, this concern with the links between specific texts and practices and larger historical forces is one of the reasons I am going back to Ortiz. He interests me not only because of his many insights on Cuba but because his work offers a perspective on the interaction between national and global transformations that helps develop the critique of Eurocentrism in three ways. First, his analysis of Cuban culture presents an appreciative view of the Americas *from* the Americas that questions the usual stories of modernity as the heroic epic of a self-contained and self-produced Europe. Second, his work engages with and transforms metropolitan theory and allows us to see that theory itself need not be treated just as a European or Western achievement, but as a transcultural product. Third, his approach helps bridge the persistent gap between political economy and culture, a gap that has been further widened, I believe, by the divide between modernist and postmodernist approaches, and provides a model for analyzing the dynamic interaction between cultural texts and historical contexts.

As I hope will become evident, through Ortiz I am seeking inspiration to explore an emerging landscape. With this chapter, I wish to trace a few tentative lines in this direction. If I were to represent this chapter visually—you already know why I am thinking visually—I would choose to represent it as a Magritte painting, a painting that would have an image of an academic paper—I leave to Magritte's imagination to decide how to do that—and below it a text would say, "Ceci n'est pas un presentation." It would not be the "real pipe" or even its image, but a pipe-in-the-making, perhaps a pipe-seed, if such a thing exists.

To provide a clearer idea of how I plan to explore this landscape, let me give you a sense of what I find exciting. As I begin to do fieldwork in Cuba and continue my ongoing research in Venezuela, I continually encounter a growing gap between our analytical categories and the world we study. One of the sources for this gap or methodological inadequacy, I believe, is our disciplinary neglect of what is generally called "the economy." One of the unintended effects of the recent posts and turns (linguistic, historic, etc.) has been that our growing attention to phenomena that readily lend themselves to modes of analysis that draw on the image of the world as a text has led to the reinscription of the separation between "culture" and "political economy." As social geographer Doreen Massey has noted, "in the move towards a greater engagement with the social and the cultural which itself was part of wider and positive rejection of a previous economism, we have moved away from looking seriously at the economy at all." As a result, we tend to treat economic activities not as one set of discursive practices among many, but as facts. When we look at the economy, we often treat it as factual background in the naturalized manner that economists talk about it.

This concern was brought home to me in January 2001 in Cuba, when I attended a conference called "Globalization and the Problems of Development." The meeting, organized by Cuban economists, was called by Fidel Castro as an effort to understand the changes that are taking place in the world today. It lasted five days, from 10 A.M. till midnight, and attracted the constant attendance of Fidel Castro and over five hundred delegates from all over the world, plus several hundred Cubans. I found it remarkable that all these people, including Fidel Castro, despite their different perspectives, national origins, and languages, could listen and talk to each other during five extremely long days; and most people, including Castro, attended regularly from morning to midnight. I feel that part of what made this meeting in Cuba possible was not just shared thematic concerns but a shared conceptual language, the language of economics.

While I learned a lot in the meetings, I found this language at once empowering and limiting, a low common denominator that reproduced rather than examined the dominant assumptions. The papers and discussions reminded me of Goethe's complaint about gray descriptions of a vibrant green world.

Despite the flatness of its language, however, the meeting made me feel envious, for at least all of these people managed to engage in lively discussions, foregrounded big problems rather than narrow issues, and discussed them with extraordinary intensity, with a sense of urgency. In this respect, the meeting intensified my concern that our accounts may indeed be less gray, even brilliantly green, but that this achievement frequently occurs through a focus on individual trees, at the expense of our ability to see the forest of which they are part, the global landscape which surrounds us all.

In his own time, Ortiz produced *Cuban Counterpoint* as a reaction against the dark politics of his day, as well as in response to "gray" economic accounts of Cuban history. Seeking inspiration in Ortiz, this chapter stands, shakily, as it were, on three uneven legs. The first will offer a brief description of Ortiz's use of transculturation in *Cuban Counterpoint*. The second will discuss how transculturation was received by Malinowski. The third, the longest and also the most speculative, is an attempt to chart globality. Unlike the previous two, which summarize extensive research, the latter consists of some speculations about a subject I find puzzling and elusive. The three sections, united by Ortiz's spirit, explore a hunch. If, building on Ortiz, what I have called a transcultural anthropology is going to be as useful a tool in my work in Cuba today, I must open it up to exchanges with theoretical reflections produced elsewhere, including the visual images I seek to study.

FIRST LEG: *CUBAN COUNTERPOINT*

Cuban Counterpoint was published in 1940 when sixty-year-old Fernando Ortiz was at the height of his creative activity and Cuba was at the end of a tumultuous decade marked by numerous ruptures: domestic upheavals routinely arbitrated by the United States; sharp swings in its U.S.-dependent economy; the collapse of a short-lived revolutionary civilian regime in 1933, which Ortiz had supported; the consolidation of the army's power under Fulgencio Batista, who ruled Cuba until the revolution of 1959 (except for eight years); the defeat of the Spanish Republic, which Ortiz had supported; and the rise of fascism throughout Europe.

Written in this dark political context, *Cuban Counterpoint* was the product of a career that sought to interpret Cuban society, analyze the sources of its "backwardness," and extol the distinctive aspects of its culture. I cannot herein trace the evolution of his thought. Suffice it to say that his first book, *Los negros brujos* (*The Black Sorcerers*), published in 1906 when Ortiz was twenty-six years old, focused on the conditions that promoted criminality and "backward" beliefs among practitioners of *brujería* (sorcery) in Cuba. The book was framed by evolutionary positivist theories and by the biological reductionism of the Italian criminologist Cesare Lombroso, who prefaced it. In contrast, *Cuban Counterpoint* embraces a conception of race as a social construction, and presents a historical interpretation of Cuban culture that seeks to appreciate its different cultural traditions.

Cuban Counterpoint is divided into two complementary, counterpoint sections written in contrasting styles. The first is a relatively brief allegorical tale of Cuban history narrated as a counterpoint between tobacco and sugar. This is a rather conventional essay that provides masses of information about the history of tobacco and sugar in Cuba.

The allegorical essay is the core of the book, which is based on a playful counterpoint between sugar and tobacco, modeled on medieval Spanish poet Juan Ruiz's allegorical poem about the contest between lent and carnival, and inspired by Cuban popular traditions. It includes the antiphonal prayers of the liturgies of both whites and blacks, the erotic controversy in dance measures of the rumba, the versified counterpoint of peasants and urban Afro-Cubans.[1] This part is deceptively simple. It is as if, through his playful evocation of the pleasures associated with sugar and tobacco's consumption, Ortiz wishes to seduce us into enjoying the text with sensuous abandon. Yet it is also as if, through his telling of a history of colonial and neocolonial domination, he wishes us to read Cuban history the way he reads tobacco and sugar: as a complex hieroglyph that invites constant decoding.

Ortiz opens this section by introducing tobacco and sugar as "the two most important personages in the history of Cuba."[2] He emphasizes their contrasting properties. Let me give you a taste of Ortiz's writing:

> Sugar cane lives for years, the tobacco plant only a few months. The former seeks the light, the latter shade; day and night, sun and moon. Food and poison,

waking and drowsing, energy and dream, delight of the flesh and delight of the spirit, sensuality and thought, the satisfaction of an appetite and the contemplation of a moment's illusion, calories of nourishment and puffs of fantasy.

Ortiz, however, soon complicates this description. As metaphorical constructs that condense a multiplicity of meanings, he makes tobacco and sugar stand for themselves, as agricultural products, as well as for the changing conditions under which they are produced. Tobacco comes to represent a native plant from which is made a product of great individuality and uniqueness, but also relations of production marked by domestic control over the labor process, individual craftsmanship, and the flexible rhythms of seasonal time. Sugar, on the other hand, represents not only a generic product derived from an imported plant but also industrial capitalist relations of production that reduce people to commodities, homogenize social relations and products, and subject labor to the impersonal discipline of machine production and to the fixed routines of mechanical time. Symbols both of commodities and of productive relations, tobacco and sugar become defined reflexively by the conditions of production that they represent. This reciprocal interplay between products and their generative historical contexts constitutes a second counterpoint. As both products come under the impact of the capitalist forces, they become less differentiated and their attributes converge. They represent not only distinctive qualities or identities but also their mutability under changing conditions.

Thus, the initial contrasts between tobacco and sugar—which emphasize such critical oppositions as between indigenous/foreign, black and white, tradition/modernity, national independence/foreign dependence, Europe and America—come to have unexpected alignments that destabilize notions of fixed identity. While at the beginning of the book these characterizations are described almost in Lombrosian fashion as deriving from the "biological distinction" between tobacco and sugar,[3] later they unfold not as fixed qualities but as historical, hybrid products themselves. Tobacco is variously linked to the native (as an indigenous plant), to the European (as cultivated by white small holders), to the uniquely Cuban (as Cuban made Cigars), and to the imperial (as the U.S.-controlled cigarette industry). Similarly, sugar's attributes also change: It is seen both as an enslaving force identified with foreign domination as well as with the vital energy associated with Afro-Cuban labor. As paradigmatic metaphors, they acquire new meanings by being placed within a syntagmatic structure through which they express a changing historical flow.

At the end, what becomes important is the way history is made, not the biological composition of its main "actors." Except for certain aspects of their gendering, there is little that remains essential about them, for their biological attributes are mediated by social activity and modified by evolving patterns of production and consumption. As we come to the contemporary period, the playful contrasts between tobacco and sugar are reduced by the homogenizing force of capital's growing domination over Cuban society and culture.

The second part of the book, the historical essay, begins with an unusual introduction of close to seven pages divided into two chapters, one of which has one paragraph where he introduces the term "transculturation." Contrasting it with the unidirectional and static denotations of the term acculturation, Ortiz suggests that transculturation provides a more dynamic framework to understand cultural transformations, or, as he calls it, "the extremely complex transmutations of culture in all domains either in the economic or in the institutional, legal, ethical, religious, artistic, linguistic, psychological, sexual, or other aspects of its life." Ortiz explains that transculturation suggests two phases, the loss or uprooting of a culture ("deculturation") and the creation of a new culture ("neoculturation"), thus making visible the destruction of cultures as well as the creativity of cultural encounters.

While in the allegorical section of the book he introduced tobacco and sugar as the main personages of Cuban history, in this theoretical introduction to the historical chapters, he asserts that "The real history of Cuba" is the history of the "intermeshed transculturations" of the array of "human groups" that have populated the island over its history, from Indians to contemporary immigrants.

This shift from commodities to people as well as the brevity and placement of this theoretical introduction here, after he has demonstrated how he uses the term *transculturation*, suggests that for Ortiz the significance of transculturation is to be discerned through its use rather than formal definition. In the earlier section Ortiz had shown the workings of transculturation through a highly metaphorical treatment of the dynamic interactions of tobacco and sugar throughout Cuban history. I argue that by treating tobacco and sugar as fetish-things and using their fetish-power to enchant reality (à la Benjamin) rather than to demystify it, as in most Marxist treatments of fetishism, his fetishized rendering of Cuban culture actually resulted in a counterfetishistic interpretation that challenged essentialist understandings of Cuban history. By treating tobacco and sugar not as mere things but as social actors, Ortiz in effect manages to bring them back to the social world that creates them, resocializes them as it were, and in so doing illuminates the society that has given rise to them. The relationships concealed through the real appearance of commodities as independent forces become visible once commodities are treated as what they are—social things impersonating autonomous actors.

Without referring to parties, groups, or personalities, Ortiz depicts the dynamics of colonial and neocolonial Cuba, the malleable loyalties and identities of its major actors, the provisional character of its arrangements and institutions, and the absence of control over its productive relations. He had seen how no political principle was secure; nationalists asked the U.S. ambassador to intervene, procivilians allied themselves with the military, advocates of honesty became masters of corruption. In Ortiz's narrative, no names need to be mentioned, for tobacco and sugar act as a mirror in which one could see reflected familiar social identities.

SECOND LEG: TRANSCULTURAL
ANTHROPOLOGY—MALINOWSKI AND ORTIZ

Now I want to discuss Malinowski's reaction to Ortiz's book in his introduction in order to examine a second counterpoint, not between tobacco and sugar but between Ortiz and Malinoswki, and suggest that this counterpoint reveals a process of transculturation at the level of theory formation itself.

Just as it is reasonable to assume that Ortiz hoped to receive international validation by having Malinowski introduce his book, we may surmise that Malinowski sought to consolidate his own reputation by supporting, while aligning with his own position, the work of a noted anthropologist from the periphery. Malinowski's introduction reflects the tension between his two aims. At one level, Malinowski highlights the importance and originality of the book, offers an appreciative exegesis of the book's argument as he understood it, and recognizes the validity of the term *transculturation*. He declares in the introduction that he will use it ever after.

At another level, however, the introduction assimilates Ortiz's project into Malinowski's own, blunting its critical edge and diminishing its originality. This assimilation takes place through three related moves, which I can only describe here briefly. First, Malinowski aligns Ortiz's transculturation with his own ideas concerning cultural contact, even citing his own work to indicate that it anticipated Ortiz's argument. Second, he defines Ortiz as a functionalist, despite the fact that there was every indication that this was not the case. Third, he reads *Cuban Counterpoint*, literally as a book on tobacco and sugar, as material objects, without attending to their complex cultural structure as commodities and to the critical use Ortiz made of this complexity. It must be remembered that Malinowski saw himself as no ordinary anthropologist, but as one who combined literary sensitivity with theoretical ambition—he aspired to be the "Conrad of anthropology" (not Kottack, but Joseph). In Malinowski's introduction, there is little receptivity to a reading of *Cuban Counterpoint* as a critical intervention in Cuban historiography and, least of all, as a text that could develop metropolitan anthropology. He reads *transculturation* narrowly as a technical term that expresses certain dynamism in cultural exchanges, not as a critical category intended to reorient both the ethnography of the Americas and anthropological theory.

I think Malinowski's contradictory attitude toward Ortiz's work is confirmed by the fact that despite his promise to use transculturation ever after, in the multiple articles and books that he published after 1940, he only used this term twice.

Elsewhere I have discussed in detail how Ortiz's ideas have traveled, showing how the reception of transculturation has been marked by remarkable silences and omissions. Here I wish to build on Edward Said's plea that we read the formation of identities and cultures contrapuntally in order to suggest the possible presence of Ortiz's ideas in Malinowski's growing acceptance of a more dynamic conception of cultural change. Critical of the tendency to view identities and cultures as self-fashioned and essential, Said concludes *Culture and Imperialism* by offering, with a sense of urgency, a contrapuntal perspectivism:

> Survival in fact is about the connections between things, in Eliot's phrase, reality cannot be deprived of the "other echoes [that] inhabit the garden." According to Said: It is more rewarding and more difficult to think concretely and sympathetically, contrapuntally, about others than only about "us."[4]

If transculturation is indeed a two-way process, could we find Ortiz's echo in Malinowski's evolving ideas about cultural change? I think that in the care that Malinowski took to contain *Cuban Counterpoint* within functionalist anthropology, perhaps we can observe certain ambivalence, a veiled desire to domesticate its power. I read this ambivalence as a tension between denial and disavowal, between totally repressing and fleetingly recognizing Ortiz's originality as an ethnographer, an originality that challenged metropolitan assumptions about "home" and "abroad," "science" and "fiction," "civilized" and "savage cultures." Ortiz looked at Cuba, his "home," not from a detached Archimedean point, as Malinowski demanded in the Argonauts, but from within; his integral vision of the whole was developed by being *in* it and *of* it. As an intellectual from the periphery, developing a critical perspective from within did not preclude, but rather was conditioned by, a view from without. Yet his critical distance entailed a critique of distance and of the view from afar. Detachment was thus not the opposite of commitment but its necessary condition. Implicitly challenging the notion of the detached observer, his work encourages anthropologists and intellectuals, at the center or at the periphery, to recognize our position; the historicity of what Walter Mignolo has theorized as "the locus of enunciation."[5] With particular urgency in postcolonial societies, this task involves taking a critical stance with respect to the available standpoints. Ortiz's work reflects a creative struggle of a postcolonial intellectual to construct rather than merely to occupy a critical locus of enunciation from the margins.

It is difficult for me to imagine that Malinowski did not even glimpse the significance as well as the challenge represented by Ortiz's achievement. If I am right in perceiving a tension in Malinowski's introduction between repressing and fleetingly recognizing Ortiz's contribution, perhaps we may see this tension on the two occasions when Malinowski used the term *transculturation*.

The first appears in Malinowski's attempt to lay the foundations of functionalist anthropology in his *A Scientific Theory of Culture and Other Essays*.[6] In the second chapter, "A Minimum Definition of Science for the Humanist," he briefly mentions the word *transculturation* in a passage that does not attach any significance to the term and does not recognize Ortiz (ironically, the *Oxford English Dictionary* credits Malinowski as introducing this neologism in this book and does not distinguish it from *acculturation*, which was Ortiz's reason for coining it).

In striking contrast to Malinowski's minimal use of *transculturation* in this canon-setting book, in the last article he wrote before his death in 1942, "The Pan-African Problem of Culture Contact,"[7] he mentions the term several times, fully crediting Ortiz and referring to him as "the great Cuban scholar," one of the most passionate friends of the Africans in the New World, and a very effective spokesman of their cultural value and sponsor of their advancement. In this article, Malinowski takes an unusually strong critical stance with respect to "the onslaught of white civilization on native cultures." In response to the ravages of colonialism, Malinowski makes an extraordinary proposal: the establishment in Africa of "an equitable system of segregation, of independent autonomous development."[8]

How to explain Malinowski's exceptional use of Ortiz's transculturation, his emotional denunciation of colonial destruction, his strong critique of white civilization, his proposal for empowering Africans at this time? We may find a clue to this puzzle in the way Malinowski justified his proposal for a system of "autonomous" African development:

> Speaking as a European, and a Pole at that, I should like to place here as a parallel and paradigm the aspirations of European nationality, though not of nationalism. In Europe, we are members of oppressed or subject nationalities, and Poland was in that category for one hundred and fifty years, since its first partition, and has again been put there through Hitler's invitation do not desire anything like fusion with our conquerors and masters. Our strongest claim is for segregation in terms of full cultural autonomy that does not even need to imply political independence. We claim only to have the same scale of possibilities, the same right of decision as regards our destiny, our civilization, our careers, and our mode of enjoying life.[9]

In this unusual statement, Malinowski places himself in the text, but this time not as an impartial observer standing on an Archimedean point outside history, as in his early texts, or as a concerned anthropologist, as in some of his later writings, but as a positioned historical actor, a kindred victim of history's atrocities. A decentered and fragmented Europe seems to have enabled Malinowski to locate himself *in it*, to *be of it*, to speak *from it*. It is as if at the zenith of his life, the advance of fascism in Europe, the occupation of Poland, the destruction of his own "home," had made him receptive to the claims and experience of other oppressed groups. At that moment, he was able to acknowledge Ortiz, to fulfill, at the end, the promise he once made him. Malinowski's acknowledgment suggests how Ortiz's ideas helped him view cultural transformations from a nonimperial perspective.

As we seek useful theories to understand today's world, Malinowski's reception of Ortiz's ideas raises critical questions concerning the relationship between theory production, understood as self-critical forms of thought produced anywhere, and canon formation. It suggests that while theory formation is often a transcultural process, the canonization of theory is fundamentally a power-laden metropolitan operation that, through silencing and selective appropriation, conceals the complicity between knowledge and power. Yet even canons, as this example shows, often bear the traces of their historical formation and are inhabited by subaltern echoes.

Today, just as much as in the forties, when no place can be safe from history's horrors or innocent of its effects, it is necessary to place knowledge at the service of decolonization. The recognition of the existence of a dynamic exchange between dominant and subaltern knowledge may enable us to move beyond canonical social sciences toward "transcultural social sciences"—that is, social sciences open to their own decolonization through worldwide transactions between centers and borders, the dominant and the subaltern.

Cuban Counterpoint was published in 1940, at a time when "nations" and "development" were fundamental categories; within this cultural landscape, Ortiz explored how tobacco and sugar had been and could continue to be, the basis of Cuban nationality. This book has circulated, until recent years, in a world divided into modern and backward nations and socialist and capitalist camps; for so-called backward or postcolonial nations, capitalism and socialism offered not only different visions of society but different paths to modernity.

Now we face a world where cultural differences and political inequalities cannot be mapped in terms of old polarities. The second world has drastically contracted and transformed, while the first world is decentering and diversifying. Third world "development" programs of neoliberal design are accelerating the fractures within and among the nations of the "periphery." A number of intimately related processes, in which globalizing forms of capital accumulation and communication are both met with transnationalizing and reconfigured nationalist responses, have unsettled certainties associated with the belief in modernity.

In this new context, does the concept of transculturation hold some use? Ortiz used it in narratives that show the brutal force of colonizing powers as well as the play of human creativity in the making of history. While Ortiz developed the concept of transculturation to grasp this counterpoint between violence and creativity in the formation of Cuban nationality, the concept need not be confined to the consolidation of a national formation. As a concept, transculturation has no intrinsic positivity, no inherent geographic boundaries, and it offers no guarantees. As an open category developed to examine the complex dynamic of historical transformations, I believe transculturation can be used to examine national transformations in today's globalized landscape.

THIRD LEG: GLOBALITY

This shaky leg is my attempt to trace some outlines of this global landscape. There has been much discussion about globalization, about its origins, its various phases, and its current characteristics. It seems that what distinguishes globalization now is not the extent of transnational flows of trade and capital, for these have occurred in similar degrees in other periods (particularly at the beginning of this century), but certain transformations in the concentration and character of these flows, enabled by new technologies of communication. I am going to summarize two accounts of the current phase of globalization, written from rather different perspectives, each of which describes this phenomenon by highlighting seven of its features.

The first is a recent (1997) report of the United Nations Conference on Trade and Development.[10] The report, concerned that rising inequalities pose a serious threat of a political backlash against globalization, is presented as a "wake up call to policymakers." The report describes seven "troublesome features" of the contemporary global economy. I'll summarize them briefly: First, the global economy is growing slowly. Second, the gap between the developed and developing countries, as well as the income gap between rich and poor within countries, are widening steadily. I give you a critical statistic: in 1965, the average GNP per capita for the top 20 percent of the world's population was thirty times that of the poorest 20 percent; by 1990, it had doubled, to sixty times. Third, the rich have gained everywhere, and not just in comparison to the poorest sections of society, but also by hollowing out the middle class. Fourth, finance has gained an upper hand over industry, and rentiers over investors. Fifth, the share of income accruing to capital has gained over that assigned to labor. Sixth, increasing job and income insecurity is spreading worldwide. Finally, the growing gap between skilled and unskilled labor is becoming a global problem.

The second report, titled "The Fourth World War has begun," was written by subcomandante Marcos from the mountains of Chiapas and published in *Le Monde Diplomatique*.[11] According to Marcos, neoliberal globalization must be understood "as a new war of conquest of territories." His typology of four twentieth-century world wars decenters metropolitan conceptions of contemporary history. Marcos renames the Cold War the "Third World War," because for the third world it was really a hot war, made up of 149 localized wars that claimed 23 million lives. The Fourth World War is the current neoliberal globalization that, according to Marcos, is claiming the lives of vast numbers of people subjected to increasing poverty and marginalization.

While World War III was waged between capitalism and socialism with varying degrees of intensity in localized territories in the third world, World War IV is taking place between metropolitan financial centers and the world's majorities in global scenarios with constant intensity.

According to Marcos, the Fourth World War has torn the world into multiple pieces. He selects seven of these broken pieces in order to put together what he calls the *rompecabezas* or "puzzle" of neoliberal globalization. I will briefly list them (some of the titles are self-explanatory), omitting most of the abundant data he offers to support his claims:

Concentration of wealth and distribution of poverty, which synthesizes well-known data revealing the extent to which global wealth is being polarized worldwide.

The globalization of exploitation, which discusses how this polarization goes hand in hand with the increasing power of capital over labor worldwide.

Migration as an errant nightmare, which reveals not only the expansion of migratory flows forced by declining conditions of production in the third world—it also reveals the local wars which have multiplied the number of refugees (from two million in 1975 to over twenty-seven million in 1995).[12]

Globalization of finances and generalization of crime, which shows the growing complicity between megabanks, financial corruption, and hot money coming from the illegal traffic in drugs and arms.

The legitimate violence of an illegitimate power, which argues that the "strip-tease" of the state in many third world nations has reduced the state into an agent of social repression rather than of social welfare, turning it into a protection agency at the service of megaenterprises.

Megapolitics and dwarfs, which argues that strategies directed at eliminating trade frontiers and uniting nations lead to the multiplication of social frontiers and the pulverization of nations, turning politics into a conflict between giants and dwarfs, between the megapolitics of financial empires and the national policies of weak states—unlike the United Nations' report, Marcos ends on a positive note, in arguing point 7.

Pockets of resistance, that in response to the pockets of concentrated economic wealth and political power, there are emerging multiple and multiplying pockets of resistance, whose richness and power resides in their diversity and dispersion.

Despite their different perspectives, both accounts present similar data suggesting that one of the distinguishing features of contemporary globalization is the polarization of wealth worldwide not only among nations but within them. While the gap between the first and third worlds is widening, wealth is concentrating in fewer global hands, including those of third world elites. In this reconfigured global landscape, the "rich" can no longer be identified with metropolitan nations. Moreover, given this worldwide concentration of private power and the deregulation of the world economy, the territories that made up the third world are increasingly being treated as sources of cheap labor and natural resources.

In some respects, we can see this process of reprimarization—that is, of increased exploitation of primary products—as a regression to older forms of colonial control. Yet, this process is taking place within a technological and geopolitical framework that transforms the character of the exploitation of nature and labor. As I argue in *The Magical State*, this process of reprimarization goes hand in hand with the increasing abstraction and depersonalization of power through the figure of the market. A telling sign of this change is the tendency not only to treat all forms of social wealth as capital in practice but to conceptualize them as such in theory.

In effect, while in the past "produced assets" were considered the "traditional measure of wealth," now the World Bank suggests that we also include "natural capital and human resources." In two recent books, *Monitoring Environmental Progress*[13] (1995) and *Expanding the Measure of Wealth: Indicators of Environmentally Sustainable Development*[14] (1997), the World Bank proposes a reconceptualization of the measure of the wealth of nations and of development objectives as a paradigm shift. The reports note that:

> Expanding the measure of wealth suggests a new paradigm of economic development: development objectives are to be met by portfolio management, where the constituents of the portfolio are natural resources, produced assets, and human resources.

Now development objectives are to be defined as the management of this portfolio by experts. It could be argued that this new "paradigm" builds on an older conception according to which land, labor, and capital were treated as factors of production. What is new is the attempt to homogenize them, to treat natural resources, produced assets, and human resources directly as capital. By subsuming them under the abstract category capital, these resources are then treated as equivalent constituents of a "portfolio" to be managed by "experts." Ironically, as nature is being privatized and held in fewer hands, it is being redefined as the "natural capital" of increasingly denationalized nations.

This redefinition of wealth, its growing abstraction as homogenized capital, has yet another feature connected to a transformation in the character of the global market. In a wonderful book that examines the joint evolution of the market and the theater in England from the sixteenth to the eighteenth centuries, Jean Cristphe Agnew has argued that the "market" evolved during this period from a place to a process, from the fixed locations in the interstices of feudal society, to fluid transactions anywhere. In this shift from place to process, the market, however, remained placed, as it were, within existing geographic space.

Analysts of globalization have noted how its contemporary forms result not in the extension of the market in geographical space but to its concentration in social space. According to Hoogvelt, as international capital becomes more mobile and detached from its previous social locations, the "structure of core-periphery becomes a social division rather than a geographic one." She describes this change as a shift from a geographically expanding capitalism to an economically imploding one, characterized by "financial deepening."

The *New York Times*[15] series on "Globalization" of February 1999 corroborated this observation, noting the growing detachment of financial transactions from the trade of real goods. In a typical day, according to the *New York Times*, "the total amount of money changing hands in the world's foreign exchange markets alone is $1.5 trillion, an eightfold increase since 1986, an almost incomprehensible sum, equivalent to total world trade for four months." It quotes a Hong Kong banker: "it is no longer the real economy driving the financial markets, but the financial markets driving the real economy." According to the *New York Times*, the amount of investment capital has "exploded." In 1995, institutional investors controlled $20 trillion, ten times more than in 1980. As a result, the global economy is no longer dominated by trade in cars, steel, and wheat but by trade in stocks, bonds, and currencies. This wealth is increasingly stateless, as national capital markets are merging into a global capital market. Moreover, these investments are increasingly channeled through derivatives, which have grown exponentially: In 1997, they were traded at a value of $360 trillion, a figure equivalent to a dozen times the size of the entire global economy.

As I see things, financial deepening implies a significant transformation of the market—not just its concentration in social space, but its extension in time. Now capital travels not only within the geographic constraints of existing boundaries but in cyberspace—that is, in time. This temporal expansion of the market, or if you prefer, its extension into cyberspace, perhaps a further development of what Harvey and others describe as the transformation of space into time, gives new significance to the redefinition of nature as capital. Thus, it is not just that fewer private hands, largely unconstrained by public controls, hold more wealth, but that in these hands "wealth" is being transformed through a process of growing homogenization and abstraction.

I have come to think of this process as a transmaterialization of wealth. In a recent issue of *Time*[16] magazine on the future of money, the authors highlight the significance of new forms of wealth and new ways of thinking about them. Wealth, according to this article, is increasingly treated by investors and bankers not just in terms of tangible commodities but in terms of risks assumed on them, such as derivatives. The Magna Carta of this new form of thinking, the *Time* article suggests, is a speech delivered in 1993 by Charles Sanford, then CEO of Bankers Trust.

After much searching, two weeks ago I found this speech, an impressive document in style and content. In this speech, titled "Financial Markets in 2020," Sanford humbly recognizes that reality is moving faster than our categories, that a combination of art and science will be required to develop theories that correspond to the changes that are taking place in the world. He feels that these theories will develop in the future. He suggests it will happen in 2020—a number he chose because it indicates perfect vision, compared to the blurred vision of the present—but anticipates the nature of this shift in perspectives:

> We are beginning from a Newtonian view, which operates at the level of tangible objects (summarized by dimension and mass) to a perspective more in line with the nonlinear and chaotic world of quantum physics and molecular biology.

Building on this analogy with quantum physics and modern biology, he calls this theoretical reconceptualization "particle finance."

This reconceptualization will permit us to bring together all wealth, all investments, into wealth accounts, and then to break down these accounts into particles, particles of risk derived from the original investment, that can be sold as bundles in a global, computerized network. To help us visualize the nature of the change, Sanford says, "We have always had transportation—people walked, eventually they rode donkeys—but the automobile was a break from everything that came before it. Risk management will do that to finance. It's a total break."

Echoing Sanford, *Time* magazine states that derivatives "have changed the rule of the game forever." In order to imagine the new game, *Time* asks us

> to think of the world as a landscape of opportunity, everything from distressed Japanese real estate to Russian oil futures, marketed and packed by giant banks like BankAmerica or by Fund companies like Fidelity Investments and the Vanguard Group.

(The example of Russian oil futures is a general trope; it can also represent as well Venezuelan oil futures, Cuban sugar or tourism futures, etc.)

Echoing Sanford almost to the end, *Time* says that "E-[lectronic] cash, wealth accounts, and consumer derivatives will have made these firms as essential as cash itself once was." If business immortality can be purchased, *Time* concludes, now taking the perspective of the common reader, "these are the people who will figure out how to finance it. And they will be doing so with your money."

I am in no position to judge these interpretations, which I suspect are hyperbolic and self-serving. But it seems to me that the changes taking place today, of which these narrations are a part, suggest that the critique of Eurocentrism must be modified. Two related processes have shifted the commanding heights of colonial or neocolonial power from "the West" to the "globe." On the one hand, neoliberal globalization has homogenized and abstracted diverse forms of "wealth," including nature, which has become the third world's major source of foreign exchange and its most secure comparative advantage. On the other hand, the deterritorialization of "Europe," or the West, has entailed its reterritorialization as a figure or as a metaphor (as Noam Chomsky would call it) that now refers to more geographically diffuse, more socially concentrated, but less visible global financial and political transnational networks that include such non-Western entities as Japan, the elites of third world countries. These two interrelated processes are linked to a host of cultural transformations that both express and help shape different modes of articulating the relation among markets and nations, citizens and states, and individual and collective life projects.

In light of these changes, I would like to suggest that current forms of globalization make it necessary for us to move beyond the critique of Eurocentrism toward that of, for lack of a better word, what I would call the critique of globalcentrism. This shift also entails expanding the critique of old colonialisms, which has been so productive in our field, toward the critique of imperialism, or if you prefer, new colonialism, which is impressively absent. Just as the old colonialisms and Eurocentrism entailed the marginalization of the cultures and societies of non-European peoples, globalcentrism and the new colonialisms entail the exclusion of large sectors of the world population, but now defined less in terms of their territorial location than of their links to the international market. And just as the critique of Eurocentrism has sought to provincialize Europe and to question its pretended universality, the critique of globalcentrism must now regionalize and heterogenize the globe in order to show its highly differentiated distribution of power, and to demystify the univeralizing and homogenizing discourses of globalization that mask its polarizing effects.

Let me now briefly return to Cuba. On the basis of what I learned in Cuba, it was the need to understand these changes that most likely prompted Fidel Castro to call an international meeting on globalization in Cuba. Beyond the political show, there was a certain pathos in the meeting. As one of Castro's top economic advisers told me in relation to Cuba's ability to survive the economic crisis that began in 1989, "it is a miracle—we don't understand it ourselves." One could see, as Castro asked questions about derivatives, hedge funds, exchange rates, and the actual location of dollar deposits in Argentina or Brazil, that he was trying to sustain this miracle, trying to understand the world that Cuba is being obliged to enter after the fall of the Soviet bloc. At times the meeting seemed like Fidel's private workshop, as if he were using it to think of ways of managing the Cuban economy in an increasingly un-regulated global market, as a way of holding Cuban society together against the pull of the global market.

As I seek to define my project about the politics of visual semantics in revolutionary Cuba, it is clear to me that in this new global landscape, Cuban history cannot be seen as Ortiz saw it in 1940. Neither can it be seen as Ortiz imagined it in the sixties, during the euphoric or romantic phase of the revolution. I found one of the few statements he made about the revolution in the archives of the national library in Havana. In response to a question about the opportunities that researchers have in revolutionary Cuba, Ortiz answered that the "Cuban revolution offered anthropologists and historians a new and wide open field of work to study this *crisis of transculturation*, that is, the human change from an old pluriclassist structure to one moving toward a non-class society."[17] I cannot at this point discern the significance of the Cuban economy's growing dependence on dollars coming from tourism and remittances, and even less of the possible transformation of sugar and tobacco into bundles of risks in the international market. But it is clear that Cuba's integration into the world market and the dollarization of its economy—now over 50 percent of Cubans have access to ever more essential dollars—has drastically intensi-fied social differences and sharply commodified private activities, including the arts. What Ortiz called "the crisis of transculturation" entailed in the cre-ation of a classless society, threatens to become the crisis of creating a hierar-chical society within the context of socialist institutions and ideals, unless the Cuban state and its people manage to counter these tendencies.

In Cuba and elsewhere, neoliberal globalization's reconfiguration of pop-ulations, states, production, and culture has modified the contexts of politi-cal action and intellectual and artistic production. I suspect that in these con-ditions, as the periphery implodes in the center, and the center in the periphery, cultural transformations and reflections about them will take place, not only through counterpoints like the ones I examined here, but through a multiplicity of exchanges among collectivities and scholars who are imagining anew their location in this shifting social landscape.

If these exchanges are to be informed, as Said suggests, by a contrapuntal perspectivism, they should involve, as in Ortiz's work, an openness to the way individuals and communities form their visions of life and aspirations within, as well as beyond, national imaginings.

At the end of the nineteenth century, when Cuba was seeking to free it-self from Spanish colonialism and from U.S domination, Cuba's poet leader of independence Jose Martí coined the term "Nuestra America" to express pan–Latin American aspirations of political and cultural autonomy in oppo-sition to the United States. Now Nuestra America is being redefined from the outside and inside.

I would like to conclude by recognizing the vision of the future expressed by Cherrie Moraga, whose discussion of her position as a Chicana artist in America inspired the title of this chapter. Seeking to define an enabling American geopolitical imaginary, Cherrie Moraga rejects the categories that divide Latinos from each other and from other peoples of the Americas, and she asserts her desire to see Latinos as members of "a larger world community composed of many nations of people, and no longer give credence to the geopolitical borders that have divided us." Seeking a sign to represent this desired identity—treating labels not so much as signs of identity but as signs for identity—she adds an accent to the word *América* and defines herself, in the closing line of her article, as "an American, *con acento*"—with an accent.

NOTES

1. Fernando Ortiz, *Cuban Counterpoint* (New York: Knopf, 1947): 4. The term *curros* referred to freed Afro-Cubans who roamed the streets of Havana during the first half of the nineteenth century and were considered part of the underworld. Ortiz examined this topic in *Los negros curros*, a posthumous book (Havana: Editorial de Ciencias Sociales, 1986).

2. Ortiz, *Cuban Counterpoints*, 4.

3. Ortiz, *Cuban Counterpoints*, 4.

4. Edward Said (1992), 336.

5. Walter Mignolo (1993).

6. Bronislaw Malinowski, *A Scientific Theory of Culture and Other Essays* (Chapel Hill: University of North Carolina Press, 1944).

7. Bronislaw Malinowski, "The Pan-African Problem of Culture Contact" (1943). This is the article that disappeared as a citation in Kaberry's introduction to the second edition of Malinowski's *The Dynamics of Cultural Change*.

8. Malinowski, "The Pan-African Problem," 665.

9. Malinowski, "The Pan-African Problem," 665.

10. UNCTAD, *Report of the United Nations Conference on Trade and Development* (New York: Author, 1997).

11. Comandante "Marcos," "The Fourth World War Has Begun," *Le Monde Diplomatique* (1997).

12. United Nations' figures.

13. World Bank, *Monitoring Environmental Progress* (Author: 1995).

14. World Bank, *Expanding the Measure of Wealth: Indicators of Environmentally Sustainable Development* (Author: 1997).

15. *New York Times*, February 1999.

16. *Time*.

17. Fernando Ortiz, quote from the archives of the national library in Havana.

12

Poetry in the Presidio

Toward a Study of *Proyecto de Código Criminal Cubano*

Alejandra Bronfman

De la justicia actual en son de guerra	From current justice in state of war
La Ley, contra el delito se levanta	Law raises against crime
Y en su código nuevo Cuba canta	And Cuba sings in its new code
Un himno de equidad sobre la tierra	A hymn of equity over the land
La sanción del Derecho que él encierra	The sanction itself of Right
Reduce el mal con la virtud que implanta	Reduces evil and virtue implants
sentando Ortiz la noble, pura y santa	Ortiz lays a noble, pure, saintly
"doctrina racional" para el que yerra	"rational doctrine" for he who errs
Salva al Hombre y persigue su delito	Saving Man, and pursuing offense
Si juzgado lo fatal halla lo adverso	If judging adversely over the fatal
Del mal innato, por fatal, maldito	Of innate, deadly evil condemned
Pero siempre, fallando entre lo humano,	However, always a human finding
Neutraliza en su forma lo perverso	Neutralizes what is perverse in form
Cual lo equívoco, el Código Cubano[1]	As what mistaken, the Cuban Code

The opening poem renders tribute to Fernando Ortiz's *Proyecto de Código Criminal Cubano*.[2] Intending to replace the penal code adopted under the colonial regime in 1870, Ortiz wrote and presented the *Proyecto* to Cuban legislative bodies in early 1926. This chapter is a preliminary analysis of this relatively unexamined aspect of Ortiz's work. If the contours of Ortiz's work as an anthropologist and ethnographer are emerging more clearly as a result of growing interest,[3] the shape and substance of Ortiz as lawyer and criminologist have remained in the shadows. By now *Negros brujos*[4] is a familiar if continually challenging text, as are his writings on music or *Contrapunteo cubano*. Yet the relationship between these texts remains a matter of speculation. What happened to Ortiz's initial impulses to link observations concerning the practices of Cubans of African descent with his understandings of the origins and etiology of crime? As is clear in *Negros brujos*, Ortiz's training as a lawyer and criminologist imbued his work. One might assume that these early paradigms evolved or shifted. It would be harder to claim, I will try to argue, that Ortiz rejected them outright. The *Código* suggests that Ortiz continued to apply his legal training to the problems of social order and the regeneration of delinquency well after his career bulged with the proliferation of other interests.

Ortiz wrote the *Proyecto* in the early years of General Gerardo Machado's regime. Although the regime ended in a violent tyranny that led to Machado's overthrow in the revolution of 1933, historians have argued that initially Machado appealed to many Cubans with his nationalist, reformist platform. Given growing discontent, especially after the economic crisis of 1920 perceived to emanate from the particular and peculiar relationship among foreign (mostly U.S.) capital, Cuban sugar production, and the ambiguous boundary between Cuban and U.S. sovereignty, Machado's Liberal Party platform in 1924 drew wide appeal from disenchanted sectors. When he ran for president in 1924, claiming to be committed to a "revision of the Permanent Treaty, eliminating the appendix to the Constitution, and winning Cuba an independent place in the world," his spoken concerns resonated with those groups already organized around a commitment to "national regeneration."[5]

Machado's plans included domestic reforms, as well as those in the sphere of international relations. He initiated a series of projects, expanding the role of the state in public life even as it aimed to remedy economic distress as it offered jobs to many Cubans. It was during his regime that the replica of the U.S. Capitol was built in downtown Havana, as well as the seven-hundred-mile central highway that runs across the entire island, part of a new public works program. The Presidio Modelo, built on the Isle of Pines on the site of the same colonial prison that housed José Martí for a time, evinced Machado's interest in extending his reformist agenda to the control of crime and criminality.[6]

An overlooked moment of coinciding purpose between Machado and Ortiz, the *Proyecto de Código Criminal Cubano* brought together both Machado's interest in reform and Ortiz's criminological leanings. When Ortiz presented his *Proyecto* to the Comisión Codificadora, he prefaced his remarks with an acknowledgment of the mutual endeavor, noting that the new code would be a product of "el esfuerzo de todos, secundando el impulso reformador del Gral Machado, muy interesado en la renovación legislativa."[7]

The most important innovation in the *Proyecto de Código Criminal Cubano*, from the point of view of the history of criminology, was Ortiz's introduction of a new social type: the delinquent. He defined a delinquent, in the first instance, as someone who had committed a crime. But a delinquent was also someone who might potentially break the law. Those who, according to Ortiz, show by their external conduct to be notoriously against good customs or the laws of public security, a state of extraordinarily mental, moral, or legal inadaptation that incline them to delinquency and social fear,[8]

were deemed *personas peligrosas*, even if they had not committed a crime. They were to be treated in the same way as delinquents: Both rights conceded and obligations imposed, which were inviolable for delinquents, were also inviolable for dangerous persons. But the differences between them mattered: Ortiz disaggregated delinquents into different types. Depending on the nature of their responsibility for the crime committed, they would be classified into the following subcategories: "habituales, alienados, psicopáticos, toxicómanos, vagos, políticos, menores, y corporativos."[9] A notable array of different "orders of things" comprises the list. The inclusion of biological, psychological, social, and political factors reflected perhaps early twentieth-century criminology's confidence in its ability to encompass and address the problem of crime in its multifaceted entirety.

This focus on the criminal rather than the crime reflected a shift from classical to positivist criminological theories. Instigated principally by the Italian school of criminology, it rejected the notion of the free will of the criminal and replaced it with a view of the criminal as both constrained and impelled by environmental, biological, and psychological factors. One of the principal proponents of this theory was Enrico Ferri, whose lecture on "The Positivist School of Criminology" in 1885 provides a landmark for historians of criminology.[10] In the succinct analysis of one historian,

> the person who commits a crime, says Ferri, is a criminal. . . . It is no use looking for the motive of his act: the reason for his crime is precisely, his criminality. In a sense these few peremptory words mark the registering of a new object of penal science and practice: homo criminalis, a new figure engendered outside the sphere of classical penal thought, but which in the course of the nineteenth century gradually advances to its forefront.[11]

The line of influence between Ortiz and Ferri may be drawn through their connections to Césare Lombroso, whose influence on Ortiz's early work has been well documented. Ferri made a name for himself during his student years as a vociferous critic of the notion of free will in crime. When he went to Turin in the 1880s to study with Lombroso, who was professor of legal medicine at the university there, he hoped to add empirical weight to some of his beliefs through the studies of prisons and inmates that Lombroso was sponsoring at the time. He and Lombroso became friends and colleagues, working together on key positivist concepts such as the born criminal, the use of anthropological data, and the importance of a preventive approach. Ferri proposed a reform of penal law in 1921, which was in many ways a model for Ortiz's *Proyecto*.[12]

Following Ferri, the *Proyecto* envisioned punishment as designed to match the delinquent, his crime, and his potential to reform. The *Proyecto* listed ten types of confinement and their respective institutions, ranging from the *presidio*, with a regimen of work and nightly isolation; through the *arresto*, in which inmates could choose between work and isolation during the day; the reformatory, which was to make provisions for education as well as labor; and finally the insane asylum, directed at therapy and education for its inmates.[13] Article 150 stated the basic principle: "las sanciones criminales se adecuarán al delincuente individualizándolas en vista de su peligrosidad como el tribunal, a su prudente arbitrio y de acuerdo con los límites y reglas de este Código, estime más eficaz parala readaptación e inocuización de aquél."[14]

The proposal included provisions for the method by which data on inmates was to be gathered. The role of anthropologically derived knowledge was key.[15] In an oral presentation of his *Proyecto* to the Comisión Certificadora, Ortiz emphasized the newly conceived delinquent as the most important aspect of his proposal. In an effort to underscore the scientific aspect of his views, he drew an analogy to changing medical practices: "en criminología esta sucediendo lo que ha sucedido en medicina. Aunque no puede decirse que el delincuente es un enfermo en el sentido estricto de este vocablo, no es desacertada la comparación entre uno y otro . . . ya la ciencia médica no cura enfermedades sino enfermos, y asi hay que hacer en criminología." Ortiz traced this development to the challenge to absolutism brought about by the French Revolution, and the ensuing humanization of penal practices, undergirded by a newly legitimized belief in the Rights of Man. Thus, a theory emerged that acknowledged different types of delinquents, and corresponding penalties, gradiated in severity.[16] Yet at the same time this approach presented a potential contradiction, one that plagued positivist conceptions of penal reform. How would a positivist criminology reconcile faith in the potential of delinquents to reform and shed their dangerous tendencies with the drive to classify criminal types and categorize some as irredeemable?

Ortiz held specific ideas about the ways this code, if adopted, ought to be promulgated. Again, anthropological inquiry formed a critical component of his plan. He recommended the creation of university courses, the training of a body of penitentiary personnel, and of medical anthropologists.[17] In a formal proposal, he later called for the institutionalization of instruction in the University of Havana, envisioning the creation of three new professorships in the Law School: "para la enseñanza de la Criminología y Penología," "para la enseñanza de la Antropología Criminal y Policiologia," and "para la enseñanza de Enjuiciamiento Criminal y Ley Penitenciaria." He also called for the creation of a doctorate in criminology.[18] Once inculcated with knowledge of the most recent technologies and theories, these new experts would run the new institutions Ortiz proposed.

All of this new criminological energy would be channeled by a Junta Nacional de Prevención y Represión de la Delincuencia, which he envisioned as analogous to the Junta Nacional de Sanidad y Beneficencia, as an "Estado Mayor de la defensa y guerra contra la criminalidad."[19] This Junta would direct and oversee any operations involved in the repression of crime, including general administration, gathering of statistics, daily operations in corrections centers, and the control over recently released inmates. The Junta would join together government officials and experts in pursuit of greater control over the penological landscape. Ortiz envisioned a committee comprised of a member of the judiciary, preferably at the level of Presidente de la Audiencia, a number of academics, including those named to the chairs of Derecho Penal, Criminología y Penología, Antropología Criminal y Policiología, and Enjuiciamiento Criminal y Legislación Penitenciaria. In addition, the Junta would include those involved in more practical matters: the inspector of all corrections establishments, the director of the Gabinete Nacional de Identificación, and the chiefs of personnel of corrections. Finally, he proposed that the three remaining members should be, for an unstated reason, women.[20]

The proposal generated a wide range of responses, with various degrees of enthusiasm. His colleague and friend Israel Castellanos, the director of the Gabinete Nacional de Identificación at the time, entered the forum with a proposal of his own for expanding the role of state institutions and the experts who would run them. Castellanos wrote from the perspective of a participant within this evolving apparatus, sketching out a plan that would fit the needs of the Cuban penal system and a national ambition to acquire the trappings of modernity. Castellanos praised Ortiz's plan as a step in the direction of a positivist overhaul of Cuba's penal system. He pointed out, however, that some practices within the penitentiary system had already begun to change in that direction, regardless of the state of the theoretical enterprise. He and others had begun to conduct anthropological studies of inmates. Ortiz's plan would support and legitimize his own plan for a Laboratorio de Antropología Penitenciaria. Through it he would obtain, in as much detail as its techniques allowed, the *diagnóstico moral* and *pronóstico correcional* of each inmate. Once the diagnosis was obtained, it would formulate a plan by which the inmate would be redeemed socially, to whatever extent possible.[21]

Castellanos accepted the premises of Ortiz's *Proyecto* and encouraged their extension beyond the confines of formal law, onto the bodies and psychologies of inmates. Ortiz himself was somewhat doubtful that the general public would accept this modernizing impulse, just as they had resisted the modernization of medical practices to a certain extent. He noted in a letter to a Supreme Court judge that it had taken the trauma of war and the overpowering authority of the U.S. presence to promulgate adequate and scientific measures against yellow fever. Likewise, he believed that

> to scientifically implant the defense system of criminality in Cuba, the pressure of a high authority would also be necessary. I doubt this would happen and therefore we will continue immersed in the useless chores of the current criminal justice while criminality increases in a terrifying way.[22]

Perhaps this doubt about the appeal of his ideas rendered him amenable to a proposal, found among his papers, for a survey that would gauge the amount of interest among the educated public "en relación con la reforma de la legislación criminal." A questionnaire would be sent out to teachers, doctors, judges, lawyers, institutes of *beneficencia* and *correción*, employees of corrections centers, the military, and politicians. The responses would help him not only to determine what they thought, but also the degree to which they could be brought into the project as participants. Ortiz agreed to design the questionnaire. Whether he did so and what kinds of results he obtained have yet to be uncovered.[23]

Ortiz did send out his *Proyecto* to dozens of colleagues and acquaintances, both in Cuba and abroad. In Cuba, the president of the Asociación Pedagogica Universitaria received a copy, as did José Tapis, Pedro Pablo Rabell, Juan Clemente Vivanco, and Juan Gutierrez Quirós, all judges sitting on Cuba's Supreme Court. Of non-Cubans, one prominent recipient was E. H. Crowder, then the ambassador to Cuba from the United States, who sent a note acknowledging the receipt of the volume and his support of its intention. "It will be a great pleasure to cooperate with you in securing the enactment of this new criminal code," wrote Crowder in June 1926, not long after Ortiz's completion of the project.[24]

The response from the criminologist who had inspired the project, Enrico Ferri, was prompt and positive.[25] Another article from a journal of criminology published in Milan, *La Scuola Positiva*, asserted its praise for Ortiz's general theoretical thrust and the rigor of his work, faulting it only for an excessive attention to detail. In its view, Ortiz's project was far more successful than similar projects in its shift from a penal to criminal approach, aiming to defend society against criminal activity, rather than simply organizing punishment using abstract principles.[26]

Ortiz ensured that the knowledge of Ferri's affirmation was widely disseminated. He sent copies of Ferri's laudatory comments to several newspaper editors, including Gustavo Gonzalez Beauville, Alberto Lamar Schweyer, Juan O'Naghten, Enrique Serpa, and Jorge Mañach, asking that they take note in their respective newspapers.[27] As a result, the *Proyecto* was widely publicized, and generated a variety of responses.

A letter from Ramiro Cabrera expressed one kind of response: unadulterated enthusiasm. In florid prose, quoting Sophocles, Quevedo, and Cicero, Cabrera thanked Ortiz for his contribution, which as he saw it, was a "código revelador de los males atávicos que rodean nuestro ambiente social." Ortiz was a worthy colleague of the positivists in Europe: according to Cabrera, he was "as brilliant in the fight for the improvement of nations and men" as were the "enlightened Lombroso, Ferri, Garofalo, and Ottolenghi." Not only was Ortiz in tune with European criminological strains, he was also in line with the aims of the president of Cuba. "General Gerardo Machado y

Morales," wrote Cabrera, "like you suffers the most intense, incurable, and beneficial fever in favor of the advancement, morality, and progress of the Republic." Ortiz's proposal had a bright future: "Your Penal Code will be from now on in Cuba THE CODE OF MACHADO!!"[28]

Likewise, admiring law students wrote in. With studious precision they located Ortiz within the canon of penal law they had spent the year learning. Referring to recent political change as a "process of renovation," they suggested that Ortiz's "modern and scientific" contribution would bring that process to fruition. With lofty language they described the extent to which Ortiz would help them achieve their obligations to "defend, prosecute, and judge those cases of conflict between individuals and society, according to the high criteria of Humanity and Justice in brotherhood." Due to Ortiz's intervention they, as new lawyers, would be spared wrestling with the obsolete and rigid norms of classical penal law. They thanked him for this and for his "intense, well-directed, intellectual, and nationalist labor."[29] These kinds of responses perhaps indicate a sense of optimism and faith in the possibility of progress, a sense that at this moment Machado and Ortiz shared a perspective on the path toward regeneration of Cuban politics and society.

Not all the letters were as uncritically adulatory. A colleague, who signed with the initials "LJA," mentioning that he had published extensively on the subject of criminal law, and wrote in with his reservations. He quibbled over the length of the project, the casuistic penchant for drawing needless distinctions, and Ortiz's analysis of the significance of the kinds of crimes committed by the insane. One of his principal objections challenged Ortiz's notion of guilt. Yet acceptance of the progressive aims and acknowledgment of the project's importance informed even this critical response. Despite the complaints, the writer of the letter insisted that none of this was meant to criticize the code. Rather he meant only to point out differences, in the hopes of discussing them and clarifying them sometime in the future. Deferential, especially for someone who claimed to have written thirty-five books and hundreds of articles on criminal law, he closed with an effusive expression of friendship and admiration.[30]

It is perhaps not surprising that Ortiz would have gained the consent of a liberal elite, pleased with a proposal that posited a move toward modernity even as it envisioned the elimination of a source of disorder. Likewise, the scientific and academic establishment might have welcomed their projected status elevation. They might all have been attracted to his intention to "centralize all the defensive organization of the state against criminals, as it has been done in all civilized countries, under the jurisdiction of the ministry of Justice."[31] Lest this become an exercise in fitting the Cuban case into a Foucauldian template, however, it is important to note that Ortiz also drew consent from the targets of his project: Some inmates found much to praise in his *Proyecto*.

The response received from detained Cubans speaks volumes with regard to the perception and dissemination of this project as a humane, reformist attempt to help rather than punish delinquents. Perhaps most remarkable is the poem, dedicated to "el eminente penalista Dr. Fernando Ortiz," with which I opened this chapter. Its author was Luis Branovel, writing from the *presidio* on December 29, 1926. He preceded his sonnet with a letter, asking if Ortiz had already received it as he had sent it for the first time a few weeks earlier. To ensure its arrival, he was enclosing it a second time. He meant it, he wrote, as a token of his "spontaneous penitentiary congratulations."[32]

Another letter from prison thanked Ortiz for his efforts more extensively. Alejo Hernandez de la Noval, convicted for bigamy, listed the numerous ways in which Ortiz's plans would serve the population within the prison walls. He had managed to obtain a copy of the code, he wrote, after coming across reviews in Cuban and foreign presses. It was an honor for him as a Cuban citizen to see Ortiz's name mentioned in foreign newspapers. Elevating himself above most of the inmates in his company, he alluded "to any number of moral conditions and dark souls who were on a constant lookout for victims for their unsavory ideas." It was clear that these unsavory types carried an inherited stain in their blood, and he was grateful that Ortiz had begun to bring this to the attention of the general public. Furthermore, the personnel were not adequately trained to deal with inmates. When and if the code was approved by Cuba's legislative bodies, it would fill a void, one created by the lack of attention to scientific principles in the present code. It was very satisfying, he wrote, to know, even from within the depths of his cell, that Cuba was not just constituted by men "who are busy searching for benefits, asking favors, and who know by heart the retirement law." There was at least one citizen, Ortiz, who held humanity's best interests in mind. Hernández signed off most affectionately and then closed with a postscript: Would it be too much trouble for Ortiz to explain the way his own crime of bigamy was to be understood within the new criminal code?[33]

I hope this preliminary interrogation of the material, rather than drawing conclusions, has opened new avenues of inquiry. Here I will focus on two questions. First, how can students of Ortiz's legacy integrate his work as a legal reformer into a broader interpretation of his intellectual trajectory? Second, how would a more profound study of Cuban criminology engage an emerging historiography of criminology in Latin America?

One way to address the first question might be to look at what Ortiz himself said about this moment in his intellectual career. On the question of the influences on his work, he was ambivalent. In a 1928 letter to a Spanish criminologist Mariano Ruiz-Funes, he claimed to be an "old Lombrosian." Yet he sent copies of *Negros brujos* to friends that year, suggesting that he was not prepared to completely disavow his Lombrosian roots.[34] By 1944, he was even further removed from his previous endeavors. Writing to Rafael Portuondo in the Audiencia de Oriente in Santiago de Cuba, he thanked Portuondo for mentioning the Código Criminal in a recent text, and assured him that his interpretation had been correct. Yet it was as if he had to be reminded of something long gone: "I am presently so distant from those studies that when they talk to me about penal problems it seems they remind me of another life."[35] These remarks suggest that he did not want to link penitentiary and cultural anthropology too closely.

Some commentators, on the other hand, see this as one of Ortiz's most important contributions. Berta Becerra y Bonet wrote of his contribution to the "science of Law," that it was one of his "most deeply rooted callings . . . on which he has been one of the greatest masters of our people."[36] Israel Castellanos, a close interlocutor, imagined a direct link between the earlier and later Ortiz, arguing that the criminal code grew out of his interest in *la mala vida*, in both instances fueled by reformist impulse. His interpretation is of a life work that followed a certain logic and consistency.[37]

On the other hand, the seeming multiplicity of Ortiz's projects might suggest a less cohesive view, one that is satisfied, like Benítez-Rojo, to note the polyphonic quality, not only within texts but between texts, or, rather, between all of his intellectual endeavors.[38] In this regard locating the Código Criminal within the corpus of Ortiz's work might entail assuming, like Ortiz himself hinted at, that he engaged several simultaneous but not necessarily consistent projects. An intermediate view might rely on Fernando Coronil's elegant suggestion that "his scholarly work was marked at once by a continuity of concerns and a shift in perspectives."[39] The fate of the *Proyecto* in the Cuban legislature and Ortiz's ongoing involvement with criminology remains relatively unexamined. Further study might add to the richness of Coronil's proposed continuities and shifts.

A recent volume on criminology and prison reform in Latin America sets a research agenda for further understanding the relationships "between prison and society and between technologies of punishment and culture in Latin America."[40] The authors raise a few issues that are relevant to the issues raised by Ortiz's endeavors to reform the criminal code. The nature of positivism, they argue, was somewhat at odds with the reformist impulse, which initially drove prison reform. For if prison reform focused on the regeneration and transformation of criminals into productive, or at least less dangerous, members of society, positivism held to a certain degree that some types were not reformable. This tension is present, and indeed, informs Ortiz's work, as well as Castellanos. How did these tensions resolve themselves, if in fact they did? Was Ortiz's vision a "humanitarian critique of existing prisons" or what Aguirre and Salvatore call part of emerging "imaginaries of total institutional control"?[41]

Salvatore and Aguirre's attention to periodization suggests that the example of Cuba is an important case study. Throughout most of Latin America, liberal reformist projects preceded the height of the legitimacy of positivism. Yet in Cuba, these currents, as we have seen, converged in the early 1920s. How does this convergence impinge on general narratives of the history of liberalism and state formation in Latin America?

Similarly, the authors posit a significant resonance between politics and prisons, using the construction of the *Presidio Modelo* as their example. They suggest a paradox in the way the *Presidio*, built by Machado as a symbol of modernity, came to be an emblem of the tyranny and cruelty of his regime. There is much about this process that we do not know, including the role of Ortiz, whose position toward Machado changed radically during the regime. Ortiz's own words provide probably the best guide toward further understanding his complex work and legacy. Cuban writer Lino Novás Calvo recalled Ortiz's remarks regarding an African icon in his hand:

> This doll has, first of all, individuality; it also has a place in time, space, and environment. We cannot understand this doll without understanding all these dimensions. It is not sufficient to study one of its measurements; one needs to study all of them. Ultimately, it is very interesting to observe how these measurements and dimension interact and what the result is.[42]

NOTES

1. Letter from Luis Branovel, December 29, 1926. Biblioteca Nacional José Martí, Colección Manuscrita Fernando Ortiz (hereafter BNJM, C.M. Ortiz), Carpeta 356, Proyectos de leyes.

2. Fernando Ortiz, *Proyecto de código criminal cubano (Libro primero o parte general)* (Havana: Librería Cervantes, 1926). See also "El proyecto de código criminal cubano," *Revista Bimestre Cubana* XXI, no. 5 (September–October): 681–705.

3. The literature on Ortiz is extensive. The list includes but is not limited to Thomas Bremer, "The Constitution of Alterity: Fernando Ortiz and the Beginnings of Latin American Ethnography Out of the Spirit of Italian Criminology" in Thomas Bremer and Ulrich Fleischmann, eds., *Alternative Cultures in the Caribbean* (Frankfurt am Main: Vervuert, 1993); Fernando Coronil, "Introduction" to Ortiz's *Cuban Counterpoint* (1995); Diana Iznaga, *Transculturación en Fernando Ortiz* (Havana: Editorial de Ciencias Sociales, 1989); Aline Helg, "Fernando Ortiz ou la pseudo-science contre la sorcellerie Africaine à Cuba," in *La pensée métisse: Croyances africaines et rationalité occidentale en questions* (Paris: Presses Universitaires de France, 1990); Jorge Ibarra, "La herencia cientifica de Fernando Ortiz," *Revista Iberoamericana* (1990): 56. See also Araceli García Carranza, Norma Suárez Suárez, and Alberto Quesada Morales, *Cronología Fernando Ortiz* (Havana: Fundación Fernando Ortiz, 1996).

4. Fernando Ortiz, *Los negros brujos* (Madrid: Libréria de Fernando Fe, 1906).

5. Louis Pérez, *Cuba under the Platt Amendment, 1912–1934* (Pittsburgh: Univeristy of Pittsburgh Press, 1986), 252; Marifeli Pérez-Stable, *The Cuban Revolution: Origins, Course, and Legacy* (New York: Oxford University Press, 1993); Jorge Domínguez, "Seeking Permission to Build a Nation: Cuban Nationalism and U.S. Response under the First Machado Presidency," *Cuban Studies* v16 (1986): 33–48.

6. Gerardo Machado y Morales, *Ocho Años de Lucha* (Miami: Ediciones Históricas Cubanas, 1982); Foreign Policy Association, *Problems of the New Cuba: Report of the Commission of Cuban Affairs* (New York: Foreign Policy Association, 1935).

7. "Ponencia a la Comisión Certificadora," BNJM, C.M. Ortiz, Carpeta 356, Proyectos de leyes.

8. Ortiz, *Proyecto*, 14.

9. Ortiz, *Proyecto*, 13–14.

10. See Piers Beirne, "Adolphe Quetelet and the Origins of Positivist Criminology," *American Journal of Sociology* 92: 1140–69; and Pasquale Pasquino, "Criminology: The Birth of a Special Savior," *Ideology and Consciousness* 7: 17–32, both reprinted in Piers Beirne, ed., *The Origins and Growth of Criminology: Essays on Intellectual History, 1760–1945* (Brookfield: Dartmouth, 1994).

11. Pasquino, "Criminology," 18.

12. On Ferri, see Thorsten Sellin, "Enrico Ferri," in Hermann Mannheim, ed., *Pioneers in Criminology* (Montclair, N.J.: Paterson Smith, 1972): 361–84.

13. Ortiz, *Proyecto*, 40–41.

14. Ortiz, *Proyecto*, 65.

15. "En cada reclusorio se llevará con las formalidades y requisitos que fijen las Ordenanzas Criminales un 'Registro Diario de Conceptuación' de la conducta, moralidad, correctivos disciplinales, ventajas premiativas, trabajo, instrucción, aseo, salud y categoría de cada recluso. Todo recluso estará sometido al examen antropológico en la extensión y condiciones que establezcan las Ordenanzas Criminales": Ortiz, *Proyecto*, 50–51.

16. "Ponencia a la Comisión Certificadora," BNJM, C.M. Ortiz Carpeta 356, *Proyectos de leyes*.

17. "Ponencia a la Comisión Certificadora" BNJM, C.M. Ortiz, Carpeta 356, *Proyectos de leyes*.

18. "Proyecto de ley" BNJM, C.M. Ortiz, Carpeta 356, *Proyectos de leyes*.

19. "Proyecto de ley" BNJM, C.M. Ortiz, Carpeta 356, *Proyectos de leyes*.

20. "Ponencia a la Comisión Certificadora" BNJM, C.M. Ortiz, Carpeta 356, *Proyectos de leyes*.

21. "Solamente sobre la doble base del diagnóstico moral y del pronóstico correcional puede establecerce el plan correcional o curativo moral, que es tipo individualizado de un tratamiento científico de reforma física y moral, para la readaptación a la vida social de un preso": Saldaña, cited in Israel Castellanos, *Un plan para reformar el regimen penal cubano* (Havana: Imprenta La Universal, 1927), 15.

22. Letter to Gabriel Vandama, July 26, 1926. BNJM, C.M. Ortiz, Carpeta 356, Proyectos de leyes.

23. BNJM, C.M. Ortiz, Carpeta 356, *Proyectos de leyes*.

24. Letter from E. H. Crowder, June 22, 1926, BNJM, C.M. Ortiz, Carpeta 356, *Proyectos de leyes*.

25. "El fondo del Proyecto de Código Criminal de Cuba constituye una magnífica y excelente afirmación del principio de defensa social, superando las normas tradicionales, ya desacreditadas por sus resultados de plena insuficiencia en el terreno práctico . . . es decir, que el proyecto cubano, mejor que el Código ruso, regula legalmente una clasificación antropológica de los criminales que es idéntica a la establecida en nuestro proyecto de 1921": BNJM, C.M. Ortiz, Carpeta 195, Juicios críticos de su obra.

26. BNJM, C.M. Ortiz, Carpeta 195, *Juicios críticos de su obra*.

27. BNJM, C.M. Ortiz, Carpeta 356, *Proyectos de leyes*.

28. Letter from Ramiro Cabrera, October 16, 1926, BNJM, C.M. Ortiz, Carpeta 356, *Proyectos de leyes*.

29. Letter from law students, November 22, 1926, BNJM, C.M. Ortiz, Carpeta 356, *Proyectos de leyes*.

30. Letter from 'LJA', June 12, 1926, BNJM, C.M. Ortiz, Carpeta 356, *Proyectos de leyes*.

31. Letter to Jesús Barranque, Secretaria de Justicia, November 11, 1926, BNJM, C.M. Ortiz, Carpeta 356, *Proyectos de leyes*.

32. Letter from Presidio Nacional, December 29, 1926. BNJM, C.M. Ortiz, Carpeta 356, *Proyectos de leyes*.

33. Letter from Carcel, October 9, 1927, BNJM, C.M. Ortiz, Carpeta 356, *Proyectos de leyes*.

34. Letter to Sr. Dr. Mariano Ruis-Funes, March 16, 1928, BNJM, C.M. Ortiz, Carpeta 403, *Correspondenca variada*.

35. Letter to Rafael M. Portuondo, November 2, 1944, BNJM, C.M. Ortiz, Carpeta 325, *Correspondencia*: P. I thank Consuelo Naranjo Orovio for bringing this letter to my attention.

36. Berta Becerra y Bonet, "El Doctor Ortiz, Periodista," in *Miscelanea de estudios dedicados a Fernando Ortiz* (Havana: Sociedad Económica de Amigos del País, 1955), 1: 160.

37. "Explorando la mala vida cubana, estudiando sus causas históricas, sus factores étnicos, antropológicos, psicológicos y sociales, así como la profilaxis y la represión de la brujería, Ortiz reconoció en el mismo campo de investigaciónes *criminológicas* la urgencia de la reforma penal y penitenciaria, que cuatro lustros más tarde abordó con su Proyecto de Código Criminal Cubano. En sus apuntes criminológicos de los afrocubanos, ya bullía el reformador que más tarde se revelara con las normas del más acendrado postivismo": Israel Castellanos, "Fernando Ortiz en las ciencias criminológicas," in *Miscelanea* (1955), 1: 313.

38. Antonio Benítez-Rojo, *The Repeating Island: The Caribbean and the Postmodern Perspective* (Durham, N.C.: Duke University Press, 1992), chap. 4.

39. Fernando Coronil, "Introduction" in *Cuban Counterpoint* (1995), xvii.

40. Ricardo D. Salvatore and Carlos Aguirre, "The Birth of the Penitentiary in Latin America: Towards an Interpretive Social History of Prisons," in Ricardo D. Salvatore and Carlos Aguirre, eds., *The Birth of the Penitentiary in Latin America: Essays on Criminology, Prison Reform, and Social Control, 1830–1940* (Austin: University of Texas Press, 1996), 34. On criminology in Latin America see also Rosa del Olmo, *America Latina y su criminología* (México: Siglo XXI, 1981). On Cuba, see Mariano Ruiz-Funes, "La antropología penitenciaria en Cuba," in *Delito y Libertad: Ensayos* (Madrid: Javier Morata, 1930).

41. Salvatore and Aguirre, "Birth of the Penitentiary," 19.

42. Lino Novás Calvo, "Cubano de Tres Mundos," in *Miscelanea de estudios dedicados a Fernando Ortiz* (Havana: Sociedad Económica de Amigos del País, 1956), vol. 2: 1136.

IV

RACIAL DIVERSITY, RELIGION, AND NATIONAL IDENTITY

Fernando Ortiz's contribution to the study of racial relations and their impact on the Cuban sense of identity is a polemic issue of contemporary relevance. Tomás Fernández Robaina considers the history of the much-debated term *Afro-Cuban,* with valuable insights relevant to innovative bibliographic classifications. Patricia Catoira critiques the Ortizian theory of transculturation as applied to his evolving intellectual proposals for Cuban national unity. These debates are not new in Latin American literature. Recent theoretical reinterpretations can profit significantly from the major insights on race and national identity gained by Ortiz. Ortiz's increasingly diverse interdisciplinary interests led him also to seminal studies on Afro-Cuban religions, with an original anthropological trend, as highlighted by Jorge Ramírez Calzadilla in his study of the influence of Spanish anticlericalism and Afro-Cuban religions on Cuban religiosity.

13

The Term *Afro-Cuban*: A Forgotten Contribution

Tomás Fernández Robaina

The term *Afro-Cuban* was first used in 1847, according to the information supplied by Fernando Ortiz in 1942, in reference to his *Hampa Afro-cubana: Los negros brujos* (1906):

> In this book I introduced the term, Afro-Cuban, which eliminated prejudice and accurately conveyed the original duality of the social phenomena we wanted to study. Antonio de Veitía had already used that term in Cuba for the first time in 1847, according to the gentle and erudite information of Francisco González del Valle; but this term had not been incorporated into the common language as it is today.[1]

Unfortunately, Ortiz does not explain how Veitía used this term. He does not explain the concept behind the term, either, although he uses the term several times. In the book's summation, where Ortiz describes the content of one of its chapters, he uses the subtitle "Triple Aspect of Afro-Cuban Witchcraft."[2] On the following page, at the beginning of the second paragraph, Ortiz writes, "The Afro-Cuban, even if he calls himself a Catholic, . . . remains a fetishist."[3]

This statement probably made sense at that moment and reflected Ortiz's own experiences. However, there were then and are now Afro-Cuban Catholics who refuse and even condemn religions of African origins. To state or insinuate that they were fetishist because they were black was to pretend and consider that Afro-Cuban religions, especially *santería*, were practiced exclusively by blacks. We cannot ignore that many blacks and mulattoes fully assimilated into Euro-centric cultural, religious, and social standards in order to advance toward equal conditions with the white population.

171

Ortiz also argues that "the Afro-Cuban fetishist in general, since the time in which slavery impeded his de-Africanization, was also a priest, a wizard, and a superstitious man."[4] He initially refers in general to male or female using the term *Afro-Cuban*. In two of the three references provided earlier, he uses the term as an adjective and once as a noun. In the first reference he terms the group of religious beliefs of Africans and their descendants as Afro-Cuban "witchcraft," indicating, however, that "Afro-Cuban witchcraft, as it exists today, does not normally inspire homicide."[5] This observation is relevant since the general notion at the time was that many of the crimes committed by blacks were motivated by religious beliefs. Two decades later, in an important text, he explains:

> it is important to remind here that, although the ethnic influences of the black population who reached Cuba were many, they have all blended their fundamental contributions to the extent that today one can speak of a specific psychology and set of Afro-Cuban customs without referring to their particular ethnic origins.[6]

It is clear that he conceived the Afro-Cuban character as the result of mutual influences between the different cultures of the slaves forcefully transferred from various parts of Africa, as well as similar influences between the slaves' cultures and the dominant colonial culture. However, Ortiz believed in a process of integration or dissolution of the slaves' original cultures, and their assimilation or absorption of the Euro-centric culture of slavery. He thus emphasizes:

> A psychological community was formed once the African divisions ended, and once all blacks from various origins mingled—initially in the narrow limits of the slave quarters (*barracón*) and the sugar mill buildings (*batey*), the old sugar mill (*cachimbo*) and the coffee plantation, later in the small towns, provinces or the island itself. It was then relatively easy, though necessary, for the blacks to gradually abandon their different languages and seek a common one, which could hardly be any of their own.[7]

And, of course, as a product of that assimilation and integration of the slaves into the dominant colonial culture, the conquering language "could not be any other than Spanish."[8] In *Los negros brujos* he has already stated:

> The spirit that preserves Latin and Hebrew among white religious persons helps to explain the preservation of African languages among fetishists, despite having been almost completely forgotten by the large majority of Afro-Cuban blacks.[9]

Currently, the conservation of some of those African languages in Cuba is one of the traits that most attracts language students. Not only is the old

Yoruba preserved, but also the language of the *Abakuás* is still used for "social communication" and ritualistic purposes among the members of the Abakuá secret society, or *ñáñigos* as they are popularly known.

I regard the idea behind the term *Afro-Cuban* as used by Ortiz in his famous lecture at the Club Atenas as highly relevant. The use of the term "eliminated prejudice and accurately conveyed the original duality of the social phenomena we wanted to study."[10] The term continued to be employed intellectually to refer to blacks and their cultures and beliefs. I say "intellectually" because at the time, as today, the majority of blacks of the various social classes did not and do not consider themselves Afro-Cubans. This classification or sociological, anthropological category reincorporated by Ortiz has not been widely adhered to among the majority of the Cuban population, especially among blacks and mulattoes. This makes sense if we realize that within all Cubans, and deeply within blacks and mulattoes, is embedded Martí's view that to be Cuban is to be more than white, more than black, more than mulatto; or Maceo's dictum not to ask for anything as a black but for everything as a Cuban.[11]

In texts addressing the issues of black Cubans, the term *Afro-Cuban* was used with the Ortizian original meaning of identifying blacks and their culture. It was used mainly among white and black intellectual circles involved in the social movement of black Cubans. In their struggle, these intellectuals endeavored to demonstrate that blacks had achieved the same intellectual level as whites who dominated the public, professional, artistic, and all other types of positions in Cuban society. Examples of this approach are the two important works of Gustavo E. Urrutia (1881–1958), the black intellectual who probably had the most profound insights on the racial problem within the context of Cuban nationality and identity.[12] In his *Cuatro charlas radiofónicas* (1935) that included four articles originating from radio broadcasts, he used the term *Afro-Cuban* several times, to refer to the cultures and ancestors of African origin.[13] In reply to the criticisms made to his radio program *Sensemayá*, the first to transmit the ritual music of *santería*, he firmly argued for the revendication of Afro-Cuban culture. Unlike others, Urrutia's efforts went beyond the social and economic struggle and courageously addressed mainly educated blacks with the intention of promoting the racial and cultural self-esteem of the African legacy. Thus, he stated:

> As the black population of the country is usually accused of having a savage and barbaric ancestry; as it is the Afro-Cuban who is scorned and shamed due to a supposed inheritance of inferiority, and denigrating racial flaws; so it is the Afro-Cuban who must urgently address and explain the religious, moral, and artistic values of his black forefathers, having absolutely nothing to envy, in moral and spiritual matters, of his white forefathers.[14]

It is clear that he refers to the black Cuban, as well as to the culture inherited from Africans as Afro-Cuban. Urrutia never regarded this as a danger to Cuban national identity and nationality. With full conviction he wrote:

> In my view, the problem must be dealt with as follows: within *cubanidad* and creole ethnology, and as long as white racism remains, the Afro-Cuban should be interested in upholding his free choice in the mental direction of his own race. He must begin by knowing what he wants and what is convenient to the overall progress of Cuba; he must point out, define, and transmit this to the white person so that there may be a cultured and fraternal debate.[15]

In 1937, a year in which the Afro-Cuban question was widely discussed in the midst of a debate on whether to revive the traditional parades of Havana's neighborhoods, Urrutia delivered a lecture that I consider to be of mandatory reference to all whites and blacks. I am referring to "Points of View on the New Black." Here he again used the term *Afro-Cuban*, but on this occasion he addressed economic and social issues:

> The New Black is the Afro-Cuban—male or female, young or old—who is convinced that our current demo-liberalism is unsuitable by itself in correcting the social and economic subordination and underestimation of people of color, inherited through our history of colonial slavery; being this regime incompetent in overcoming the dramatic disadvantage in the living conditions of the Cuban proletariat and middle classes, to which the race of color mainly belongs.[16]

Urrutia did not reject Cuban nationality and identity. On the contrary, he referred to the organization of a convention of the existing black societies at the time, in order to discuss Cuban problems and the racial issue. He firmly underscored:

> The New Black contemplates the global solution of the Cuban problem with the statesman's view and the spirit of justice for all, blacks and whites. Once the Convention has defined a collective program, an expression of the Afro-Cuban perspective on national problems, I believe that its leadership will contrast this view with that of the "New Whites," today's authentic revolutionaries, with the objective of uniting these views and embarking together the New White and the New Black, as the black and white separatists did in the past, a new liberating crusade: economic and social justice for all the inhabitants of our country.[17]

Fernando Ortiz witnessed the social struggle of the black man, the struggle of Urrutia and others, and participated in those debates through his writing and studies, and as member of societies such as the Society of Afro-Cuban Studies.[18] That is probably why Ortiz clearly explained the reason why he used the term *Afro-Cuban* and why he considered such use very convenient.

But not all intellectuals at the time, as indeed some today, viewed the term *Afro-Cuban* favorably. One of the most stern opponents of the term was Alberto Arredondo, the author of *El negro en Cuba* (1939).[19] In one of the chapters of the book, he passionately expresses his views, clearly arguing against the Afro-Cuban trend. Arguments similar to those elaborated by Arredondo are still being used:

> When speaking of nationality it is clearly established that when referring to a Cuban it is to include both blacks and whites. To pretend to refer to Afro-Cubans is to cause reference to Hispanic-Cubans. This would revive old and counterproductive conflicts at a time when Cuba needs the most the union of all its children.[20]

Arredondo perceived the Afro-Cuban issue as something that had been overcome; for him, all those who hailed from the island were Cubans at the time. Therefore, the term *Afro-Cuban* clashed with what he considered to be nationality and Cubanity. In this regard, he repeated notions expressed in colonial times, when the independence movement was being forged. In specific historical moments that involved political or social issues, a national cohesion has been demanded above other social demands, which could have threatened that union. Arredondo did not perceive the term *Afro-Cuban*, as Ortiz brilliantly conceived it, as conveying the original duality of the social phenomena he wanted to study. Obviously, the Afro-Cuban phenomenon could not be considered finished.

Rómulo Lachatañeré was another Cuban researcher to use the term *Afro-Cuban* as an adjective or a noun. He published his important essay on "The Lucumis Religious System and other African Influences in Cuba" in the *Revista de Estudios Afrocubanos*, edited by Ortiz.[21] In Lachatañeré's "Manual de Santería," the meaning given to the term *Afro-Cuban* is clear:

> [W]e do not know of any publication that studies the Afro-Cuban beliefs in accordance to Afro-Cuban interpretations, logical deductions, and philosophical speculations applied in the performing of their cults.[22]

Lachatañeré was also very critical of false interpretations of Afro-Cuban singing and dancing, at a time when almost every creation was classified as Afro-Cuban. He averred, "Today terms like conga, rumba, and Afro-Cuban are as popular in the United States as North American vernacular music itself."[23] The commercialization of African culture, especially the Afro-Cuban culture, had a good market at the time in the United States coinciding with the ongoing "discovery" of African cultures. The existence of this market for products of African origin might explain the adoption of the term *Afro-Cuban*, in the same way as the term *Afro-Brazilian* was adopted. In 1906, Ortiz himself had used the term *Afro-Bahian* in reference to San Salvador de

Bahía.[24] The prefix *Afro-* is very common in literature on the black person and his or her culture, not only in Brazil but also in Uruguay, Argentina, Ecuador, and other countries. Despite Arredondo's debatable but understandable objections in the context of his time, the term continued to be used with more or less assiduity.

One of the positive aspects of the Cuban revolution in its initial stages was that it provided a space for the study of all Cuban historical and cultural roots. And, of course, work started prominently toward the recovery of artistic, dancing, cultural, and musical values of the different African cultures. These cultures had mutually influenced each other and mixed with the dominant cultures, thus developing other cultures, some with the visible imprint of their original roots, others with less visible vestiges. The Conjunto Folklórico Nacional was created with the mission of preserving the dancing and musical values of the popular sectors in the country, among which those of African origin were fundamental. The Academy of Sciences of Cuba, through its Institute of Folklore and Ethnology, endeavored the rescue of aboriginal, African, and other popular religious traditions.

In 1968, there was a conference of a group of specialists in Afro-American cultures meeting in Havana and Santa Clara. On that occasion the Biblioteca Nacional José Martí compiled the first bibliography on the "Afro" theme, published as a short book of the revolutionary period.[25] For that task, I consulted musicologist and ethnologist Argeliers León. At the time I was beginning to gain interest in research, despite the fact that I was very surprised that the methodology that I was advised to follow explicitly discouraged the use of terms such as *Afro-Brazilian*, *Afro-Mexican*, *Afro-Cuban*, and others. Paradoxically, the title of that project was "Bibliography of Afro-American Studies." However, the compilation work soon provided sufficient elements for me to disagree with that methodology. The lack of an updated mechanism to compile information on African heritage in Latin America at the Biblioteca Nacional contributed to my disagreement on methodological issues. I was being advised not to use epigraphs or descriptors with the prefix *Afro-*, as was the practice used in books on classification, and especially in the printed catalog of the U.S. Library of Congress, the bible of all librarians.

I could understand that the prefix was not used, according to the explanation given to me. But nowhere in the Biblioteca Nacional was there a "see also" that could guide me to the various headings where I could find equivalent information. I concluded that it was essential to use the term *Afro-Cuban* as an adjective, because of the need that all librarians have of providing information. There was the need to simply refer to the cultural and historical phenomena that Africans and their forefathers had left and still maintained in the American soil. Regardless of whether anyone sympathized or not with the term *Afro-Cuban*, practical life and its laws imposed its use. How could one ignore this reality?

In 1992, I had the opportunity to work at the New York Public Library's Schomburg Center for Research in Black Culture in Harlem. As a result of my work there making use of the "Afro" material in the different branches of that library, and given the fact that these materials were not accessible through the conventional headings used in that library, I elaborated a new list on the basis of the Latin American "Afro" resources cataloged in the Biblioteca Nacional. I also provided that list to the Biblioteca Nacional so that their catalogers could provide a better service to library visitors. However, as far as I know, nothing of that sort has been implemented. One is still unable to find the novel *Cuando la sangre se parece al fuego*[26] by Manuel Cofiño through the heading "Afro-Cuban novels" or "Santería in novels" or any other indicator that may suggest its content. This is the case for both the New York Public Library in New York and the Biblioteca Nacional José Martí in Havana.

More recently, I had another experience with someone who was against the use of the term *Afro-Cuban*. His objections were firm. He expressed his views after I had invited him to participate in a debate on a course I had given on Gustavo E. Urrutia and the Afro-Cuban movement of the 1930s. His arguments were similar to those upheld by Arredondo: *Afro-Cuban* distinctions prevented Cuban unity. Instead, the term *Cuban culture* already implied all of our roots. For that person, the Cuban culture is one and finite. As far as I am concerned, though I also believe the Cuban culture to be one, I consider that we must interpret it in consideration of the roots still alive in many of its expressions. In order to appreciate these roots we must use the term *Afro-Cuban*, or *Sino-Cuban*, or *Hispanic-Cuban*, or any other that is appropriate. I see no danger in referring to objective phenomena by their names.

This is why I believe that the term *Afro-Cuban*, as Fernando Ortiz conceived it, is still current. If today one refers to *Afro-Brazilian*, *Afro-Ecuadorian*, and *Afro-Peruvian* cultures, then why is it that in Cuba, which is one of the countries in Latin America with the most prominent black population and heritage, one is unable to use the term? In the New York Public Library's Schomburg Center for Research in Black Culture, one can consult dozens of books using the prefix *Afro-* to describe a noun or an adjective relating to a specific country, continent or city, such as *Afro-Brazilian* music, *Afro-Mexicans*, *Afro-Bahian*, among others. This can be extracted simply from the titles of some of the chapters that appear in *Afro-Brazilian Culture and Politics* (1998)—for example, "A Mixed-Race Nation: Afro-Brazilians and Cultural Policy;" [27] also those terms in *Faces de tradiçao afro-brasileira* (1999): "Afro-Recife religions; Afro-Brazilian syncretism," among others relating to specific countries.[28]

I consider that the term *Afro-Cuban*, used as an adjective or a noun, although an intellectual construction incorporated in the research lexicon of Ortiz, and subsequently adopted in other professional fields, tends to consolidate rather than separate. *Afro-Cuban* is a term that illustrates the result of an ongoing process of influences among African cultures in Cuba and the dominant Euro-centric cultures. I consider that we are still a young country, in all senses, with a young republican history. We must approach that history using the entire legacy that researchers have provided on Cuban history and culture, especially the significant contribution of Fernando Ortiz toward the use of the term *Afro-Cuban*.

NOTES

1. Fernando Ortiz, "Por la integración cubana de blancos y negros," *Revista Bimestre Cubana* 51, no. 2 (1943): 258.
2. Fernando Ortiz, *Hampa afro-cubana: Los negros brujos*, 2d ed. (Madrid: Editorial-América, 1917), 17.
3. Ortiz, *Negros brujos*, 42; he also uses the term in some phrases on pages 61, 89, 141, 146, 167, 173, 176, 180, 181, 182, 187, 188, 193, 195, 212, 220, 229, 231, 239, 356, 357, 361, 366, 368, 382, and 393.
4. Ortiz, *Negros brujos*, 45.
5. Ortiz, *Negros brujos*, 357.
6. Fernando Ortiz, "Los afronegrismos de nuestro lenguaje," *Revista Bimestre Cubana* 17, no. 6 (1922): 321.
7. Ortiz, "Afronegrismos," 321.
8. Ortiz, *Negros brujos*, 31.
9. Ortiz, "Por la integración cubana," 258.
10. José Martí, "Mi raza," in *Obras completas* (Havana: Editorial de Ciencias Sociales, 1975), vol. 2: 298.
11. Gustavo E. Urrutia (1881–1958), was one of the most important black reporters and intellectuals in Cuba. His work is barely known due to his dispersed body of articles, mainly published in *Diario de la Marina* between 1928 and 1958.
12. Gustavo E. Urrutia, *Cuatro charlas radiofónicas* (Havana: n.p., 1935): 20.
13. Urrutia, *Cuatro charlas*, 17.
14. Urrutia, *Cuatro charlas*, 15.
15. Gustavo E. Urrutia, *Puntos de vista del nuevo negro* (Havana, 1937), 38.
16. Urrutia, *Puntos de vista*, 4.
17. Urrutia, *Puntos de vista*, 36–37.
18. *Estudios Afrocubanos*—a journal founded by Ortiz and other intellectuals at the time when there was an extensive public debate in Brazil regarding black presence and their culture. It published superb texts, including those of Rómulo Lachatañeré.
19. Alberto Arredondo, El negro in Cuba (Havana: Editorial Alfa, 1939),170.
20. Arredondo, *El negro en Cuba*, 103.
21. Rómulo Lachatañeré, "El sistema religioso de los lucumí y otras influencias africanas en Cuba," in *El sistema religioso de los afrocubanos*, 149–362 (Habana: Editorial de Ciencias Sociales, 1992). This text includes all of Lachatañeré's works published during his permanence in Cuba as well as his later contributions to weekly publications of the United States.
22. Rómulo Lachatañeré, "Manual de santería," in *El sistema religioso de los afrocubanos*, 95.

23. Rómulo Lachatañeré, "Congas y afrocubanismos de exportación," in *El sistema religioso de los afrocubanos*, 382.

24. Ortiz, *Los negros brujos*, 61. He also refers to "negros-criollos," 8.

25. Tomás Fernández Robaina, comp., *Bibliografía de estudios afroamericanos*, prologue by Argeliers León (Havana: Biblioteca Nacional José Martí, 1968), 96.

26. Manuel Cofiño, *Cuando la sangre se parece al fuego* (Havana: UNEAC, 1975), 244.

27. Hendrik Kaay, ed., *Afro-Brazilian Cultures and Politics: Bahia 1790s to 1990s* (Armonk, N.Y.: Sharpe, 1998), 208.

28. Carlos Caroso and Jeferson Bacelar, eds., *Faces de tradição afro-brasileira: religiosidades, sincretismo, antisincretismo, reafricanização e práticas terapêuticas, etnobotânicas e comida* (Salvador: Pallas, 1999), 346.

14

Transculturation à la *Ajiaco*

A Recipe for Modernity

Patricia Catoira

Throughout his essays, Ortiz referred to a well-known Cuban dish, *ajiaco*, a Creole stew that incorporates American, European, and African ingredients. For him, the mixture of the *ajiaco* provided an excellent metaphor for the cultural processes that have shaped Cuban society since colonization. Ortiz proposed that *cubanidad*—the identity of the Cuban people—should be thought of in terms of the *ajiaco*, since the encounter of different cultures in Cuba contributed to the development of a hybrid culture. The term he used to describe this cultural process was *transculturation.*

In this way, Ortiz was part of a long line of Latin American intellectuals who have taken it upon themselves to study and formulate the identity of their countries and their continent. In this essay, I intend to show how Ortiz's concept of cultural change related to his preoccupation with *cubanidad*. Ortiz considered *cubanidad* a necessary foundation for the creation of an independent nation in every sense of the word: politically, socially, economically, and culturally. Although Ortiz attempted to create a meaningful place in the national story for Cubans from marginal races and cultures, I have found that, in the end, he gravitated toward a homogenizing cultural project.

While most of Spain's colonies in Latin America became independent in the first decades of the nineteenth century, Cuba, Puerto Rico, and the Philippines were the last ones to gain their independence in 1898. In Cuba, Spain's defeat did not bring about the end of foreign involvement in Cuban society. Scholars have described the military, political, economic, and cultural presence of the United States on the island in the early twentieth century as "neo-colonialism": the period when American power supplanted the Spanish and frustrated the nationalist desire for a completely independent country. The

Peace Treaty of Paris (1898) between Spain and the United States installed an American provisional military government in Cuba to ensure social order on the island. This occupation lasted until 1902, when the first Cuban republic was formed. Even then, independence from the northern neighbor was not total. In exchange for political independence, American interests forced the Cuban Congress to include the Platt Amendment in its 1901 Cuban constitution.[1]

Ortiz found three main internal faults (*fallas internas*) that he thought were responsible for the state of national disintegration in Cuba and that were, therefore, impeding the realization of a national and universal culture. These faults included political corruption, imperialism, and racism. In 1919, in "La crisis política cubana," Ortiz denounced the lack of unity among Cubans as the main problem affecting the country. He stressed the amorality of politicians and the lack of culture of the popular classes as causes of this disintegration. After the formation of the first republic in 1902, a series of corrupt governments contributed to the frequent instability of the new nation. Historian Louis Pérez registers this in the following way:

> During the administrations of José Miguel Gómez [1908–1912] and Mario G. Menocal, a total of some 372 indictments were brought against public officials, dealing with a wide range of offenses, including embezzlement, fraud, homicide, infraction of postal regulations, violation of lottery law, misappropriation of funds, and violation of electoral laws. By 1923, the number of indictments had increased to 483.[2]

For Ortiz, this corruption also symbolized the deficient culture of the ruling class. In his view, their personal interests conflicted with the progress and the interests of the nation and the world.[3]

Ortiz saw American involvement in Cuban affairs as another internal fault. Backed by the Platt Amendment, the United States intervened politically and militarily several times in the island during the first decades of the republic under the pretext of quelling social unrest.[4] The regional power's economic penetration became even more prominent after the period called "the dance of the millions" in the 1920s. The euphoria resulting from the rise in sugar prices encouraged many plantation owners to ask for loans to expand production. Overproduction of sugar caused a drop in prices and the subsequent ruin of Cuban landowners. As a result, American companies appropriated bankrupt haciendas, plantations, and factories.[5] According to Ortiz in "La crisis política cubana," this foreign presence mirrored the spiritual debility of the national character whose heart was being bought by fast enrichment. Foreign capital could not feel "the patriotic vibration" and, therefore, endangered national progress.[6]

Even so, Ortiz had ambiguous feelings toward the United States. While he criticized the increasing American takeover of the island, in 1923, as president of the Revolutionary Junta, Ortiz made a call for the "moral intervention" of the United States in the island in order to stabilize the social chaos under the Machado government.[7] Similarly, in his essay "Imperialismo y buena vecindad," Ortiz showed a contradictory position by denouncing the intentions of the United States but declaring, at the same time, the need to keep close relations between both countries through a reformulation of the term "panamericanism." In this essay, he emphasized that

> the "American unity" . . . will be nothing but a positive economic reordering, built with "science and conscience." . . . It is necessary to start another inter-American New Deal, a Renew Deal to bring all American states abundant crops, mines, machines, laboratories, schools, universities, and civic values.[8]

Therefore, Ortiz suggested that the presence of the United States could play a major role in the modernization of Cuba and Latin America.

According to Ortiz, the third internal fault that was ripping Cuban society apart was racism. The Ten Years' War (1868–1878) had united blacks and whites against the Spanish colonial regime. Slavery was finally abolished in 1886, but this structural change marked the change from a slave system to a racist one. At the same time, the popularity of deterministic ideas about the inferiority of the black race once again relegated the Afro-Cuban to a lower place in society. Furthermore, the American military and administrative presence reinforced the racism of Cuban Creoles. Cuban historian Julio Le Riverend explains the situation in the following way:

> It was stressed that blacks and colored Cubans should not be allowed to appear prominently in the institutional life of the country, for reasons of "patriotism" so as to calm the racist worries of the new ruler, named with euphemism or surrender "our friends."[9]

Racial tension intensified in the first years of the republic. The appropriation of land by American companies created general malaise throughout the island, especially in Oriente province, where the population of blacks and whites was almost evenly balanced. In 1912, the Independent Party of Color's political revolt against the Morúa Law ignited the spark that lit up the lower classes' accumulated frustrations.[10] There were uprisings across the island, but they were more intense in Oriente. Due to the great number of participants of color, the revolt was called a "race war." For Pérez, this appellation covers up the true motivations behind the uprising: the pervasive political, economic, and administrative marginality of the peasantry. In fact, "the view that the protest was a race war," Pérez argues, "served to divide the peasantry along racial lines. . . . The construct served to unify the white majority in Oriente, and this unity tended to cut across class lines. . . . It served as the basis for repression."[11]

This state of national disintegration was in Ortiz's eyes comparable to a state of "barbarism" and "semiculture," an argument that he developed in his essay "La decadencia cubana." The only way to overcome such a state, Ortiz proposed, lay in a self-evaluation of the faults in Cuban society and in the definition and diffusion of a true Cuban national culture. For him, economic and political independence was to be obtained through a national unity based on culture: "Only in true culture can be found the necessary strength to live a life without servitude."[12]

In Ortiz's body of essays, one notices a transformation between his initial ethnological positivist phase and his posterior cultural phase. Following the positivist influence, he considered blacks responsible for the poor state of Cuban society. He believed that blacks introduced such elements as *ñañiguismo*,[13] superstition, and dialects that disintegrated Cuban culture. Ortiz also argued that blacks had developed their race thanks to their miscegenation with other races. However, in the second edition of *Los negros brujos* (1917), Ortiz reformulated his argument. The black subject, which he saw as a disruptive marginal force in 1906, was now reinterpreted in a more complex historical and social context. The essentialist association of the Afro-Cuban with the underworld disappeared from this edition. Ortiz now claimed that the term "bad life" (*mala vida*) was used by the dominant group to marginalize and contain a way of life that was different from, or that could challenge, theirs. Ortiz adapted his methodology for studying Cuban society to an approach more in tune with his developing idea of national progress. He abandoned the ethnological perspective to focus on a totalizing social study that would allow Cuba to reach the level of or the category of "universal civilization," which according to him only strong nations possessed:

> Undoubtedly, one of the first tasks of the advancing modern generation must be the precise, emotionless, objective, unprejudiced, detailed, and informed analysis of the multiple factors that each race has contributed to our customs and national character, and the evolution of each of those specific factors in relation to the others.[14]

In order to establish a unifying discourse around an all-encompassing idea of Cuban culture, Ortiz attacked the racialist thought from the nineteenth century and its intellectual offspring, such as Nazism. "Racism," Ortiz stated, "is an anachronistic concept of barbarism, incompatible with the contemporary demands of culture and enemy of the Cuban nation."[15] Ortiz emphasized the difference between the concepts of race and culture by using a theory of counterpoint:

> Certainly, culture does not signify what race signifies. The former is a human classification based on typical means of life, a social behavior; the latter is an attempt at a morphological and physical classification. . . . Culture is an essentially

human and sociological concept; race is of an exclusive zoological nature. And today we attempt to use the word *culture* precisely because of its social and effective significance, free of any mythological and deceptive burden imposed on the term race.[16]

Therefore, for Ortiz, the ruling elite manipulated the pseudoscience of racialism to its own ends. The effect was to exacerbate divisions in Cuban society, which Ortiz saw as an impediment to a national progress toward modernity.

In Ortiz's opinion, culture was the key to understanding socio-historical developments and he would follow several steps in analyzing them. Diana Iznaga delineates Ortiz's steps in the following way: isolate the cultural elements that form Cuban culture; study the evolution of each element separately in Cuba; analyze the relation of each element with the rest; study the evolution of those relations until the present day; and compare the original manifestations to the Cuban amalgams in order to draw conclusions.[17] With this methodological process, Ortiz was able to formulate a Cuban cultural discourse around the concept of transculturation.

In his masterpiece, *Cuban Counterpoint*, Ortiz introduced transculturation in order to counteract the racialist discourse and other theories of cultural contact that were in vogue at the beginning of the twentieth century. The term *transculturation* alludes to an effort to decolonize the language of social science. With it, Celina Manzoni argues, Ortiz implanted a space of resistance in language.[18] The term sought to replace others—especially *acculturation*—that were based on ideologies of cultural superiority propagated by "high-cultured," imperialist powers.[19]

Acculturation, as Bronislaw Malinowski points out in the introduction to the first edition of *Cuban Counterpoint*, supposes a cultural contact in which the "uncultivated" group, the Other, loses elements of its culture in order to assimilate itself to the dominant group. For the Polish anthropologist, the term *acculturation* was ethnocentric.[20] Acculturation reflects, then, an unequal relation between two cultures already predetermined as inferior and superior. In contrast, *transculturation* was, according to Ortiz, a more suitable term for the process of contact:

> It is used to express the multiple phenomena, which are generated in Cuba due to the complex transmutation of cultures existing here. Ignoring them prevents us from understanding the evolution of the Cuban people, in the economic as well as the institutional, legal, ethical, religious, artistic, linguistic, psychological, sexual, and the rest of its aspects.[21]

This is the reason why Ortiz believed that Cuban culture was "creative, dynamic, and social." Manzoni also considers *Cuban Counterpoint* to be a hybrid text in itself. The amalgam of genres, the incursion of appendices, the illustrations, and the tables of statistics along with the use of different types of language and narrative styles create, in the whole, "a scientific analysis contaminated by mixture, heterogeneity, crossings, ruptures, changes of direction and rhythm, which make the Caribbean culture so different and unique."[22]

Ortiz found four main instances of transculturation in Cuba based on interethnic contacts. The first instance took place with the substitution of the Paleolithic Indian (*siboney* and *guanajabil*) by the Neolithic Indian (*taino*), and the subsequent disappearance of the latter when he was not able to "accommodate himself to the new Castillan culture."[23] The second transculturation process occurred with the arrival of Spanish colonizers and immigrants who came from different cultures and regions of the Iberian peninsula and its islands. These Spaniards, according to Ortiz, had to adjust to the cultural backgrounds of their compatriots but also to the culture forming overseas. The third instance happened in a similar manner with the arrival of African slaves who belonged to different tribes and ethnic groups. Lastly, the sporadic immigration of other groups such as the Chinese and the Portuguese contributed to another transculturation. The feelings of being uprooted (*desarraigo*) and transitory, which each community experienced, were, in Ortiz's judgment, transcendental factors for *cubanidad* and, consequently, for national unity. These periods of contact constituted a series of adjustments and maladjustments in the cultural exchanges among different groups that produced a new syncretic culture. For Ortiz, this new culture was *cubanidad*.

In the analysis of these processes of adjustment during transculturation, Ortiz seemed to forget that the feeling of transitoriness and uprooting that he considered characteristic of the process of transculturation was not felt in the same way by all groups. While for the Spaniards the arrival to Cuba could cause psychological uprooting from the *madre patria*, for many this was a chance to thrive and prosper. The position of social and economic power that many Spaniards held established unequal cultural exchanges. The transculturation of the Spaniards with other ethnic groups was part of a strategy of power and domination.

This phenomenon can be observed clearly in the explanation of the transculturation of tobacco that Ortiz mapped out in *Cuban Counterpoint*. While he considered the development of tobacco in Cuba as an example of (spontaneous) transculturation, from his own explanation one can deduce that it was, instead, a process of transculturation that culminated in the appropriation of a cultural practice propelled by economic and power motivations. Here lies one of the contradictions in Ortiz's analysis. Tobacco, Ortiz argued, was at first taboo, a thing of savages and devils. Indians used it in religious and medicinal practices. Africans adopted the unknown plant for the same uses and began to cultivate it in small plots of land in the plantation. In the sixteenth century, with the disappearance of the Indian population, the sale of tobacco became a black business. However, due to the incipient demand of tobacco by certain groups of the white community (sailors, merchants, etc.), the Spanish soon realized the lucrative possibilities of this plant. As a result, in 1557, the municipal council in Havana passed a law prohibiting blacks from selling tobacco and it became a white business. From that point on, tobacco use was accepted and began to spread among white Creoles.

In contrast, Africans lived under an oppressive slave regime and this meant that assimilation of the culture of power (the Spanish) was an act of cultural appropriation as a means to thrive socially. For instance, learning the Spanish language facilitated work in the slavemaster's house. Therefore, in a way, Ortiz seemed to forget that the "painful transculturations" mirrored the cultural hierarchy existing in Cuba. Cultural exchanges were unequal because they developed within a power framework. Angel Rama admits his certain uneasiness with Ortiz's formulation of the transculturation process.

> This design does not comply with the requirements of selectivity and invention that must apply in all cases of "cultural plasticity," because that state certifies the energy and creativity of a cultural community. If this is a lively one, it will meet the requirement of selectivity, within itself and through external contributions, and it will necessarily invent through an "*ars combinatorio*" fitting with the autonomy of the cultural system itself.[24]

Therefore, Rama recognizes that cultural exchange is not spontaneous but selective from each point of contact. The Uruguayan critic contextualizes the process of transculturation within the practices of modernity since he considers that such selection responds to a desire to create or invent a cultural identity that is *viable*—in other words, a cultural model that allows access or functionality to the new power dynamics. In a similar way, Mary Louise Pratt proposes in her book *Imperial Eyes* that in many instances the processes and the dynamics of transculturation take place in "contact zones," which she defines as social spaces where different cultures interact from asymmetric positions of domination and subordination.[25]

Ortiz paid special attention to the study of transculturation between whites and blacks. He believed that it was in this phenomenon where Cuba could find the unifying base from which to build a modern nation. The most important essay in this regard is "Por la integración cubana de blancos y negros" from 1943. It is in this text where Ortiz is most problematic. In the first place, his analysis of culture in terms of white and black reinforced the presence of a racial discourse and ignored the cultural diversity within those racial categories. Therefore, Ortiz created a contradiction in his central argument—identity through cultural unity—because he overlooked the cultural project and the agency of, for instance, the Galician community as well as those of racial minorities such as the Chinese. It is true, as mentioned earlier, that Ortiz recognized the presence of this diversity in the phases of transculturation in Cuba, but he discussed these groups as part of the past rather than as living, dynamic cultures. In other words, Ortiz was inscribing the presence of, let's say, the Haitian in the moment of his arrival on the island as a historical fact instead of as a contributing participant of the modern Cuban society. It is as if Ortiz were proposing that the contribution of each ethnocultural group consolidated with time, through transculturation, into two big cultural blocks defined by the two majority races: black and white. Ortiz was therefore hiding racial parameters behind his idea of cultural unity. These parameters, as a result, were contradicting the base of his argument.

In the second place, in "Por la integración cubana de blancos y negros," one can notice once again how the concept of transculturation reflects an unequal relation in the adjustments resulting from cultural contact. Ortiz proposed that the transculturation between the culture of whites and blacks had taken place in five distinct phases: hostility, accommodation, adaptation, self-affirmation, and integration. The explanation of each phase centers around how, little by little, blacks became assimilated in the culture of power—the white culture. This display of the process denotes by itself the inequality of the components. In the hostility phase, blacks rebelled, fled to *palenques* or communities of runaway slaves, or committed suicide as response to their slavery. The accommodation phase developed during the first generation of Creoles; blacks began adapting to the new land and became attached to it. It is also in this phase when *mestizaje* occurred at a larger scale than before. Also, Ortiz made the black an exotic subject by linking him to dancing and singing: "the black person can now dance and the white person has fun with him," "Ya el negro puede bailar y el blanco con él se divierte," and by speaking of the "sensual" love embodied in black women that allowed for their *mestizaje* with whites.[26]

Ortiz judged adaptation to be the most difficult phase. This occurred during the second generation of Creoles. Blacks denied their color and wanted to imitate whites for their own benefit. In the next phase, blacks had the opposite feeling and were proud of their race and heritage. This period of self-affirmation happened at the end of the nineteenth century and the beginning of the twentieth. Ortiz argued that, at this point, there was mutual respect between blacks and whites, but racial prejudices persisted. Ortiz longed for the last phase, integration, to be realized in Cuba:

> It is the last one in which cultures have fused together and conflict has ceased; they have given way to a *tertium quid*, a third entity and culture, to a new community culturally integrated in which merely racial factors have lost their divisive malice.[27]

The essay "Por la integración de blancos y negros" is the transcription of a conference delivered in 1942 in which Ortiz stated:

In that [integrating phase] there is exists only a reduced minority. In that phase is where we are those who meet here today. . . . That is why the present event by a group of Cubans of diverse races, who gather for a rite of social commun-ion, consecrates the need for reciprocal understanding on the objective basis of truth, in order to approach the definitive integration of the nation. For its pro-found and consequential sense this meeting represents a new moment in the history of the homeland and as such we need to interpret it.[28]

Here the project of national unity that Ortiz proposed finally reveals itself as an intellectual project. For him, the intellectual minority was charged with spreading and promoting the national culture—*cubanidad*—to the rest of the nation. Cultural diffusion, then, does not seem to be as dynamic and spontaneous as Ortiz theorized. Moreover, Ortiz established cultural cate-gories depending on the degree of "development" of the nation.[29] Conse-quently, he considered the culture of the Cuba of his time inferior to the cul-ture of the United States because Cuba had not reached the level of civilization and material progress of its northern neighbor.

Many contemporary critics question the models of transculturation, *mesti-zaje*, or multiculturalism that are lately so popular. Antonio Cornejo Polar criticizes these discourses as falsifications of the Latin American racial and cultural reality:

The idea of transculturation becomes more and more the most sophisticated cover for the category of miscegenation [*mestizaje*]. After all, the symbol of the "ajiaco," defined by Rama, can well be the highest emblem of the false harmony in which the process of multiple mixtures ends up.[30]

In his analysis of the cultural creolization in the Caribbean, the Jamaican critic Edward Kamau Brathwaite states that these terms of intermixing and heterogeneous projects can be applied to the formation of a national culture, but they must not be taken as a base for a national identity or as a privileged model of the future. For him, the idea of social unity is incompatible with the idea of cultural diversity; he considers Caribbean reality to be "cracked, frag-mented, ambivalent, not certain of itself."[31]

At the end, there are contradictions in Ortiz's proposal of *cubanidad* as remedy for the problems of the Cuba in the first decades of the twentieth century. On the one side, Ortiz proposed *cubanidad*—the feeling of being Cuban—as a remedy for the political corruption, the "civic anemia," and the passivity of the Cuban people regarding foreign presence and national deca-dence. On the other side, he suggested immigration from Europe and "ad-vanced countries to enhance the importance of the manual force and . . . the *importation of ideas*" (my italics), and proposed that Cuba open up to the "cultural breeze" coming from its neighbor in the north.[32]

In sum, although Ortiz believed culture to be dynamic and constantly changing, his intellectual project imposed a model of cultural integration that had not happened yet in the society of his time and that, according to him, was only present in the Cuban intellectual minority. Ortiz was anticipating a cultural identity—*cubanidad*—that, at that time, Cuban people did not yet feel. In this sense, the presupposed dynamism and spontaneity of the process of transculturation proved to be limited. Ortiz sought national unity to promote economic, political, and cultural progress in Cuba and, in this way, be independent and able to compete with other nations like the United States.

However, the concept of transculturation that Ortiz invented served, in fact, homogenizing purposes at a cultural level. It is true that he took into account the contribution of Indians, Africans, and others to *cubanidad*, but that contribution was only discussed as part of the past. Ortiz reduced the cultural plurality to two groups defined by race, blacks and whites, and with this he left behind the projects of cultural or racial minorities.

Furthermore, according to his model, the integration between both groups responded more to a cultural "whitening" of blacks than to transculturation. Therefore, the project of national unity that Ortiz proposed was a homogenizing project dressed in cultural rhetoric, which claimed to include all the diverse elements of the Cuban *ajiaco*.

NOTES

1. The Platt Amendment addressed the United States' political, economic, and military goals in Cuba. It imposed restrictions on foreign relations and on the management of the national budget: the United States had the power to intervene in the country if it feared social unrest.

2. Louis A. Perez, Jr. *Cuba under the Platt Amendment, 1912–1934* (Pittsburgh: University of Pittsburgh Press, 1986), 217.

3. Ortiz, "La crisis política cubana," in Julio Le Riverend, ed., *Orbita de Fernando Ortiz*, (Havana: UNEAC, 1973), 101.

4. The United States took control of the island from 1906 to 1909 and had different degrees of intervention in four occasions during the period 1909–1921.

5. Edwin Williamson, *The Penguin History of Latin America* (London: Penguin, 1992), 440.

6. Ortiz, "La crisis política cubana," in *Orbita de Fernando Ortiz*, 99–120.

7. Pérez, *Cuba under the Platt Amendment*, 293.

8. Fernando Ortiz, "Imperialismo y buena vecindad," in *Orbita de Fernando Ortiz*, 318.

9. Julio Le Riverend, "Prólogo," in *Orbita de Fernando Ortiz*, 17.

10. The Morúa Law, passed in 1910 by José Miguel Gómez's liberal government, prohibited the organization of political parties based on racial criteria.

11. Louis A. Perez, Jr. "Politics, Peasants, and People of Color: The 1912 'Race War' in Cuba reconsidered," *Hispanic American Historical Review* 66, no. 3 (1986): 539.

12. Ortiz, "La decadencia cubana," in *Orbita de Fernando Ortiz*, 73.

13. The *ñáñigos* integrated black secret societies that tried to preserve African culture and religion. In some cases, these societies had the social role of providing economic or emotional help to their members.

14. Ortiz, "Las supervivencias africanas en Cuba," in Julio Le Riverend, ed., *Entre cubanos: psicología tropical* (Havana: Editorial de Ciencias Sociales), 87.

15. Ortiz, "Por la integración cubana de blancos y negros" [from Salvador Bueno, ed., *Los mejores ensayistas cubanos* (Lima: Imprenta Torres Aguirre, 1959)], in *Orbita de Fernando Ortiz*, 185.

16. Fernando Ortiz, *El engaño de las razas* (Havana: Editorial de Ciencias Sociales, 1975), 401–2.

17. Diana Iznaga, *Transculturación en Fernando Ortiz* (Havana: Editorial de Ciencias Sociales, 1989).

18. Celina Manzoni, "El ensayo ex-céntrico: el *Contrapunteo* de Fernando Ortiz (algo más que un cambio de nombre)," *Filología* 29 (1996): 151–56.

19. One of the most important works was *Acculturation. The Study of Culture Contact* (1838) from the anthropologist Melville J. Herskovits.

20. Bronislaw Malinowski (1884–1942) is considered the founder of the functionalist school in anthropology.

21. Ortiz, *Contrapunteo*, 137.

22. Manzoni, "Ensayo ex-céntrico," 155.

23. Ortiz, *Contrapunteo*, 137.

24. Angel Rama, *Transculturación narrativa en América Latina* (Mexico: Siglo XXI, 1982), 38.

25. Mary Louise Pratt, *Imperial Eyes: Travel Writing and Transculturation* (London: Routledge, 1992).

26. Ortiz, "Por la integración," in *Orbita de Fernando Ortiz*, 186–87.

27. Ortiz, "Por la integración," in *Orbita de Fernando Ortiz*, 188.

28. Ortiz, "Por la integración," in *Orbita de Fernando Ortiz*, 188.

29. Ortiz, "La decadencia cubana," in *Orbita de Fernando Ortiz*.

30. Antonio Cornejo Polar, "Mestizaje e hibridez: los riesgos de las metáforas. Apuntes," *Revista Iberoamericana* vol. 63 (1997): 341.

31. Brathwaite Edward Kamau, *Contradictory Omens: Cultural Diversity and Integration in the Caribbean* (Mona: Savacou Pulbications, 1974), 6.

32. Ortiz, "La crisis política cubana," in *Orbita de Fernando Ortiz*, 113.

15

Religion in the Work of Fernando Ortiz

Jorge Ramírez Calzadilla

One of the greatest contributions of Fernando Ortiz's work, some of it yet unpublished, is no doubt his innovative study of African influence in Cuban culture and religion. However, Ortiz's contribution in this field was not limited to the study of African religions and their Cuban derivatives. He elaborated important descriptions, reflections, and evaluations of other religious forms or currents that resulted in Cuba's complex and heterogeneous religious framework. The specialist who studies religion in Cuba must necessarily consider Ortiz's references to Catholicism and the modalities it adopted through time. In Ortiz's opinion, these Catholic adaptations were very close to the religions of African origin or to modern spiritualism, which Ortiz had studied thoroughly.

Ortiz regarded Cuban culture and religion as the result of a synthesis of diverse contributions. This give-and-take process formed a cultural *ajiaco*, an accurate term in describing the Cuban cultural and religious phenomena. In this way a more realistic understanding of religious issues can be reached for different periods, particularly in the present. However, Ortiz's work in this regard must not be viewed as a finished product. Doing so leads to regrettable mistakes. The analysis of his work should follow a diachronic course as his knowledge on the subject evolved. Ortiz moved from being influenced by criminological schools toward a more integrating and flexible perspective to establish the foundations of Cuban ethnology, anthropology, and sociology of religion. His early works were full of prejudice and erroneous appreciations that he later revised and corrected as he matured intellectually.

In this essay, I will first summarize the main characteristics of the religious background operating before Ortiz's research began. I will then analyze his considerations of different religious forms and their origins and evolution in Cuban society using a series of categories present in his work. I contend that this analytical approach contributes to a better understanding of the current situation of religion in Cuban society. These arguments are designed to present suggestions for debates and reflection on the matter.

RELIGIOUS BACKGROUND TO ORTIZ'S STUDIES

The complexity, heterogeneity, and contradictory issues of Cuban religion are mainly due to their diversity of origin and cultural multiplicity. The first and oldest social and cultural model established in Cuba is the indigenous. The indigenous groups on the island never achieved the levels of development of the Inca and Meso-American cultures; their aboriginal religion did not intervene as significantly in the reproduction of a society in which power and essential resources for life (land, crops, water) were sacred. Even Spanish domination in Cuba failed to have the repercussions it had in other parts of Spanish America. While the colonial system allowed the preservation of the indigenous cultural heritage and its ritual in the mainland, in Cuba, enslavement led to the disappearance of entire ethnic communities. However, certain indigenous vestiges could not be erased, and somehow their contributions filtered into Cuban religion, as recent studies suggest.[1]

The Spanish version of Western culture, a long-established dominant culture that imposed Catholicism as the official and exclusive religion, remained in Cuba longer than in other Spanish colonies in the Americas. After Cuban independence, Spanish influence was prolonged by Spaniards who remained active in trade and agriculture, by additional immigrations, and by Catholicism being imposed as the official and exclusive religion.

It is important to understand three factors that conditioned Catholicism in Cuba. First, the church was subject to a strong dependence on the Spanish Crown, and its local ecclesiastical organization and style were subordinated to those of Spain. Second, the behavior of the clergy in the colony was not particularly ethical or dedicated, a claim for which there is plenty of evidence. Finally, the type of Catholicism that was imported to Cuba rejected the renovating tendencies of the Reformation, and was strongly influenced by Jewish, Moorish, and Medieval superstitions. It was not the Catholicism of the great mystics, not even that of the official ecclesiastical hierarchy; it was, in fact, closer to so-called Spanish popular Catholicism.

In summary, orthodox Catholicism did not develop strong roots in Cuban society. Consequently, an anticlerical position permeated the most advanced ideas of the nineteenth century, finding its way into the Cuban sense of nationality even up to our own days. These leading, foundational ideas were antidogmatic and freethinking, but without being atheistic or antireligious.

This line of thought was espoused by Sanguily, Mestre, Varona, and others, and it was synthesized in Martí. Its legal expression is contained in the Cuban constitutions dating back to the early independence struggle.

The African sociocultural model contributed different forms of religion, and gradually modified to form the current Cuban manifestations, among them Regla Ocha or saint cult of yoruba origin; the Regla Conga or *"palo monte,"* a *bantú* origin; the Abakuá male secret societies, similar to the Nigerian societies; and other less widespread forms such as the Regla Arará and Regla Iyesá.[2]

The inefficient work of the clergy and the inconvenient consequences of Christianizing African slaves and their descendants led to the ineffective evangelical education of slaves. The Christianization of the slave would give him or her an equal status inimical to the foundation of slavery: the unequal condition of men believed to be primitive, pagan, idolatrous, and fetishist. It was also inconvenient to reduce labor hours among slaves for Christian religious teaching or for holidays. In addition, the preservation of ethnical, religious, and linguistic differences prevented unification and revolts among slaves. Consequently, a certain tolerance of formal religious norms allowed a syncretic relationship between the Catholic devotion of saints and the African mythology as a device of resistance against identity change.

Although widespread among the population, the religious beliefs of African origin could not become the main Cuban religion due to the absence of proper organizational structures. Also, the African religions were part of the dominated culture subject to long-term underestimation and discrimination. The Western bias to recognize the significant differences of the African model contributed to a prejudiced view of it as a conglomerate of amoral religions. Recent investigations of these religions show the existence of a system of values, very different from those of the Christian codes.[3]

The North American version of the Western model arrived in Cuba during the second half of the nineteenth century, and with greater force in the twentieth century, once the neocolonial project erected the republic formed after the U.S. intervention of 1898.[4] This new arrival brought spiritualism, which, although theorized in France, was adopted among the Cuban population in nontheoretical versions of a fundamentally utilitarian nature, that were also syncretic with Catholicism and the religions of African origin.[5]

Likewise, Protestantism was introduced to Cuba in the various ways it was fractioned in the United States, as the fifty-four evangelical denominations currently existing in Cuba demonstrates. Protestantism was initially introduced by Cubans engaged in pro-independence activities toward the end of the nineteenth century. For this reason they were called "missionary patriots," who were soon replaced by North Americans and their missionary organizations. They gave Protestantism a North American characteristic in its social and liturgical activities.[6]

Its late arrival, foreign seal, and alien ritual meant that Protestantism did not constitute the main Cuban religion. Only later, into the latter part of the twentieth century, were charismatic forms of religion introduced, with participatory and active rituals, experimentation, "possession," and cures. Only then was Protestant religiosity able to gain popular acceptance as it was more in line with the way in which Cubans expressed their religious feelings.

Cuban culture has also received other influences with religious implications that, although less widespread, have made the religious scene in Cuba even more complex. Haitian workers immigrating to satisfy labor demand were the bearers of the so-called voodoo religion, which reflects the syncretisism of African religions and Catholicism within the Haitian slave society. Chinese peasants, hired under conditions of semislavery, had their own set of religious values and rituals, which are unfortunately not very well researched in Cuba. Jewish immigrants brought their religion through various organizations and synagogues. Other philosophical religious forms, such as Baha'ism and theosophy, are also currently practiced and studied.

A first conclusion that can be drawn from the religious complex in Cuba is that no organized religious expression has managed to constitute the characteristic religion of society in general. This is true even though Catholicism, spiritualism, and *santería* have managed to have more influence than others. However, the Cuban people are not primarily Catholic, even if many who do not have a constant religious practice and beliefs consider themselves to be Catholics. Nor are they primarily Protestant, because membership to this religion was never very high. Nor are they *santero, palero,* or *ñáñigo,* nor spiritualist, despite the level of diffusion that these forms of religion have achieved, frequently in mixed forms.

ORTIZ'S RESEARCH AND EVALUATION OF RELIGION IN CUBA

Ortiz began studying Cuban society through a framework of evident rationalist and positivist influences. He found religion to be an especially interesting field. From an early stage, he acknowledged the religious multiplicity and the lack of prevalence of any one religion, a phenomenon he summarized in the following manner:

> In Cuba, three religious currents struggle to survive and prevail: African fetishism, especially the Lucumí, Christianism in its various more or less pure versions, especially Catholicism, and contemporary religious philosophism, especially spiritualism.[7]

On these three religious forms, concentrating perhaps on some above others, Ortiz followed a changing course of analysis and came to accumulate an unceasing amount of information. Guided by criminal anthropology, Ortiz analyzed the religious issue from a criminological standpoint, searching for the relationships between religion, crime, and vicious or bad life. This is the case of his first texts, *Los negros brujos* (1906) and *Los negros esclavos* (1916), part of the series *El hampa afro-cubana* (a project he abandoned later as he matured his perspective), and *La filosofía penal de los espiritistas* (1915), which again made associations between crime and religion. These texts reveal prejudice, erroneous appreciations, and imprecisions regarding fetishism, witchcraft, amoral religions, religious indifference, Afro-Cuban religions, and negative racial bias.

Ortiz would gradually introduce new theoretical and methodological perspectives in his studies, gathered from the anthropological and sociological research available at the time. Ortiz found that direct contact with the religious context, and the use of sources reached through his own experience and religious practice were both particularly useful research methods, as they allowed him to gain contact with the people. He was thus able to understand his deficiencies and improve upon his analysis. By the 1940s, he had matured his approach and abandoned his initial criminological perspective. In 1936, he had already discussed the changes he was adopting in a public lecture entitled "How I Thought 30 Years Ago." In 1942, he admitted, "I began to investigate, but gradually I began to understand that, like all Cubans, I was confused."[8]

RELIGIOUS INDIFFERENCE:
MORE APPARENT THAN GENUINE

Ortiz acknowledged the limited importance religion had in Cuba in comparison to the rest of Latin America. This somewhat precipitated observation led him to assume a weak religiosity in Cuba, a product of "religious indifference."[9] Other analysts, observers, and religious authorities in different stages of Cuban history shared this view.

Throughout the colonial period there were opinions concerning a weak religious life or religiosity expressed in not properly Catholic ways. In the sixteenth century,

> Bishop Almendáriz verified, when he performed ecclesiastical visits, [that] the blacks and Indians were so mixed and involved with the Spaniards and with the land, that there is no reason for them to have a different doctrine, . . . stating that the population lived without knowing what it was to go to mass or any other Christian rite.

Bishop Pedro Morell de Santa Cruz wrote that report in the first quarter of the eighteenth century. References of this kind were also repeatedly present in the report, regarded his pastoral visit to the island. Bishop

Morell persistently brought up the numerous foundations, appointments, and religious celebrations that had been abandoned or forgotten. His account of the Virgin of Regla is particularly interesting since he described the superstition surrounding this cult and the miracles attributed to it, all of which the bishop gave little credit to.

In various opportunities, Bishop Morell regretted the absence or inefficiency of the clergy, and the scant education people received on "the eternal truths." A good seventeenth-century example was the invention of the presence of demons, concocted by the priest of Remedios to force the transfer of the town's location to lands that belonged to him. This ingenuity inspired Fernando Ortiz to write the ingenious *Historia de una pelea cubana contra los demonios*, where he also noted that this "superstitious fantasy far surpassed any analogy among the African blacks."[10]

Other visitors, writers, and chroniclers during the nineteenth century also expressed their impressions on religiosity in Cuba. In 1853, Nicolás Tarrea Armero stated:

> A procession in Popayán, Seville, or Rome is sumptuous, magnificent; in Havana, it is the most ridiculous that can take place. . . . People in Havana should be Catholics but many of them are indifferent towards religion.[11]

The prestigious Swedish novelist Fredrika Bremer remarked: "Among foreigners of different nationalities who have settled in Cuba, there is only one and the same opinion on the absolute absence of religious life in the island."[12] Toward the middle of the same century, another observer noted that

> the country is not very religious or rather not very pious. It is odd that families only attended mass on the first day of January and regard it as being enough for the rest of the year. . . . It is colored people who practice religion with more faith and even fanaticism.[13]

Ortiz also noted the opinions of foreign visitors in his research. One of them, according to his reference, stated, "Not even the religion of the state . . . has influence on the masses," and another assured, "There is no other country on earth that can adapt so well religion to its lifestyle; they turn it into a complacent friend that succumbs to all of their fantasies."[14]

In a letter to the Spanish queen, dated September 14, 1866, the Bishop of Havana, Jacinto María Martínez Sáenz, reported:

> The picture is awful, but accurate; here, where there are over two hundred thousand inhabitants, only about fifteen thousand attend the Sunday mass, and hardly anyone takes communion during Lent, and there isn't a single employee of Your Majesty taking communion on Easter Thursday.

Complaining about the predominant desacralization, a Catholic publication in 1948 noted, "Catholic and spiritual feasts are degenerating into paganism and materialism; and Midnight Mass and Holy Communion are second to a splendid banquet and a scandalous dance." When analyzing the structure of believers in Cuba, a group of Cuban Christians referred to "[t]he masses of followers and believers who do not participate actively and constantly in Christian communities." Later, the archbishop of Havana commented on "[t]he small Christian communities, because our Church of followers was always small in numbers."[15]

In 1952, the Franciscan priest P. Biaín noted what I believe to be an accurate summary of religiosity among Cuban believers:

> [E]xperience tells us that if we conducted a poll to discover which religion the Cubans favor, a vast majority would say that they are Catholics. . . . But if we then analyzed the content of this declaration, we would reach very pessimistic results. The majority of those who pride themselves of being Catholic do not know what that means or what it is. . . . On more than one occasion, supposedly learned men have said to me: "I am a Catholic. I too believe in God." That is what many people's religion has been limited to: a well-rooted deism expressed in rituals and formulas created by Christianity.

In a poll conducted by the Agrupación Católica Universitaria (ACU) in 1953, the concluding assessments on religiosity stated that

> the issues driving the majority of people towards the Church, or away from it, are never theoretical or abstract, but concrete and specific. . . . That tendency towards the concrete characterizes the popular minds . . . in many cases the devotion to the Holy Virgin is reduced to a series of meaningless practices and sometimes even superstitions.[16]

In research compiled by the American University, published in 1987, it is noted that "Cuba was predominantly a non-religious country." According to historian Margaret E. Crahan, "pre-revolutionary religious practice in Cuba was only relatively significant."[17]

In 1985, Rafael Cepeda, a Presbyterian priest and ecumenical leader, evaluated the scarce statistical results in the spread of Protestantism in Cuba reported by missioners. He agreed with the view that "there was religious indifference among the Cuban people," who mainly "preferred other magical and animistic religions" since the Christian faith was "a very heavy burden."[18] Soon afterward, a Cuban priest stated, "The Cuban people are a radically mixed [*mestizo*] group in racial, cultural, and religious terms." He observed "a very lax and ethically uncommitted religiosity" and a "popular religiosity, both Catholic and syncretic, in which Catholicism, African animism, and, more recently, spiritualism, are all intermixed." He also noted that, especially among young people there was a neopagan current that "had hues of religious syncretism."[19]

In these opinions and in sociological data, the lax nature of religious conscience and practice in Cuban society is clearly characteristic; in other words, this feature is not exactly proper of a specific religious expression. Certain opinions indicate religious indifference as a feature or cause in the observed religious laxity. In my view, those who consider indifference as a central characteristic base their conclusion on the erroneous assumption that religiosity should be structured and systematic such as in the Catholic model. A lax religiosity of any kind is not the same as religious indifference, though it may perhaps be an indicator of a low-level religious intensity. That indifference may not be caused, as it can also be a consequence.

More recent studies reveal that toward the end of the 1980s, 85 percent of the Cuban population had religious notions rooted in their mind, even though those beliefs did not correspond to a specific, orthodox religious current, and were spontaneous nature.[20] In the context of an increase in religious beliefs in the 1990s, certain modifications must account for an increase in the intensity and significance of religion in society. However, there are reasons that suggest that in previous periods, a similar behavior ignor the Cuban people have not been distant from or indifferent toward religion.

According to Ortiz's transculturation hypothesis for the Cuban religious scenario, there is a process of religious interrelation, specifically between Catholicism and religions of African origin, and spiritualism. What Ortiz did not realize, or was unable to do given the research resources available to him, was the generation of a new religious product constructed along the years. In this new process, all the major religious forms intervene, along with other, minor forms to a lesser degree. There is also another important component: the popular imagination; the creative capacity of the people to develop particular interpretations of the supernatural and ways of assimilating these beliefs in their lives. This is the religiosity that we can classify as popular, most significantly due to its extent and vitality in the Cuban context throughout time, and different in form and content from the organized religious systems.

ORTIZ'S VIEWS ON CATHOLICISM AND SPIRITUALISM

Ortiz's views on Catholicism are dispersed throughout his work. Although he acknowledged Catholic influence on Cuban society, history, culture, and nationality, Ortiz distanced himself from, and criticized, the church and Catholicism in pejorative terms:

> The permanent inefficiency of traditional Catholic teachings, especially in the slave quarters, the stubbornness of Borbon colonialism and its adverse repercussions on popular ideology, the prolonged abandonment of the missionary work.[21]

Elsewhere he avers that "the Catholic cult practiced in Cuba was not, in fact, essentially different from the fetishist cult."[22] Insisting on the closeness between Cuban Catholicism and religions of African origin, he also commented on the need for certain Catholics to search for "the supernatural issues in fetishists."[23] Lydia Cabrera, one of Ortiz's most important followers, wrote in *El Monte* of "a Catholicism that adapts perfectly to their beliefs and has not really altered the religious beliefs of the majority."

Ortiz's criticism against the clergy was strong because of their behavior during the colonial period; he accused the clergy of being stubborn, ignorant, mean-spirited, and selfish.[24] In condemning the bad life of whites, which in his view contributed to that of the blacks through compulsion, he stated, "Even the clergy of the time, composed almost exclusively by immigrants, suffered from an identical immorality that some virtuous and illustrious ecclesiastical authorities could not repress."[25] He added, "The clergy, therefore, was suffering the evil and deleterious effects of slavery, which demoralizes and corrupts the people who accept it and establish it."[26]

The first Diocesan Synod celebrated in Cuba toward the end of the eighteenth century should have adopted measures adequate to the type of clergy that arrived to the island, a group of uncultured men with doubtful morality. In 1887, Raimundo Cabrera stated that "There is plenty of evidence on the general ignorance of the clergy."[27] In 1954, as recorded by the ACU poll, 39 percent of those polled made 2,760 objections against the clergy and the Catholic Church.

> The favorable predisposition of the vast mass of Creoles towards a doctrine presenting itself as modern philosophy, in line with science, adopted by prominent whites, originating in the most civilized nations, advocating the elimination of Hispanic or African expressions, customs, rituals, hierarchies, and submissiveness typical of the colony and slavery. Spiritualism, in its original Kardecist form, was introduced as a new and freeing element of Cuba Libre.[28]

In regard to spiritualism, Ortiz had a different approach from the one he used to discuss Catholicism. Although he declared several times that he was not a spiritualist, Ortiz gave spiritualism preferential treatment with ill-disguised sympathy. He published several articles and books on the subject and discussed it in several of his works. Between February 1949 and June 1950, he published ten articles specifically on spiritualism in the magazine *Bohemia*. In his lecture "The Phases of Religious Evolution in 1919," when he was practically beginning his research on the topic, he referred to spiritualism as "pretending to be the faith of the future, based on science," an idea that he would repeat in other texts and lectures. In a later, mature work that encapsulated his view on spiritualism, he evaluated the factors that contributed to its rapid spread.

Ortiz observes a new form of spiritualism in its Cuban expression, the cordon spiritualism (*espiritismo de cordón*) or, as he names it, *espiritismo cordonero de orilé.* This spiritualist version emerges from the eastern region of Cuba, apparently from the area of Bayamo. In it there is a mixture of the more ritualistic and practical, rather than theoretic, Kardecian doctrine with Catholicism and, to a lesser degree, with religions of African origin. Its name is owed to the way in which they organize their cult standing around, forming a human cordon or belt. The *orilé, olilé,* or *oringué* element in its name is because in their chants they repeat this word, which has no defined manner of pronounciation and unknown meaning.

In the recent work of Ileana Hodge, Minerva Rodríguez, and Yalexy Castañeda, spiritualism in the Cuban context has been defined along two great currents. The first is the traditional current, known as orthodox spiritualism or table spiritualism, which is more in line with the doctrine of its sytematizer, Allan Kardec. Although intending to be scientific, spiritualism emerged as a religious expression of North American society and its strong sense of empiricism and pragmatism. The second current is the Cuban adaptation or contextualization, influenced by other forms of religious expression and centered on the everyday life. This current is the most widespread in the country.

ORTIZ AND RELIGIONS OF AFRICAN ORIGIN

Fernando Ortiz's extensive and pioneering research on African presence in Cuban culture has contributed to the better-known religions of African origins. Given the relationship between these religions and artistic forms of expression—especially music, dance, and musical instruments—that Ortiz studied with interest, his work on religion was greatly facilitated. Also, in Ortiz's published and unpublished works, there is a direct treatment of African religions.

As we know, the initially biased approach by the young Ortiz established links between African religions, bad life, theft, fetishism, witchcraft, and even human sacrifice, especially in children, which he discussed in his article "Los comedores de niños" (1913). He also makes associations with violence and fierceness and its aesthetic qualities, as evidenced in "Los africanos dientimellados" (1929).

But if during Ortiz's time there were still Africans with sharpened teeth, today there are none in Cuba. In the same manner, even if at the beginning of the twentieth century it was still possible to talk about "religions of blacks," it is currently no longer part of reality, as indeed it is even less possible to talk about ethnic-religious relationships.

Two factors account for this change. In the first place, the Cuban people have gone through a process of intense racial mixture in about 80 to 90 percent of its total population, according to Cuban ethnologists. Second, people of different racial types have been incorporated, as practitioners or authorities, to the popularized religious forms such as religions of African origin and spiritualism, widely present among the poorer social sectors.[29]

Even among certain Christian churches that used to recruit mainly white believers, the proportion of mixed-race or black recruits has increased significantly. This phenomenon is more noticeable in the recent growing trends of the Pentecostal churches. Previous Protestant communities with mainly members of Jamaican or other Caribbean origin, never significantly large, have ceased to make sense. Since its origin, the more widespread popular religiosity emerged without distinction of race or color.

In any case, it must be understood that racial classifications are very difficult in Cuba, especially due to the intense racial mixture. Today the Cuban nation is monoethnical though multiracial or *mestiza*, and this feature is reflected in the religious realm.

I would like to delve into two realms briefly: amorality and the term *syncretic cults*, precisely because they reveal a conception, conscious or not, perhaps uncritically inherited from Western ethnocentrism and European anthropology. Young Ortiz regarded religions of African origin as "amoral" or deprived of regulatory values and norms. This view results from applying Western values to a culture that had an entirely different vision of the world, different from the one organized on ethical codes. This culture of African origins had its own system of values based on the balance of all forces of good and evil; it held nature at the center of its cosmology approaching life on earth with no eschatological concerns.

Referring to these religions as cults is also a Westernizing reductionism that applies the term *religion* only for its own cultural traditions. The cult is a part of a religious system; as in the case of other religions, African religions and their Cuban derivatives have, apart from their rituals, a system of ideas and rules, as well as an organization that does not necessarily follow the ecclesial model. Moreover, classifying them as synergetic is also a condescending notion by alluding to a lack of originality or authenticity; no religion that has gone beyond regional borders is free from the incorporation of elements of other cultures it comes in contact with.

On the other hand, the term *Afro-Cuban* applied to religious systems such as Regla Ocha or *santería*, Regla Conga or *palo monte*, Abakuá societies or *ñañiguismo*, the Regla Arará, or any other, is imprecise and does not correspond to reality. Despite their strong African roots, these religions have evolved through time under Cuban conditions and have acquired components that differentiate them from their African origins. Consequently, these religions can be more appropriately regarded as undoubtedly Cuban. Perhaps the term *Afro-* followed by another denoting place may be used in other contexts but not in the Cuban case. However, due to the controversy that this issue generates, it is worth discussing it in greater depth.

A FINAL CONSIDERATION

To be fair, it is necessary to acknowledge not only the changes in perspective introduced by Fernando Ortiz in dealing with these religious issues over time; one should also understand that even in his early works the critical approach he adopted was mainly toward the system and conditions generating crime, violence, and bad life, rather than toward African culture, religions, and heritage. As early as 1913, after stating that "the religion of witchdoctors is entirely amoral" (note that he does not say immoral), he underscored that his criticism was against witchcraft, not against the Abakuá cultural contribution, music, dance, mutualism, and rituals, which "even though fetishist they are harmless."[30] Ortiz's task was difficult, as he himself acknowledged. According to Ortiz, studying "the intricate contacts" between "uprooted" black cultures and white cultures "also bereaved of their original trunks" in "any aspect of Cuban social life," is "as difficult a task as extracting all the mixtures of racial blending [*mulatez*] from pigmental mixtures."[31]

In summary, I believe that a better evaluation of Ortiz's views, regarding the situation of slavery and the alien and alienating context in which Africans were placed in Cuba, can be achieved by reading his own words:

In religion, the black man, not trusting the foreign and colonial clergy that exploited him and subjected him to slavery, began comparing his myths with those of whites, thus creating within the large mass of our nation a syncretism of such lucid and eloquent equivalents, worth sometimes like a critical philosophy is. . . .
It also moves towards agnosticism or Presbyterian, Methodist, or Baptist Protestantism; and bewildered by the unsolved mystery of spiritual possession, begins to believe in the experimental and ethical beliefs of metempsychosis, and the mediumistic and reincarnationist spiritualism.[32]

NOTES

1. Fariñas, M. Daisy. 1995. "The Religion of the Antilles," Editorial Academy, Havana.

2. Aníbal Argüelles Mederos and Ileana Hodge, *Los llamados cultos sincréticos y el espiritismo* (Havana: Editorial Academia, 1991).

3. A. C. Perera, *El sistema de valores de la regla de ocha* (Havana: Departamento de Estudios Socioreligiosos, 1998).

4. J. Berges, "El protestantismo histórico en Cuba" in *La religión en la cultura* (Havana: Editorial Academia, 1993).

5. Ileana Hodge and Mineria Rodríguez, "El espiritismo en Cuba. Percepción y exteriorización," in *Colección religión y sociedad* (Havana: Editorial Academia, 1997).

6. Rafael Cepeda, "Análisis de los juicios de los misioneros sobre Cuba (1894–1925)," in *La herencia misionera en Cuba* (San José, Costa Rica: DEI, 1980).

7. Fernando Ortiz, "Las fases de la evolución religiosa," lecture at the Teatro Payet on April 7, 1914 (Havana: Tipografía Moderna, 1919).

8. Franco, José Luciano. 1985. Apuntes para una historia de la legislación y administratión colonial en Cuba, 1511–1800. La Habana: Editorial de Ciencias Sociales.

9. Fernando Ortiz, *Los negros brujos* (Madrid: Editorial-América, 1917), 252.

10. Fernando Ortiz, *Historia de una pelea cubana contra los demonios* (Havana: Editorial de Ciencias Sociales, 1975), 325.

11. Tarrea, N. 1981. "La isla Cuba", en *Juan Pérez de la Peña: La isla de Cuba en el siglo XIX vista por un extranjero*. La Habana: Editorial Ciencias Sociales.

12. Bremer, Fredrika. 1981. *Cartas desde Cuba*. Ciudad de La Habana: Editorial Arte y Literatura.

13. Barras y Prado, Antonio de las. La Habana a mediados del siglo XIX. Memorias de A. de las Barros y Prado, las publica su hijo Francisco de la Barras de Aragón. Madrid, Spain: Impr. De la ciudad lineal.

14. Ortiz, *Historia de una pelea*, 261–62.

15. *Encuentro Diocesano de pastoral*,1982, folleto publicado por la arquidiocesis de La Habana. En él aparecen una intervención del arzobispa, Mons. Jaime Ortega, actualmente y desde noviembre de 1994, cardenal, en la que hace referencia a la religiosidad en el pueblo, que en su opinión tiene un fundamento católico, aunque admite contradictoriamente con una ausencia de práctica ortodoxa que es lo que en verdad se constata.

16. Agrupación Católica Universitaria (ACU), *Encuesta nacional sobre los sentimientos religiosos* (Havana: Buró de Información de la ACU, 1954).

17. J. D. Rudolp, *Cuba: A Country Study*, 3d ed. (Washington, D.C.: Foreign Area Studies, American University, 1987).

18. Cepeda, R. 1985. "Lasiglesias protestantes nortamericanas en la política expansionista de 1898, sureflejo en Cuba," en *Cristianismo y sociedad* núm. 86, México: 60.

19. Carlos M. Céspedes, "Ideología, mentalidad y fe cristiana," *Revista Ateísmo y Diálogo* 21, no. 3 (1986): 265–70.

20. Colectivo del DESR, *La conciencia religiosa. Características y formas de manifestarse en la sociedad cubana contemporánea* (Havana: Departamento de Estudiso Sociorreligiosos, Academia de Ciencias de Cuba, 1993).

21. Fernando Ortiz, "Una moderna secta espiritista de Cuba," *Bohemia* 42, no. 3 (1950): 9.

22. Ortiz, *Los negros brujos*, 252.

23. Ortiz, *Los negros brujos*, 283.

24. Ortiz, *Los negros brujos*, 21, 29.

25. Fernando Ortiz, *Los negros curros* (Havana: Editorial de Ciencias Sociales, 1986), 204.

26. Ortiz, *Los negros curros*, 205.

27. Raimundo Cabrera, *Cuba y sus juices (retificaciones oportunas)* (Havana: Imprenta El Retiro, 1887).

28. Ortiz, "Una moderna secta espiritista," 9.

29. Colectivo DESR, *La conciencia religiosa*.

30. Ortiz, *Entre cubanos . . . (Psicología tropical)* (Paris: Librería P. Ollendorff, 1913) 5–6.

31. Ortiz (1946a).

32. Fernando Ortiz, "Por la integración cubana de blancos y negros," *Ultra* 77 (1943): 74.

V

LITERATURE AND MUSIC

The dominant trends in contemporary Latin American and Caribbean literature and arts can be situated within the Ortizian notion of transculturation as a process. Twentieth-century literary statements in Latin America and the Caribbean have recognized the complex terms of cultural exchange. This is especially true from the midcentury to the present, when writers and artists from the region asserted, actively and without apology, that the literature of the Old World had been shaped by that of the New, just as New World letters and arts had received the influence of the Old. The mature work of Ortiz addressed the need for an inclusionary literary practice, in both creation and theory, and the continued innovation and exploration of new territory. That is the spirit in which the chapters in this section were conceived and developed.

Roberto González Echevarría examines Ortiz's relationship to literature, as well as the links between the practices of anthropology and literary creation, and the ways in which discourse and method are appropriated from one practice to the other. Ricardo Viñalet takes Fernando Ortiz's response to Spanish novelist Benito Pérez Galdós's novel *El caballero encantado* (1909) as a central theme in his own, *El caballero encantado y la moza esquiva: Versión libre y americana de una novela española de Benito Pérez Galdós* (1910), an "interpretative rewriting" undertaken to explore essential questions that emerged from Spain and Latin America in the aftermath of 1898. Antonio Fernandez Ferrer's contribution explores the symbolic infrastructure used by Ortiz in his written work, and he ponders the connection between concepts and images at the center of literary creation. Maria Teresa Linares Savio relates the important ethnomusicological contributions of Ortiz with those of his most distinguished disciple, Lydia Cabrera. Finally, Benjamin Lapidus explores Ortiz's approach to the study of original Cuban musical genres.

16

The Counterpoint and Literature

Roberto González Echevarría

During his productive and lengthy career, Fernando Ortiz engaged in a deep and complex relationship with literature.[1] I would even claim that literature was for him both a temptation and something to be rejected, a means of arriving as well as escaping all questions that troubled him, and all solutions that captivated him. Ortiz was aware of the literature of his time: vanguard literature and modernism (not to be confused, of course, with *modernismo* in Latin American literature). To those who consider Ortiz a social scientist, it will be surprising to find in his books, even the most technical on dancing or Afro-Cuban music, precise and opportune allusions to authors such as James Joyce. His literary culture was vast and active, and always present in all his meditations, observations, hypotheses, and theories. This is where Ortiz distanced himself from the ordinary social scientists, but not from the masters of those disciplines who often found suggestions, answers, and even models of approach and analysis in literature and art in general. Like them, Ortiz soon found that anthropology was the flexible and porous frontier between the social sciences and literature. Instead of making his relationship with literature easier, this realization made it more complicated and dramatic.

The first works of Ortiz appear at a crucial moment of Cuban history. It was the time when the political and legal bases of the republic, formed in 1902, were being formulated. A decisive moment when the political and cultural projects that had led to independence now collided with the nation's realities, and were subjected to tough tests, programs, and national myths. One of those realities was the presence of a large, poor, and marginalized black population of relative but obvious cultural autonomy. This fact could endanger the precarious social and political integrity of Cuba.

Young Ortiz (he was twenty-one in 1902) was a pragmatic man, educated in law and the emerging social sciences, especially criminology or criminal sociology. Therefore, his initial studies on the black population in Cuba, original and even daring by their mere existence, made him a renowned figure. He had an ideological bias and tone different from those he would later develop. What was novel and daring in texts such as *Los negros brujos* (1906) was, in the first place, that someone like Ortiz should approach the topic in a conscientious and serious manner.

But we cannot deceive ourselves or allow even well-intentioned revisionisms to blind us. Ortiz initially became interested in the African cultures in Cuba because of what they could reveal about crime on the island, especially in the large cities. In his earlier texts, Ortiz is a criminologist, as indicated by the complete title of his book: *Hampa afrocubana: Los negros brujos (apuntes para un estudio de etnología criminal)*. With a preface by Cesare Lombroso, of whom Ortiz considers himself a disciple and admirer, the book is a meticulous study of witchcraft among Cuban blacks, written with the clear intention of understanding this phenomenon in order to eliminate it with greater efficiency. Ortiz got interested in the criminal aspect of witchcraft—ritual murders, necrophilia, extravagant sexual practices—and its moral impact on Cuban society, given that many whites were converting to or at least practicing it. The physiological-genetic conception of psychology and race professed by Ortiz, derived from his master Lombroso and from a large part of nineteenth-century science, perceived blacks as people with a primitive mentality and strong inclination to lust and violence. It was a race that had to be "civilized" to ensure the country's progress and well being.

While Ortiz initially perceived many elements of Afro-Cuban culture as damaging to society, the young vanguard literati soon exalted those same elements. The warlock (*brujo*), for example, a type studied attentively by Ortiz and an important element of the Afro-Cuban movement, was defined as:

> usually a criminal, always a defrauder, often a thief, a rapist and murderer in some cases, desecrator of graves when given the chance. Lustful to the most savage extremes of sexual corruption, collector of concubines and a polygamist, lascivious in cult rituals and outside them, and an encourager of prostitution. Truly a social parasite, exploiting ignorant minds and especially those of his concubines.

This initial Ortiz was a biological determinist and a social Darwinist. This is evidently why Alejo Carpentier comments on the difference of ages, in reference to Ortiz, in the midst of recollecting of the origins of the Afro-Cuban movement in *La música en Cuba* (1946):

> Fernando Ortiz, despite the difference in age, socialized closely with the young. His books were read. Folkloric values were exalted. Suddenly, the black man was the center of attention. For the same reason that it annoyed the intellectu-

als of the old school, the secret *ñáñigo* oath was ceremoniously taken, the dance of the *diablito* was praised.

There was a difference of twenty-three years between Ortiz and Carpentier: The former was almost fifty years old when the Afro-Cuban movement began. Ortiz was an old school intellectual, a young member of the so-called First Republican Generation, concerned with the social and economic progress of the nation in the context of the newly established state.

The fact that Ortiz went through a conversion, which I suggest was triggered by the young Afro-Cubanist literati and the vanguard in general, has blurred his initial years and the nature of his influence on the movement and on literature. During his first period, Ortiz shared much of Domingo Sarmiento's ideological position. Just as the famed Argentinian regarded Indians as an obstacle to his program of civilization, Ortiz believed blacks to be a retrograde group. In a short book published in 1913 entitled *Entre cubanos . . . (Psicología tropical)*, Ortiz wrote the following on the demographic composition of Cuba:

> Transformism [i.e., evolution] is today the law of life in all of its manifestations. . . . Perhaps our national future lies really in nothing but a complex problem of ethnic selection in physiological and psychical terms. [Humanity] continues to be abandoned to itself, subject to the most basic physical and social laws, struggling against the biologically general promiscuity of inferior species barely counter-balanced by the action of the germs from cold countries [i.e., of white persons], in the strong gales of immigration and political cyclones.

Ortiz's early work was important to the Afro-Cuban movement because he discovered and analyzed the salient aspects of African culture in Cuba. This work is the first systematic account of the myths, rituals, and beliefs of that culture. However, and paradoxically, Ortiz was also important to Afro-Cuban movement because his initial work represented, given their tone and philosophical inclination, all the factors that vanguard studies rejected: positivism, rationalism, and progress according to the political and social ideals of the republic.

During the 1920s, Ortiz's studies began to approach topics less solemn, without the ominous punitive aura of criminology and the pious preservation of social order. At the time, he began studying music, dance, games, feasts, and, above all, Cuban language. He studied the latter from different angles, from tongue twisters to, of course, the detailed filological analysis of the African origin of many terms. These linguistic studies resulted in the publication of *Un catauro de cubanismos* in 1923, a text that, starting from its title, displayed a newly found humorous and irreverent tone. Let us remember that the *Catauro* is almost the direct contemporary of James Joyce's *Ulysses*, published in 1922 and abundant in Irish slang and word tricks. A study that could check and compare Ortiz's new work in detail with that of the initial literary vanguard, and above all, the Afro-Cuban movement would, reveal that the author of the grave *Los negros brujos* had been influenced by this new spirit. Vanguardism was radically opposed to the study of crime, conformism, and the preservation of social integrity and political stability. Through this new perspective, Ortiz arrived at the *Contrapunteo* (1940), a text in which he produced more literature than science.[2]

Although *Contrapunteo cubano del tabaco y el azúcar* is a work of serious intellectual ambitions, and not less serious political ambitions, it is a far cry from the sapient and magisterial tone found in his first texts. It is not in vain that the author invokes the most satirical of Spanish writers, the jocular and ribald Arcipreste de Hita, as an inspiration for the *Contrapunteo*. The first and perhaps more important thing that Ortiz's text shares with the vanguardist literature is humor. In great measure, this humor arises from the automatism of the contrasts established between the two main products of Cuba. It is as if sugar and tobacco rejoiced in an amusing and entertaining conflict that turns into a game of contrasts (the *contrastar opósitos* of the old courtier poetry), in which if one zigs, the other would predictably zag; if one ticks, the other tocks, and so on. Ortiz knows this, and his winks at the reader (of which there are many) make him or her an accomplice of the notion that things can not be so symmetrical and mechanical, and that the "counterpoint" is a baroque and gracious conceptual game from where poetic truths emerge. It is a witticism, a *jeu d'esprit*, typical in vanguardist art and literature; the *Contrapunteo* is a long, detailed Joycean game of words and concepts, as found in Joyce's contemporary text, *Finnegans Wake*.

I believe it is reasonable to further suggest that its irreverent tone, mockery, frequent jokes, and predictability of the contrasts, place the text within that which it wishes to define. This feature therefore abolishes science's methodological distance between the observer and the object observed, between analytical discourse and the matter studied. The *Contrapunteo* defines Cubanity from what is Cuban, through a Cuban discourse and methodology. What is Cuban in this text is expressed through the choteo, which Jorge Mañach had analyzed only a decade before in his famous essay. The *Contrapunteo* is therefore a choteo, a relaxation, to which we would have to respond, if we were to meet its author in another world, in these terms: "Yes, Fernando, all of that is very nice, witty, and brilliant, but let's talk seriously now." We would never have that serious talk, of course, after losing ourselves in the labyrinthic witticisms, jokes, quotes, eternally condemned to a Cuban counterpoint, a controversy, like those demons who play tennis striking books set afire in the Quijote.

The work of Cuban vanguardist authors, especially that of poets and novelists such as Nicolás Guillén and Alejo Carpentier, was no less important to Ortiz than his was to them. It was the argumentative, mocking spirit of the

Afro-Cuban and vanguard movement that led Ortiz to change his perspective and the *Contrapunteo*. Without this change, Ortiz would have been confined to writing solemn prose, a mixture of patriotism and academics, like most contemporary Latin American essay writers. Ortiz abandoned the magisterial tone used by Rodó, Martínez Estrada, Vasconcelos, and even Mañach, who writes about the *choteo* without practicing it. Ortiz's book is irreverent even in the way it describes, from the very beginning, the pleasant nature of tobacco and sugar. Flavors, pleasure, vice; both Cuban products are like drugs, which promote physical well-being, ignoring morals and crime. These inherent forms of decadence are part of vanguardism and *modernismo*. One associates this with the symbolic and physical pleasures of Joyce's *Ulysses*, in the food, drink, and verbal gloating: Ireland is defined by its food, drink, irreverent banter, and sexual coarseness. It is also associated with oral pleasures, of the mouth, like the literary discourse of Ortiz. The *Contrapunteo* is a Creole speech (*labia*), a mouth pleasure, like sugar and tobacco themselves.

Erudition and knowledge in the *Contrapunteo* are consigned to a final collection of documents, lengthier than Ortiz's essay itself. That archive of documents is a sort of supplement, prior or posterior, to the essay. It is an invitation for the reader to make his or her own interpretation of the documents, not to verify Ortiz's text and its erudite footnotes. Those archival documents beg the reader to participate in the counterpoint, much as the supplementary chapters in Julio Cortázar's *Rayuela* encourage alternative, parallel, or marginal interpretations of that novel. The mere existence of that archive proclaims that the argument is unfinished, and it admits it is unfinished and merely in the process of being built: a work-in-progress, another Joycian metaphor. The wealth or treasure of documents at the end of the *Contrapunteo* is like the archive-novel that I have described elsewhere: it is *arché*, origin, deposit of the law, a building or monument designed to harbor it. However, in this case, the law has been displaced from the center of authority and the production of knowledge, except in a remote original sense, a faraway melody, the alternate song of the essay's gay knowledge. In appealing to literature, in practicing it, Ortiz makes a contradictory or, better still, dialectic gesture. On the one hand, he discards the rigorous verification of science, but on the other hand, he aspires to a deeper, lasting, and shareable poetic knowledge. In the *Contrapunteo*, the archive is a ciphered collective memory, which demands interpretation, in both a hermeneutical and musical sense.

In the *Contrapunteo*, the dialogical core is thematic, not formal; it is evoked, not represented, interpreted or executed, except in the implicit textual dialogue between the essay and the archive. We can imagine the dialogue between tobacco and sugar as that of Don Carnal and Doña Cuaresma, but it does not actually appear like this in Ortiz's text. Instead, there is a mirror between the evoked counterpoint and that of texts, which repeats the one discovered by the essay in Cuban culture.

There are many other elements that characterize the text as literary: alliterations and numerous rhetorical and poetic resources, as in the personification of cane and sugar. However, its most literary aspect is the way the text shapes itself and realizes that process. In doing so, the *Contrapunteo* reaches a level of originality that has not been highlighted enough. As an essay, the *Contrapunteo* is one of the most innovative, experimental texts of Latin American vanguard literature. Recent essayists such as Octavio Paz have not matched it in audacity. I am unable to find a parallel except for the experiments of Julio Cortázar in his books *Ultimo round* and *La vuelta al día en ochenta mundos*. In this sense, the only thing that Ortiz's text lacked was a more complex and daring typographical design. In order to perceive Ortiz's originality, one must view his text in relation to the Latin American essay writing centered on issues of cultural identity.

In terms of literary style, the essay does not have a particular generic mold; therefore, it must declare its own setting, assume it, and act it as part of the process of making a statement. The decision over which type of discourse an essay should parasitically adhere to, is essential for its being properly understood. *Ariel*, to use a very well-known example, represents a school's end-of-year magisterial lecture. That selection is not naïve. There are subgenres that adapt well to essays or essays that adapt well to subgenres: the public lecture, the journalistic article, the letter, and so on. These subgenres have already been naturalized by the essay and thus do not constitute a manifest gesture of literary style. But, of course they are, given that not every letter is an essay. When pretending to be a letter, an essay adopts a wide range of rhetorical hues that are deliberate. All this perhaps derives from the original essay-writing literary genre, the classic dialogue of the Renaissance. Why does the *Contrapunteo* mold itself around musical traces and echoes? Why did Ortiz not write an erudite, academic, scientific article, like so many he had published before? What is the sense of the *Contrapunteo*'s form that suggests a fake genre?

To Ortiz, literature was a discourse to channel his research through the Cuba he lived in, avoiding the rhetorical and ideological traps of anthropology. Literature enabled him to elaborate on Cuban issues from his own perspective, without objectifying them, without turning them into an abstraction or construction that follows a method alien to them. In fact, literature was not a panacea for Ortiz. He distanced himself from the promoters of a national or Latin American identity based on inert cultural retentions, frozen in an ideal past, and accessible only through abstract thinking. Instead, he searched that identity in a dynamic and material process of evolution and *mestizaje* where nothing is static but always in motion, mixture, and transmutation. In the *Contrapunteo*, what is Cuban is the result of Cuban factors, not an idealization of Spanish, African and, least of all, indigenous ones. What is outstanding in Ortiz's use of literature is the fact that, of all the Latin

American authors who ventured to write on the theme of identity, he was the only one with a genuine anthropological formation. Vasconcelos, Martínez Estrada, Ramos, Reyes, and several others based their views on philosophy or literature. In contrast, Ortiz emerged from anthropology, the only discipline with the ability and authority to embark on such an inquiry.

I believe that in turning to literature Ortiz acknowledged that he could not escape his own culture. He recognized that he was incapable of being an anthropologist studying himself, an integral part of the myths he analyzed. Compelled by literature, he realized what anthropology would only gradually later acknowledge: that as a discourse it was part of the modern and contemporary mythology from which it emerged, and that the expression, or the interpretation of that mythology was literature. Thus, in *Contrapunteo*, scientific and poetic knowledge intermix, but the wrapping (to use the terminology of tobacco) is that of poetry. In this sense, Ortiz distanced himself from literature's approach to the study of identity and instead adopted literature as a discourse. In other words, he would not have entertained the approximate, impressionistic analysis of the authors who dealt with the issue; he would rather write literature than write from literature.

This, however, does not mean that his research was less rigorous. In comparison to other essayists, Ortiz was able to understand the material nature and contingency of the objects expressed in culture, from within literature. He rejoiced in the concreteness of such culture, and its products, not its idealizations. His *Contrapunteo* aspires to be one of those concrete, tangible, subject-to-consumption objects of the Cuban self, not their reflection or representation. Appealing to the terminology of Lezama, one can say that Ortiz creates the image from the image. The *Contrapunteo* is presentation, performance, acting, séance, function, and show. Perhaps the most inherently literary factor in the essay is that it sets the textual dialogue that constitutes it and makes it theatrical in motion. The dialogical is thematic but also formal or textual. It is evoked but also interpreted or executed, especially in the explicit dialogue between the essay and the archive. Being and culture only exist as dialogue, in correspondence and counterpoint. This counterpoint also involves negation, contrast, counterchant—not just echo, repetition, chorus. There is a game of reflections between the "discovered" counterpoint, at the center of Cuban culture, and the counterpoint of the texts that repeats and rehearses the former cultural counterpoint. The *Contrapunteo* becomes Cuban when it becomes counterpointing. It is a text-archive and a foundational text, not only for its theme but also its form. This is why it has had so many reflections, echoes, and counterpoints in literature. Like *Paradiso*, it is a summa that has the ability to conceive the Cuban nature of its character as the synthesis of two families, one of tobacco growers and the other of sugar planters.

NOTES

This article was published in Spanish in *La Gaceta de Cuba* 2 (May–April 1996). The text is based on the inaugural lecture of the Primera Conferencia Internacional sobre Fernando Ortiz, delivered on December 7, 1995, at the Sociedad Económica de Amigos del País, Havana. I thank the president of the Fundación Fernando Ortiz, Miguel Barnet, for the invitation and hospitality.

1. In this essay, I make use of ideas discussed in my following works: *Alejo Carpentier: The Pilgrim at Home* (Ithaca, N.Y.: Cornell University Press, 1977), translated into Spanish as *Alejo Carpentier. El peregrino en su patria* (Mexico: Universidad Autónoma de México, 1993); *The Voice of the Masters: Writing and Authority in Modern Latin American Literature* (Austin: University of Texas Press, 1985); *Myth and Archive: A Theory of the Latin American Narrative* (New York: Cambridge University Press, 1990); and "Lo cubano en Paradiso," in *Coloquio Internacional sobre la obra de José Lezama Lima*, (Madrid: Editorial Fundamentos, 1984), vol. 2: 31–51, now incorporated in my *Isla a su vuelo fugitiva. Ensayos críticos sobre la literatura hispanoamericana* (Madrid: Porrúa, 1983), 69–90.

2. I acknowledge here my debt to two recent rereadings of the *Contrapunteo*: Gustavo Pérez Firmat, "Cuban Counterpoint," in *The Cuban Condition: Translation and Identity in Modern Cuban Literature* (New York: Cambridge University Press, 1998), 47–66; and Antonio Benítez Rojo, "Fernando Ortiz: el Caribe y la posmodernidad," in *La isla que se repite: El Caribe y la perspective posmoderna* (Hanover: Ediciones del Norte, 1989): 149–85. I endorse especially the latter interpretation with the caveat that I consider the *Contrapunteo*, anchored undoubtedly by the imperative of identity, as a text based on a notion of origin tracing back to romanticism. It is an archetypical work of modernity and not postmodernity.

17

Of How Fernando Ortiz Found an Elusive Maiden for an Enchanted Gentleman

Ricardo Viñalet

In 1909, the Spanish writer Benito Pérez Galdós (1843–1920) published a strange novel entitled *El caballero encantado, cuento real . . . inverosímil* (1909).[1] Despite being well received by specialized critics and readers of high cultural circles, this novel remains one of his least read texts. The wide specter of critiques have made it a controversial work. An interesting example of these discordant reactions produced by the novel is an article by Peter Bly published on the seventieth anniversary of the novel's publication.[2] Bly considers the diversity of perspectives used to interpret and evaluate the novel since its publication. Bly cites more than ten authors and incorporates quotes from them in his own discourse to support his own thesis. Bly establishes links between the views of Galdós and those of Joaquín Costa, the spirit of the so-called Generation of 1898 of Spanish intellectuals, and their programmatic ideals for a new and different national life for Spain.

However, Bly's references and evidence contrast markedly with his conclusion. According to Bly, *El caballero encantado* is limited in its social approach because its characters, especially the main ones, are to be faulted for their decisively individualistic tendency. They have exaggerated emotions of their own personalities, lead a lifestyle largely revolving around sexual appetite, and pay more attention to the practical factors of their existence than to the spiritual ones. All this weakens the social intention of the regeneration spirit. These factors lead him to value the text more for its moral propositions than its social ones.

In my view, Bly's interpretation is perhaps the result of a previous, erroneous assumption. He reads *El caballero encantado* too literally, as if analyzing any other of Galdós's conventionally realistic creations. Bly is therefore unable to read the novel in tune with its fantastic tone and symbolic nature. He regrets that the novel's fiction is not credible. He is unable to understand the fantasy behind the text, which Galdós makes explicit in the title. The social dimension of *El caballero encantado* is very clear if the reader goes along with its factual implausibility. Bly appears to acknowledge the weakness of his analysis when he states, "My interpretation of Galdós' examination of these social problems could be criticized for its failure to take into account the fantastic frame in which the examination is held."[3] Perhaps realizing that he had gone too far, he tries to be conciliatory in concluding his essay: "*El caballero encantado* may be the work of a tired sixty-six-year-old professional novelist, but its theme remains eternally relevant to youth's idealistic social reformers. Its subtlety of composition is worthy of a younger writer."[4] He is acknowledging the social significance of *El caballero encantado*, the shrewdness of its creation, the artistic value of the text, and even the youthful vigor emerging from it.

However, despite the differences in the criticisms of his novel, there is a certain consensus regarding the intentions that drove Galdós to pose a reflection about Spain, its history, its present, and its perspectives. The text reedits with irony the style of the old chivalric stories, where enchantments, spells, and similar happenings are commonplace. In the novel there is also room for various fifteenth- and sixteenth-century narrative modes, such as the pastoral, sentimental, and picaresque novels. Given its fortuitous nature and its condition of fable, the quixotic aura of Cervantes is immediately perceived behind the apparent naiveté of linked adventures that hide more significant thoughts. Thus, Pérez Galdós inscribes his creation with symbolic clues and develops a parabolic literary discourse around the specific conditions of his time and the situation of Spain. However, in *El caballero encantado*, one does not find Cervantes's mockery, humor, parody, and ability of subtle irony. Galdós's novel is more irascible, severe, and explicit. These intentions of Galdós are reflected throughout the novel, from its subtitle to the conception of characters.[5]

El caballero encantado is a concrete and anxious meditation of a sensitive spirit, not a novel of intellectual old age. In this sense, the text is consistent with the life pattern of its author. This is why Saínz de Robles considers:

> It is an exquisite narrative. . . . [Galdós's] symbolism is always the same: history, Spain. . . . Galdós was always a passionate Spaniard. I can safely assert that he was the most Spanish of all the great nineteenth-century authors. He was immensely proud to be Spanish and was always optimistic about future generations of Spaniards. With time, Galdós's unconditional patriotism was exalted to limits that cause vivid emotion. It is in the final series of *Episodios Nacionales* and in *El caballero encantado* . . . where he most strongly displayed his faith. Blind, clumsy, a bit disillusioned of everything, he takes refuge in his everything: Spain. And he focused it better than ever. And he penetrates it and understands it better than ever.[6]

"Exquisite" is the word used by Saínz de Robles to characterize the novel, several decades before the Cuban Fernando Ortiz described it as "divine." Inspired by it, Ortiz published a free American version he entitled *El caballero encantado y la moza esquiva*. Ortiz's sympathy toward Galdós's novel is due to both literary and nonliterary reasons.

There is plenty of evidence showing that Ortiz admired Perez Galdós as a writer. Ortiz acknowledged the mastery of the Canarian author in creating a novel of fantasy; a supernatural or oneiric journey in which time proceeds capriciously and carries the characters through various levels of time and space, enveloped in magic and mystery. Ortiz enjoyed the text's essential symbolic proposition that encourages a diversity of readings to arrive at one's own interpretation. From that interpretation, he elaborated his own free version, giving his readers advice on what he believed was the key to Galdós's text and the translation he was embarking in:

> Wake up the understanding reader who wishes to proceed and is not experi-
> enced in symbolisms. The master Pérez Galdós demands from us a cautious and
> keen imagination to become aware of what lies behind the folds of his language
> and the veil of his personifications and events, sometimes blurry due to the at-
> tractive mystery which surrounds them like mist. *El caballero encantado* should
> be read twice, first glancing over and then pausing between the lines.[7]

The nonliterary aspects of the novel that attracted Ortiz related to its theme and significance. *El caballero encantado* poses the issue of Spanish regeneration from a social, historical, and ethical perspective. These issues delved squarely into questions that concerned Ortiz for their importance to Cuban life in those early years of the twentieth century. His interpretation, therefore, followed that sense, and with it, he wrote his own version from the other side of the Atlantic and with an American focus.

The Spanish disaster and the Cuban independence movement lie at the center of the problem. In Cuba, the events of 1898 had violent repercussions. For Cubans, the notion of disaster was also a painful reality. The ideals and struggles for freedom ended in massive frustration. The end of Spanish dominance coincided with U.S. intervention, and only in 1902 was the republic established, mutilated of all its dreams by the Platt Amendment, as is well known. That was the situation in those early years. History accounts for the civil disputes, military revolts, the second U.S. military intervention, and so-cial, administrative, and political corruption. These were tough times when skepticism and disappointment became strong. The preservation of national identity and the nation itself was the nucleus of the worries and actions of notable Cubans. It was the realization that was necessary to solve that criti-cal situation, a search for a cultural identity that could not be postponed. The questions of who, what, and how the Cubans were had to be answered. This was a way of facing the challenge.

Fernando Ortiz's first intellectual efforts were immersed in that process of self-examination and self-knowledge of being Cuban. He also embarked on a crusade to defend the dignity of citizenry in that artificial and exhausted republic, torn apart in terms of sovereignty and urgently needing ethical, social, and political progress. Ortiz took up the gauntlet. He realized that this was the path for achieving objectives: regeneration from within defeat, poverty, and identity. He established the affinity of the situation in both Spain and Cuba. It was a regenerationism from the opposite shore, a transcultured regenerationism. Ortiz had creatively assimilated that spirit of renewal during his residence in Spain. It became the genesis of his work on Cuba and its problems and culture. The relationship between regenerationism and national and cultural identity was the backbone of his work from beginning to end.

However, among certain Spanish regenerationists were certain dark zones, which Ortiz strongly criticized. One of these areas was pan-Hispanism, a true neocolonial attempt to subject Spanish America to the former metropolis's tutelage. Entirely defeated in military terms, it occurred to some that Spain should return to dominate its former territories through influence and economic privileges. However, Spain was deteriorated and lagging behind, longing to Europeanize itself to escape its troubles, including high levels of illiteracy, lack of education, and serious political and social conflicts. Spain was a poor model for the Spanish American republics. From these verifications, Ortiz rejected the frenzy of pan-Hispanism.

Several spokesmen for pan-Hispanism elaborated an opportunistic discourse. They argued that if Spain did not exercise its tutoring mission in Spanish America, it would fall under the hegemony of the United States. Thus, the old empire was destined to rescue its daughters from the claws of the young and puissant Yankee imperialism. This pan-Hispanist maneuver only offered a choice between two imperialisms. Like other lucid Cubans, Ortiz understood the situation. He discussed these matters in *La reconquista de América: Reflexiones sobre el panhispanismo* (1910) and *Entre cubanos . . . (Psicología tropical)* (1913). These books compiled a selection of articles, the majority published in periodicals between 1905 and 1913, and often forged in the heat of debate. Attacking the roots of the problem of bipolar formulations, he insisted on solutions:

> Anemic creatures of a dying imperialism, we have been stultified by tropical sleepiness, awakening late and only when another growing imperialism has ravaged us . . . only an intense and widespread civilization can save us. Being cultured we would be strong. Let us be so.[8]

Salvation through culture and education was a proposition of Krausist-positivist origins and the ideological banner of regenerationism and the group of the Generation of 1898. However, in the Cuban version that Ortiz proposes, the claim is for the existence of a nation shielded by a national identity defined as cultural identity. Ortiz, fully aware of the Cuban national identity, would not form ideas subservient to the former metropolis but rather about the important task Spain had ahead:

> This is what Spain ought to do: bring us culture, a lot of culture, because when Spain prevails through the culture and the scientific genius of its people, then and only then all of America will be truly Spanish, even that part that speaks English, since during times like these it is civilization that brings nations together.[9]

Ortiz's strategic thought sought the integration of the Spanish American republics, away from pan-Hispanism's attempts, trying to prevent absorption into the United States. He was very explicit: "If we convince ourselves of this and manage to make a reality . . . the association for struggle, we will one day be able to present an Iberian-American mental barrier, resistant and well defined."[10]

This context motivated Ortiz to write *El caballero encantado y la moza esquiva*. The title, but especially the subtitle, *versión libre y americana*, would lead one to think of Ortiz as a narrator. There are also the antecedents of a short story, published in Minorca when he was a high school student, as well as the pamphlet *Principi i prostes* (1895), a narrative on local customs in Minorcan.[11] If such a perspective was assumed, *El caballero encantado y la moza esquiva* would require literary criticism, and the text as a novel would lack the quality to distinguish itself in the genre. However, the essential point is that Ortiz did not intend to write a novel. The work is rather an interpretation, a reconsideration, a rewriting that had the objective of developing a regenerationist political discourse opposed to pan-Hispanism. This is why it can be considered part of *La reconquista de América*. He has manipulated literature; he toyed with it and the result was a kind of satire and parody, which showed Ortiz's aesthetic consciousness (something very common in his work). This is far different from trying to write novels. Furthermore, Ortiz was very clear in stating his intentions. In the prologue he wrote, "Search for the book and read the most peculiar and instructive account of Spanish history. . . . Here it is, plainly, without the makeup and colors given by its first narrator."[12]

He will shorten it, he tells us; he must summarize and simplify because his work is a different one and seeks to provide access to the original text, where supplementary, and even totally different arguments are to be found. He then declares, "This is the purpose. The author of these lines submits the master novel to his own fantasy . . . and interprets it from American viewpoints, underscoring the principal episodes and passages that would most interest the sons of America."[13] In the most literal and delightful sense, we are standing before a tendentious text.

There are three parts in *El caballero encantado y la moza esquiva*: a short prologue with clues for interpretation, the Ortizian version of Galdós's novel with titles and chapters different from those of the original text, and an epilogue that goes beyond the arguments of the Spanish writer. We have already analyzed the first part. The second part reduces the extension of the narrative to approximately two-thirds of the original and the number of chapters decreases from twenty-seven to fourteen. In a footnote in chapter 1, Ortiz explains, "Neither the chapters nor the titles of this translation correspond to those of the Spanish original."[14] Thus, Ortiz insists on his free inspiration in presenting the bare bones, often condensing in few words that which is lengthy in Galdós's text; always defining his role as translator and interpreter. The tone of this précis is humorous and even ironic, and Ortiz reveals his ability to depict characters and situations, sometimes even through the use of simple adjectives:

> Don José Augusto del Becerro was a sticky, quarrelsome, and wise high-brow, engaged deeply in documents and folios, impassioned by heraldic jigsaws, maniatic for historical eruditions, searches in archives and libraries, papyri, parchments, and incunables, until he fell in the wacky custom of calling the Middle Ages, the Stone Age, and the Phoenician and Roman ages his dear sisters and many other periods the daughters of the prolific Spanish history.[15]

This fragment condenses several chapters of Galdós's novel and adopts a different narrative viewpoint since it does not judge the attitudes of the character. There are other instances in which Ortiz inserts Galdós himself as a character in his version, with the same spirit of the previous example: "On the date in which the narrative begins, when Pérez Galdós began to deal with Don Pueblo, I mean, with Don Carlos de Tarsis, the latter felt desperate, sad, pessimistic."[16] Ortiz also resorts to textually cite relatively short passages from the original text to support his perspective and qualifications, a true work of intertextuality in 1910. The skeptical Tarsis laments:

> Classical theater, with Lope and Tirso, also burdens me, and every time I go to such performances I have the bad idea of sleeping on my seat. A theatre performance should be named as all performances: *Life is a dream*. I again state with full conviction that we do not have agriculture, in the same way that we do not have politics or finance. All of this here is purely nominal, figurative, a work of imitating monkeys, of actors who do not know their parts. There is nothing here. All that you see is fake jewelry from foreign sales.[17]

In another part, again quoting Galdós, the character argues:

> Work! What for? The sparks, the fatuous fire in literature, graphic arts, and other orders of intellectual life do not invite us to work. Everything incites us to rest, to remain passive, to allow the days to pass by without making the slightest at-

tempt to fight against the Hispanic inertia. If I were faced with the dilemma of choosing between working or dying, I would choose death. The Spaniard who has a rent these days must save it and increase it if possible. Live well while life lasts, and while the last drop of oil remains in the lamp of well-being. I am not trying to say that I am better than everyone else. I am the worst, laziest, last priest or altar boy of inertia. My only merit is in the brutal sincerity of my pessimism.[18]

After Tarsis has fallen in love with a beautiful South American, she rejects him, and new adventures follow until the enchantment of the main character occurs. The cynical, lazy, pessimistic, and wealthy man turns into a poor youth by an act of magic. He experiences countless vicissitudes that will make him realize how empty, decadent, and exploitative his previous life was. This leads him to reconsider his life and adopt a more active, regenerating attitude, with a commitment to aid the poor whom he had previously despised and exploited. In this process, the character named Madre plays an essential role. She is a magician with limited powers, a kind of reincarnation of the bruised Hispanic culture. The enchanted man will remain in her hands until he completes his positive transformation.

During a long dialogue between Tarsis (now transformed into poor Gil) and Madre, he lists a number of defects that decadent Spaniards have. Even though he is conscious of the abuse the rich give the poor, Gil does not intend to subvert the system. He calls on the powerful to remain good though rich, so that poor men can be less poor and also good; he calls on them to give without taking from anyone, even if that wealth had been the result of the most abusive practices. Here Ortiz again looks at Galdós in revealing such idealized notions: "We are equal, the poor man and the rich man, the plebian and the noble, we are all in fortunate brotherhood; we live for it."[19] Even if this sublime trail of thought is not a part of Ortiz's opinions, he respects the good intentions behind it, does not quarrel with it, and, when the story continues, in his own words he comments: "A graceful lesson . . . that we could all take advantage of. The wordy Spaniard can use it in his new, tough working life, and the talkative American to build his dreams."[20] The American projection intended in Ortiz's version is thus inserted.

However, on occasions Ortiz must disagree, especially when touching American issues. The woman Tarsis loved is also transformed by a spell from Cintia to Pascuala, from a beautiful South American capable of rejecting Tarsis for his defects to a teacher in a rural area of Spain. Ortiz would admit this if it was symbolically meant to show just how much Spaniards had to learn from their former colonial subjects. However, Ortiz does not allow the opportunity to pass by, humorously and ironically noting:

Although we were aware of Tarsis's mistakes and stupidities that prompted Madre to cast him under a spell to correct them, we were unaware that Cintia had her defects too . . . nor did we know that she had strayed from the good path and that love for Madre would straighten her ways. . . . Therefore this chapter should in fact be labeled: Where a Pascuala suddenly appears and where enchantment either is or is not unjust, or is only that of the gentleman.[21]

This is a lashing attack on any pan-Hispanist intention. The spell would only end when Madre considers that her mission of regeneration has been achieved. Within Galdós's spirit this would occur in a context of harmony: Cintia and Tarsis will love each other, will be happy, and will have a son. The reading between the lines that Ortiz suggested in the prologue becomes handy at this stage. Would Pérez Galdós avoid exercizing the Hispanic mission of tutelage? Here Ortiz required a strictly American epilogue, where he can abandon the original text to dive into his own discourse without losing the novelesque aura. He opted to do this in an epistolar style with an almost allegoric form of symbolism.

It begins with an intimate letter that América Andina writes to her younger sister Juanita Antilla, written in Buenos Aires on the significant date of May 25, 1910. The sender regrets the scarce communication between the two: "We are so far away and the post is so slow, family is so dispersed! But, although we do not share the same surname, we are daughters of the same mother and sisters all the same, and it is fair that we should love each other and tell each other our troubles."[22] From the very beginning, Ortiz thus establishes the concept of Ibero-Americanism, and its need, and calls for union. The elder sister continues: "You must have heard from our old friend Benito Pérez Galdós, who despite never meeting us personally knows our joys and sorrows well, . . . about the new craze that has possessed Carlitos de Tarsis." She continues to say that the good-looking youth had visited those lands and "was prowling our door, speaking our language, and whispering words sweeter than honey."[23]

América Andina's letter is a warning call in regard to the neoimperialist intentions of pan-Hispanism, addressed to Juanita Antilla who had only been able to free herself from the maternal authoritarianism much later. América tells about Tarsis's jealousy of other suitors, especially Samuel Johnson, and concludes, "Please advise me. Tell me if I should succumb to this unhappy lover, if I should say goodbye to friends and admirers, and if I should resign to my luscious freedom of rich female and give in to a union with him, a marriage whim of our downtrodden cousin."[24]

Transparent in his objectives and concerns, Ortiz then inserts the confidential reply to the elder sister. Written in Baracoa on July 4, the letter begins by greeting the never forgotten América and, after congratulating her for receiving the news, says: "We are in festivities here in celebration of the birthday of a rowdy neighbor who you know." Juana, absorbed in a spirit of identity, writes to her sister:

I am in this town where my cradle used to rock because, after hearing profusely of my race and heritage, I burn with desire to learn of the feats of my elders. I have come here in search of documents and chronicles of the Indies that can serve as fuel for the flames of my zeal for study. I hardly find anything but searching alone is a relief and soon I will rejoice.[25]

She confesses that she knows of Tarsis's delirium. He also courts her and the rest of their sisters: "Look at this sultan! Sister, it is obvious that the blood of a moor boils in his veins!" The Don Juan cousin does not accept any rivals, and she is not surprised of "the grudge that Carlitos holds against Sam, as we call our neighbor here."[26] She admits to having a certain sympathy toward Sam, although he is also a relentless suitor, because he has different qualities compared to Carlitos. At this point, Ortiz makes a comparison between the two, which could not be understood out of context. Defeated, dated, uncultured, illiterate, and pretentious Spain was incapable of reconquering America. Only through its own development could Spain reestablish a relationship of equality, respect, and mutual benefit with Spanish America.

Ortiz understood that prosperity for the Cuban nation was feasible if adequate relations with the United States were established. He wanted Cuba to capitalize on all the opportunities that the ties with that country could provide. Perhaps he was too benevolent. Perhaps during those initial years of the illusory republic, he did not understand the essence of the puissant empire and may have even granted the neighbor some traces of goodness. It is true that even then there were protests against Yankee greed. It is also true that later in his life Ortiz did not deceive himself on this, as his actions and his work later showed. The idea that he was a man awestruck or conciliatory with any imperialist desire, not even in 1910 on that Fourth of July when Juana wrote to América Andina. She knows three different concepts: sister, neighbor, and suitor. In *El caballero encantado y la moza esquiva*, in the rest of what is included in *La reconquista de América,* and in many other works of that period, Ortiz processed the attitudes that filtered form Washington and understood their meaning and essence.

Juana Antilla advises América Andina:

Flirt with Carlos as much as you like, and even entertain yourself with his romanticism. It is not bad to look back once we can look firmly forward; but ensure that you do not allow him to be irreverent or audacious.

Ortiz is clearly stating his views on pan-Hispanism. He is also able to define his position regarding the other threat:

I will do the same, although I am closer than you to my friend Sam owing needs of gratitude and neighborhood proximity. If due to this you should hear Carlos say that I have given up my honor, tell him that he is lying, that pure I continue my honest life, firmly looking toward the future. I am anxious given my inexperience, but nonetheless resolved to die rather than to take a step backwards.[27]

Patriotic, worthy, and incorruptible in Cuba facing Spain and the United States, this free version of the novel is much more: It is a declaration of identity and a lesson of it. Ultimately, it is the expression of the right to be, against any attempt at absorption. It is a model of an interpretative rewriting inspired by the mysterious vessels connecting life and art, and a blueprint of historical destiny.

NOTES

A shorter version of this essay under the title "El caballero encantado en la óptica cubana de Fernando Ortiz: un enfoque sociopolítico regeneracionista e intertextual en 1910," was delivered at the "6to. Congreso Internacional Galdosiano: Galdós y el 98" in Las Palmas, Gran Canaria, Spain, June 16–20, 1997.

1. Benito Pérez Galdós, *El caballero encantado*, in *Obras completas de Benito Pérez Galdós* (Madrid: Editorial Aguilar, 1951), vol. 4: 223–343.

2. Peter A. Bly, "Sex, egotism, and social regeneration in Galdós' *El caballero encantado*," *Hispania* 2, no. 1 (1979): 20–29.

3. Bly, "Sex, egotism," 24.

4. Bly, "Sex, egotism," 28.

5. For a summary of the novel's argument and meaning, see the opinion of Emilio Gutiérrez Gamero, literary critic and Galdós's biographer, cited by Federico Carlos Saínz de Robles, "Nota preliminar a *El caballero encantado*," in *Obras completas de Benito Pérez Galdós* (Madrid: Editorial Aguilar, 1951), 221–23.

6. Saínz de Robles, "Nota preliminary," 221–22.

7. Fernando Ortiz, *El caballero encantado y la moza esquiva: Versión libre y americana de una novela española de Benito Pérez Galdós* (Havana: Imprenta La Universal, 1910), 256.

8. Fernando Ortiz, *Entre cubanos: Psicología tropical* (Havana: Editorial de Ciencias Sociales, 1986), 77–78.

9. Ortiz, *Entre cubanos*, 107.

10. Ortiz, *Entre cubanos*, 17–18.

11. Araceli García Carranza, *Bio-bibliografía de Don Fernando Ortiz* (Havana: Instituto del Libro, 1970), 15.

12. Ortiz, *El caballero encantado*, 255–56.

13. Ortiz, *El caballero encantado*. 256.

14. Ortiz, *El caballero encantado*, 257.

15. Ortiz, *El caballero encantado*, 259.

16. Ortiz, *El caballero encantado*, 259–60.

17. Ortiz, *El caballero encantado*, 261.

18. Ortiz, *El caballero encantado*, 263. The corresponding part is in Galdós, *El caballero encantado*, 233.

19. Ortiz, *El caballero encantado*, 276. The corresponding part is in Galdós, *El caballero encantado*, 256.

20. Ortiz, *El caballero encantado*, 276.

21. Ortiz, *El caballero encantado*, 287.

22. Ortiz, *El caballero encantado*, 321.

23. Ortiz, *El caballero encantado*, 322–23.

24. Ortiz, *El caballero encantado*, 329.

25. Ortiz, *El caballero encantado*, 329–30.

26. Ortiz, *El caballero encantado*, 331.

27. Ortiz, *El caballero encantado*, 333.

18

Comparative Analysis of Theoretical Symbols

Antonio Fernández Ferrer

I was born in Paris in 1910. My father was a gentle, easygoing person, a salad of racial genes: a Swiss citizen of French and Austrian ancestry, the current of the Danube circulated in his veins.[1]

With this tasty metaphor, "a salad of racial genes," the main character describes his father in Vladimir Nabokov's popular novel, *Lolita*. But, who isn't a salad? Let us also remember that, many centuries ago, the *ensaladilla* was a form of Golden Age Spanish literature: Sor Juana Inés de la Cruz (who was of the opinion that "if Aristotle had cooked, he would have written much more") left us several masterpieces of this genre of mixed languages. However, gastronomic metaphors are not exclusive of everyday language and literature; they are fundamental and inescapable parts of literary and anthropological theories, and, for that matter, of any other theoretical language.

For his profound erudition, Fernando Ortiz could have been nicknamed "Doctor Ocean," as was Lima's encyclopedic Don Pedro Alejandrino de Peralta Barnuevo Rocha y Benavides. It is a vain enterprise even to start alluding to Ortiz's oceanic production. I will only study two important metaphors, which Ortiz used in his research as a symbolic frame for his theories: the *ajiaco* and the symbol of Janus.

In refusing to simplify traditional discourses and academic disciplines, Fernando Ortiz prided himself of being an "explorer" of the forest, jungle, or Cuban *manigua*. In this sense, he adopted imaginative emblems, symbols, and metaphors. These symbols provide important clues for understanding the theoretical reach of his erudite research, as well as debating essential aspects of their currency.

Let us remember that, from a criminological standpoint, Ortiz started from the concept of the black *brujo* or "witch doctor," the inhabitant of *Hampa afro-cubana* (1906), in a similar way as the Brazilian Raymundo Nina Rodrigues had treated the black person and his "fetish" (in this case from the perspective of the "alienist"). The illustrations of the first edition of Ortiz's text, *Los negros brujos*, a text we ought to read today as a foundational writing milestone, are revealing of the initial stages of this approach toward a metaphorical crossroads. This effort was at the center of Ortiz's thoughts and was useful to ordering the oceanic, erudite vastness of his research through successive and different conformations. Other metaphorical concepts were, in succession, the xylophone key (1935) (an allegorical symbol or articulation of crucial resonance that includes the conscious use of the word *key* in its meaning of a device to open the intricate Cuban cultural labyrinth); the *ajiaco* as a metaphor for transculturation; the symbol of the two-headed Janus; the explorer of the intricate jungle; the notion of "counterpoint" always symbolizing the latent dialectic in the dichotomy of Ortiz's theoretical thought; the lexical creations such as *cubanía* or *africanía* (1950); and others.

The theoretical path dotted with conceptual metaphors has always been a bit sinuous and intricate. In its more evident extremes, José Juan Arrom has aggressively criticized three metaphors used for symbolizing relations between Spain and Spanish America from the standpoint of the paternalistic mentality of chauvinist colonizing attitudes: "the Motherland" (*la Madre Patria*), "the branches of the Spanish trunk," and Julián Marías, coarse "Spain as the *Plaza Mayor* of Spanish America." "Metaphors" warned Arrom "are both valuable and dangerous given their suggestive power and force to penetrate the imagination."[2]

We are well aware that the most famous dishes, essential elements in the gastronomic imagery, have often been used as metaphors of identity for nations. We could almost state that they are a conceptual "archetype" if we were to trust the Jungian archetypal theories. Despite these doubts, let us quote a classic example of this custom of using gastronomic metaphors for the purposes of national mythical interests in Latin American literature. The example is from the Argentinian Esteban Echeverría in his famous "Apology of the *matambre*":

> Let the taciturn Englishmen shout, roast-beef, plum pudding; the Italians cry, macaroni, and let them remain as thin as an I or the spire of a gothic tower. Let the Frenchmen say *omelette souflée, omelette au sucre, omelette au diable*; let the Spaniards pronounce with sarcasm, *chorizos, olla podrida*, more putrid and rancid than their secular enlightenment. All of you scream freely, as we press our sides and let the big word *matambre* escape, sealing off your mouths completely. Antonio Pérez used to say: "Only great stomachs can digest poison," and I say: "Only great stomachs can digest *matambre*." This is not to say that all Argentinian *porteños* have great stomachs; but merely that only the *matambre* feeds and nurtures robust stomachs, which according to Perez mean magnanimous hearts.[3]

The gastronomic emblems that often coalesce in true "national dishes" are invested with the values of the most ennobled tradition expressed concretely in individual life. We can recognize this in the following passage of the Spanish novelist Carmen Laforet when she describes the smell of the *cocido madrileño* as an ancient sediment:

> He arrived home like a dream, through the narrow streets of Madrid's old city center. He arrived to his large and cool home, with a smell of food that was embedded in the staircase of footstep holes in the middle. . . . An indescribable, most ancient smell of pot stew. The smell of *cocido madrileño* that had been settling for over two centuries.[4]

As an analogy, Ortiz's work refers to the value of the *ajiaco* as an experience of history. Ortiz is especially interested in using this metaphor for illustrating what could be described as an archeological permission. The symbol of the *ajiaco* clearly enables him to compare the Cuban enigma and its aboriginal ancestral precedent. The tag of indigenous, pre-Columbian, prehistoric, and atemporal, lying at the bottom of the *ajiaco* pot is similar to that which we find in the description of the *cocido madrileño* by someone also interested in conveying the historical resonance of ennobled archaeology:

> There is no doubt that the *cocido* itself, through its simplicity of throwing into a single pot anything which comes to hand and cooking it with water for hours, until it's ready, while the reindeer or bison is hunted, for example, thanks to the time it takes for the chickpeas to soften. It is perhaps the only dish remaining from the stone age, as almost inevitable the *gabrieles* remain hard as stone if the privileged water of Madrid does not soften them up, that water as fine as wind, and capable of working through silicon as its colleague the air is capable of killing a man, so impassive is Madrid water to the soap's foam.[5]

Already in his first book on Minorcan traditions, Fernando Ortiz used gastronomic metaphors. Let us remember the title itself: *Principi y prostes: Collecció d'aguiats menorquins que s'espera cauran bé a's ventrell.* But, without a doubt, the *ajiaco* pot as the emblem of the inextricable labyrinth of Cuban transculturations would be the most famous metaphor of all of Ortiz's erudite contributions. Furthermore, as often happens with the use of theoretical emblems, a troubling ambiguity unravels its contradictory problematic essence. In the gastronomic metaphor of the *ajiaco* pot, those elements of negative resonance often found in the inventory of symbols are also present. A sinister symbology of the cauldron:

> If the skull is the container of superior forces, the cauldron is the container of inferior ones. This is why cauldrons and potions are present in tales of magic and stories of folklore linked to the forces of evil (remember the wizard, Merlin, Morgana, the druids . . . or the identification of hell with an enormous cauldron). Antagonically, the chalice sublimates and makes sacred the notion of a container.[6]

Different languages also alert us to the contradictions inevitably associated with conceptual metaphors. In English, "gone to pot" indicates either a spoiled or rotten thing, which needs to be improved by returning it to the pot or rejected as in a bargain.[7] Remembering an Argentinian saying, "in every big pot," there is a traumatic confusion also derived from the metaphorical image of a stew that confuses and mixes everything. Ortiz himself notes another meaning of the term *ajiaco* related to these problematic repercussions: "In Cuba, there is also another sense [for *ajiaco*]: tumult, scandal, a mess or knot."[8]

Ortiz uses the cooking pot of the *ajiaco* to replace the traditional melting pot. However, it is inevitable to establish the relationship between the "melting" and the always incomplete process of fusion. It is not strange, therefore, that the metaphor of the *ajiaco* pot produced a number of contrary opinions. For example, Gastón Baquero points to this troubling ambiguity by associating Ortiz's pot with the jar of the mythical Danaids, a metaphor conveying both a negative result (with the sinister invocation of infernal torment) and the impossibility of theoretically fulfilling the Cuban problem. Certainly in the myth of the Danaids many issues coincide: food, founding genealogy, and ancestral crimes.[9] Likewise, Iván de la Nuez, in alluding to the Barthesian relationship between flavor and knowledge, also deals with the ambiguity of Ortiz's gastronomic metaphor:

> In 1940 Fernando Ortiz conceived in Cuba the term transculturation—eventually more effective than multiculturalism—as a way of understanding the exchanges between cultures. Malinowski adopted it as a great contribution to anthropology, which he always considered to be the science of sense of humor. To illustrate his term, Ortiz used the gastronomical metaphor of *ajiaco* (a Cuban stew that mixes meats, vegetables, and other very diverse ingredients). The success of the *ajiaco* consists of a final product of the mixing that ought to taste better than each of the original ingredients by themselves. I have always been suspicious of Ortiz, especially when I imagine him with a ladle stirring the pot. This however does not invalidate that over half a century later, his term and his stew can still aid us to obtain a good tasting knowledge and critical perspective.[10]

Apart from his famous *ajiaco* pot, in his relentless exploring of the Cuban labyrinth, Ortiz also uses the janiform vases from pieces of ancient classic Greco-Roman pottery. The opposed, double face of the metaphor depicting Janus is therefore another basic allegory in Ortiz's theories. It was adopted as an emblem for the Sociedad de Estudios Afrocubanos (founded and headed by Ortiz in 1937). Ortiz explains the sense behind the emblem in one of his articles: "Our symbol is ultimately the reproduction of the two-headed janiform glass of the sixth century B.C. attributed to the potter Charinus."

In classic Greece, the figure of the black man was artistically depicted with relative frequency in pottery, statues, cameos, and coins according to Beardsley's research. But it is in a single Janus-type vase that we find the best expression of the social cooperation between the black and white races in pleasant harmony based on equality. As Beardsley indicates, there is no prejudice in those Athenian works of art; on the contrary, the contrast is merely employed for artistic purposes. This motif of the union of a black face and a white face, in the shape of Janus, appears in classic ceramic pieces around the seventh century B.C. in Naveratis, and from there it is adopted by Attic ceramists in the sixth century. This would appear to suggest that the Janus motif in vessels was not originally Hellenic but in fact African. It is also probable that the bifacial morphology of the vessel was based on sacred and ritual reasons of a propitiatory nature.[11]

But, as it often occurs in Ortiz's considerations during deep theoretical thinking, the African origin will be decisive. He was careful to underscore that the double face of Janus is an essentially African motif, immediately related to the representation of the *orisha Elegguá*. Ortiz concluded:

> Given all of this background, it is easy to understand how the emblem adopted by our Sociedad de Estudios Afrocubanos obeys allegorically, aesthetically, and historically to the two ethnic ancestries whose union in Cuba constitutes the path for the new intellectual association.[12]

The double face of the God Janus is a classical symbol for historians and politicians. It has been used, among others, by Arthur Koestler as a symbol of his anthropological endeavors.[13] One of the most recent researchers on this topic, José Forné, uses it to examine the contradictions of the nationalist movements in Europe today. Based on the Janus symbol, Forné carries on a comparative analysis between the various European nationalisms, especially focusing on the contradictions in their discourses of identity.[14]

In the study of the characteristics, functions, and risks of conceptual metaphors in cultural theory, there are several approaches. George Lakoff and Mark Johnson analyze "ontological metaphors" and "container metaphors."[15] For the case of Ortiz, as for many other scholars, it would be necessary to relate this use of the conceptual metaphor with the construction of the anthropologist's style, following the insights of Clifford Geertz in dealing with the style and the images of three renowned anthropologists.[16] And, if we were to deepen the analysis, we would need to travel through complex areas such as those dealt with by Derrida.[17] Lacan criticized the excessive "idolatry" in cultural investigation as "the propensity of using excessive imagery":

> The need to use images is valid in scientific writing as in other fields, but perhaps not as much as one thinks. And nowhere is it more dangerous than in the domain we are now at: subjectivity. When we talk about subjectivity, the difficulty lies precisely in not identifying the subject.[18]

But perhaps the most interesting aspect of Ortiz is not so much the unraveling of a series of fairly identifiable contradictions, but rather the tenacious output of his capacity for scrutiny: from criminologist-filologist to collectionist; from the fetishist witch doctor to the troubling double face of Janus. They are original metaphors that become the drive behind his erudite oceanic contributions. Yvette Sánchez's recent work studies the relationship between collectionism and literature; in this sense, Ortiz's vastly erudite contribution is a fundamental component of contemporary research.[19] His conceptual metaphors are decisive components in the consolidation of his theory on the Cuban cultural jungle, its guiding talismans as well as the emblems that guide his voyage.

It is significant to note that if we attempt even the most superficial comparative analysis, we will find the contrast between the two symbols analyzed here: the *ajiaco* cauldron against the Janus figure. In the first conceptual metaphor, we have the notion of sublimation by mixture and concocted transubstantiation; in the Janus figure, two entities remain confronted. Additionally, the Janus metaphor has a classicistic valorative component absent in the *ajiaco*. Everything seems to indicate that there is an oscillation between Utopia and nightmare: the cauldron of the exquisite mixture turned into the barrel of the Danaids and the irreducible Cuban dichotomy. To escape this cul-de-sac, Ortiz appeals to the infinity of his work, the complexity of his objectives, and, at this point, the use of other metaphors such as "explorer" of the jungle or infinite island. The perhaps impossible mixture of the two emblems, the *ajiaco* cauldron and the figure of Janus, could be the idea of the explorer of the "infinite island," another useful metaphor for describing an endless enigma.

Thus, the island could be a metonym for intellectual efforts and contributions that are as vast as Ortiz's work. In a way, all theoretical efforts involve an expedition through the intricate jungles of an island, the problematic contours of a theoretical insularity or hermeneutics. As Lezama Lima stated, "The distinct island in the Cosmos or, what mounts to the same, the indistinct island in the Cosmos." Here we encounter the infinite island, a clever title that Cintio Vitier and Fina García Marruz gave to a rescued fragment of a text that reads, "Columbus asked the local Indians whether he was on mainland or on an island, and they replied that it was an infinite land of which no one had seen the end although it was an island."[20] Nothing stops us from imagining that this paradoxical infinite island (seemingly a Cuban version of the Cheshire cat) may help us understand the work of Fernando Ortiz and any ethnological, aesthetic, or literary theory: any theoretical intention is an expedition through an infinity, inevitably thinking in its contradictory finiteness. After all, the tribes in the eastern woodlands use the term *island* to refer to the universe. The infinite island is useful not only as a metaphor for illustrating the Cuban enigma, the prodigious crossroads of cultures, but also theoretical research itself. Furthermore, if we start from that image of the "explorer" of the cultural jungle, we could remember Ortega's notion of the "vertical explorer" in reference to another great founder of the literature of transcultured labyrinths (and inevitably linked to problematic comparisons of original concepts and current theoretical perspectives).[21] In this sense, Ortiz's emblems are the cipher of the contributions of a ceaseless "vertical exploration."

NOTES

1. Vladimir Nabokov, *Lolita* (Buenos Aires: Sur, 1959), 16.

2. José Juan Arrom, "Tres metáforas sobre España e Hispanoamérica," in *Certidumbre de América: Estudio de letras, folklore y cultura*, 2d ed. (Madrid: Editorial Gredos, 1971), 167–71.

3. Esteban Echevarría, "Apología del matambre," in *Obras completas* (Buenos Aries), 325–26.

4. Carmen Laforet, *La mujer nueva* (Barcelona: Ediciones Destino, 1955), 233.

5. Joaquín de Entrambasaguas, *Gastronomía madrileña*, 2d ed. (Madrid: Instituto de Estudios Madrileños, 1971), 17.

6. Monserrat Escartín Gual, *Diccionario de símbolos literarios* (Barcelona: PPU, 1996), 80.

7. See Gertrude Jobes, *Dictionary of Mythology, Folklore, and Symbols* (New York: Scarecrow, 1962), vol. 2: 1288.

8. Fernando Ortiz, *Glosario de afronegrismos* (Havana: Editorial de Ciencias Sociales, 1991), 18.

9. "En fin, me parece que voy a verter agua en la tinaja de las Danaides, y que en vano trataré de llenarla, al no retenerla el fondo, ya que antes de fluir en su interior se derramará el contenido: tan ancho es el agujero de vertido de la tinaja e incoercible su salida": Luciano de Samosata, *Timón o el misántropo* (Madrid: Gredos), 445–46. "El negro es la rémora de Cuba, decía en privado Fernando Ortiz, según Jorge Mañach, hombre que a su vez tenía miedo al negro. Es el tonel de las Danaides. Es la roca de Sísifo. Es el buitre rasgando las entrañas de Prometeo . . .": Gastón Baquero, "El negro en Cuba," in *Indios, blancos y negros en el caldero de América* (Madrid: Ediciones de Cultura Hispánica, 1991), 115.

10. Iván de la Nuez, *La balsa perpetua: Soledad y conexiones de la cultura cubana* (Barcelona: Editorial Casiopea, 1998), 116.

11. Fernando Ortiz, "El emblema de la Sociedad de Estudios Afrocubanos," *Estudios Afrocubanos* 1, no. 1 (1937): 11–14.

12. Ortiz, "El emblema," 14.

13. Arthur Koestler, *Janus: A Summing Up* (New York: Vintage Books, 1979).

14. "Trop souvent l'on jugue que les phénomènes identitaires sont des reminiscences archaïques. Mais le sont-ils vraiment? Ne sont-ils pas, au contraire, la manifestation de la fragmentation sociale, du sauve-qui-peut géneralisé, du modèle inaccesible de la réussite individuelle prôné par les néo-libéraux? Les mouvements identitaires jouent sur l'affectif, sur l'émotion, sur les images d'une collectivité pacifique qui retrouve enfin son épanouissement dans une convivialité créatrice. C'est le

visage souriant de la figure antique de Janus. L'autre inquiétant et troublant, est celui qui reste dans l'ombre, celui de la perpétuation des clivages sociaux et de l'exclusion envers de nouvelles minorities": José Forné, *Les nationalismes identitaires en Europe: les deux faces de Janus* (Paris: Éditions L'Harmattan, 1994).

15. George Lakoff and Mark Johnson, *Metaphors We Live By* (Chicago: University of Chicago Press, 1980), 68, 78.

16. Clifford Geertz, *El estilo del antropólogo* (Barcelona: Paidós).

17. Jacques Derrida, "La mitología blanca: La metáfora en el texto filosófico," in *Márgenes de la filosofía* (Madrid: Ediciones Cátedra, 1989), 247–311. See also his "La retirada de la metáfora," in *La deconstrucción en las fronteras de la filosofía. La retirada de la metáfora*, trans. Patricio Peñalver Gómez (Barcelona: Paidós/ICE, Universidad Autónoma de Barcelona, 1989), 35–75.

18. Jacques Lacan, *El seminario, libro 2. El Yo en la teoría de Freud y en la técnica psicoanalítica 1954–1955*, ed. Jacques-Alain Miller, trans. Irene Agoff (Buenos Aires: Paidós, 1983), 87.

19. Yvette Sánchez, *Coleccionismo y literatura* (Madrid: Cátedra, 1999).

20. Andrés Bernaldes, "Historia de los Reyes Católicos," in Cintio Vitier and Fina García Marruz, eds., *Flor oculta de poesía cubana (siglos XVIII y XIX)* (Havana: Editorial Arte y Literatura, 1978), 63.

21. José Ortega y Gasset used the expression "vertical explorer" in a cycle of conferences at the Residencia de Estudiantes in Madrid: "Es curioso advertir que Africa, desde el Ecuador hasta el Mediterráneo, pareció predestinada a ser conquista científica de los alemanes. Los grandes descubridores de sus tierras han sido gente germánica, y ahora Frobenius, cuando ya apenas queda nada que explorar en la superficie, logra ser el zahorí de un Africa subterránea, de un pasado africano. Por que ésta ha sido, en última abreviatura, la hazaña máxima de Frobenius: descubrir en un continente, en que parecía no haber habido nunca movimientos históricos, perspectiva de un ayer distinto de un hoy, un profundo pasado. Frobenius ha sido un explorador en vertical: bajo el presente, que parecía, hacia atrás, haber sido invariable y eterno, ha encontrado hondos estratos de pretérito": "Las ideas de León Frobenius," in *Obras completas*, 6th ed., vol. 3 (Madrid: Revista de Occidente, 1966), 246.

19

Stirring the *Ajiaco*

Changüí, Son, and the Haitian Connection

Benjamin L. Lapidus

In his best-known works on Cuban music, Fernando Ortiz looked beyond Cuba's shores to the Caribbean, the Americas, and Africa to find similarities and analogues that could explain the origins of a given Cuban musical or nonmusical cultural practice. One of the ways that Ortiz deepened his understandings was by exchanging ideas with other researchers throughout the world. Robin Moore's excellent analysis and problematization of Ortiz's writings on Afro-Cuban music demonstrates how Ortiz's later texts show a familiarity with works on folklore and anthropology written by contemporaries such as Herskovits and Courlander who worked in various regions of the Caribbean.[1]

Within Cuba, Ortiz collaborated with Guantánamo-based musicologists Rafael Inciarte Brioso (1909–1991) and Luis Morlote Ruiz (1903–1994) concerning music and musical instruments in Oriente. The result of these collaborations was an emphasis on the Haitian origins of many of the region's instruments. Ortiz recognized the historical contact between Cuba and Haiti and how the process of transculturation contributed to the particularities of Oriente's music and the resulting Afro-Haitian folklore found in the region.

This chapter focuses on several points. First, I argue that the Haitian presence in Oriente has contributed significantly to the development of the Cuban *son,* the ultimate Cuban musical product. The Afro-Haitian component of *son* has been all but ignored in the telling of the genre's history. Second, I present *changüí,* a genre performed mostly by Cubans of Afro-Haitian descent, as the best musical evidence to support this argument. In his well-known concept of the *ajiaco,* Ortiz likens Cuban culture to a stew possessing both tasty and putrid elements. As Moore explains, "to Ortiz the tastier elements are those which have been added more recently, and . . . the older or more 'primitive' elements associated with Spanish- or African-derived 'atavisms' are those which need to be discarded."[2] Ortiz's position vis-à-vis these elements would change in the 1950s, but the notion as originally conceptualized is relevant to this discussion.

First, it would appear that, because Afro-Haitian elements are both relatively recent arrivals and established traditions in Cuban culture, there are multiple possibilities for interpreting their qualitative value and impact within this framework. Haitians and other non-Cuban Caribbean migrants to Cuba were often vilified and used as scapegoats for the economic and social problems that plagued numerous Cuban administrations; from this standpoint Afro-Haitian culture was seen negatively. At the same time, Haitian culture was celebrated for its contribution of the *contradanza* to Cuban music, as well as various musical practices in Oriente. Afro-Haitian folklore is currently celebrated and supported by the state like other genres of Cuban folklore. By studying *changüí* and other musical practices in Oriente, it is possible for us to examine and raise questions about the transculturative process that created *son*.

Through focusing on *changüí* and using Ortiz's ideas, I will argue that we must look beyond Cuba's shores, viewing both *changüí* and *son* in a broader pan-Caribbean context. In fact, it will be useful and necessary to create new genre/ensemble categories that include the transculturative process reflected in Caribbean music. I propose that studying the string band as a Creole genre can further our understanding of the historical and cultural connections in the Caribbean region.

THE FIRST WAVE OF HAITIAN
MIGRATION TO CUBA AND ITS RELATED MUSIC

Haitian migration to Cuba took place in two major waves. At the beginning of the Haitian revolution in 1791, white planters began to flee the island of Hispaniola. Some settled in New Orleans, while most others remained in the Caribbean. Juan Pérez de la Riva estimates that between 1795 and 1805, more than thirty thousand people from Hispaniola settled in Oriente. Approximately twenty thousand were not white.[3] The white planters brought their domestic slaves and agricultural laborers with them. Within a short time, the planters used their technical ingenuity and expertise to create a thriving coffee industry, and to improve the quality of the crop in their new country.

This large influx of French Creole and Afro-Haitian immigrants created a vibrant community in Oriente. Shortly after the arrival of white planters, free blacks and mulattoes began arriving in large numbers and continued to do so throughout the nineteenth century. French planters and *mayorals* (overseers) had reputations as being especially harsh.[4] Nevertheless, the slaves of Haitian descent found ways to express themselves and maintain their culture in this new environment. Cultural practices such as the Creole language and voodoo were maintained, even though they changed. *Tumba francesa* and *tajona* are two of the main genres that originate from this period.

The music and dance of the *tumba francesa* have strong French and Afro-Haitian elements. First, the society has a specific hierarchy, which mimics French aristocracy. The *mayor* or *mayora de plaza* directs and chooses all of the orders of the dances and the changing of the dance steps. They also decide which dancers will perform and maintain a sense of royalty through curtsies and similar actions. The *composé* is the lead vocalist, and he leads songs in Creole. As his name suggests, he composes and improvises songs. The chorus is usually made up of women, although I have seen men participate. The chorus uses metal rattles called *chachás*. Ortiz confirmed the Haitian origin of the *chachá* and wrote that "Sin duda, ese tipo cubano de *maruga cilíndrica o chachá* procede de Haití y otras islas de influencia francesa" (without a doubt, this Cuban type of rattle comes from Haiti and other French islands)."[5] Judith Bettleheim has also noted that the names of the instruments in the *tumba francesa* battery (which include the *premiér*, *bulá*, *ségon*, and *catá*) and their specific rhythms take their names from Haitian instruments and genres.[6]

The two main styles for the ensemble are *masón* and *yubá*; each has its own dance. The *masón* is danced by couples and is thought to be based on the *contredanse* of the French plantocracy.[7] During the *masón*, another small double-headed drum, the *tambora*, is added. The dance that accompanies this style is a side-to-side movement with each shift in body weight occurring at the beginning of the *catá* pattern.

Ortiz wrote about the Haitian origins of congas in Santiago de Cuba as well, further evidence of this link between the two islands. Just as one can see Haiti from the coast of Guantánamo, one hears Haiti in the music of Guantánamo. Miguel Barnet affirms this when he says, "Oriente is like another country, so close to Haiti."[8]

THE SECOND WAVE OF HAITIAN
MIGRATION TO CUBA AND ITS RELATED MUSIC

The second major wave of Haitian migration to Cuba took place during the twentieth century. Mats Lundahl attributes this wave to economic factors such as the need for laborers in Cuba after the war of 1895–1898, the growth of the Haitian population, and the lack of land available to Haitian peasants as a result of the U.S. occupation of Haiti (1915–1934).[9] Pérez de La Riva estimates that more than half a million Haitians came to Cuba between 1902 and 1930.[10] Haitian *braceros* (day laborers), along with Jamaican laborers, were brought in under unfavorable conditions to cut sugarcane. Compared to the Jamaican laborers, the Haitians were mistreated and forcibly repatriated during times of economic depression. They often kept to themselves and settled in remote mountain areas near Santiago de Cuba.[11] In Guantánamo, Haitians settled near the sugar *centrales* (plantations) and in the city. This heritage is tangible in culinary, religious, linguistic, and musical traditions such as *méringue, tambuyé, gagá,* and voodoo, among others.[12] Contact with Haiti was also maintained during the 1970s and 1980s, as boatloads of Haitians visited Guantánamo for medical care. Space does not allow for an explanation of each musical style associated with more recent Haitian migration, but one rhythmic pattern, the *tresillo,* is central to many of them, particularly *gagá* and *méringue.*

CHANGÜÍ'S HISTORICAL
BACKGROUND AND MUSICAL CHARACTERISTICS

Don Fernando Ortiz cited G. A. Cavazzi's seventeenth-century reports of a similarly named genre in Africa. Cavazzi observed Congolese musicians performing a dance and music called *quisangüí.* Ortiz wrote that the verb *sanga* means "to dance or jump with joy," and the prefix *qui* marks a quality in Angolan and Congolese languages.[13] From this linguistic perspective, Ortiz defined the Cuban word *changüí* as a joyous dance. Additionally, Ortiz gave several definitions of the word *changüí* on page 192 of his *Nuevo catauro de cubanismos,* emphasizing the multiple meanings of the word: a dance and gathering of lower classes, to jump with joy, to trick or deceive someone, among others.[14] The word is used to indicate a party and is often interchanged with words such as *cumbancha, cucalambé, parranda, bachata, rumba,* and *rompía,* among others.

Changüí is a musical genre that is specifically linked to certain modes of behavior, which have changed over time. For about a century before the 1959 revolution, a *changüí* was a rural party at which participants consumed large quantities of rum, ate roasted pigs, danced, and engaged in musical duels (*controversias*) that included *treseros* (*tres* players) and *trovadores* (improvising singers).[15] Often the *treseros* would accompany themselves as they sang. According to Inciarte, one occasion for *changüí* gatherings was the period between Christmas Eve and Three Kings Day (January 6), when musicians and revelers would begin traveling from house to house. From around the 1930s, these events would be advertised on the radio because the participants lived so far from one another. Participants would each bring a chicken, a pig, or some rum, and often arrived with their clothes dirty from the trip. Many *changüíseros* distinguished themselves as great vocal improvisers and *tres* players; songs by and about these musicians form a large part of the *changüí* repertoire that is performed today. All of these musicians from the legendary past were black, and, with few exceptions, each had a French surname. There were numerous informal *changüí* groups in the city of Guantánamo throughout the first half of the twentieth century. In 1945, Rafael Inciarte Brioso urged some of these musicians to form a formal group, and thus the Grupo Changüí de Guantánamo was born.[16]

During the first thirty years after the revolution, Grupo Changüí de Guantánamo became an official professional musical group performing *changüí* locally, nationally, and internationally. The music underwent a folklorization process in which many of its elements were stabilized. Many musicians from the surrounding rural areas such as Yateras, Las Cidras, Salvador, and Manuel Tames moved to the city of Guantánamo, and some learned to read and write music. By this time, most *treseros* already had electric pickups on their instruments and the music was performed on stages with microphones.

Since the start of the post-Soviet "special period" in 1990, more local groups have received professional status from the state musical bureaucracy as have stage folkloric presentations of *changüí* and its variants, such as *kiribá* and *nengón*. The shift to a tourist-based economy after the collapse of the Soviet bloc and the loss of its subsidies brings tourists to experience authentic *changüí* parties in the mountains. Furthermore, the quest for the roots of Cuban music and the Buena Vista phenomenon have brought foreign record companies and film crews to Guantánamo as well. Due to the severe rationing of gas and food, the kind of parties that would have been normal during the early years of *changüí* are restricted to special occasions such as birthdays or weddings. Smaller, private gatherings are more conducive for long vocal improvisations and *controversias*, but some singers sing longer improvisations, such as *décimas*, regardless of the performance context. Most of the people who knew the great musicians of the legendary past, and/or the musicians who participated in that past, are deceased.

The most active and prominent *changüí* musicians in Guantánamo have been of Haitian descent. The same family names have appeared in local song and history for several generations. Many of the best-known musicians and composers have surnames such as Cadete, Speck, Lescaille, Planche, Creagh, Cobás, Logát, Latamblé, Masó, Arnaud, Mustelier, Durand, Durruthy, Vichí, and Moreaux.[17] Some of these musicians were among the first generation born in Cuba to Haitian parents while others confirmed that their grandparents were Haitian. There have also been a few musicians whose English surnames, such as Wilson and Brown, reflect an Anglophone-Caribbean heritage. All of the important musicians playing this genre of music are of African descent. In fact, there have been few nonblack *changüiseros*.

Many *changüiseros* played and continue to play Afro-Haitian genres such as *tumba francesa*, *tambuyé*, and *montompolo*. Others still speak Creole, and many actively participate in voodoo. Many of the musicians who came from the mountains to the city were active in Afro-Haitian musical and cultural activities in the villages surrounding the city of Guantánamo.

CHANGÜÍ AND TUMBA FRANCESA

Ortiz's methodology generally pursues connections between Cuban and non-Cuban music based on the physical characteristics of musical instruments, similarities in performance practice, and linguistic relationships. Let us apply Ortiz's comparative approach to the study of *changüí*. Close examination of *changüí bongó* patterns reveals a striking similarity to *tumba francesa premiér* improvisational patterns. The low pitch of *changüí* bongos is similar to the low pitch of the *tumba francesa's premiér*. One local musicologist, Ramón Gómez Blanco, finds that the *changüí marímbula, guayo*, and maracas patterns are related to the *catá* pattern in *tumba francesa* by way of a common Bantu heritage rather than an explicit Afro-Haitian connection.[18]

The Haitian connection is more apparent if one focuses on dance. *Changüí* dancers step with the *marímbula*, and *tumba francesa* dancers often step with the *catá*. Furthermore, the *masón tambora* pattern in *tumba francesa* is the same as the *changüí bongó* part during the climax and decrescendo. Both could be derived from the *cinquillo* pattern or the Haitian *gagá* pattern.

Interestingly, *tumba francesa* music is organized around time lines played by the *catá*. In contrast, *changüí* has no parts that act as timelines. *Tumba francesa* was originally danced in *cafetales* (coffee plantations). Similarly, the dance step for a style older than *changüí*, called *nengón*, requires moving one's foot in a circle. Some regional dance specialists have explained this motion as mimetic, as if one were spreading coffee to dry. *Changüí* and *nengón* come from the same rural coffee regions (Las Cidras, Yateras, etc.) where there were many people of Haitian descent and *tumba francesa* groups. There might be a relation between the two based on this evidence, but as of this writing it remains hypothetical.

CHANGÜÍ AND *SON*

Thus far I have emphasized the differences between *changüí* and *son*; now it is time to invoke Ortiz and consider their connectedness. From a musical perspective, the claim that *changüí* is the direct predecessor to *son* has some merit. Comparing the rhythmic patterns and roles of the instruments reveals a few interesting points that support this argument. Our best sources of knowledge of early *son* are recordings by groups such as Sexteto Boloña, as well as Sexteto and Septeto Habanero.[19] Early recordings demonstrate that the first *son* groups were organologically similar to the *changüí* ensemble.

When listening to early recordings of El Sexteto Habanero and other groups (ca. 1925–1931), one can hear the *bongó* player make much use of the *bramido* (gliss). This is a howling or moaning sound characteristic of the climax section during a traditional *changüí* performance. It is also interesting to hear that, like a *changüí bongocero*, El Sexteto Habanero's *bongocero* plays few time-keeping patterns and mostly improvises. This seems to have been the dominant style for playing the *bongó* in a *son* context at that time.

The rhythm of the *changüí marímbula* begins to appear in the *tumbadora* (conga) patterns in recordings of *son* from the 1940s and 1950s, and is now an established trait of *son*.[20] Second, the rhythm of the *bongó de monte* during the *climax de despedida* (climax before ending the song), a variant of the *tresillo*, is found in the bass patterns of *son* recordings from the same period, becoming the standard *bajo anticipado* figure that characterizes *son* bass lines. In addition, the cowbell pattern commonly heard in *son* recordings of the 1940s and 1950s, and in today's *son,* is identical to the *changüí guayo* pattern. Finally, these same patterns have endured in contemporary performance practice of *son*, salsa, and other genres, both in Cuba and beyond its shores.

If one follows the argument of most theories and chronologies of Cuban musical development, specifically that the *son* as performed in eastern Cuba was brought westward by soldiers and migrants, then it is conceivable that *changüí* developed into *son* as it traveled west. Sometime during this transformation and geographic shift at the end of the nineteenth century and beginning of the twentieth (1898–1920), the difficult patterns of the *tres* and *bongó*, normally found in *changüí*, became less syncopated. In recordings, one can hear the use of the *bramido* as late as the 1920s, but it disappears in later recordings of *son*. Similarly, vestiges of the free, improvised style of the *changüí bongó* are audible in early *son* recordings of the 1920s, only to disappear in the 1930s with a shift to *martillo*, the steady, time-marking *son bongó* pattern. Most scholars agree that the clave figure in *son* derives from rumba clave as heard in Havana and Matanzas; the only difference between *son* and rumba clave is one eighth note.

Perhaps as musical characteristics from other genres and regions were added to *son* during the course of its development, these elements were altered and made less syncopated. Thus, the clave figure found in rumba is smoothed out and transformed by one eighth-note so that it is less syncopated when used in *son*. One possible consequence of this transformative process is that the high degree of syncopation in *changüí* was significantly diminished when it encountered the rigid timeline of the *son* clave, resulting in the rhythmic uniformity and smoothness of the *son*'s choreography and music. The high degree of syncopation in *changüí* makes it more difficult to dance to in comparison to *son*. Fewer dancers dance *contratiempo* to *son*, and most Cuban genres do not emphasize dancing *contratiempo* as *changüí* does. Is this a positive indicator of *changüí*'s older age? These are all hypotheses, but *changüí*, more so than *son*, is a genre that exploits highly syncopated musical ideas and movements.

CONCLUSION

One goal of this study was to present the varying narratives regarding the development of the *son*. These national and local perspectives present a linear, evolutionary development of the foremost Cuban musical genre. However, the evidence presented in this chapter suggests a more complex history; *changüí* and *son* are both related and distinct. *Changüí* and the dominant style of Cuban *son* (which developed in 1920s Havana and continues to thrive to this day) share some basic traits: use of string instruments such as the *tres*, emphasis on percussion instruments, simple chordal harmony, call and response vocal patterns, syncopated Afro-Caribbean rhythms, and an accompanying dance performed by male-female couples touching one another throughout the dance choreography (unlike in rumba). There, the similarity ends; both have similar ingredients, but the resulting swing or groove created by the *changüí* ensemble's interlocking parts does not resemble the *son* groove. Each genre has its own system of coordinated movements. In current practice, musical competition and vocal dueling remain key components of *changüí* while they have subsided in *son*. These characteristics are also found in rumba and *música campesina*, thus calling into question the nature of current Cuban genre classification.

Another goal of this study was to show how the Haitian presence in Oriente contributed, via *changüí*, to the development of *son*. The implications of the musical and historical evidence presented thus far warrant further investigation and study in Oriente. First, *changüí* has strong links to *tumba francesa* and other Afro-Haitian genres. Second, the absence of clave and the high degree of syncopation indicate that it probably came before *son*. An examination of dance styles supports the view that *son*'s choreography is smoother and more "creolized" than the choreography for *changüí*, which emphasizes "offbeat aesthetics" and is closely related to the choreography for *tumba francesa*.

Finally, this essay raises questions about the current system of Cuban genre classification by utilizing Ortiz's concept of the transculturation process, coupled with a new interpretation of his writings. Ortiz's studies of Cuban music can be interpreted in such a way as to encourage a broad pan-

Caribbean perspective that organizes Caribbean and African-diasporic musical traditions into larger groups across national borders. By studying *changüí*, we can begin to establish one such pan-Caribbean genre/ensemble category: the string band. Looking beyond Cuba toward the rest of the Caribbean, it is appropriate to see *changüí* as part of a loosely related group of Creole genres such as Jamaican *mento* and Haitian *méringue*, among others. Texture, instrumentation (emphasis on strings and percussion), basic harmonic conventions, emphasis on syncopated Afro-Caribbean rhythms, tempo, call and response vocal patterns, and couple dance choreography are a few of the ways in which these seemingly disparate genres could arguably be viewed as part of a broader category.

NOTES

1. Robin Moore, "Representations of Afrocuban Expressive Culture in the Writings of Fernando Ortiz," *Latin American Music Review* 15, no. 1 (1994): 45.

2. Moore, "Representations," 42.

3. Juan Pérez de la Riva, "Cuba y la migración antillana 1900–1931," *Anuario de Estudios Cubanos* 2 (1979): 17.

4. Olga Portuondo Zuñiga, "La región de Guantánamo: de la producción de consumo a la de mercancias," *Del Caribe* IV, no. 10 (1987): 12.

5. Fernando Ortiz, *Los Instrumentos de la música afrocubana, vol. 1* [1952] (Madrid: Editorial Música Mundana Maqueda; Havana: Fundació Fernando Ortiz, 1996), 305–6.

6. Judith Bettleheim, "The *Tumba Francesa* and *Tajona* of Santiago de Cuba," in Judith Bettleheim, ed., *Cuban Festivals: An Illustrated Anthology* (New York: Garland, 1993), 178. For transcriptions of tumba francesa, see Olavo Alén Rodríguez, *La música de las sociedades de tumba francesa en Cuba* (Havana: Casa de las Américas, 1986), 136–81.

7. Bettlheim, "*Tumba Francesa*," 179.

8. *What's Cuba Playing At?* [¿Qué se toca Cuba?] Arena/BBC LMA L024H, 1985; videocassette.

9. Mats Lundahl, "A Note on Haitian Migration to Cuba, 1890-1934," *Cuban Studies* 12, no. 2 (1982): 24–26.

10. Pérez de la Riva, "Cuba y la migración antillana," 53.

11. Marc C. McLeod, "Undesirable Aliens: Race, Ethnicity, and Nationalism in the Comparison of Haitian and British West Indian Immigrant Workers in Cuba," *Journal of Social History* 31, no. 3 (1998): 606.

12. Manriela Méndez Ceballo, María Cubeira Palomo, and Lourdes San Fat, "Influencias de las inmigraciones haitianas en el ámbito cutual y costumbrista de la provincia de Guantánamo," *El Managüí* 2, no. 4 (1987): 27.

13. Fernando Ortiz, *Los bailes y el teatro de los negros en en el folklore de Cuba* (1951; reprinted Madrid: Editorial Arte y Literatura, 1998), 53.

14. The liner notes and public relations campaign for *Changüí: Grupo Changüí* and *Estrellas Campesinas* (Traditional Crossroads CD4290, 1999) promote these definitions.

15. The *tres* is a traditional Cuban guitarlike instrument with three pairs of double courses.

16. José Cuenca Sosa, "Una fiesta interminable," *Debate* 1, no. 1 (1995): 10.

17. Carlos Padrón, *Franceses en el suroriente de Cuba* (Havana: Universales Unión, 1997), 68–100.

18. Ramón Gómez Blanco, *Rasgos étnicos unificados en la formación del changüí* (Guantánamo: Centro Provincial de la Música, Departamento de Programación, Trabajo Investigativo, 1996), 11–13.

19. *Sexteto y Septeto Habanero, Grabaciones Completas 1925–1931* (1998), Tumbao Cuban Classics TCD300; four CDs with accompanying liner notes and photos; *Las raíces del son* by Sénen Suárez.

20. Arsenio Rodríguez, Dundunbanza (1994) [1946–1951], Tumbao Cuban Classics TCD043.

20

Fernando Ortiz, Founder

María Teresa Linares Savio

More than sixty years of exploring the entrails of Cuban culture enabled Ortiz to supply us with elements from all the disciplines that assisted his work. But in his relentless task he must have thought he was unable to complete the work of his life, and modestly stated:

> I have lived, read, written, always in a hurry and without rest because the Cuban foliage was too thick and almost unexplored, and with my limited strength I was only able to open a small trail and try to establish some directions. And that has been my life. Nothing more.

This he said in 1955, when he completed his great *Los instrumentos de la música afrocubana*. At the time, he already had many disciples who would follow in his footsteps along the paths. A few years later, in 1959, *Una pelea cubana contra los demonios* appeared, his last publication during his lifetime. In each of his works, he dealt with a number of problems and hypotheses to which he would return in subsequent studies. In each one of them, he analyzed new angles so that his followers could continue the investigation.

In 1923, he published an article in *Revista Social* where he proclaimed the urgent need to recover the heritage of our ancestral cultures, especially those preserved by oral tradition. Later, in 1938, he insisted on these arguments in *Archivos del Folklore Cubano*. He had realized the urgency of rescuing all the oral history of the approximately one thousand remaining Africans brought to Cuba by the slave trade and their direct descendants. He had compiled a series of histories and texts of prayers and called for anyone who had the chance to transcribe for posterity those sources of African oral tradition. His friend Lydia Cabrera followed up on this idea; she collected and published *Cuentos negros de Cuba*, published in Havana in 1940. This text has been a most studied work. Ortiz wrote the prologue to it where he informed the reader, "This is the first book written by a woman from Havana, to whom we introduced the appreciation of Afro-Cuban folklore years ago." Lydia had penetrated the deep layers of black legends and found the bases of these in the stories that she had heard as a child. She published these stories in a literary language that was not distant from its naïve, original version.

She continued with *Porqué*, another compilation of black stories and legends, published in 1948. This work served as an editorial support to the texts that followed: *Anagó. Vocabulario lucumí, el yoruba que se habla en Cuba* (1957) with a prologue by Roger Bastide, and the following year *La sociedad secreta abakuá, narrada por viejos adeptos* (1958). In this text, as the author points out, the forms of expression of her informants are preserved. She then quoted other texts that were probably a product of the same research, which must have supplied her with unique material: *Vocabulario abakuá*, the secret language of *ñáñigos*; *Ritual abakuá y anaforuana*, which were not published in Cuba. In 1954, she published her paramount work, *El monte*, and would then add essential ethnographic studies such as *La laguna sagrada de San Joaquín*. This work was preceded by the collection "La música de los cultos africanos en Cuba" consisting of fourteen records of musical recordings of original groups from the extensive area of Mantanza's bembé drums. This work, carried out between 1956 and 1957, with the aid of María Teresa de Rojas and Josefina Tarafa, counted with the participation of professional Italian technicians who brought the latest recording equipment to Cuba and edited the work in Rome. This collection of records was presented together with a booklet of photographs by Josefina Tarafa and Pierre Verger, a French ethnologist and photographer who was a friend of the author. The booklet also includes a description of the religious activities during which the recordings took place, in a both interesting and beautiful narrative that allows the student to understand a real fact of historical and ethnographical accuracy.

The booklet's information can be complemented with the reading of *La laguna sagrada de San Joaquín*, a beautiful narration of a series of ceremonies perhaps using notes taken at the time the recordings were made. We intend to work with old informants of the mentioned zones in order to identify certain aspects of the recordings that have not been duly explained but are essential for musicological analysis. The merit of this impressive collection is that it was the first work to register the music of a specific zone and all the ritual chants of one particular ceremony in an organized fashion. The making of this pioneer work was again a response to a call from the master:

There is still the need to explore the current situation of Afro-Cuban music. It is to be expected that musicologists will undertake this task scientifically; their work, if done properly and if reaching beyond simple passing excursions, will no doubt reveal many interesting findings.[1]

Ortiz recommends "a serious and systematic process that goes beyond the recording of records for commercial purposes," and he added that the learned specialist "must study religious music and Afro-Cuban music in general, their characteristics, intricate rhythms, rustic scales, musical forms, harmonies, and typical instruments, as well as Creole instruments invented or transformed" in Cuba.

Ortiz was concerned with the difficulties that Cuban historians faced in their research due to the scarcity or lack of written sources on black music, which, much like the *guajira* or peasant music, was never considered an integral part of the Cuban culture. He considered at the time (1950) that the descendants of original Africans still preserved the character of the music of different ethnic groups, yet there were no memories of their original chants and beats. Ortiz had encouraged this research, opening up another path for musicologists to follow. Tape recorders were still not used in his time, and Ortiz had to rely on piano transcriptions by Gaspar Agüero, even with the inaccuracies inherent in that method.

He also recommended interdisciplinary research that could produce a more encompassing understanding of the economic, social, geographic, and historical context: "The ethnographic field in Cuba still has to be explored, geographically, historically and culturally. The ethnic map of Cuba has yet to be done, the ethnic layers resulting from successive immigrations over several centuries is still to be described." He believed that only through a general perspective could scientific research on Afro-Cuban music be properly oriented. He realized the existence of cultural zones or areas, which had been influenced by the ethnic groups settled there. When he recommended the study of "the intricate contacts, links, and mixtures of the different black cultures that preserved their ancestral complexity," he was recommending that transculturation be considered a concept applied by all of his followers.

Argeliers León, in the prologue to the second edition of *Los bailes y el teatro de los negros en el folklore de Cuba*, centers on the comments made by the Mexican author Alfonso Reyes in the first edition. León acknowledges the role of Fernando Ortiz as a founder of the *Revista Bimestre Cubana, Revista de Estudios Afrocubanos, Cuadernos de Estudios Afroamericanos*, and *Archivos del Folklore Cubano*. He emphasizes Ortiz's tenacious editorial work to ensure that every magazine dealing with Cuban and Latin American culture in general paid tribute to his eternal memory. That is the first premise of Revista Catauro published by the Fundación Fernando Ortiz. Its very name is inspired by the term *catauro*, which denotes an aboriginal container, used by Ortiz in *Archivos del Folklore Cubano, Catauro de cubanismos,* and *Glosario de afronegrismos*, to deposit short pieces of news, games, riddles, and word games. Likewise, the *Revista Catauro*'s sections follow Ortiz's basic theoretical lines, compilation efforts, and publication of anthropological studies and rare archival sources.

In his own prologue to the first edition of *Los bailes y el teatro de los negros*, Alfonso Reyes pointed out its comparative method also used in *La africanía de la música folklórica de Cuba* and *Los instrumentos de la música afrocubana*. Ortiz also treated the processes of social contact, their impact on the historical effects of the slave trade, and different African ethnic groups and their transculturation.

Don Fernando Ortiz contributed to the spreading of Afro-Cuban music by inviting original groups from the Havana provinces to his lectures. The first such lecture was held in 1936 in the Campoamor theater with the participation of members of drummer Pablo Roche's school. Afterward, at the summer courses of the University of Havana, Ortiz lectured on the ethnographic factors in Cuba with Merceditas Valdés and other musicians as guests. Many young intellectuals who followed his teachings registered for the course, among them Argeliers León, Isaac Barreal, and Salvador Bueno. Then the University Extension Department of the Instituto de Investigaciones Científicas was created; Argeliers was awarded a scholarship there to continue his second phase of research under Ortiz, and also joined research groups trained by Ortiz in the fieldwork of Havana's environs. Armed with a small Kodak camera and a tape recorder, Argeliers obtained the basic information for Ortiz's course projects. In the meantime, Argeliers had also registered in a course on folklore music, taught by María Muñoz de Quevedo, collaborating with her in the morphological analysis of Cuban music pieces, case studies, and fieldwork. When María fell ill, she asked him to lecture the summer courses, which he did from 1946 to 1957. During this time, Argeliers continued to befriend Don Fernando and work with him at his home processing the product of his research, photographs, essays, and primary sources aided by Ortiz's observations and comments. On one occasion, pleased with the progress his student was making, Ortiz told him, "Young man, I see you have found your own keys." On more than one occasion he recommended the young man as his distinguished disciple.

Argeliers continued Ortiz's research directions: He used Ortiz's research methodology and indexing of materials; adopted the term *transculturation* and applied it to all the changes in the evolution of Cuban music and the ethnographic process of the Cuban nation; and transmitted this knowledge to his musicology and ethnography students. In collaboration with his wife and student, María Teresa Linares, he conducted fieldwork in several provinces, recording music in performances and festivals, peasant song sessions, rumba parties, and popular dances. They also worked in the morphological analysis of the music they recorded and that of old records they collected. He subsequently published a book on Cuban musical genres that included the text of his lectures in the university's summer courses on peasant music, rumbas, yuka and Matanza's Iyesá drum beating, and dance music of palomonte and kimbisa.

After several years of combining teaching work and investigation, and after an initial project in the Department of Folklore of the Teatro Nacional de Cuba, Argeliers, with the aid of other professors, organized a seminar on folklore for young advanced students. Miguel Barnet and Rogelio Martínez Furé participated in that seminar, and contributed to research on original music groups presenting Afro-Cuban chants and dances of different ethnic groups. This research material became part of the database of the Instituto de Etnología y Folklore of the Cuban Academia de Ciencias. Fernando Ortiz was the honorary president of that institute, and many works produced there were sent to him at his home. Barnet met with Ortiz on several occasions for interviews that were magisterial lectures. Thus, the master was informed on the progress of the guiding seeds he had planted in his courses, lectures, and texts.

As a result of that more recent research work, other investigators emerged, more fieldwork was carried out, along with surveys on popular feasts and the publication of magazines like *Actas del Folklore* of the Teatro Nacional de Cuba and *Etnología y Folklore* of the Academia de Ciencias. The Academia also published the original case study that resulted in the novel-document *El cimarrón* by Miguel Barnet, which has been translated into more than sixty languages. Likewise, the records *Viejos cantos afrocubanos* and *Cancionero hispanocubano*, based on field recordings of groups of old Spanish and African traditions, were edited by María Teresa Linares, who also wrote a prologue for them, left in the academy's archives abundant documents, recordings, and unpublished works. In the Recording Studios EGREM in 1978, María Teresa began working on the collection "Antología de la música afrocubana." The collection's first volume was "Viejos cantos afrocubanos," and then continued with "Toques de tambores batá en un Oro de Igbodú," recorded during a ceremony held by one of the most orthodox groups in Matanzas, in the casa of Julio Suárez. The ceremony begins with a salute to sixteen gods, with no chants or prayers. A series of chants to Changó follows. Another of the records was also the recording of a complete ritual toque with the chants and beats to all the deities of the Iyesá pantheon, unique to Matanzas; an original Bembé feast as well as a saint's day, also unique to the province of Matanzas; beats from peasant fiestas; Yuka drums from Pinar del Río; and a fiesta of Tumba Francesa recorded in Guantánamo by an interdisciplinary team of researchers trained by Argeliers León. In the latter production, he counted with the collaboration of Olavo Alén, a researcher who wrote his doctoral thesis at Humboldt University on that same group of Tumba Francesa in Guantánamo, and with that of Danilo Orozco, from the same university.

This "Antología" continued the one Lydia Cabrera had begun in Matanzas. Each record is a monographic study of the musicological and ethnological event of a specific area. Some female musicology students from the Instituto Superior de Arte contributed notes, analysis, and description of the drums, the ceremonies, and other elements. The Instituto Superior de Arte was established in 1976 with Argeliers as a founding member. Many who had been his musicology students at the Instituto de Etnología, and others who had attended his lectures on black cultures at the University of Havana, joined research centers, participated in cultural exchanges programs, graduated, wrote doctoral theses, and began new projects. Olavo Alén became the director of the Centro de Investigación y Desarrollo de la Música. From there and with the aid of students and graduates of the Instituto Superior de Arte, he organized the interdisciplinary team that produced the *Atlas de instrumentos de la música cubana*, a monumental work in two volumes and a set of maps. This work was inspired by the idea that Ortiz had insisted on: to draft maps showing characteristics of black cultures. Only an interdisciplinary team could have achieved that task requested by Don Fernando.

The *Atlas de los instrumentos de la música cubana*, completed in 1996 after many years of research throughout the whole island, contains all the components of musicological analysis required by such a work. This work involved the previous analysis of the five volumes of Ortiz's *Los instrumentos de la música afrocubana* (1952–1955). Also, for the adequate research of the *Atlas*, courses and lectures on organology and transcription were given, the methods and classifications of Sachs and Hornbostel were studied, and the adaptations made by Ortiz himself were considered. Its first stage was a laboratory study of sources, followed by fieldwork in all locations in Cuba where there were traces of traditional and folkloric music.

From the fieldwork for the *Atlas* there resulted statistics, changes in organological classifications, master's essays, and doctoral dissertations in musicology. Many of the researchers of the interdisciplinary team participated in the musicology competition of the Casa de las Américas and were awarded prizes. Apart from the *Atlas*, much photographic material and musical recordings still remain in the archives. Records, monographic studies, and essays on these topics have been published. In my view, Fernando Ortiz would be proud of encouraging what can be considered the most important musicological work of the last decades of the twentieth century in Cuba, perhaps even in Latin America.

Only recently another important work, the *Atlas etnográfico*, was completed by another interdisciplinary team headed by Jesús Guanche, a student of Argeliers León in the University of Havana and a doctor of ethnology in Moscow. The *Atlas etnográfico* was a joint effort by the Centro de Investigación y Desarrollo de la Cultura Cubana "Juan Marinello" and the Department of Anthropology of the Academia de la Ciencias. Partial results have been published, such as *Artesanía popular cubana* and *El tambor arará* by Dennis Moreno, *Entre brujas, pícaros y consejas, un estudio de la tradición oral en Cuba* and *Cuentos tradicionales* by María del Carmen Víctori, and others to be published, such as the study on *nanas* and romances by Martha Esquenazi. There will be a multimedia edition of the *Atlas etnográfico*, covering all the studies, with musical examples; it will be a work of essential reference.

The Instituto Cubano de Arte e Industria Cinematográfica (ICAIC), has released a series of documentaries on the ethnographical components of the Cuban people, its rumba fiestas, toques, religious ceremonies, carnival parades and music, and musical genres such as the *danzón* and the *cancionística*. These documentaries are of course guided by artistic criteria but count on the aid of consultants supplying the scientific and musical knowledge required. The films are also a form of dissemination and preservation of Cuban traditional culture, following in the ethnographical footsteps of Fernando Ortiz.

The genius of Fernando Ortiz is well known throughout the cultural world as the founder of the Cuban social sciences, for which he worked for a large part of his life without discrimination. We are in debt to him for what he taught us. We believe that all the events that evoke his name, his research, and his work cannot cover all the essays and researchers he inspired. His work continues to inspire those interested in studying Cuban culture and already has several generations of followers.

NOTES

1. Fernando Ortiz, *La africanía de la música folklórica de Cuba* (Havana: Ministerio de Educación, Dirección de Cultura/Ediciones Cárdenas y Cía, 1950), 103–4.

Bibliography

WORKS BY FERNANDO ORTIZ

1895   *Principi y prostes: Folleto de artículos de costumbres en dialecto menorquín.* Ciudadela, Menorca: Imprenta Fábregas.

1901   *Base para un estudio sobre la llamada reparación civil. Memoria para optar el grado de doctor en Derecho.* Universidad Central de Madrid. Madrid: Librería de Victoriano Suárez.

1903   "'El alcoholismo,' folleto por C. Bernaldo de Quirós." *Azul y Rojo* 2: 8.

1904   "Los modernos criminólogos americanos." *Cuba y América* 14, no. 6: 154–56; no. 11: 277–80; no. 12: 322–24.

1905   *Las simpatías de Italia por los mambises cubanos: documentos para la historia de la independencia de Cuba.* Marseilles: Instituto Sordomuti.

1905   "La criminalitá dei negri in Cuba." *Archivio di Psichiatria, Neuropatologia, Antropologia Criminale e Medicina Legale* 26, no. 2: 594–600.

1906   *Hampa afro-cubana. Los negros brujos (apuntes para un estudio de etnología criminal), con una carta prólogo del Dr. C. Lombroso.* Madrid: Librería de Fernando Fe.

1906   "A Unamuno." *El Fígaro* 22, no. 38: 481.

1908   *Para la agonografía española: estudio monográfico de las fiestas menorquinas.* Con un prólogo por Juan Benejam y trece fotogafías y dibujos del natural. Havana: Imprenta La Universal.

1908   "Desde Salamanca. Cultura de Ultramar." *Cuba y América* 25, no. 21: 3.

1909   *Los mambises italianos: apuntes para la historia cubana.* Havana: Imprenta Cuba y América.

1910   *El caballero encantado y la moza esquiva; versión libre y americana de una novela española de Benito Pérez Galdós.* Havana: Imprenta La Universal.

1910   *Las rebeliones de afrocubanos.* Havana: n.p.

1910 *La Reconquista de América: reflexiones sobre el panhispanismo.* Paris: Librería P. Ollendorff.

1911 "Sales y Ferré." *El Fígaro* 27, no. 4: 47.

1913 *Entre cubanos . . . (Psicología tropical).* París: Librería P. Ollendorff.

1913 *La identificación dactiloscópica. Informe de policiología y derecho público.* Havana: Imprenta La Universal.

1914 *Seamos hoy como fueron ayer.* Discurso leído el día 9 de enero de 1914 en la Sociedad Económica de Amigos del País. Havana: Imprenta La Universal.

1915 *La filosofía penal de los espiritistas: estudio de filosofía jurídica.* Havana: Imprenta La Universal.

1916 *Hampa afro-cubana.* Los negros esclavos; estudio sociológico y de derecho público. Havana: Revista Bimestre Cubana.

1917 [1906] *Hampa afro-cubana; Los negros brujos. (Apuntes para un estudio de etnología criminal).* Con una carta prólogo de Lombroso. 2d ed. Madrid: Editorial-América.

1918 *Las actuales responsabilidades políticas y la nota americana.* (Carta al Hon. Sr. Ministro de los Estados Unidos. Havana: n.p.

1919 *La crisis política cubana; sus causas y remedios.* Havana: Imprenta La Universal.

1919 "Las fases de la evolución religiosa." Lecture at the Teatro Payet on April 7, 1919. Havana: Tipografía Moderna.

1920 *Cuba en la Paz de Versailles.* Discurso pronunciado en la Cámara de Representantes en la sesión del 4 de febrero de 1920. Havana: Imprenta La Universal.

1920 "La fiesta afro-cubana del 'Día de Reyes.'" *Revista Bimestre Cubana* 15, no. 1: 5–26.

1921 "Los cabildos afro-cubanos." *Revista Bimestre Cubana* 16, no. 1: 5–39.

1922 *Historia de la arqueología indocubana.* Havana: Imprenta El Siglo XX.

1922 "Los afronegrismos de nuestro lenguaje." *Revista Bimestre Cubana* 17, no. 6: 321–36.

1923 "Las nuevas orientaciones históricas e inmigratorias de Cuba." In *En la tribuna: discursos cubanos,* ed. Rubén Martínez Villena. Havana: Imprenta El Siglo XX.

1923 [1914] "Seamos hoy como fueron ayer." In *En la tribuna: discursos cubanos,* ed. Rubén Martínez Villena, 37–56. Havana: Imprenta El Siglo XX.

1923 *En la tribuna: discursos cubanos.* Prol. and ed. Rubén Martínez Villena. 2 vols. Havana: Imprenta El Siglo XX.

1923 *Un catauro de cubanismos: apuntes lexicográficos.* Colección Cubana de Libros y Documentos Inéditos o Raros no. 4. Havana: n.p.

1924 *La decadencia cubana: conferencia de propaganda renovadora pronunciada en la Sociedad Económica de Amigos del País la noche del 23 de febrero de 1924.* Havana: Imprenta La Universal.

1924 *Glosario de afronegrismos.* Havana: Imprenta El Siglo XX.

1924 *Recopilación para la historia de la Sociedad Económica Habanera.* Havana: Imprenta El Universo.

1925   [1920] *La fiesta afrocubana del "Día de Reyes."* Havana: Imprenta El Siglo XX.

1926   *Proyecto de código criminal cubano.* (Libro primero o parte general). Ponencia oficial con un proemio del autor, un juicio de Enrique Ferri y un apéndice con los primeros comentarios. Havana: Librería Cervantes.

1926   "El proyecto de código criminal cubano." *Revista Bimestre Cubana* 21, no. 5: 681–705.

1926   *El derecho internacional en el nuevo proyecto de código criminal cubano.* Havana: Imprenta El Siglo XX.

1926-   "Los negros curros." *Archivos del Folklore Cubano* 2: 209–22; 2: 285–35; 3: 27–50; 3: 160–75; 3: 250–56; 3, no. 4: 51–53.

1927   "Prólogo." In *Historia de la isla de Cuba by Pedro José Guiteras.* Colección de Libros Cubanos nos. 1 and 3, 1: i–xxiv. Havana: Cultural.

1928   "Prólogo." In *Contra la anexión by José Antonio Saco*, 1: v–xcvi. Havana: Cultural.

1929   *José Antonio Saco y sus ideas cubanas.* Colección Cubana de Libros y Documentos Inéditos o Raros no. 8. Havana: Imprenta El Universo.

1929   *Ni racismo ni xenofobias: discurso en la sesión solemne del 9 de enero de 1929, conmemorando el 136o. aniversario de la fundación de d   i   c   h   o patriótico instituto.* Havana: Imprenta El Universo.

1929   "El cocorícamo y otros conceptos teoplásmicos del folklore afrocubano." *Archivos del Folklore Cubano* 4, no. 4: 289–312.

1931   *American Responsabilities [sic] for Cuba's Troubles.* New York: n.p.

1932   *Las responsabilidades de los Estados Unidos en los males de Cuba.* Washington, D.C.: Cuban Information Bureau.

1932   *Lo que Cuba desea de los Estados Unidos.* Discurso pronunciado por el Dr. Fernando Ortiz en Washington el día 10 de diciembre de 1932. Havana: n.p.

1935   *La "clave" xilofónica de la música cubana.* Ensayo etnográfico. Havana: Molina y Cía.

1937   "El emblema de la Sociedad de Estudios Afrocubanos." *Estudios Afrocubanos* 1, no. 1: 11–14.

1937   "La religión en la poesía mulata." *Estudios Afrocubanos* 1, no. 1: 15–62.

1938   "Prólogo." In *¡Oh, mío Yemayá! Cuentos y cantos negros by Rómulo Lachatañeré*, vii–xxvii. Manzanillo, Cuba: Editorial El Arte.

1939   "La cubanidad y los negros." *Estudios Afrocubanos* 3: 3–15.

1940   *Contrapunteo cubano del tabaco y el azúcar. Advertencia de sus contrastes agrarios, económicos, históricos y sociales, su etnografía y su transculturación.* Prol. by Herminio Portell Vilá. Introd. by Bronislaw Malinowski. Havana: Jesús Montero.

1940   "Los factores humanos de la cubanidad." *Revista Bimestre Cubana* 14, no. 2: 161–86.

1940   *Los factores humanos de la cubanidad.* Havana: Molina y Cía.

1942   *Martí y las razas.* Havana: Molina y Cía.

1942   "Cuba, Martí, and the Race Problem." *Phylon* 3: 253–76.

1943   *Las cuatro culturas indias de Cuba.* Havana: Arellano y Cía.

1943   *La hija cubana del iluminismo.* Recopilación para la Historia de la
        Sociedad Económica Habanera, no. 5. Havana: Sociedad Económica de
        Amigos del País.
1943   "Por la integración cubana de blancos y negros." Lecture at Club Atenas
        on December 12, 1942. *Ultra* 13, no. 77: 69–76.
1943   [1943/1942] "Por la integración cubana de blancos y negros." *Revista
        Bimestre Cubana* 51, no. 2: 256–72.
1945   "Martí y 'las razas de librería.'" *Cuadernos Americanos* 4, no. 3: 185–98.
1946   *El engaño de las razas.* Havana: Editorial Páginas.
1946   [1945] "Martí y las razas." In *José Martí: obras completas.* Edición con-
        memorativa del cincuentenario de su muerte, ed. Manuel Isidro Menén-
        dez, 1: xxiv. Havana: Editorial Lex.
1947   [1940] *Cuban Counterpoint: Tobacco and Sugar.* Trans. Harriet de Onís.
        Prol. by Herminio Portell Vilá. Introd. by Bronislaw Malinoski. New York:
        Knopf.
1947   *El huracán, su mitología y sus símbolos.* Mexico City: Fondo de Cultura
        Económica.
1950   *La africanía de la música folklórica de Cuba.* Havana: Ministerio de
        Educación, Dirección de Cultura/ Ediciones Cárdenas y Cía.
1950   "Una moderna secta espiritista de Cuba." *Bohemia* 42, no. 3: 8–9, 137–39.
1950   "Las espirituales 'Cordoneros del Orilé.'" *Bohemia* 42, no. 5: 20–22,
        118–19, 122–23.
1951   *Los bailes y el teatro de los negros en el folklore de Cuba.* Havana: Min-
        isterio de Educación, Dirección de Cultura/ Ediciones Cárdenas y Cía.
1952–1955   *Los instrumentos de la música afrocubana.* 5 vols. Havana: Ministerio
        de Educación.
1955   *Dirección de Cultura/Ediciones Cárdenas y Cía.*
1953   [1942] *Martí y las razas.* Havana: Comisión Nacional Organizadora de
        los Actos y Ediciones del Centenario y del Monumento de Martí.
1955   "El Panhispanismo." *Revista Bimestre Cubana* 70, no. 1: 55–59.
1955   "Presentación y glosa de Fray Bartolomé." Revista *Bimestre Cubana* 70,
        no. 1: 184–210.
1959   *Historia de una pelea cubana contra los demonios.* Havana: Universi-
        dad Central de LasVillas, Departamento de Relaciones Culturales.
1959   [1943/1942] "Por la integración cubana de blancos y negros." In *Los mejores
        ensayistas cubanos,* ed. Salvador Bueno. Lima: Imprenta Torres Aguirre.
1963   [1940] *Contrapunteo cubano del tabaco y el azúcar.* 2d rev. ed. Santa
        Clara: Universidad Central de las Villas-Dirección de Publicaciones.
1973   *Orbita de Fernando Ortiz.* Ed. Julio Le Riverend. Havana: UNEAC.
1973   "Imperialismo y buena vecindad." In *Orbita de Fernando Ortiz,* ed.
        Julio Le Riverend, 311–19. Havana: UNEAC.
1973   [1940] *Contrapunteo cubano del tabaco y el azúcar.* Barcelona: Editorial
        Ariel.
1974   *Nuevo catauro de cubanismos.* Ed. Angel Lluis Fernández Guerra and
        Gladys Alonso. Posthumous ed. Havana: Editorial de Ciencias Sociales.
1974   [1946] *El engaño de las razas.* Havana: Editorial de Ciencias Sociales.
1975   [1959] *Historia de una pelea cubana contra los demonios.* Prol. by Mar-
        iano Rodríguez Solveira. 2d ed. Havana: Editorial de Ciencias Sociales.

1978	[1940] *Contrapunteo cubano del tabaco y el azúcar.* Prol. by Julio Le Riverend. Caracas: Biblioteca Ayacucho.
1986	[1926–1928] *Los negros curros.* [1926–1928]. Prol. and ed. by Diana Iznaga. Havana: Editorial de Ciencias Sociales.
1987	[1913] *Entre cubanos . . . Psicología tropical.* Prol. by Julio Le Riverend. 2d ed. Havana: Editorial de Ciencias Sociales.
1991	[1940] *Contrapunteo cubano del tabaco y el azúcar.* Havana: Editorial de Ciencias Sociales.
1991	*Estudios etnosociológicos.* Prol. by Isaac Barreal. Havana: Editorial de Ciencias Sociales.
1991	*Glosario de afronegrismos.* Havana: Editorial de Ciencias Sociales.
1993	*Etnía y sociedad.* Havana: Editorial de Ciencias Sociales.
1993	"For a Cuban Integration of Whites and Blacks." In *AfroCuba: An Anthology of Cuban Writing on Race, Politics and Culture,* ed. Pedro Pérez Sarduy and Jean Stubbs. Melbourne: Ocean.
1995	[1940, 1947] *Cuban Counterpoint: Tobacco and Sugar.* Prol. by Herminio Portell Vilá. Introd. by Bronislaw Malinowski. New introd. by Fernando Coronil. Durham, N.C.: Duke University Press.
1996	[1952–1955] *Los instrumentos de la música afrocubana.* 2 vols. Madrid: Música Mundana Maqueda.
1998	[1950] *La africanía del folklore cubano.* Madrid: Música Mundana Maqueda.
1998	[1951] *Los bailes y el teatro de los negros en el folklore de Cuba.* Madrid: Música Mundana Maqueda.
1999	[1940] *Contrapunteo cubano del tabaco y el azúcar.* Prol. by María Fernanda Ortiz. Madrid: Música Mundana Maqueda.

GENERAL BIBLIOGRAPHY: REFERENCES CITED

Agrupación Católica Universitaria (ACU). 1954. *Encuesta nacional sobre los sentimientos religiosos.* Havana: Buró de Información de la ACU.

Aguilar, Luis E. 1974. *Cuba 1933.* New York: Norton.

Alén Rodríguez, Olavo. 1986. *La música de las sociedades de tumba francesa en Cuba.* Havana: Casa de las Américas.

Altamira y Crevea, Rafael. 1911. *Mi viaje a América.* Madrid: Librería General de Victoriano Suárez.

———. 1924. *La huella de España en América.* Madrid: Editorial Reus.

Amado Blanco, Luis. 1937. "Biología de la moda." *Lyceum* 8: 28–45.

Antón, Manuel. 1923. "Don Rafael Salillas. Nota necrológica." *Actas y Memorias de la Sociedad Española de Antropología, Etnografía y Prehistoria,* vol. II: 89–93.

Arendt, Hannah. 1990. *Hombres en tiempos de oscuridad.* Barcelona: Gedisa.

Argüelles Mederos, Aníbal, and Ileana Hodge. 1991. *Los llamados cultos sincréticos y el espiritismo.* Havana: Editorial Academia.

Arocena, Berta. 1949. "El primer año en la vida del Lyceum." *Lyceum* 17: 58–62.

Arquiola, Elvira. 1981. "Anatomía y antropología en la obra de Olóriz." *Dynamis* I: 165–77.

Arredondo, Alberto. 1939. *El negro en Cuba.* Havana: Editorial Alfa.

Arrom, José Juan. 1971. "Tres metáforas sobre España e Hispanoamérica." In *Certidumbre de América: estudio de letras, folklore y cultura*, 2d ed., 167–71. Madrid: Editorial Gredos.

Azcárate, Gumersindo de. 1891. *Concepto de sociología*. Madrid: Imp. de Fortanet.

———. 1899. "Plan de la Sociología." *Boletín de la Institución Libre de Enseñanza*.

Azcárate, Patricio de. 1968. *Gumersindo de Azcárate: estudio biográfico documental*. Madrid: Tecnos.

Baldrich, Juan José. 1988. *Los que sembraron la no-siembra*. San Juan, Puerto Rico: Ediciones Huracán.

Baquero, Gastón. 1991. "El negro en Cuba." In *Indios, blancos y negros en el caldero de América*. Madrid: Ediciones de Cultura Hispánica.

Barnet, Miguel. 1966. *Biografía de un cimarrón*. Havana: Academia de Ciencias de Cuba, Instituo de Etnología y Folklore.

Basso, Enrico, and Giustina Olgiati, eds. 1989. *Fernando Ortiz*. Atti del convegno (Genova, 11–12 maggio 1988). Genoa: Civico Istituto Colombiano.

Becerra y Bonet, Berta. 1955. "El Doctor Ortiz, Periodista." In *Miscelánea de estudios dedicados a Fernando Ortiz*, I: 155–60. Havana: Sociedad Económica de Amigos del País.

Beirne, Piers. "Adolphe Quetelet and the Origins of Positivist Criminology." *American Journal of Sociology* 92: 1140–69.

Beirne, Piers, ed. 1994. *The Origins and Growth of Criminology: Essays on Intellectual History, 1760–1945*. Brookfield: Dartmouth.

Benítez-Rojo, Antonio. 1989. "Fernando Ortiz: el Caribe y la posmodernidad." In *La isla que se repite: el Caribe y la perspective posmoderna*, 149–85. Hanover: Ediciones del Norte.

———. 1992 [2d ed. 1996]. *The Repeating Island: The Caribbean and the Postmodern Perspective*. Durham, N.C.: Duke University Press.

———. 1998. *La isla que se repite*. Barcelona: Editorial Casiopea.

Berges, J. 1993. "El protestantismo histórico en Cuba." In *La religión en la cultura*. Havana: Editorial Academia.

Bernaldes, Andrés. 1978. "Historia de los Reyes Católicos." In *Flor oculta de poesía cubana (siglos XVIII y XIX)*, ed. Cintio Vitier and Fina García Marruz. Havana: Editorial Arte y Literatura.

Bernaldo de Quirós, Constancio. 1907. *La picota*. Madrid: V. Suárez.

———. 1913. "Bandolerismo y delincuencia subversiva en la Baja Andalucía." In *Anales JAE*.

———. 1919. *El espartaquismo agrario andaluz*. Madrid: Reus.

Bettelheim, Judith, ed. 1993. *Cuban Festivals: An Illustrated Anthology*. New York: Garland.

Blanco Rodríguez, Juan Andrés. 1982. *El pensamiento sociopolítico de Dorado Montero*. Salamanca: Centro de Estudios Salmantinos-CSIC.

Bloom, Harold. 1995. *El canon occidental: la escuela y los libros de todas las épocas*. Barcelona: Anagrama.

Bly, Peter A. 1979. "Sex, egotism, and social regeneration in Galdós' El caballero encantado." *Hispania* 2, no. 1: 20–29.

Bolívar Aróstegui, Natalia. 1990. *Los orishas en Cuba*. Havana: Ediciones Unión.

Bremer, Thomas. 1993. "The Constitution of Alterity: Fernando Ortiz and the Beginnings of Latin American Ethnography Out of the Spirit of Italian Criminology." In

Alternative Cultures in the Caribbean, ed. Thomas Bremer and Ulrich Fleischmann. Frankfurt am Main: Vervuert.

Brown, David Hilary. 1989. "The Garden in the Machine: Afro-Cuban Sacred Art and Performance in Urban New York and New Jersey." Ph.D. diss., Yale University.

Bure, Michael, and Mary Ellen Moore. 1981. *Tampa: Yesterday & Tomorrow.* Tampa, Fla.: Mishler King.

Burke, Peter. 2000. *Formas de historia cultural.* Madrid: Alianza Editorial.

Caballo, Giuglielmo, and Roger Chartier. 1998. *Historia de la lectura en el mundo occidental.* Madrid: Taurus.

Cabrera Infante, Guillermo. 1985. *Holy Smoke.* London: Faber & Faber.

Cabrera, Lydia. 1940. *Cuentos negros de Cuba.* Havana.

———. 1954. *El monte.* Havana.

———. 1970. *La sociedad secreta abakuá narrada por viejos adeptos.* Miami: Colección del Chicherekú.

Cabrera, Raimundo. 1887. *Cuba y sus jueces (rectificaciones oportunas).* Havana: Imprenta "El Retiro."

———. 1922. *Cuba y sus juices: rectificaciones necesarias.* Havana: Librería Cervantes.

Cacho Viu, Vicente. 1969. *La Institución Libre de Enseñanza.* Madrid: Rialp.

Campa, Román de la. 1999. *Latin Americanism.* Minneapolis: University of Minnesota Press.

Campbell, A. Stuart. 1939. *The Cigar Industry of Tampa.* Tampa, Fla.: University of Tampa Press.

Camprubí, Zenobia. 1991. *Diario. 1: Cuba (1937–1939).* Madrid: Alianza Tres–EDUPR.

Cárdenas, Carlos F. 1938. "Presentación del profesor Gustavo Pittaluga." *Revista de Medicina Tropical, Parasitología, Bacteorología Clínica y Laboratorio* (January–February).

Caroso, Carlos, and Jeferson Bacelar, eds. 1999. *Faces de tradicao afro-brasileira: religiosidades, sincretismo, antisincretismo, reafricanizao e practicas teraupeticas, etnobotanicas e comida.* Salvador: Pallas.

Carpentier, Alejo. 1988. *La música en Cuba.* Havana: Letras Cubanas.

Carrión, Miguel de. 1921. "El desenvolvimiento social de Cuba en los últimos veinte años." n.p.

Castellanos, Isabel. 1987. "Abre kutu wiri ndinga: Lydia Cabrera y las lenguas afrocubanas." In *En torno a Lydia Cabrera*, ed. Isabel Castellanos and Josefina Inclán. Miami: Ediciones Universal.

Castellanos, Israel. 1927. *Un plan para reformar el régimen penal cubano.* Havana: La Universal.

———. 1955. "Fernando Ortiz en las ciencias criminológicas." In *Miscelánea de estudios dedicados a Fernando Ortiz*, vol. 1: 298–332.

Cepeda, Rafael. 1980. "Análisis de los juicios de los misioneros sobre Cuba (1894–1925)." In *La herencia misionera en Cuba.* San José, Costa Rica: DEI.

Céspedes, Carlos M. 1986. "Ideología, mentalidad y fe cristiana." *Revista Ateísmo y Diálogo* 21, no. 3: 265–70.

Chacón y Calvo, José M. 1937. "Los días Cubanos de Menéndez Pidal." *Lyceum* 5–6: 5–8.

Chapman, Charles A. 1969. *A History of the Cuban Republic.* New York: Octagon.

Chomsky, Aviva. "'Barbados or Canada': Race, Immigration, and Nation in Early Twentieth-Century Cuba." Unpublished manuscript.

Cofiño, Manuel. 1975. *Cuando la sangre se parece al fuego.* Havana: UNEAC.

Colectivo del DESR. 1993. *La conciencia religiosa. Características y formas de manifestarse en la sociedad cubana contemporánea.* Havana: Departamento de Estudiso Sociorreligiosos, Academia de Ciencias de Cuba.

Cornejo Polar, Antonio. 1997. "Mestizaje e hibridez: los riesgos de las metáforas. Apuntes." *Revista Iberoamericana* 63: 341.

Cornudella, José. 1973. "Obra científica y sanitaria del académico honorario prof. Luis Sayé." *Anales de Medicina y Cirugía* 53, no. 233: 247–53.

———. 1976. "Lluis Sayé i Sempere." *Anales de Medicina y Cirugía* 56, no. 243: 46–50.

Coronil, Fernando. 1995. "Introduction." In Fernando Ortiz, *Cuban Counterpoint: Tobacco and Sugar.* Durham, N.C.: Duke University Press.

Corrêa, Mariza. 1999. *As ilusões da liberdade: a escola Nina Rodrigues e a antropologia no Brasil.* Bragança Paulista: Instituto Franciscano de Antropologia–Universidade São Francisco.

Cuenca Sosa, José. 1995. "Una fiesta interminable." *Debate* 1, no. 1: 10–13.

Deleuze, Gilles, and Félix Guattari. 1997. *Mil mesetas: capitalismo y esquizofrenia.* Valencia: Pretextos.

Derrida, Jacques. 1975. *La diseminación.* Madrid: Editorial Fundamentos.

———. 1989. "La mitología blanca. La metáfora en el texto filosófico." In *Márgenes de la filosofía,* 247–311. Madrid: Ediciones Cátedra.

———. 1989. "La retirada de la metáfora." In *La deconstrucción en las fronteras de la filosofía: la retirada de la metáfora,* trans. Patricio Peñalver Gómez, 35–75. Barcelona: Ediciones Paidós/ICE, Universidad Autónoma de Barcelona.

Deschodt, Eric, and Philippe Morane. 1998 [1996]. *The Cigar.* Cologne: Könemann Verlagsgesellschaft.

Diggs, Ellen Irene. 1944. "Fernando Ortiz: la vida y la obra." M.A. thesis, Facultad de Filosofía y Letras, Universidad de La Habana.

DiMaggio, Paul. 1994. "Culture and Economy." In *The Handbook of Economic Sociology,* ed. Neil Smelser and Richard Swedberg. Princeton, N.J.: Princeton University Press.

Dixit, Avinash, and Barry Nelabuff. 1991. *Thinking Strategically.* New York: Norton.

Doeringer, Peter, and Michael Piore. 1971. *Internal Labor Markets and Manpower Analysis.* Lexington, Mass.: Heath.

Domingo Sanjúan, Pedro. 1976. "En recuerdo de Luis Sayé Sempere." *Anales de Medicina y Cirugía* 56, no. 243: 19–28.

Domínguez, Jorge. 1986. "Seeking Permission to Build a Nation: Cuban Nationalism and U.S. Response Under the First Machado Presidency." *Cuban Studies* 16: 33–48.

Dorado Montero, Pedro. 1898–1899. "Sobre el último libro de Salillas y la teoría criminológica de este autor." *Revista General de Legislación y Jurisprudencia* XCIII: 483–99; XCIV: 46–78.

Dumont, Henri. 1915–1916. "Antropología y patología comparada de los negros esclavos." *Revista Bimestre Cubana* X, no. 3; XI, no. 2.

Dunn, Hampton. 1974. *Yesterday's Tallahassee.* Miami: Seeman.

Echevarría, Esteban. "Apología del matambre." In *Obras completas*, 325–26. Buenos Aires.

Entrambasaguas, Joaquín de. 1971. *Gastronomía mardileña*. 2d ed. Madrid: Instituto de Estudios Madrileños.

Escartín Gual, Monserrat. 1996. *Diccionario de símbolos literarios*. Barcelona: PPU.

Espino Marrero, Eumelio, and Gilberto Torrecilla Guerra. 1999. *El tabaco cubano: recursos fitogenéticos*. Madrid: Instituto Cubano del Libro/Editorial Científico-Técnica.

Ewald, Francis, and Jean-Jacques Brochier. 1984. "Una vie pour l'histoire." *Magazine Littéraire* 212: 22.

Fernández Ferrer, Antonio, ed. 1998. *La isla infinita de Fernando Ortiz*. Alicante: Instituto de Cultura Juan Gil-Albert.

Fernández Robaina, Tomás, ed. 1968. *Bibliografía de estudios afroamericanos*. Prol. by Argeliers León. Havana: Biblioteca Nacional José Martí.

Fernández Rodríguez, M. D. 1976. *El pensamiento penitenciario y criminológico de Rafael Salillas*. Santiago de Compostela: Universidad de Santiago de Compostela.

Fernandez, Nadine T. 1996. "The Color of Love: Young Interracial Couples in Cuba." *Latin American Perspectives* 23, no. 1: 99–117.

Ferrer, Ada. 1999. *Insurgent Cuba: Race, Nation, and Revolution, 1868–1898*. Chapel Hill: University of North Carolina Press.

Florida's Cuban Heritage Trail/Herencia cubana en la Florida. n.d. Tallahassee: Florida Department of State.

Foreign Policy Association. 1935. *Problems of the New Cuba: Report of the Commission of Cuban Affairs*. New York.

Forné, José. 1994. *Les nationalismes identitaires en Europe: les deux faces de Janus*. Paris: Éditions L'Harmattan.

Foucault, Michel. *La arqueología del saber*. Mexico City: Siglo XXI.

Freyre, Gilberto. 1974. "Toward a Mestizo Type." In *The Gilberto Freyre Reader*, 110–11. New York: Knopf.

———. 1980. *New World in the Tropics: The Culture of Modern Brazil*. Westport, Conn.: Greenwood.

Frisby, David. 1992. *The Alienated Mind*. New York: Routledge.

Galera Gómez, Andrés. 1986. "Rafael Salillas: medio siglo de antropología criminal española." *Llull* IX: 81–104.

———. 1991. *Ciencia y delincuencia*. Sevilla: CSIC.

———. 1994. "Dorado Montero, Pedro." In *Diccionario histórico de la antropología española*, ed. Carmen Ortiz García and Luis Ángel Sánchez Gómez, 264–66. Madrid: CSIC.

García Carranza, Araceli. 1970. *Bio-bibliografía de Don Fernando Ortiz*. Havana: Instituto del Libro.

García Carranza, Araceli, Norma Suárez Suárez, and Alberto Quesada Morales. 1996. *Cronología Fernando Ortiz*. Havana: Fundación Fernando Ortiz.

García Delgado, J. L. 1973. "Estudio preliminar." In *El espartaquismo agrario y otros ensayos sobre la estructura económica y social de Andalucía*, ed. Constancio Bernaldo de Quirós, 10–51. Madrid: Ediciones de la Revista de Trabajo.

Geertz, Clifford. *El estilo del antropólogo*. Barcelona: Paidós.

Geertz, Clifford, James Clifford, et al. 1992. *El surgimiento de la antropología posmoderna*. Barcelona: Gedisa.

Giner de los Ríos, Francisco. 1899. *La persona social: estudios y fragmentos*. Madrid: Suárez.

Giró, Radamés. 1995. "Los motivos del son: hitos en su sendero caribeño y universal." In *Panorama de la música popular cubana*, 219–30. Havana: Editorial Facultad de Humanidades, Editorial Letras Cubanas.

Gómez Blanco, Ramón. 1996. *Rasgos étnicos unificados en la formación del changüí*. Guantánamo: Centro Provincial de la Música.

González Echevarria, Roberto. 1977. *Alejo Carpentier: The Pilgrim at Home*. Ithaca, N.Y.: Cornell University Press.

———. 1983. *Isla a su vuelo fugitiva: ensayos críticos sobre la literatura hispanoamericana*. Madrid: Porrúa.

———. 1984. "Lo cubano en Paradiso." In *Coloquio Internacional sobre la obra de José Lezama Lima*, vol. 2: 31–51. Madrid: Editorial Fundamentos.

———. 1985. *The Voice of the Masters: Writing and Authority in Modern Latin American Literature*. Austin: University of Texas Press.

———. 1990. *Myth and Archive: A Theory of the Latin American Narrative*. New York: Cambridge University Press.

———. 1993. *Alejo Carpentier: el peregrino en su patria*. Mexico ity: Universidad Autónoma de México.

González Sierra, José. 1987. *Monopolio del humano: elementos de la historia del tabado en México y algunos conflictos de tabaqueros veracruzanos: 1915–1930*. Xalapa, Mexico: Universidad de Veracruz.

Goodman, Jordan. 1993. *Tobacco in History: The Cultures of Dependence*. London: Routledge.

Granovetter, Mark. 1985. "Economic Action and Social Structure: The Problem of Embeddedness." *American Journal of Sociology* 91: 481–510.

———. 1993. "The Nature of Economic Relationships." In *Explorations in Economic Sociology*, ed. Richard Swedberg, 4–5. New York: Russell Sage Foundation.

Grasso Gonzalez, Nancy. 1989. "Folklore y profesionalismo en la rumba matancera." M.A. thesis, Facultad de Música, Instituto Superior de Artes, Havana.

Greenbaum, Susan. 1985. "Afro-Cubans in Exile: Tampa, Florida, 1886–1984." *Cuban Studies/Estudios Cubanos* 15, no. 1.

Grismer, Karl H. 1950. *Tampa: A History of the City of Tampa and the Tampa Bay Region of Florida*. St. Petersburg: St. Petersburg Printing.

Guanche, Jesus, and Idalberto Suco. 1982. "Consideraciones teóricas sobre la caracterización de las agrupaciones musicales y danzarias de carácter popular tradicional." Paper presented at the colloquium "La elaboración artistica del folklore: aspectos corográficos y teatrales," Havana, May 12.

Guibernau, Montserrat. 1996. *Los nacionalismos*. Barcelona: Editorial Ariel.

Guilbault, Jocelyne. 1993. *Zouk: World Music in the West Indies*. Chicago: University of Chicago Press.

Guiral Moreno, Mario. 1917. "El saneamiento de las costumbres públicas y la educación cívica del pueblo." *Cuba Contemporánea*: 109.

Gutiérrez-Vega, Zenaida, ed. 1982. *Fernando Ortiz en sus cartas a José M. Chacón (1914–1936, 1956)*. Madrid: Fundación Universitaria Española.

Habermas, Jürgen. 1989. *El discurso filosófico de la modernidad*. Madrid: Taurus.

Hall Proby, Kathryn. 1981. *Mario Sanchez: Painter of Key West Memories*. Key West, Fla.: Southernmost.

Hanke, Lewis. 1949. *Bartolomé de las Casas: pensador político, historiador, antropólogo*. Havana: n.p.

Harner, Charles F. 1975. *A Pictorial History of Ybor City*. Tampa, Fla.: Trend Publications.

Helg, Aline. 1990. "Fernando Ortiz ou la pseudo-science contre la sorcellerie africaine á Cuba." In *Cahiers de L'Institut Universitaire D'Etudes du Développement*, 241–49. Paris: Presses Universitaires de France.

———. 1995. *Our Rightful Share: The Afro-Cuban Struggle for Equality, 1886–1912*. Chapel Hill: University of North Carolina Press.

Herkovits, Melville J. 1838. *Acculturation: The Study of Culture Contact*. n.p.

Hernández, José M. 1993. *Cuba and the United States: Intervention and Militarism, 1868–1933*. Austin: University of Texas Press.

Hetherington, M. F. 1971. *History of Polk County, Florida*. Chulmota, Fla.: Mickler House.

Hewitt, Nancy A. 1990. "Varieties of Voluntarism: Class, Ethnicity, and Women's Activism in Tampa." In *Women, Politics, and Change*, ed. Louise Tilly and Patricia Gurin. New York: Russell Sage Foundation.

Hewitt, Nancy A. 1991. "'The Voice of Virile Labor': Labor Militancy, Community Solidarity, and Gender Identity among Tampa's Latin Workers, 1880–1921." In *Work Engendered: Toward a New History of American Labor*, ed. Ava Baron. Ithaca, N.Y.: Cornell University Press.

Hodge, Ileana, and Minerva Rodríguez. 1997. "El espiritismo en Cuba. Percepción y exteriorización." In *Colección religión y sociedad*. Havana: Editorial Academia.

Ibarra, Jorge. 1990. "La herencia científica de Fernando Ortiz." *Revista Iberoamericana* 152–53: 1339–51.

Inciarte Brioso, Rafael. n.d. "Various notes on changüí and music in Guantánamo." Unpublished manuscript. Guantánamo: Casa Inciarte.

Infante Urivazo, Enzo A. 1997. *Havana Cigars 1817–1960*. Neptune City, N.J.: T.F.H. Publications.

InterAmericas. 1998. *Miscelanea II of Studies Dedicated to Fernando Ortiz (1881–1969)*. Introd. by Jane Gregory Rubin. Foreword by Miguel Barnet. New York: InterAmericas, Society of Arts and Letters of the Americas.

Iznaga, Diana. 1982. *El estudio del arte negro en Fernando Ortiz*. Havana: Instituto de Literatura y Lingüística.

———. 1989. *Transculturación en Fernando Ortiz*. Havana: Editorial de Ciencias Sociales.

James, Winston. 1998. *Holding Aloft the Banner of Ethiopia: Caribbean Radicalism in Early Twentieth-Century America*. London: Verso.

Jerez Mir, Rafael. 1980. *La introducción de la sociología en España: Manuel Sales y Ferré, una experiencia frustrada*. Madrid: Ayuso.

Jiménez-Landi, Antonio. 1972. "Luis de Zulueta y Escolano." In *Cartas, 1903–1933* by Miguel de Unamuno and Luis de Zulueta, ed. Carmen de Zulueta, 343–73. Madrid: Aguilar.

———. 1973. *La Institución Libre de Enseñanza y su ambiente: los orígenes*. Madrid: Taurus.

Jobes, Gertrude. 1962. *Dictionary of Mythology, Folklore, and Symbols*. New York: Scarecrow.

Junta para Ampliación de Estudios e Investigaciones Científicas. 1929. *Memoria correspondiente a los cursos 1926–7 y 1927–8*. Madrid: JAE.

Kaay, Hendrik, ed. 1998. *Afro-Brazilian Cultures and Politics: Bahia 1790s to 1990s*. Armonk, N.Y.: Sharpe.

Kautsky, Karl. 1925. *Los fundamentos del cristianismo*. New York.

Kelley, Robin D. G. 1990. *Hammer and Hoe: Alabama Communists during the Great Depression*. Chapel Hill: University of North Carolina Press.

Kiernan, V. G. 1991. *Tobacco: A History*. London: Hutchinson Radius.

Kirshenblatt-Gimblett, Barbara. 1991. "Objects of Ethnography." In *Exhibiting Cultures: The Poetics and Politics of Museum Display*, ed. Ivan Karp and Steven D. Lavine. Washington, D.C.: Smithsonian Institution Press.

Koestler, Arthur. 1979. *Janus: A Summing Up*. New York: Vintage.

Lacan, Jacques. 1983. *El seminario, libro 2. El Yo en la teoría de Freud y en la técnica psicoanalítica. 1954–1955*. ed. by Jacques-Alain Miller, trans. Irene Agoff. Buenos Aires: Ediciones Paidós.

Lachatañeré, Rómulo. 1992. "El sistema religioso de los lucumí y otras influencias africanas en Cuba." In *El sistema religioso de los afrocubanos*, 149–362. Havana: Editorial de Ciencias Sociales.

———. 1992. "Manual de santería." In *El sistema religioso de los afroCubanos*, 95–148. Havana: Editorial de Ciencias Sociales.

———. 1992. "Congas y afrocubanismos de exportación." In *El sistema religioso de los afrocubanos*. Havana: Editorial de Ciencias Sociales.

Laforet, Carmen. 1955. *La mujer nueva*. Barcelona: Ediciones Destino.

Lakoff, George, and Mark Johnson. 1980. *Methaphors We Live By*. Chicago: University of Chicago Press.

Laporta, Francisco J., Alfonso Ruiz Miguel, Virgilio Zapatero, and Javier Solana. 1987. "Los orígenes culturales de la Junta para la Ampliación de Estudios." *Arbor* 126, no. 493: 17–87.

Le Riverend, Julio. 1973. "Prólogo." In *Orbita de Fernando Ortiz*, ed. Julio Le Riverend. Havana: UNEAC.

León, Argeliers. 1991. "Notes toward a Panorama of Popular and Folk Musics." In *Essays on Cuban Music: North American and Cuban Perspectives*, trans. and ed. Peter Manuel, 1–23. Lanham, Md.: University Press of America.

Lombroso, Cesare. 1876. *L'uomo delinquente*. Torino: Bocca.

Long, Durward. 1965. "La Resistencia: Tampa's Immigrant Labor Union." *Labor History* 6, no. 3.

———. 1966. "The Historical Beginnings of Ybor City and Modern Tampa." *Florida Historical Quarterly* 45, no.1.

———. 1968. "The Open-Closed Shop Battle in Tampa's Cigar Industry, 1919–21." *Florida Historical Quarterly* 47, no. 3.

———. 1971. "The Making of Modern Tampa: A City of the New South." *Florida Historical Quarterly* 49, no. 4.

———. 1971. "Labor Relations in the Tampa Cigar Industry, 1885–1911." *Labor History* 12, no. 4.

López-Morillas, Juan. 1980. *El krausismo español: perfil de una aventura intelectual*. 2d rev. ed. Madrid: Fondo de Cultura Económica.

Lundahl, Mats. 1982. "A Note on Haitian Migration to Cuba, 1890–1934." *Cuban Studies* 12, no. 2: 21–36.

Machado y Morales, Gerardo. 1982. *Ocho Años de Lucha*. Miami: Ediciones Históricas Cubanas.

Malinowski, Bronislaw. 1944. *A Scientific Theory of Culture and Other Essays*. Chapel Hill: University of North Carolina Press.

———. 1945. *The Dynamics of Cultural Change*. New Haven, Conn.: Yale University Press.

Manresa Formosa, G. 1973. "Obra científica y sanitaria del académico honorario prof. Luis Sayé Sempere en Hispanoamérica." *Anales de Medicina y Cirugía* 53: 260–65.

Manuel, Peter. 1995. *Caribbean Currents: Caribbean Music from Rumba to Reggae*. Philadelphia: Temple University Press.

Manzoni, Celina. 1996. "El ensayo ex-céntrico: el Contrapunteo de Fernando Ortiz (algo más que un cambio de nombre)." *Filología* 29: 151–56.

Marcos. 1997. "The Fourth World War Has Begun." *Le Monde Diplomatique*.

Maristany, Luis. 1973. *El gabinete del doctor Lombroso (delincuencia y fin de siglo en España)*. Barcelona: Editorial Anagrama.

Márquez Sterling, Carlos. 1986. *A la ingerencia extraña, la virtud doméstica: biografía de Manuel Márquez Sterling*. Miami: Ediciones Universal.

Márquez Sterling, Manuel. 1933. *Las conferencias del Shoreham*. Mexico City: Ediciones Botas.

———. 1937. *Doctrina de la República*. Havana: Secretaría de Educación.

Martí, José. 1975. "Mi raza." In Obras completas. Havana: Editorial de Ciencias Sociales.

Martinelli, Alberto. 1987. "The Economy as an Institutional Process." *Telos* 73: 131–46.

Martínez Ortiz, Rafael. 1929. *Cuba: los primeros años de independencia*. 2 vols. Paris: Editorial Le Livre Libre.

Masó, Calixto C. 1998. *Historia de Cuba*. Miami: Ediciones Universal.

Matory, J. Lorand. 2000. "The New Yoruba Imperium: Texts, Migration, and the Rise of the Trans-Atlantic Lucumi Nation." Paper presented at the XXII Congress of the Latin American Studies Association.

McDaniel, Tim. 1994. "Response to Goodwin." *Theory and Society* 23: 791.

McLeod, Marc C. 1998. "Undesirable Aliens: Race, Ethnicity, and Nationalism in the Comparison of Haitian and British West Indian Immigrant Workers in Cuba." *Journal of Social History* 31, no. 3: 599–623.

Méndez Ceballo, Manriela, María Cubeira Palomo, and Lourdes San Fat. 1987. "Influencias de las inmigraciones haitianas en el ámbito cutual y costumbrista de la provincia de Guantánamo." *El Managüí* 2, no. 4: 25–34.

Menocal, Narciso. 1995. *The Tobacco Industry in Cuba and Florida: Its Golden Age in Lithography and Architecture*. Coral Gables, Fla.: Cuban National Heritage.

Moliner Castañeda, Israel. 1988. "La Rumba Columbia." *Union* 1: 25–48.

Moore, Robin. 1994. "Representations of Afrocuban Expressive Culture in the Writings of Fernando Ortiz." *Latin American Music Review* 15, no. 1: 32–54.

Morejón, Nancy. 1982. *Nación y mestizaje en Nicolás Guillén*. Havana: UNEAC.

Moreno Fraginals, Manuel. 1978 [1964]. *El ingenio: complejo económico cubano el azucar*. 3 vols. Havana: Editorial de Ciencias Sociales.

Mormino, Gary, and George E. Pozetta. 1993. "'The Reader Lights the Candle': Cuban and Florida Cigar Workers' Oral Tradition." *Labor's Heritage*.

Mullen, Edward J. 1987. "*Los negros brujos*: A Reexamination of the Text." *Cuban Studies/Estudios Cubanos* 17: 32–54.

Nabokov, Vladimir. 1959. *Lolita*. Buenos Aires: Sur.

Naranjo Orovio, Consuelo. 1988. *Cuba, otro escenario de lucha. La guerra civil y el exilio republicano español*. Madrid: CSIC.

Naranjo, Consuelo and Miguel Angel Puig-Samper. 1998. "Delincuencia y racismo en Cuba: Israel Castellanos versus Fernando Ortiz." In *Ciencia y fascismo*, ed. Carmen Ortiz and Rafael Huertas, 11–21. Aranjuez: Ediciones Doce Calles.

Neira Vilas, Xosé. 1983. *Castelao en Cuba*. La Coruña: Ediciones do Castro.

Nelson, Lowry. 1950. *Rural Cuba*. Minneapolis: University of Minnesota Press.

Nina Rodrigues, Raymundo. 1933. *Os africanos no Brasil*. São Paulo.

Nohria, Nitin, and Ranjay Gulati. 1994. "Firms and Their Environments." In *The Handbook of Economic Sociology*, ed. Neil Smelser and Richard Swedberg. Princeton, N.J.: Princeton University Press.

Novás Calvo, Lino. 1956. "Cubano de Tres Mundos." In *Miscelanea de estudios dedicados a Fernando Ortiz*, vol. 2. Havana: Sociedad Económia de amigos del País.

Nuez, Iván de la. 1998. *La balsa perpetua: soledad y conexiones de la cultura cubana*. Barcelona: Editorial Casiopea.

Núñez Encabo, Manuel. 1976. *Manuel Sales y Ferré: los orígenes de la Sociología en España*. Madrid: Edicusa.

Nuñez Jiménez, Antonio. 1998. *The Journey of the Havana Cigar*. Neptune City, N.J.: T.F.H. Publications.

Núñez Ruiz, Diego. 1975. *La mentalidad positiva en España: desarrollo y crisis*. Madrid: Túcar Ediciones.

Olmo, Rosa del. 1981. *América Latina y su criminología*. Mexico City: Siglo Veintiuno.

Olson, James S., and Judith E. Olson. 1995. *Cuban Americans: From Trauma to Triumph*. New York: Twane.

Oriol Anguera, José. 1973. "Obra científica y sanitaria del académico honorario prof. Luis Sayé Sempere." *Anales de Medicina y Cirugía* 53, no. 233: 253–59.

Ortega y Gasset, José. 1966. "Las ideas de León Frobenius." In *Obras completas*, vol. 3. 6th ed. Madrid: Revista de Occidente.

Osterman, Paul. 1988. *Employment Futures: Reorganization, Dislocation, and Public Policy*. New York: Oxford University Press.

Padilla, Napoleón S. 1982. *Cultivo del tabaco negro: sol y tapado*. Santo Domingo: Instituto del Tabaco de la República Dominicana.

———. 1988. *Memorias de un cubano sin importancia*. Hialeah, Fla.: A.C.Graphics.

Padrón, Carlos. 1997. *Franceses en el suroriente de Cuba*. Havana: Ediciones Unión.

Pasquino, Pasquale. N.d. "Criminology: The Birth of a Special Savior." *Ideology and Consciousness* 7: 17–32.

Paterson, Orlando. 1999. *Rituals of Blood: Consequences of Slavery in Two American Centuries*. Washington, D.C.: Civitas/Counterpoint.

Perera, A. C. 1998. "El sistema de valores de la regla de ocha." Havana: Departamento de Estudiso Sociorreligiosos.

Pérez Cabrera, José Manuel. 1959. *Fundamentos de una historia de la historiografía cubana*. Havana.

Pérez de la Riva, Juan. 1979. "Cuba y la migración antillana 1900–1931." In *Anuario de Estudios Cubanos* no. 2: 5–75. Havana: Editorial de Ciencias Sociales.

Pérez-Firmat, Gustavo. 1998. "Cuban Conterpoint." In *The Cuban Condition: Translation and Identity in Modern Cuban Literature*, 47–66. New York: Cambridge University Press.

Pérez Galdós, Benito. 1951 [1909]. El caballero encantado. In *Obras completas de Benito Pérez Galdós* 4: 223–343. Madrid: Editorial Aguilar.

Pérez Jr., Louis A. 1975. "Reminiscences of a Lector: Cuban Cigar Makers in Tampa." *Florida Historical Quarterly* 53, no. 4.

———. 1978. "Cubans in Tampa: From Exiles to Immigrants, 1892–1901." *Florida Historical Quarterly* 57, no. 2.

———. 1986. *Cuba under the Platt Amendment, 1912–1934.* Pittsburgh: University of Pittsburgh Press.

———. 1986. "Politics, Peasants, and People of Color: The 1912 'Race War' in Cuba Reconsidered." *Hispanic American Historical Review* 66, no. 3: 509–39.

Pérez Sarduy, Pedro, and Jean Stubbs, eds. 1993. *AFROCUBA: An Anthology of Cuban Writing on Race, Politics and Culture.* London: Ocean/Latin America Bureau/Center for Cuban Studies.

———. 2000. *Afro-Cuban Voices: On Race and Identity in Contemporary Cuba.* Gainesville: University Press of Florida.

Pérez-Firmat, Gustavo. 1989. *The Cuban Condition: Translation and Identity in Cuban Literature.* New York: Cambridge University Press.

Pérez-Stable, Marifeli. 1999 [1993]. *The Cuban Revolution: Origins, Course, and Legacy.* New York: Oxford University Press.

———. 2001. "Estrada Palma's Civic March: From Oriente to Havana, April 20–May 11, 1902." *Cuban Studies/Estudios Cubanos* 29.

Peset, José Luis, and Mariano Peset. 1963. "Positivismo y ciencia positiva en médicos y juristas españoles del siglo XIX. Pedro Dorado Montero." *Almena:* 65–123.

———. 1973. *Lombroso y la escuela positivista italiana.* Madrid: CSIC.

Pichardo, Esteban. 1836. *Diccionario provincial casi-razonado de vozes cubanas.* N.p.

Pichardo, Hortensia, ed. 1973. *Documentos para la historia de Cuba.* Havana: Editorial de Ciencias Sociales.

Pino Díaz, Fermín del. 1978. "Antropólogos en el exilio." In *El exilio español de 1939,* ed. J. L. Abellán, vol. VI: 13–155. Madrid: Taurus.

Pittaluga, Gustavo. 1937. "El libro y la cultura." *Lyceum* 2, no. 8: 9–17.

Platt, Jennifer. 1998. *A History of Sociological Research Methods in America 1920–1960.* New York: Cambridge University Press.

Polanyi, Karl. 1944. *The Great Transformation.* Boston: Beacon.

———. 1957. "The Economy as Instituted Process." In *Trade Markets in the Early Empires,* ed. by Karl Polanyi and Conrad Arensberg. New York: Free Press.

Polanyi, Karl, and Conrad Arensberg, eds. 1957. *Trade Markets in the Early Empires.* New York: Free Press.

Portes, Alejandro. 1995. *The Economic Sociology of Immigration.* New York: Russell Sage Foundation.

———. 2000. "The Hidden Abode: Sociology as Analysis of the Unexpected." *American Sociological Review* 65: 1–18.

Portuondo Zuñiga, Olga. 1987. "La región de Guantánamo: de la producción de consumo a la de mercancías." *Del Caribe* 4, no. 10: 2–22.

Poyo, Gerald E. 1979. "Key West and the Cuban Ten Years' War." *Florida Historical Quarterly* 47, no. 3.

———. 1986. "Evolution of Cuban Separatist Thought in the Emigré Communities of the United States, 1848–1895." *Hispanic American Historical Review* 66, no. 3.

———. 1986. "The Anarchist Challenge to the Cuban Independence Movement, 1895–1890." *Cuban Studies/Estudios Cubanos* 15, no. 1.

————. 1989. *With All and for the Good of All.* Durham, N.C.: Duke University Press.

Pratt, Mary Louise. 1992. *Imperial Eyes: Travel Writing and Transculturation.* London: Routledge.

Puig-Samper, Miguel Ángel, and Andrés Galera. 1983. *La antropología española en el siglo XIX.* Madrid: CSIC.

Puig-Samper, Miguel Ángel, and Consuelo Naranjo. 1998. "Fernando Ortiz: herencias culturales y forja de la nacionalidad." In *Imágenes e imaginarios españoles en el Ultramar español,* ed. Consuelo Naranjo Orovio and Carlos Serrano, 192–221. Madrid: CSIC-Casa de Velázquez.

Quintero Rivera, Angel C. 1983. "Socialist and Cigarmaker: Artisan's Proletarianzation in the Making of the Puerto Rican Working Class." *Latin American Perspectives* 10, no. 2: 3.

Rama, Angel. 1982. *Transculturación narrativa en América Latina.* Mexico City: Siglo XXI.

Roche Monteagudo, Rafael. 1908. *La policía y sus misterios en Cuba.* Havana: n.p.

Rojas, Rafael. 1998. *Isla sin fin: contribución a la crítica del nacionalismo cubano.* Miami: Ediciones Universal.

Rolph-Trouillot, Michel. 1992. "The Caribbean Region: An Open Frontier in Anthropological Theory." *Annual Review of Anthropology* 21: 19–42.

Rudolp, J. D. 1987. *Cuba: A Country Study.* 3d ed.Washington, D.C.: Foreign Area Studies, American University.

Ruiz-Funes, Mariano. 1930. "La antropología penitenciaria en Cuba." In *Delito y l ibertad: ensayos.* Madrid: Javier Morata.

Saco, José Antonio. 1928. *Contra la anexión.* Havana: Cultural S.A.

Saínz de Robles, Federico Carlos. 1951. "Nota preliminar a *El caballero encantado.*" In *Obras completas de Benito Pérez Galdós,* vol. 4: 221–23. Madrid: Editorial Aguilar.

Salillas, Rafael. 1888. *La vida penal en España.* Madrid: n.p.

————. 1901. "Los ñañigos en Ceuta." *Revista General de Legislación y Jurisprudencia* 98: 337–60.

Salvatore, Ricardo, and Carlos Aguirre. 1996. "The Birth of the Penitentiary in Latin America: Towards an Interpretive Social History of Prisons." In *The Birth of the Penitentiary in Latin America: Essays on Criminology, Prison Reform, and Social Control, 1830–1940,* ed. Ricardo Salvatore and Carlos Aguirre. Austin: University of Texas Press.

Samosata, Luciano de. "Timón o el misántropo." Madrid: Gredos.

Sánchez Ron, José M. , ed. 1989. *1907–1987: la junta para la Ampliación de Estudios e Investigaciones Científicas 80 años después.* 2 vols. Madrid: CSIC, 1989.

Sánchez, Yvette. 1999. *Coleccionismo y literatura.* Madrid: Cátedra.

Santamaría de Paredes, Vicente. 1896. *El concepto de organismo social.* Madrid: Real Academia de Ciencias Morales y Políticas.

Scarlet, Iain. n.d. *A Puff of Smoke.* London: Lewis.

Sellin, Thorsten. 1972. "Enrico Ferri." In *Pioneers in Criminology,* ed. Hermann Mannheim, 361–84. Montclair: Paterson Smith.

Serrano, Carlos. 1987. "Miguel de Unamuno y Fernando Ortiz: un caso de regeneracionismo trasatlántico." *Nueva Revista de Filología Hispánica* 35, no. 1: 299–310.

Sociedad Económica de Amigos del País de La Habana. 1955–1957. *Miscelánea de estudios dedicados a Fernando Ortiz por sus discípulos, colegas y amigos con ocasión de cumplirse sesenta años de la publicación de su primer impreso en Menorca en 1895*. Vols. I–III. Havana: Sociedad Económica de Amigos del País.

Solá, José Sixto. 1913. "El pesimismo cubano." *Cuba Contemporánea* (December): 281.

Stubbs, Jean. 1995. "Political Idealism and Commodity Production: Cuban Tobacco in Jamaica, 1987–1930." *Cuban Studies* 25.

Swedberg, Richard. 1991. "Major Traditions of Economic Sociology." *Annual Review of Sociology* 17: 251–76.

Taft, William H. 1906. *Cuban Pacification: Report of William H. Taft, Secretary of War, and Robert Bacon, Assistant Secretary of State, of What Was Done under the Instructions of the President in Restoring Peace to Cuba*. Washington, D.C.: Government Printing Office.

Toplin, Robert Brent, ed. 1976. *Slavery and Race Relations in Latin America*. Westport, Conn.: Greenwood.

Trelles, Carlos M. 1923. *El Progreso (1902 a 1905) y el Retroceso (1906–1922) de la República de Cuba*. Matanzas: Imprenta de Tomás González.

Trouillot, Michel-Rolf. 1996. *Silencing the Past: Power and the Production of History*. Boston: Beacon.

Tuñón de Lara, Manuel. 1977. *Medio siglo de cultura española (1885–1936)*. 3d ed. Madrid: Tecnos.

Turpin III, John, and B. E. Martinez. 1995. *The Batá in Cuba: Selected Writings of Fernando Ortiz*. Oakland, Calif.: Institute for the Study of Ancient African Traditions.

Unamuno, Miguel de. 1966. *Obras completas*. Madrid: n.p.

UNCTAD. 1977. *Report of the United Nations Conference on Trade and Development*. New York.

United States Department of Agriculture. 1961. *Special Study on Cigar Tobacco*. Washington, D.C.: Government Printing Office.

Urrutia, Gustavo E. 1935. *Cuatro charlas radiofónicas*. Havana: n.p.

———. 1937. *Puntos de vista del nuevo negro*. Havana: n.p.

Varela, Javier. 1999. *La novela de España: los intelectuales y el problema español*. Madrid: Taurus.

Velasco, Carlos de. 1911. "El problema negro." *Cuba Contemporánea* (February): 77.

———. 1914. "La obra de la revolución cubana." *Cuba Contemporánea* (July): 281.

Vergara, Alvarez, and Rosa Esther. 1989. "Caracterización de las agrupaciones de rumba de la Ciudad de La Habana." Trabajo de diploma, Instituto Superior de Arte, Facultad de Música.

Villoldo, Julio. 1917. "La República civil." *Cuba Contemporánea* (March): 193.

Vitier, Cintio. 1981. *Juan Ramón Jiménez en Cuba*. Havana: Ed. Arte y Literatura.

Wilde, Alexander. 1978. "Conversations among Gentlemen: Oligarchical Democracy in Colombia." In *The Breakdown of Democratic Regimes: Latin America*, ed. Juan J. Linz and Alfred Stepan. Baltimore: Johns Hopkins University Press, 1978.

Williamson, Edwin. 1992. *The Penguin History of Latin America*. London: Penguin.

World Bank. 1995. *Monitoring Environmental Progress*. Washington, D.C.

———. 1997. *Expanding the Measure of Wealth: Indicators of Environmentally Sustainable Development*. Washington, D.C.

PERIODICALS

Cigar Aficionado
Cigar World
Cuba Contemporánea (Havana)
Diario de la Marina (Havana)
El Mundo (Madrid)
El Sol (Madrid)
La Voz (Madrid)
Lyceum (Havana)
Mensajes de la Institución Hispano Cubana de Cultura (Havana)
New York Times
Revista América (Madrid)
Surco (Havana)
Tampa, Florida's Greatest City
Tampa's Hillborough County
The Tobacco Leaf
Time
Ultra (Havana)

MANUSCRIPT SOURCES

Archivo. Casa Museo Unamuno. Salamanca.
Archivo Fernando Ortiz. Sociedad Económica-Instituto de Literatura y Lingüística José A. Portuondo Valdor (SEAP-ILL). Havana.
Archivo de la Secretaría de la Junta para la Ampliación de Estudios e Investigaciones Científicas (ASJAE). Residencia de Estudiantes (RE). Madrid.
Colección Manuscrita Ortiz (C.M. Ortiz). Biblioteca Nacional José Martí (BNJM). Havana.
Sala Zenobia y Juan Ramón Jiménez. Biblioteca de la Universidad de Puerto Rico. Rio Piedras, Puerto Rico.
Sección Educación, Archivo General de la Administración. Alcalá de Henares.
University of Florida, Gainsville. Manuscript collection.
University of South Florida, Tampa. Manuscript collection.
University of Miami, Miami. Manuscript collection.

VIDEOS AND FILMS

What's Cuba Playing At? [¿Qué se toca Cuba?] Arena/BBC LMA L024H, 1985. 60 minutes. Videocassette.
Gutiérrez Alea, Tomas. 1978. *La última cena.* (The Last Supper, U.S. release).

DISCOGRAPHY

¡Ahora Sí! Here Comes Changüí. Liner notes by Danilo Orozco. Corazón Records CORA121. Compact Disc. 1994.

Antología de la música afrocubana, vol. 7: *Tumba Francesa.* Liner notes by Olvo Alén Rodríguez. Havana: EGREM/Areito LD-3606. Phonorecord. 1981.

Changüí. Liner notes by Dita Sullivan. New York: Traditional Crossroads CD 4290. Compact disc. 1999.

Cotó y Su Eco del Caribe: A mi yemayá. Havana: EGREM CD 0254. Compact disc. 1997.

Rodríguez, Arsenio. *Dundunbanza 1946–1951.* Liner notes by Max Salazar. Barcelona: Tumbao Cuban Classics TCD043. Compact disc. 1994.

Sexteto y Septeto Habanero. Grabaciones Completas 1925–1931, 4 CDs. Accompanying liner notes and photos. *Las raíces del son* by Sénen Suárez. Barcelona: Tumbao Cuban Classics TCD300. Compact disc. 1998.

Index

Contributors

Carmen Almodóvar Muñoz. Ph.D., University of Havana. Almodóvar teaches in the Faculty of History and Centro de Altos Estudios at the University of Havana and directs the Ibero-American Lecture Series at the Centro Cultural de España in Havana. She has authored and coauthored several books and edited four critical anthologies on diverse issues of Cuban history. Her specialty is Cuban historiography. The UNEAC recently granted her the Distinción Nicolás Guillén.

Alejandra Bronfman. Ph.D., history, Princeton University. An assistant professor of history at Yale University, Bronfman's current project examines the relationship between social science, race, and black political identities in early twentieth-century Cuba. Her publications include "La barbarie y sus descontentos: raza y civilización, 1912–1919," *Temas* 24–25 (2001), and "En Plena Libertad y Democracia: Los negros brujos and the Social Question," *Hispanic American Historical Review* (2002).

Patricia D. Catoira. Ph.D. candidate, University of New Mexico. Currently writing her dissertation, "Writing Cuba: Transformations of Cecilia Valdés in Martín Morúa Delgado's Sofía and in Reinaldo Arenas's La Loma del Angel," Catoira's research focuses on slavery, race, and national identity in Cuban literature.

Fernando Coronil. Ph.D., University of Chicago, 1987. Coronil is an associate professor and the director of the Doctoral Program in Anthropology and History at the University of Michigan. He specializes in historical anthropology, modernity, postcolonialism, and state formation. His publications include

The Magical State: Nature, Money, and Modernity in Venezuela (1987) and the introduction to the second English edition of Fernando Ortiz's *Cuban Counterpoint: Tobacco and Sugar* (1995).

María del Rosario Díaz Rodríguez. Education graduate, Instituto Superior Pedagógico Enrique José Varona; Ph.D. candidate in archival and information sciences. An archivist and cataloger of documents of Fernando Ortiz and José María Chacón y Calvo in Havana and Madrid, Rodríguez is writing her dissertation on the personal archive of Fernando Ortiz. She has published several articles and chapters, as well as edited books of documents by Juana Borrero and Fernando Ortiz.

Antonio Fernández Ferrer. Ph.D. in philology; professor, Universidad de Alcalá de Henares. Fernández has edited *Juan de Mairena* by Antonio Machado (1986), *Ejercicios de estilo* by R. Queneau (1987); *Borges A/Z* (1987); *La mano de la hormiga: Los cuentos más breves del mundo* (1990), *La sed de lo perdido: Antología* by Eliseo Diego (1992); and *La isla infinita* de Fernando Ortiz (1998). He has also published translations, essays, and research work on literary theory, Hispanic literatures and authors (Gastón Baquero, Borges, Cortázar, Virgilio Piñera, Gonzalo Rojas, Salarrué), literary criticism, arts, and literature.

Tomás Fernández Robaina. A graduate in library science from the University of Havana and enior researcher at the Biblioteca Nacional José Martí, Havana, Fernández teaches in the Faculty of Communication Studies, University of Havana. He has authored several books and articles: *El negro en Cuba: Apuntes para la historia de la lucha contra la discriminación racial* (1990, 1994); *La prosa de Nicolás Guillén en defensa del negro cubano* (1982); *La crítica en torno a Cecilia Valdés en el siglo XIX* (1985); and *Reflexiones sobre nuestras raíces y realidades afrocubanas* (forthcoming). Fernández has contributed to the elaboration and edition of several bibliographies, catalogs, and anthologies.

Mauricio A. Font. Director of the Bildner Center for Western Hemisphere Studies and professor of sociology, Graduate Center and Queens College, City University of New York. Font is the author of *Coffee, Contention, and Change in the Making of Modern Brazil* (1990) and *Transforming Brazil* (2003). He is the editor of Fernando Henrique Cardoso's collection of essays *Charting a New Course* (2001) and coeditor of *Toward a New Cuba? Legacies of a Revolution* (1997) and *Integración económica y democratización: América Latina y Cuba* (1998). His current research involves issues of reform and social development, including human rights, democratization, regional integration, and international cooperation in the Americas.

Roberto Gonzalez Echevarría. Sterling Professor of Hispanic and Comparative Literatures at Yale University. A member of the American Academy of Arts and Sciences, he is the author of many books on Spanish and Latin American literatures. His *Myth and Archive: A Theory of Latin American Narrative* won awards from the Moder Language Association and the Latin American Society of America, and he is coeditor of *The Cambridge History of Latin American Literature*, in three volumes. He has recently published *The Pride of Havana: A History of Cuban Baseball*. The Fondo de Cultura Económica in Mexico is publishing *Crítica práctica/Práctica crítica*, a collection of his essays. He is currently at work on a book on Cervantes.

Benjamin L. Lapidus. Ph.D. in ethnomusicology, Graduate Center, City University of New York. Lapidus has presented his research on *changüí* at national and international conferences. With his musical group, Sonido Isleño, Lapidus performed on national television, and released three albums of original compositions, *¿Quién Tiene Ritmo?* (1998), *El Asunto* (1999), and *Tres Is the Place* (2001), were recorded and released on EMI-Capitol and Envidia. For his musical talents, Lapidus received a 2001 "Meet the Composer" award. He frequently gives lectures and conducts workshops on the history and development of Latin American and Caribbean music.

Octavio di Leo. Received his Ph.D. in Spanish and Portuguese from Yale University, where he studied with Roberto González Echevarría. Di Leo published his doctoral dissertation, *El descubrimiento de África en Cuba y Brasil* [1889–1969] (Madrid, 2001), a comparative analysis of Afro-Cuban and Afro-Brazilian literature from the abolition of slavery to the independence wars in Africa, was published in Spain. He is now living and writing in Barcelona, a meaningful city in the life and work of Fernando Ortiz.

María Teresa Linares Savio studied music at the Conservatorio Municipal de Música and University of Havana. She has a B.A. in literature and Spanish, and a Ph.D. in art, and she is now an adjunct professor at the Instituto Superior de Arte, Havana. Linares is the founder of the Instituto de Etnología y Folklore de la Academia de Ciencias; director of the Museo Nacional de Música; the president of the Musicology section of the Asociación de Músicos, UNEAC; and senior researcher at the Fundación Fernando Ortiz. She has published *La música y el pueblo*, *La música entre Cuba y España*, *El punto cubano*, and *Trayecto histórico de la música cubana* (forthcoming).

José Antonio Matos Arévalos. Ph.D., philosophical sciences, assistant research fellow, Instituto de Filosofía and Fundación Fernando Ortiz, Havana. Matos has published numerous articles in Cuban and international journals. He is the author of *La historia en Fernando Ortiz* (2000) and editor of Fernando

Ortiz's previously unpublished works *La santería y la brujería de los blancos* (2001) and *Brujas e inquisidores* (2001). Matos is currently working on the edition of Ortiz's unpublished work "La virgen de la Caridad del Cobre."

Consuelo Naranjo Orovio. Ph.D., history of America, senior researcher at the Institute of History, Superior de Investigaciones Científicas (CSIC, Madrid). General editor of *Revista de Indias* and historian of the Spanish Caribbean, Naranjo has published several books and articles on Spanish immigration to Cuba, Spanish presence in Cuba, race, identity, and exile, including *Del campo a la bodega: Recuerdos de gallegos en Cuba, siglo XX* (1988); *Cuba, otro escenario de lucha: La guerra civil y el exilio republicano español* (1988); *Medicina y racismo en Cuba* (1996); and is coauthor of *Racismo e Inmigración en Cuba en el siglo XIX* (1996) and *Relaciones culturales y científicas entre España y Cuba: Fernando Ortiz y la Hispanocubana* (forthcoming).

María Fernanda Ortiz Herrera. Ortiz studied biological sciences at the University of Havana and McGill University and obtained her M.S. degree from Ottawa University. In 1969, she married the Spanish diplomat Julio López Jacoiste. Her work has included diplomatic duties and biological research and publications in the fields of genetics and biochemistry. Since 1994, she has dedicated herself to the reedition and diffusion of the works of her father, Fernando Ortiz. In Madrid, she reedited the trilogy *La africanía de la música afrocubana: Los bailes y el teatro de los negros en el folklore de Cuba*, *Los instrumentos de la música afrocubana* and *Contrapunteo cubano del tabaco y el azúcar*.

Marifeli Pérez-Stable. Professor in the Department of Sociology and Anthropology at Florida International University in Miami. Pérez-Stable's book *The Cuban Revolution: Origins, Course, and Legacy* was published by Oxford University Press in 1993. A second edition was issued in 1999, which Editorial Colibrí published in Spanish. She is currently working on a political history of Cuba and coordinating a task force on Cuban national reconciliation.

Miguel Angel Puig-Samper Mulero. Ph.D. in biological sciences, senior researcher of the Institute of History, CSIC, Madrid. A historian of science, Puig-Samper is author of several books and articles on scientific expeditions and cultural and scientific relations between Spain and Latin America, including *Las expediciones científicas en el siglo XVIII* (1991), *La obra científica de P. Löfling en Venezuela* (1993), *La Ilustración en América Colonial* (1995); *Las Flores del Paraís: La exploración botánica de Cuba en los siglos XVIII y XIX* (1999); *Historia del Jardín Botánico de La Habana* (2000); is coauthor of *Relaciones culturales y científicas entre España y Cuba: Fernando Ortiz y la Hispanocubana* (forthcoming); and is coeditor of *Ensayo político sobre la Isla de Cuba de Alejandro de Humboldt* (1998).

Enrique S. Pumar. Ph.D. in sociology; assistant professor of sociology and Latin American studies, William Paterson University; director of the MOST Program. He has published numerous academic articles and book chapters dealing with political sociology and development. Pumar is currently revising a manuscript for publication exploring the formation and institutionalization of development ideas. He is also preparing a textbook on globalization.

Alfonso W. Quiroz. Professor of history, Baruch College and Graduate Center, City University of New York. He is the author of several books and articles on the history of corruption and the financial history of colonial and modern Peru. The curator of centennial exhibitions on the Spanish-American War at the New York Public Library and New-York Historical Society, he has published articles and chapters on the history of socioeconomic repression, education, corruption, and intellectuals in Cuba. He is coeditor of a forthcoming volume on the Cuban republic and José Martí and is currently writing a book on Cuban reformists, institutions, and civil society between 1800 and 1959.

Jorge Ramírez Calzadilla. Ph.D. in philosophical sciences; professor, Faculty of Philosophy and History, University of Havana. Ramírez is the chairperson of the Department of Socio-Religious Studies at the Centro de Investigaciones Psicológicas y Sociológicas (CIPS). He has lectured widely in different international institutions. He is the author and coauthor of several books: *Religión y relaciones socials* (2000), *La religión en la cultura* (1990), *La teología de la liberación desde una perspectiva cubana* (1994), *Formas religiosas populares en América Latina* (1994), *Panorama de la religión en Cuba* (1996); he is coeditor *of Les religions á Cuba* (2001) and *Religión, cultura y espiritualidad a las puertas del 2000* (2000).

Rafael Rojas. Cuban historian and essayist, currently living in Mexico. A graduate in philosophy, University of Havana, and Ph.D. in history, El Colegio de México, he is a professor and researcher at the Centro the Investigación y Docencia Económica (CIDE, México, D.F.) He is the author of several books: *El arte de la espera: Notas al margen de la política cubana* (1998), *Isla sin fin: Contribución a la crítica del nacionalismo cubano* (1999), *Un banquete canónico* (2000), and *José Martí. La invención de Cuba* (2000); he is coauthor of *El ocaso de la Nueva España* and *Historia General de México*. He was granted the Matías Romero de Historia Diplomática prize for his book *Cuba Mexicana: Historia de una anexión imposible* (2001) and a Rockefeller fellowship.

Pamela Maria Smorkaloff. Ph.D. from New York University. She teaches in the Spanish Department at Montclair State University and is the author of *Literatura y edición de libros: La cultura literaria y el proceso social en Cuba (1900–1987)* (1987), *Readers and Writers in Cuba: A Social History of Print Culture, 1830s–1990s* (1997), *Cuban Writers on and off the Island* (1999); she is editor of *If I Could Write This in Fire: An Anthology of Literature from the Caribbean* (1994); she is coeditor of *The Cuba Reader* (forthcoming); and the author of numerous articles. She is currently working on "Ajiaco and Sancocho: Culture and Cuisine in the Spanish Antilles (Cuba, Puerto Rico, the Dominican Republic)."

Jean Stubbs. Ph.D. in history, professor of Caribbean Studies at the University of North London, and president Elect of the Caribbean Studies Association. Stubbs translated Fernando Ortiz's "The Afro-Cuban Festival 'The Day of the Kings'" into English. He has published extensively on Cuban tobacco, gender, and race and is the author of *Cuba: The Test of Time* (1989) and *Tobacco on the Periphery: A Case Study in Cuban Labour History, 1860–1958* (1985); he is coauthor of *Cuba* (Oxford 1996); and is coeditor of *Afro-Cuban Voices* (2000) and AFROCUBA (1993). He is currently working on a regional history of the Havana cigar.

Ricardo Viñalet. Professor of Spanish Literature at the University of Havana, and senior researcher and Chair of the Department of Literature at the Instituto de Literatura y Lingüística, Havana, Viñalet has been awarded the distinction Orden por la Educación Cubana. He is the author and editor of works on literary research, criticism, and university education: *Temas de literatura española,* 2 vols. (1984, 1986), *Teatro romántico español* (1990), and *Fernando Ortiz ante las secuelas del 98: un regeneracionismo transculturado* (forthcoming). He also authored the narrative works *El día de la ira* (1989), *Para sorpresa del caminante escéptico* (1993), and *Un período especial con irreverencias más o menos cordiales* (2000).